Julie C. Meloni

Sams **Teach Yourself**

HTML, CSS
and JavaScript

All in One

SAMS 800 East 96th Street, Indianapolis, Indiana, 46240 USA

Sams Teach Yourself HTML, CSS, and JavaScript All in One

Copyright © 2012 by Pearson Education, Inc.

All rights reserved. No part of this book shall be reproduced, stored in a retrieval system, or transmitted by any means, electronic, mechanical, photocopying, recording, or otherwise, without written permission from the publisher. No patent liability is assumed with respect to the use of the information contained herein. Although every precaution has been taken in the preparation of this book, the publisher and author assume no responsibility for errors or omissions. Nor is any liability assumed for damages resulting from the use of the information contained herein.

ISBN-13: 978-0-672-33332-3
ISBN-10: 0-672-33332-5

Library of Congress Cataloging-in-Publication data is on file.

First Printing November 2011

Trademarks

All terms mentioned in this book that are known to be trademarks or service marks have been appropriately capitalized. Sams Publishing cannot attest to the accuracy of this information. Use of a term in this book should not be regarded as affecting the validity of any trademark or service mark.

Warning and Disclaimer

Every effort has been made to make this book as complete and as accurate as possible, but no warranty or fitness is implied. The information provided is on an "as is" basis. The author and the publisher shall have neither liability nor responsibility to any person or entity with respect to any loss or damages arising from the information contained in this book or programs accompanying it.

Bulk Sales

Sams Publishing offers excellent discounts on this book when ordered in quantity for bulk purchases or special sales. For more information, please contact

> **U.S. Corporate and Government Sales**
> **1-800-382-3419**
> **corpsales@pearsontechgroup.com**

For sales outside of the U.S., please contact

> **International Sales**
> **international@pearson.com**

Acquisitions Editor
Mark Taber

Development Editor
Songlin Qiu

Managing Editor
Sandra Schroeder

Project Editor
Seth Kerney

Copy Editor
Mike Henry

Indexer
Ken Johnson

Proofreader
Jovana San Nicolas-Shirley

Technical Editor
Phil Ballard

Publishing Coordinator
Cindy Teeters

Book Designer
Gary Adair

Compositor
Trina Wurst

Contents at a Glance

Table of Contents

About the Author

Julie C. Meloni is the Lead Technologist and Architect in the Online Library Environment at the University of Virginia. Before coming to the library, she worked for more than 15 years in web application development for various corporations large and small in Silicon Valley. She has written several books and articles on Web-based programming languages and database topics, including the bestselling *Sams Teach Yourself PHP, MySQL, and Apache All in One*.

We Want to Hear from You!

As the reader of this book, *you* are our most important critic and commentator. We value your opinion and want to know what we're doing right, what we could do better, what areas you'd like to see us publish in, and any other words of wisdom you're willing to pass our way.

You can email or write directly to let us know what you did or didn't like about this book—as well as what we can do to make our books stronger.

Please note that we cannot help you with technical problems related to the topic of this book, and that due to the high volume of mail we receive, we might not be able to reply to every message.

When you write, please be sure to include this book's title and author as well as your name and email address. We will carefully review your comments and share them with the author and editors who worked on the book.

Email: feedback@samspublishing

Mail: Sams Publishing
            800 East 96th Street
            Indianapolis, IN 46240 USA

Reader Services

Visit our website and register this book at informit.com/register for convenient access to any updates, downloads, or errata that might be available for this book.

CHAPTER 1
Publishing Web Content

Before learning the intricacies of HTML (Hypertext Markup Language), CSS (Cascading Style Sheets), and JavaScript, it is important that you gain a solid understanding of the technologies that help transform these plain-text files to the rich multimedia displays you see on your computer or handheld device when browsing the World Wide Web. For example, a file containing markup and client-side code HTML and CSS is useless without a web browser to view it, and no one besides yourself will see your content unless a web server is involved. Web servers make your content available to others who, in turn, use their web browsers to navigate to an address and wait for the server to send information to them. You will be intimately involved in this publishing process because you must create files and then put them on a server to make them available in the first place, and you must ensure that your content will appear to the end user as you intended.

A Brief History of HTML and the World Wide Web

Once upon a time, back when there weren't any footprints on the moon, some farsighted folks decided to see whether they could connect several major computer networks together. I'll spare you the names and stories (there are plenty of both), but the eventual result was the "mother of all networks," which we call the Internet.

Until 1990, accessing information through the Internet was a rather technical affair. It was so hard, in fact, that even Ph.D.-holding physicists were often frustrated when trying to swap data. One such physicist, the now-famous (and knighted) Sir Tim Berners-Lee, cooked up a way to easily cross-reference text on the Internet through hypertext links.

NOTE

For more information about the history of the World Wide Web, see the Wikipedia article on this topic: http://en.wikipedia.org/wiki/History_of_the_Web.

This wasn't a new idea, but his simple HTML managed to thrive while more ambitious hypertext projects floundered. *Hypertext* originally meant text stored in electronic form with cross-reference links between pages. It is now a broader term that refers to just about any object (text, images, files, and so on) that can be linked to other objects. *Hypertext Markup Language* is a language for describing how text, graphics, and files containing other information are organized and linked together.

By 1993, only 100 or so computers throughout the world were equipped to serve up HTML pages. Those interlinked pages were dubbed the *World Wide Web (WWW)*, and several web browser programs had been written to allow people to view web pages. Because of the growing popularity of the Web, a few programmers soon wrote web browsers that could view graphical images along with text. From that point forward, the continued development of web browser software and the standardization of the HTML—and XHTML—languages has lead us to the world we live in today, one in which more than 110 million web servers answer requests for more than 25 billion text and multimedia files.

These few paragraphs really are a brief history of what has been a remarkable period. Today's college freshmen have never known a time in which the Web didn't exist, and the idea of always-on information and ubiquitous computing will shape all aspects of our lives moving forward. Instead of seeing web content creation and management as a set of skills possessed only by a few technically oriented folks (okay, call them geeks if you will), by the end of this book, you will see that these are skills that anyone can master, regardless of inherent geekiness.

Creating Web Content

You might have noticed the use of the term *web content* rather than *web pages*—that was intentional. Although we talk of "visiting a web page," what we really mean is something like "looking at all the text and the images at one address on our computer." The text that we read, and the images that we see, are rendered by our web browsers, which are given certain instructions found in individual files.

Those files contain text that is *marked up*, or surrounded by, HTML codes that tell the browser how to display the text—as a heading, as a paragraph, in a red font, and so on. Some HTML markup tells the browser to display an image or video file rather than plain text, which brings me back to the point: Different types of content are sent to your web browser, so simply saying *web page* doesn't begin to cover it. Here we use the term *web content* instead, to cover the full range of text, image, audio, video, and other media found online.

In later chapters, you will learn the basics of linking to or creating the various types of multimedia web content found in websites. All you need to remember at this point is that *you* are in control of the content a user sees when visiting your website. Beginning with the file that contains text to display or codes that tell the server to send a graphic along to the user's web browser, you have to plan, design, and implement all the pieces that will eventually make up your web presence. As you will learn throughout this book, it is not a difficult process as long as you understand all the little steps along the way.

In its most fundamental form, web content begins with a simple text file containing HTML or XHTML markup. XHTML is another flavor of HTML; the "X" stands for eXtensible, and you will learn more about it as you continue through the chapters. The most important thing to know from the outset is that all the examples in this book are HTML 4 and XHTML compatible, meaning that they will be rendered similarly both now and in the future by any newer generations of web browsers. That is one of the benefits of writing standards-compliant code: You do not have to worry about going back to your code sometime in the future and changing it because it doesn't work. Your code will likely always work for as long as web browsers adhere to standards (hopefully a long time).

Understanding Web Content Delivery

Several processes occur, in many different locations, to eventually produce web content that you can see. These processes occur very quickly—on the order of milliseconds—and occur behind the scenes. In other words, although we might think all we are doing is opening a web browser, typing in a web address, and instantaneously seeing the content we requested, technology in the background is working hard on our behalf. Figure 1.1 shows the basic interaction between a browser and a server.

FIGURE 1.1
A browser request and a server response.

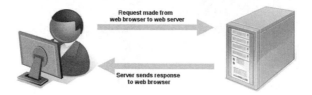

However, there are several steps in the process—and potentially several trips between the browser and server—before you see the entire content of the site you requested.

Suppose you want to do a Google search, so you dutifully type **http://www.google.com** in the address bar or select the Google bookmark from your bookmarks list. Almost immediately, your browser will show you something like what's shown in Figure 1.2.

FIGURE 1.2
Visiting www.google.com.

Figure 1.2 shows a website that contains text plus one image (the Google logo). A simple version of the processes that occurred to retrieve that text and image from a web server and display it on your screen is as follows:

1. Your web browser sends a request for the index.html file located at the http://www.google.com/ address. The index.html file does not have to be part of the address that you type in the address bar; you'll learn more about the index.html file further along in this chapter.

2. After receiving the request for a specific file, the web server process looks in its directory contents for the specific file, opens it, and sends the content of that file back to your web browser.

3. The web browser receives the content of the index.html file, which is text marked up with HTML codes, and renders the content based on these HTML codes. While rendering the content, the browser happens upon the HTML code for the Google logo, which you can see in Figure 1.2. The HTML code looks like this:

```
<img src="/logos/logo.gif" width="384" height="121" border="0"
alt="Google"/>
```

The tag provides attributes that tell the browser the file source location (src), width (width), height (height), border type (border), and alternative text (alt) necessary to display the logo. You will learn more about attributes throughout later chapters.

4. The browser looks at the src attribute in the <img/> tag to find the source location. In this case, the image logo.gif can be found in the logos directory at the same web address (www.google.com) from which the browser retrieved the HTML file.

5. The browser requests the file at the http://www.google.com/logos/logo.gif web address.

6. The web server interprets that request, finds the file, and sends the contents of that file to the web browser that requested it.

7. The web browser displays the image on your monitor.

As you can see in the description of the web content delivery process, web browsers do more than simply act as picture frames through which you can view content. Browsers assemble the web content components and arrange those parts according to the HTML commands in the file.

You can also view web content locally, or on your own hard drive, without the need for a web server. The process of content retrieval and display is the same as the process listed in the previous steps in that a browser looks for and interprets the codes and content of an HTML file, but the trip is shorter; the browser looks for files on your own computer's hard drive rather than on a remote machine. A web server is needed to interpret any server-based programming language embedded in the files, but that is outside the scope of this book. In fact, you could work through all the chapters in this book without having a web server to call your own, but then nobody but you could view your masterpieces.

Selecting a Web Hosting Provider

Despite just telling you that you can work through all the chapters in this book without having a web server, having a web server is the recommended method for continuing on. Don't worry—obtaining a hosting provider is usually a quick, painless, and relatively inexpensive process. In fact, you can get your own domain name and a year of web hosting for just slightly more than the cost of the book you are reading now.

If you type **web hosting provider** in your search engine of choice, you will get millions of hits and an endless list of sponsored search results (also known as *ads*). There are not this many web hosting providers in the world, although it might seem like there are. Even if you are looking at a managed list of hosting providers, it can be overwhelming—especially if all you are looking for is a place to host a simple website for yourself or your company or organization.

You'll want to narrow your search when looking for a provider and choose one that best meets your needs. Some selection criteria for a web hosting provider include the following"

▶ **Reliability/server "uptime"**—If you have an online presence, you want to make sure people can actually get there consistently.

▶ **Customer service**—Look for multiple methods for contacting customer service (phone, email, and chat) as well as online documentation for common issues.

▶ **Server space**—Does the hosting package include enough server space to hold all the multimedia files (images, audio, and video) you plan to include in your website (if any)?

▶ **Bandwidth**—Does the hosting package include enough bandwidth so that all the people visiting your site and downloading files can do so without you having to pay extra?

▶ **Domain name purchase and management**—Does the package include a custom domain name, or must you purchase and maintain your domain name separately from your hosting account?

▶ **Price**—Do not overpay for hosting. You will see a wide range of prices offered and should immediately wonder "what's the difference?" Often the difference has little to do with the quality of the service and everything to do with company overhead and what the company thinks they can get away with charging people. A good rule of thumb is that if you are paying more than $75 per year for a basic hosting package and domain name, you are probably paying too much.

Here are three reliable web hosting providers whose basic packages contain plenty of server space and bandwidth (as well as domain names and extra benefits) at a relatively low cost. If you don't go with any of these web hosting providers, you can at least use their basic package descriptions as a guideline as you shop around.

NOTE

I have used all these providers (and then some) over the years and have no problem recommending any of them; predominantly, I use DailyRazor as a web hosting provider, especially for advanced development environments.

- **A Small Orange (http://www.asmallorange.com)**—The "Tiny" and "Small" hosting packages are perfect starting places for the new web content publisher.

- **DailyRazor (http://www.dailyrazor.com)**—Even its Rookie hosting package is full featured and reliable.

- **LunarPages (http://www.lunarpages.com)**—The Basic hosting package is suitable for many personal and small business websites.

One feature of a good hosting provider is that it provides a "control panel" for you to manage aspects of your account. Figure 1.3 shows the control panel for my own hosting account at Daily Razor. Many web hosting providers offer this particular control panel software, or some control panel that is similar in design—clearly labeled icons leading to tasks you can perform to configure and manage your account.

FIGURE 1.3
A sample control panel.

You might never need to use your control panel, but having it available to you simplifies the installation of databases and other software, the viewing of web statistics, and the addition of email addresses (among many other features). If you can follow instructions, you can manage your own web server—no special training required.

Testing with Multiple Web Browsers

Having just discussed the process of web content delivery and the acquisition of a web server, it might seem a little strange to step back and talk about testing your websites with multiple web browsers. However, before you go off and learn all about creating websites with HTML and CSS, do so with this very important statement in mind: Every visitor to your website will potentially use hardware and software configurations that are different than your own. Their device types (desktop, laptop, netbook, smartphone, or iPhone), their screen resolutions, their browser types, their browser window sizes, and their speed of connections will be different—remember that you cannot control any aspect of what your visitors use when they view your site. So, just as you're setting up your web hosting environment and getting ready to work, think about downloading several different web browsers so that you have a local test suite of tools available to you. Let me explain why this is important.

Although all web browsers process and handle information in the same general way, there are some specific differences among them that result in things not always looking the same in different browsers. Even users of the same version of the same web browser can alter how a page appears by choosing different display options or changing the size of their viewing windows. All the major web browsers allow users to override the background and fonts specified by the web page author with those of their own choosing. Screen resolution, window size, and optional toolbars can also change how much of a page someone sees when it first appears on their screens. You can ensure only that you write standards-compliant HTML and CSS.

Do not, under any circumstances, spend hours on end designing something that looks perfect on your own computer—unless you are willing to be disappointed when you look at it on your friend's computer, on your tablet, or on your iPhone.

You should always test your websites with as many of these web browsers as possible:

- ▶ Apple Safari (http://www.apple.com/safari/) for Mac and Windows

- ▶ Google Chrome (http://www.google.com/chrome) for Windows

- ▶ Mozilla Firefox (http://www.mozilla.com/firefox/) for Mac, Windows, and Linux

- ▶ Microsoft Internet Explorer (http://www.microsoft.com/ie) for Windows

- ▶ Opera (http://www.opera.com/) for Mac, Windows, and Linux/UNIX

Now that you have a development environment set up, or at least some idea of the type you'd like to set up in the future, let's move on to creating a test file.

Creating a Sample File

Before we begin, take a look at Listing 1.1. This listing represents a simple piece of web content—a few lines of HTML that print "Hello World! Welcome to My Web Server." in large, bold letters on two lines centered within the browser window.

LISTING 1.1   Our Sample HTML File

```
<html>
<head>
<title>Hello World!</title>
</head>
<body>
<h1 style="text-align: center">Hello World!<br/>Welcome to My Web
➥Server.</h1>
</body>
</html>
```

To make use of this content, open a text editor of your choice, such as Notepad (on Windows) or TextEdit (on a Mac). Do not use WordPad, Microsoft Word, or other full-featured word-processing software because those programs create different sorts of files than the plain-text files we use for web content.

Type the content that you see in Listing 1.1, and then save the file using **sample.html** as the filename. The .html extension tells the web server that your file is, indeed, full of HTML. When the file contents are sent to the web browser that requests it, the browser will also know that it is HTML and will render it appropriately.

NOTE

You will learn a bit about text editors in Chapter 2, "Understanding HTML and XHTML Connections." Right now, I just want you to have a sample file that you can put on a web server!

Now that you have a sample HTML file to use—and hopefully somewhere to put it, such as a web hosting account—let's get to publishing your web content.

Using FTP to Transfer Files

As you've learned so far, you have to put your web content on a web server to make it accessible to others. This process typically occurs by using *File Transfer Protocol (FTP)*. To use FTP, you need an FTP client—a program used to transfer files from your computer to a web server.

FTP clients require three pieces of information to connect to your web server; this information will have been sent to you by your hosting provider after you set up your account:

- ▶ The hostname, or address, to which you will connect
- ▶ Your account username
- ▶ Your account password

After you have this information, you are ready to use an FTP client to transfer content to your web server.

Selecting an FTP Client

Regardless of the FTP client you use, FTP clients generally use the same type of interface. Figure 1.4 shows an example of FireFTP, which is an FTP client used with the Firefox web browser. The directory listing of the local machine (your computer) appears on the left of your screen and the directory listing of the remote machine (the web server) appears on the right. Typically, you will see right-arrow and left-arrow buttons—as shown in Figure 1.4. The right arrow sends selected files from your computer to your web server; the left arrow sends files from the web server to your computer. Many FTP clients also enable you to simply select files, and then drag and drop those files to the target machines.

There are many FTP clients freely available to you, but you can also transfer files via the web-based File Manager tool that is likely part of your web server's control panel. However, that method of file transfer typically introduces more steps into the process and isn't nearly as streamlined (or simple) as installing an FTP client on your own machine.

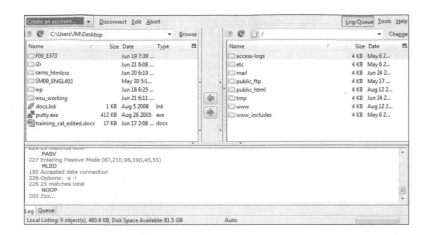

FIGURE 1.4
The FireFTP interface.

Here are some popular free FTP clients:

▶ Classic FTP (http://www.nchsoftware.com/classic/) for Mac and Windows

▶ Cyberduck (http://cyberduck.ch/) for Mac

▶ Fetch (http://fetchsoftworks.com/) for Mac

▶ FileZilla (http://filezilla-project.org/) for all platforms

▶ FireFTP (http://fireftp.mozdev.org/) Firefox extension for all platforms

When you have selected an FTP client and installed it on your computer, you are ready to upload and download files from your web server. In the next section, you'll see how this process works using the sample file in Listing 1.1.

Using an FTP Client

The following steps show how to use Classic FTP to connect to your web server and transfer a file. However, all FTP clients use similar, if not exact, interfaces. If you understand the following steps, you should be able to use any FTP client.

Remember, you first need the hostname, the account username, and the account password.

1. Start the Classic FTP program and click the Connect button. You will be prompted to fill out information for the site to which you want to connect, as shown in Figure 1.5.

FIGURE 1.5
Connecting to a new site in
Classic FTP.

2. Fill in each of the items shown in Figure 1.5 as follows:

    ▶ The site Label is the name you'll use to refer to your own site.
      Nobody else will see this name, so enter whatever you want.

    ▶ The FTP Server is the FTP address of the web server to which
      you need to send your web pages. This address will have been
      given to you by your hosting provider. It will probably be
      yourdomain.com, but check the information you received when
      you signed up for service.

    ▶ The User Name field and the Password field should also be
      completed using information given to you by your hosting
      provider.

    ▶ Don't change the values for Initial Remote Directory on First
      Connection and Initial Local Directory on First Connection
      until you are used to using the client and have established a
      workflow.

3. When you're finished with the settings, click OK to save the settings
    and establish a connection with the web server.

    You will see a dialog box indicating that Classic FTP is attempting to
    connect to the web server. Upon successful connection, you will see
    an interface similar to Figure 1.6, showing the contents of the local
    directory on the left and the contents of your web server on the right.

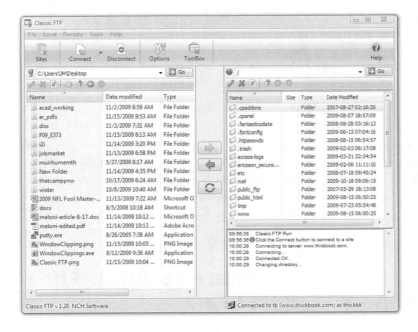

FIGURE 1.6
A successful connection to a
remote web server via Classic FTP.

4. You are now *almost* ready to transfer files to your web server. All that
    remains is to change directories to what is called the *document root* of
    your web server. The document root of your web server is the directo-
    ry that is designated as the top-level directory for your web content—
    the starting point of the directory structure, which you will learn
    more about later in this chapter. Often, this directory will be named
    public_html (as shown in Figure 1.6), www (also shown in Figure 1.6,
    as www has been created as an alias for public_html), or htdocs. This
    is not a directory that you will have to create because your hosting
    provider will have created it for you.

    Double-click the document root directory name to open it. The dis-
    play shown on the right of the FTP client interface should change to
    show the contents of this directory. (It will probably be empty at this
    point, unless your web hosting provider has put placeholder files in
    that directory on your behalf.)

5. The goal is to transfer the sample.html file you created earlier from
    your computer to the web server. Find the file in the directory listing
    on the left of the FTP client interface (navigate around if you have to)
    and click it once to highlight the filename.

6. Click the right-arrow button in the middle of the client interface to send the file to the web server. After the file transfer is completed, the right side of the client interface should refresh to show you that the file has made it to its destination.

7. Click the Disconnect button to close the connection, and then exit out of the Classic FTP program.

These steps are conceptually similar to the steps you will take anytime you want to send files to your web server via FTP. You can also use your FTP client to create subdirectories on the remote web server. To create a subdirectory using Classic FTP, click the Remote menu, and then click New Folder. Different FTP clients will have different interface options to achieve the same goal.

Understanding Where to Place Files on the Web Server

An important aspect of maintaining web content is determining how you will organize that content—not only for the user to find, but also for you to maintain on your server. Putting files in directories will help you to manage those files.

Naming and organizing directories on your web server, and developing rules for file maintenance, is completely up to you. However, maintaining a well-organized server simply makes your management of its content more efficient in the long run.

Basic File Management

As you browse the Web, you might have noticed that URLs change as you navigate through websites. For instance, if you're looking at a company's website and you click on graphical navigation leading to the company's products or services, the URL will probably change from

http://www.companyname.com/

to

http://www.companyname.com/products/

or

http://www.companyname.com/services/

In the previous section, I used the term *document root* without really explaining what that is all about. The document root of a web server is essentially the trailing slash in the full URL. For instance, if your domain is *yourdomain*.com and your URL is http://www.*yourdomain*.com/, the document root is the directory represented by the trailing slash (/). The document root is the starting point of the directory structure you create on your web server; it is the place where the web server begins looking for files requested by the web browser.

If you put the sample.html file in your document root as previously directed, you will be able to access it via a web browser at the following URL:

   http://www.*yourdomain*.com/sample.html

If you were to enter this URL into your web browser, you would see the rendered sample.html file, as shown in Figure 1.7.

FIGURE 1.7
The sample.html file accessed via a web browser.

However, if you created a new directory within the document root and put the sample.html file in that directory, the file would be accessed at this URL:

   http://www.*yourdomain*.com/newdirectory/sample.html

If you put the sample.html file in the directory you originally saw upon connecting to your server—that is, you did *not* change directories and place the file in the document root—the sample.html file would not be accessible from your web server at any URL. The file will still be on the machine that you know as your web server, but because the file is not in the document root—where the server software knows to start looking for files—it will never be accessible to anyone via a web browser.

The bottom line? Always navigate to the document root of your web server before you start transferring files.

This is especially true with graphics and other multimedia files. A common directory on web servers is called *images*, where, as you can imagine, all the image assets are placed for retrieval. Other popular directories include css for stylesheet files (if you are using more than one) and js for external JavaScript files. Or, if you know you will have an area on your website where visitors can download many different types of files, you might simply call that directory downloads.

Whether it's a ZIP file containing your art portfolio or an Excel spreadsheet with sales numbers, it's often useful to publish files on the Internet that aren't simply web pages. To make a file available on the Web that isn't an HTML file, just upload the file to your website as if it *were* an HTML file, following the instructions provided earlier in this chapter for uploading. After the file is uploaded to the web server, you can create a link to it (as you'll learn in later chapters). In other words, your web server can serve much more than HTML.

Here's a sample of the HTML code that you will learn more about later in this book. The following code would be used for a file named artfolio.zip, located in the downloads directory of your website, and link text that reads "Download my art portfolio!":

```
<a href="/downloads/artfolio.zip">Download my art portfolio!</a>
```

Using an Index Page

When you think of an index, you probably think of the section in the back of a book that tells you where to look for various keywords and topics. The index file in a web server directory can serve that purpose—if you design it that way. In fact, that's where the name originates.

The index.html file (or just *index file*, as it's usually referred to) is the name you give to the page you want people to see as the default file when they navigate to a specific directory in your website. If you've created that page with usability in mind, your users will be able to get to all content in that section from the index page.

For example, Figure 1.8 shows the drop-down navigation and left-side navigation both contain links to three pages: Solutions Overview (the section index page itself), Connection Management, and Cost Management.

The content of the page itself—called index.html and located within the solutions directory—also has links to those two additional pages in the solutions section. When users arrive at the index page of the "solutions" section in this particular website (at least at the time of the snapshot), they can reach any other page in that section (and in three different ways!).

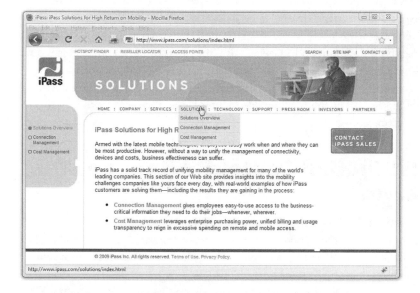

FIGURE 1.8
Showing a good section index page.

Another function of the index page is that when users visit a directory on your site that has an index page, but they do not specify that page, they will still land on the main page for that section of your site—or for the site itself.

For instance, in the previous example, a user could have typed either of the following URLs and landed on the main page of the solutions section of that website:

http://www.ipass.com/solutions/

http://www.ipass.com/solutions/index.html

Had there been no index.html page in the solutions directory, the results would depend on the configuration of the web server. If the server is configured to disallow directory browsing, the user would have seen a "Directory Listing Denied" message when attempting to access the URL without a specified page name. However, if the server is configured to allow directory browsing, the user would have seen a list of the files in that directory.

These server configuration options will have already been determined for you by your hosting provider. If your hosting provider enables you to modify server settings via a control panel, you can change these settings so that your server responds to requests based on your own requirements.

Not only is the index file used in subdirectories, it's used in the top-level directory (or document root) of your website as well. The first page of your website—or *home page* or *main page*, or however you like to refer to the web content you want users to see when they first visit your domain—should be named index.html and placed in the document root of your web server. This will ensure that when users type http://www.*yourdomain*.com/ into their web browsers, the server will respond with content you intended them to see (rather than "Directory Listing Denied" or some other unintended consequence).

Distributing Content Without a Web Server

Publishing HTML and multimedia files online is obviously the primary reason to learn HTML and create web content. However, there are also situations in which other forms of publishing simply aren't viable. For example, you might want to distribute CD-ROMs, DVD-ROMs, or USB drives at a trade show with marketing materials designed as web content—that is, hyperlinked text viewable through a web browser, but without a web server involved. You might also want to include HTML-based instructional manuals on removable media for students at a training seminar. These are just two examples of how HTML pages can be used in publishing scenarios that don't involve the Internet.

This process is also called creating *local* sites; even though there's no web server involved, these bundles of hypertext content are still called *sites*. The local term comes into play because your files are accessed locally and not remotely (via a web server).

Publishing Content Locally

Let's assume you need to create a local site that you want to distribute on a USB drive. Even the cheapest USB drives hold so much data these days—and basic hypertext files are quite small—that you can distribute an entire site *and a fully functioning web browser* all on one little drive.

NOTE

Distributing a web browser isn't required when creating and distributing a local site, although it's a nice touch. You can reasonably assume that users have their own web browsers and will open the index.html file in a directory to start browsing the hyperlinked content. However, if you would like to distribute a web browser on the USB drive, go to http://www.portableapps.com/ and look for Portable Firefox.

Simply think of the directory structure of your USB drive just as you would the directory structure of your web server. The top-level of the USB drive directory structure can be your document root. Or if you are distributing a web browser along with the content, you might have two directories—for example, one named `browser` and one named `content`. In that case, the `content` directory would be your document root. Within the document root, you could have additional subfolders in which you place content and other multimedia assets.

It's as important to maintain good organization with a local site as it is with a remote website so that you avoid broken links in your HTML files. You will learn more about the specifics of linking together files in a later chapter.

Publishing Content on a Blog

You might have a blog hosted by a third-party, such as Blogger or WordPress (among others), and thus have already published content without having a dedicated web server or even knowing any HTML. These services offer *visual editors* in addition to *source editors*, meaning that you can type your words and add visual formatting such as bold, italics, or font colors without knowing the HTML for these actions. But still, the content becomes actual HTML when you click the Publish button in these editors.

However, with the knowledge you will acquire throughout this book, your blogging will be enhanced because you will able to use the source editor for your blog post content and blog templates, thus affording you more control over the look and feel of that content. These actions occur differently from the process you learned for creating an HTML file and uploading it via FTP to your own dedicated web server, but I would be remiss if I did not note that blogging is, in fact, a form of web publishing.

Tips for Testing Web Content

Whenever you transfer files to your web server or place them on removable media for local browsing, you should immediately test every page thoroughly. The following checklist will help ensure that your web content behaves the way you expected. Note that some of the terms might be unfamiliar to you at this point, but come back to this checklist as you progress through this book and create larger projects:

▶ Before you transfer your files, test them locally on your machine to ensure that the links work and the content reflects the visual design you intended. After you transfer the pages to a web server or removable device, test them all again.

▶ Perform these tests with as many browsers that you can—Chrome, Firefox, Internet Explorer, Opera, and Safari is a good list—and on both Mac and Windows platforms. If possible, check at low resolution (800×600) and high resolution (1600×1200).

▶ Turn off auto image loading in your web browser before you start testing so that you can see what each page looks like without the graphics. Check your alt tag messages, and then turn image loading back on to load the graphics and review the page carefully again.

▶ Use your browser's font size settings to look at each page in various font sizes to ensure that your layout doesn't fall to pieces if users override your font specifications with their own.

▶ Wait for each page to completely finish loading, and then scroll all the way down to make sure that all images appear where they should.

▶ Time how long it takes each page to load. Does it take more than a few seconds to load? If so, is the information on that page valuable enough to keep users from going elsewhere before the page finishes loading? Granted, broadband connections are common, but that doesn't mean you should load up your pages with 1MB images.

If your pages pass all those tests, you can rest easy; your site is ready for public viewing.

Summary

This chapter introduced you to the concept of using HTML to mark-up text files to produce web content. You also learned that there is more to web content than just the "page"—web content also includes image, audio, and video files. All of this content lives on a web server—a remote machine often far away from your own computer. On your computer or other device, you use a web browser to request, retrieve, and eventually display web content on your screen.

You learned the criteria you should consider when determining if a web hosting provider fits your needs. After you have a web hosting provider, you can begin to transfer files to your web server using an FTP client. You also learned a little bit about web server directory structures and file management, as well as the very important purpose of the index.html file in a given web server directory. You discovered that you can distribute web content on removable media, and how to go about structuring the files and directories to achieve the goal of viewing content without using a remote web server. Finally, you learned the importance of testing your work in multiple browsers after you've placed it on a web server. Writing valid, standards-compliant HTML and CSS will help ensure your site looks reasonably similar for all visitors, but you still shouldn't design without receiving input from potential users outside your development team—it is even more important to get input from others when you are a design team of one!

Q&A

Q. I've looked at the HTML source of some web pages on the Internet and it looks frighteningly difficult to learn. Do I have to think like a computer programmer to learn this stuff?

A. Although complex HTML pages can indeed look daunting, learning HTML is much easier than learning actual software programming languages (such as C++ or Java). HTML is a markup language rather than a programming language; you mark-up text so that the text can be rendered a certain way by the browser. That's a completely different set of thought processes than developing a computer program. You really don't need any experience or skill as a computer programmer to be a successful web content author.

One of the reasons the HTML behind many commercial websites looks complicated is because it was likely created by a visual web design tool—a "what you see is what you get" or "WYSIWYG" editor that will use whatever markup its software developer told it to use in certain circumstances—as opposed to being hand-coded, in which you are completely in control of the resulting markup. In this book, you are taught fundamental coding from the ground up, which typically results in clean, easy-to-read source code. Visual web design tools have a knack for making code difficult to read and for producing code that is convoluted and non-standards compliant.

Q. All the tests you recommend would take longer than creating my pages! Can't I get away with less testing?

A. If your pages aren't intended to make money or provide an important service, it's probably not a big deal if they look funny to some users or produce errors once in a while. In that case, just test each page with a couple of different browsers and call it a day. However, if you need to project a professional image, there is no substitute for rigorous testing.

Q. Seriously, who cares how I organize my web content?

A. Believe it or not, the organization of your web content does matter to search engines and potential visitors to your site—you'll learn more about this in Chapter 28, "Helping People Find Your Web Pages." But overall, having an organized web server directory structure will help you keep track of content that you are likely to update frequently. For instance, if you have a dedicated directory for images or multimedia, you will know exactly where to look for a file you want to update—no need to hunt through directories containing other content.

Workshop

The workshop contains quiz questions and exercises to help you solidify your understanding of the material covered. Try to answer all questions before looking at the "Answers" section that follows.

Quiz

1. How many files would you need to store on a web server to produce a single web page with some text and two images on it?

2. What are some of the features to look for in a web hosting provider?

3. What three pieces of information do you need to connect to your web server via FTP?

4. What is the purpose of the index.html file?

5. Does your website have to include a directory structure?

Answers

1. You would need three: one for the web page itself, which includes the text and the HTML markup, and one for each of the two images.

2. Look for reliability, customer service, web space and bandwidth, domain name service, site management extras, and price.

3. The hostname, your account username, and your account password.

4. The index.html file is typically the default file for a directory within a web server. It allows users to access http://www.yourdomain.com/somedirectory/ without using a trailing file name and still end up in the appropriate place.

5. No. Using a directory structure for file organization is completely up to you, although it is highly recommended to use one because it simplifies content maintenance.

Exercises

▶ Get your web hosting in order—are you going to go through the chapters in this book by viewing files locally on your own computer, or are you going to use a web hosting provider? Note that most web hosting providers will have you up and running the same day you purchase your hosting plan.

▶ If you are using an external hosting provider, and then using your FTP client, create a subdirectory within the document root of your website. Paste the contents of the sample.html file into another file named index.html, change the text between the <title> and </title> tags to something new, and change the text between the <h1> and </h1> tags to something new. Save the file and upload it to the new subdirectory. Use your web browser to navigate to the new directory on your web server and see that the content in the index.html file appears. Then, using your FTP client, delete the index.html file from the remote subdirectory. Return to that URL with your web browser, reload the page, and see how the server responds without the index.html file in place.

▶ Using the same set of files created in the previous exercise, place these files on a removable media device—a CD-ROM or a USB drive, for example. Use your browser to navigate this local version of your sample website, and think about the instructions you would have to distribute with this removable media so that others could use it.

CHAPTER 2

Understanding HTML and XHTML Connections

The first chapter gave you a basic idea of the process behind creating web content and viewing it online (or locally, if you do not yet have a web hosting provider). In this chapter, we'll get down to the business of explaining the various elements that must appear in an HTML file so that it is displayed appropriately in your web browser.

By the end of the chapter, you'll learn how HTML differs from XHTML and why there are two different languages designed to do the same thing—create web content. In general, this chapter provides a quick summary of HTML and XHTML basics and gives some practical tips to make the most of your time as a web page author and publisher. It's not all theory, however; you do get to see a real web page and the HTML code behind it.

Getting Prepared

Here's a review of what you need to do before you're ready to use the rest of this book:

1. Get a computer. I used a computer running Ubuntu (Linux) to test the sample web content and capture the figures in this book, but you can use any Windows, Macintosh, or Linux/UNIX machine to create and view your web content.

2. Get a connection to the Internet. Whether you have a dial-up, wireless, or broadband connection doesn't matter for the creation and viewing of your web content, but the faster the connection, the better for the overall experience. The Internet service provider (ISP), school, or business that provides your Internet connection can help you with the details of setting it up properly. Additionally, many public spaces such as coffee shops, bookstores, and libraries offer free wireless Internet service that you can use if you have a laptop computer with Wi-Fi network support.

NOTE

Not sure how to find an ISP? The best way is to comparison-shop online (using a friend's computer or a public computer that's already connected to the Internet). You'll find a comprehensive list of national and regional ISPs at http://www.thelist.com/.

CAUTION

Although all web browsers process and handle information in the same general way, there are some specific differences among them that result in things not always looking the same in different browsers. Be sure to check your web pages in multiple browsers to make sure that they look reasonably consistent.

NOTE

As discussed in the first chapter, if you plan to put your web content on the Internet (as opposed to publishing it on CD-ROM or a local intranet), you'll need to transfer it to a computer that is connected to the Internet 24 hours a day. The same company or school that provides you with Internet access might also provide web space; if not, you might need to pay a hosting provider for the service.

3. Get web browser software. This is the software your computer needs to retrieve and display web content. As you learned in the first chapter, the most popular browser software (in alphabetical order) is Apple Safari, Google Chrome, Microsoft Internet Explorer, Mozilla Firefox, and Opera. It's a good idea to install several of these browsers so that you can experiment and make sure that your content looks consistent across them all; you can't make assumptions about the browsers other people are using.

4. Explore! Use a web browser to look around the Internet for websites that are similar in content or appearance to those you'd like to create. Note what frustrates you about some pages, what attracts you and keeps you reading others, and what makes you come back to some pages over and over again. If there is a particular topic that interests you, consider searching for it using a popular search engine such as Google (http://www.google.com/) or Bing (http://www.bing.com/).

Getting Started with a Simple Web Page

In the first chapter, you learned that a web page is just a text file that is marked up by (or surrounded by) HTML codes that tell the browser how to display the text. To create these text files, use a *text editor* such as Notepad (on Windows) or TextEdit (on a Mac)—do not use WordPad, Microsoft Word, or other full-featured word-processing software because those create different sorts of files than the plain-text files we use for web content.

Before you begin working, you should start with some text that you want to put on a web page:

1. Find (or write) a few paragraphs of text about yourself, your family, your company, your softball team, or some other subject in which you're interested.

2. Save this text as plain, standard ASCII text. Notepad and most simple text editors always save files as plain text, but if you're using another program, you might need to choose this file type as an option (after selecting File, Save As).

As you go through this chapter, you will add HTML markup (called *tags*) to the text file, thus making it into web content.

When you save files containing HTML tags, always give them a name ending in .html. This is important: If you forget to type the .html at the end of the filename when you save the file, most text editors will give it some other extension (such as .txt). If that happens, you might not be able to find the file when you try to look at it with a web browser; if you find it, it certainly won't display properly. In other words, web browsers expect a web page file to have a file extension of .html.

When visiting websites, you might also encounter pages with a file extension of .htm, which is also an acceptable file extension to use. You might find other file extensions used on the Web, such as .jsp (Java Server Pages), .asp (Microsoft Active Server Pages), or .php (PHP: Hypertext Preprocessor), but these file types use server-side technologies that are beyond the scope of HTML and the chapters throughout this book. However, these files also contain HTML in addition to the programming language; although the programming code in those files is compiled on the server side and all you would see on the client side is the HTML output, if you were to look at the source files, you would likely see some intricate weaving of programming and markup codes.

Listing 2.1 shows an example of text you can type and save to create a simple HTML page. If you opened this file with Firefox, you would see the page shown in Figure 2.1. Every web page you create must include the `<html></html>`, `<head></head>`, `<title></title>`, and `<body></body>` tag pairs.

LISTING 2.1　The `<html>`, `<head>`, `<title>`, and `<body>` Tags

```
<?xml version="1.0" encoding="UTF-8"?>
<!DOCTYPE html PUBLIC "-//W3C//DTD XHTML 1.1//EN"
  "http://www.w3.org/TR/xhtml11/DTD/xhtml11.dtd">

<html xmlns="http://www.w3.org/1999/xhtml" xml:lang="en">
  <head>
    <title>The First Web Page</title>
  </head>

  <body>
    <p>
      In the beginning, Tim created the HyperText Markup Language. The Internet
      was without form and void, and text was upon the face of the monitor and
      the Hands of Tim were moving over the face of the keyboard. And Tim said,
      Let there be links; and there were links. And Tim saw that the links were
      good; and Tim separated the links from the text. Tim called the links
```

NOTE

If you're using TextEdit on a Macintosh computer, the steps for creating an HTML file are a little different than for using Notepad on a Windows computer. Both are popular text editors, but with the latter, you must first click on the Format menu, select Make Plain Text, and then change the preferences under the Saving header by unchecking the box for Append '.txt' Extension to Plain Text Files. Also, the default preferences are set to show .html documents as they would appear in a browser, which won't allow you to edit them. To fix this, check Ignore Rich Text Commands in HTML Files under the Rich Text Processing header.

LISTING 2.1   Continued

```
        Anchors, and the text He called Other Stuff. And the whole thing together
        was the first Web Page.
      </p>
    </body>
</html>
```

FIGURE 2.1
When you save the text in Listing
2.1 as an HTML file and view it
with a web browser, only the actual
title and body text are displayed.

NOTE

Technically speaking, HTML5
will be the next web standard
but it's not quite at the point of
full adoption. Current estimates
put the full adoption of HTML
sometime in 2011. However, as
you learn about important features of HTML and XHTML in
this book, I will include notes
about how HTML5 features
might differ.

In Listing 2.1, as in every HTML page, the words starting with < and ending with > are actually coded commands. These coded commands are
called *HTML tags* because they "tag" pieces of text and tell the web browser what kind of text it is. This allows the web browser to display the text
appropriately.

The first few lines of code in the web page serve as standard boilerplate
code that you will include in all of your pages. This code actually identifies
the page as a valid XHTML 1.1 document, which means that, technically,
the web page is an XHTML page. All the pages developed throughout the
book are XHTML 1.1 pages. Because XHTML is a more structured version
of HTML, it's still okay to generally refer to all the pages in the book as
HTML pages. By targeting XHTML 1.1 with your code, you are developing
web pages that adhere to the very latest web standards. This is a good
thing!

TRY IT YOURSELF ▼

**Creating and Viewing
a Basic Web Page**

Before you learn the meaning of the HTML tags used in Listing 2.1, you might want to see exactly how I went about creating and viewing the document itself. Follow these steps:

1. Type all the text in Listing 2.1, including the HTML tags, in Windows Notepad (or use Macintosh TextEdit or another text editor of your choice).

2. Select File, Save As. Be sure to select plain text (or ASCII text) as the file type.

3. Name the file **firstpage.html**.

4. Choose the folder on your hard drive where you would like to keep your web pages—and remember which folder you choose! Click the Save or OK button to save the file.

5. Now start your favorite web browser. (Leave Notepad running, too, so you can easily switch between viewing and editing your page.)

In Internet Explorer, select File, Open and click Browse. If you're using Firefox, select File, Open File. Navigate to the appropriate folder and select the firstpage.html file. Some browsers and operating systems will also enable you to drag and drop the firstpage.html file onto the browser window to view it.

Voilà! You should see the page shown in Figure 2.1.

If you have obtained a web hosting account, you could use FTP at this point to transfer the firstpage.html file to the web server. In fact, from this chapter forward, the instructions will assume you have a hosting provider and are comfortable sending files back and forth via FTP; if that is not the case, please review the first chapter before moving on. Or, if you are consciously choosing to work with files locally (without a web host), be prepared to adjust the instructions to suit your particular needs (such as ignoring the commands "transfer the files" and "type in the URL").

HTML Tags Every XHTML Web Page Must Have

The time has come for the secret language of HTML tags to be revealed to you. When you understand this language, you will have creative powers far beyond those of other humans. Don't tell the other humans, but it's really pretty easy.

NOTE

You don't need to be connected to the Internet to view a web page stored on your own computer. By default, your web browser tries to connect to the Internet every time you start it, which makes sense most of the time. However, this can be a hassle if you're developing pages locally on your hard drive (offline) and you keep getting errors about a page not being found. If you have a full-time web connection via a LAN, cable modem, or DSL, this is a moot point because the browser will never complain about being offline. Otherwise, the appropriate disciplinary action will depend on your breed of browser; check the options under your browser's Tools menu.

Before you get into the HTML tags, let's first address the messy-looking code at the top of Listing 2.1. The first line indicates that the HTML document is, in fact, an XML document:

```
<?xml version="1.0" encoding="UTF-8"?>
```

The version of XML is set to 1.0, which is fairly standard, as is the type of character encoding (UTF-8).

The second and third lines of code in Listing 2.1 are even more complicated looking:

```
<!DOCTYPE html PUBLIC "-//W3C//DTD XHTML 1.1//EN"
  "http://www.w3.org/TR/xhtml11/DTD/xhtml11.dtd">
```

Again, the specifics of this code aren't terribly important as long as you remember to include the code at the start of your pages. This code identifies the document as being XHTML 1.1, which then allows web browsers to make sure the code meets all the requirements of XHTML 1.1.

Most HTML tags have two parts: an *opening tag*, which indicates where a piece of text begins, and a *closing tag*, which indicates where the piece of text ends. Closing tags start with a / (forward slash) just after the < symbol.

Another type of tag is the *empty tag*, which is unique in that it doesn't include a pair of matching opening and closing tags. Instead, an empty tag consists of a single tag that starts with a < and ends with a / just before the > symbol.

Following is a quick summary of these three tags just to make sure you understand the role each plays:

▶ An *opening tag* is an HTML tag that indicates the start of an HTML command; the text affected by the command appears after the opening tag. Opening tags always begin with < and end with >, as in <html>.

▶ A *closing tag* is an HTML tag that indicates the end of an HTML command; the text affected by the command appears before the closing tag. Closing tags always begin with </ and end with >, as in </html>.

▶ An *empty tag* is an HTML tag that issues an HTML command without enclosing any text in the page. Empty tags always begin with < and end with />, as in <br /> and <img />.

For example, the <body> tag in Listing 2.1 tells the web browser where the actual body text of the page begins, and </body> indicates where it ends. Everything between the <body> and </body> tags will appear in the main display area of the web browser window, as shown in Figure 2.1.

The very top of the browser window (refer to Figure 2.1) shows title text, which is any text that is located between <title> and </title>. The title text is also used to identify the page on the browser's Bookmarks or Favorites menu, depending on which browser you use. It's important to provide titles for your pages so that visitors to the page can properly bookmark them for future reference.

You will use the <body> and <title> tag pairs in every HTML page you create because every web page needs a title and body text. You will also use the <html> and <head> tag pairs, which are the other two tags shown in Listing 2.1. Putting <html> at the very beginning of a document simply indicates that the document is a web page. The </html> at the end indicates that the web page is over.

Within a page, there is a head section and a body section. Each section is identified by <head> and <body> tags. The idea is that information in the head of the page somehow describes the page but isn't actually displayed by a web browser. Information placed in the body, however, is displayed by a web browser. The <head> tag always appears near the beginning of the HTML code for a page, just after the opening <html> tag.

The <title> tag pair used to identify the title of a page appears within the head of the page, which means it is placed after the opening <head> tag and before the closing </head> tag. In upcoming chapters, you'll learn about some other advanced header information that can go between <head> and </head>, such as style sheet rules that are used to format the page, as well as the JavaScript you'll learn to write and embed.

The <p> tag used in Listing 2.1 encloses a paragraph of text. You should enclose your chunks of text in the appropriate container tags whenever possible.

Organizing a Page with Paragraphs and Line Breaks

When a web browser displays HTML pages, it pays no attention to line endings or the number of spaces between words. For example, the top version of the poem shown in Figure 2.2 appears with a single space between

NOTE

You no doubt noticed in Listing 2.1 that there is some extra code associated with the <html> tag. This code consists of two attributes (xmlns and xml:lang), which are used to specify additional information related to the tag. These two attributes are standard requirements of all XHTML web pages; the former defines the XML namespace, whereas the latter defines the language of the content. Throughout this book, a standard namespace is defined, and the English language is used. If you are writing in a different language, replace the "en" (for English) with the language identifier relevant to you.

TIP

You might find it convenient to create and save a bare-bones page (also known as a *skeleton* page, or *template*) with just the opening and closing <html>, <head>, <title>, and <body> tags, similar to the document used in Listing 2.1. You can then open that document as a starting point whenever you want to make a new web page and save yourself the trouble of typing all those obligatory tags every time.

all words, even though that's not how it's entered in Listing 2.2. This is because extra whitespace in HTML code is automatically reduced to a single space. Additionally, when the text reaches the edge of the browser window, it automatically wraps to the next line, no matter where the line breaks were in the original HTML file.

FIGURE 2.2
When the HTML in Listing 2.2 is viewed as a web page, line and paragraph breaks only appear where there are <br /> and <p> tags.

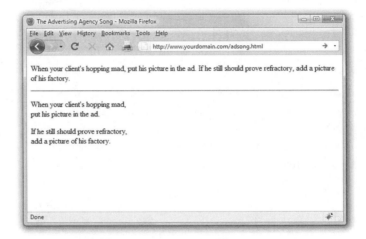

LISTING 2.2   HTML Containing Paragraph and Line Breaks

```
<?xml version="1.0" encoding="UTF-8"?>
<!DOCTYPE html PUBLIC "-//W3C//DTD XHTML 1.1//EN"
  "http://www.w3.org/TR/xhtml11/DTD/xhtml11.dtd">

<html xmlns="http://www.w3.org/1999/xhtml" xml:lang="en">
  <head>
    <title>The Advertising Agency Song</title>
  </head>

  <body>
    <p>
      When your client's    hopping mad,
      put his picture in the ad.

      If he still should    prove refractory,
      add a picture of his factory.

    </p>

    <hr />

    <p>
      When your client's hopping mad,<br />
      put his picture in the ad.
```

LISTING 2.2   Continued

```
    </p>
    <p>
      If he still should prove refractory,<br />
      add a picture of his factory.
    </p>
  </body>
</html>
```

You must use HTML tags if you want to control where line and paragraph breaks actually appear. When text is enclosed within the <p></p> container tags, a line break will be assumed after the closing tag. In later chapters, you will learn to control the height of the line break using CSS. The <br /> tag forces a line break within a paragraph. Unlike the other tags you've seen so far, <br /> doesn't require a closing </br> tag—this is one of those empty tags discussed earlier. Although HTML 4 does not require the / in empty tags, XHTML does and future standards will, so it's important for you to stick to the latest standards and create web pages that are coded properly. Always code empty tags so that they end with />.

The poem in Listing 2.2 and Figure 2.2 shows the <br /> and <p> tags being used to separate the lines and verses of an advertising agency song. You might have also noticed the <hr /> tag in the listing, which causes a horizontal rule line to appear on the page (see Figure 2.2). Inserting a horizontal rule with the <hr /> tag also causes a line break, even if you don't include a <br /> tag along with it. Like <br />, the <hr /> horizontal rule tag is an empty tag and therefore never gets a closing </hr> tag.

CAUTION

You might come across a lot of web content that includes <br> instead of <br />. Or you might see other content that does not include the closing </p> tag. Just remember there is a lot of antiquated web content floating around the Internet, and just because you see it in use doesn't mean it's correct. Save yourself a lot of future work and frustration by adhering to the standards you learn in this book. Developing clean HTML coding habits is a very important part of becoming a successful web designer.

TRY IT YOURSELF ▼

Formatting Text in HTML

Take a passage of text and try your hand at formatting it as proper HTML.

1. Add <html><head><title>My Title</title></head><body> to the beginning of the text (using your own title for your page instead of My Title). Also include the boilerplate code at the top of the page that takes care of meeting the requirements of XHTML.

2. Add </body></html> to the very end of the text.

3. Add a <p> tag at the beginning of each paragraph and a </p> tag at the end of each paragraph.

4. Use <br /> tags anywhere you want single-spaced line breaks.

5. Use <hr /> to draw horizontal rules separating major sections of text, or wherever you'd like to see a line across the page.

▼ TRY IT YOURSELF

Formatting Text in HTML

continued

CAUTION

If you are using a word processor to create the web page, be sure to save the HTML file in plain-text or ASCII format.

6. Save the file as mypage.html (using your own filename instead of mypage).

7. Open the file in a web browser to see your web content. (Send the file via FTP to your web hosting account, if you have one.)

8. If something doesn't look right, go back to the text editor to make corrections and save the file again (and send it to your web hosting account, if applicable). You then need to click Reload/Refresh in the browser to see the changes you made.

Organizing Your Content with Headings

When you browse through web pages on the Internet, you'll notice that many of them have a heading at the top that appears larger and bolder than the rest of the text. Listing 2.3 is sample code and text for a simple web page containing an example of a heading as compared to normal paragraph text. Any text between <h1> and </h1> tags will appear as a large heading. Additionally, <h2> and <h3> make progressively smaller headings, and so on as far down as <h6>.

LISTING 2.3   Heading Tags

```
<?xml version="1.0" encoding="UTF-8"?>
<!DOCTYPE html PUBLIC "-//W3C//DTD XHTML 1.1//EN"
  "http://www.w3.org/TR/xhtml11/DTD/xhtml11.dtd">

<html xmlns="http://www.w3.org/1999/xhtml" xml:lang="en">
  <head>
    <title>My Widgets</title>
  </head>

  <body>
    <h1>My Widgets</h1>
    <p>My widgets are the best in the land. Continue reading to
    learn more about my widgets.</p>

    <h2>Widget Features</h2>
    <p>If I had any features to discuss,  you can bet I'd do
    it here.</p>

    <h3>Pricing</h3>
    <p>Here, I would talk about my widget pricing.</p>
```

LISTING 2.3   Continued

```
  <h3>Comparisons</h3>
  <p>Here, I would talk about how my widgets compare to my
  competitor's widgets.</p>

  </body>
</html>
```

As you can see in Figure 2.3, the HTML that creates headings couldn't be simpler. In this example, the phrase "My Widgets" is prominently displayed using the <h1> tag. To create the biggest (level 1) heading, just put an <h1> tag at the beginning and a </h1> tag at the end of the text you want to use as a heading. For a slightly smaller (level 2) heading—for information that is of lesser importance than the title— use the <h2> and </h2> tags around your text. For content that should appear even less prominently than a level 2 heading, use the <h3> and </h3> tags around your text.

However, bear in mind that your headings should follow a content hierarchy; use only one level 1 heading, have one (or more) level 2 headings after the level 1 heading, use level 3 headings directly after level 2 headings, and so on. Do not fall into the trap of assigning headings to content just to make that content display a certain way. Instead, ensure that you are categorizing your content appropriately (as a main heading, a secondary heading, and so on), while using display styles to make that text render a particular way in a web browser.

NOTE

By now you've probably caught on to the fact that HTML code is often indented by its author to reveal the relationship between different parts of the HTML document. This indentation is entirely voluntary—you could just as easily run all the tags together with no spaces or line breaks and they would still look fine when viewed in a browser. The indentations are for you so that you can quickly look at a page full of code and understand how it fits together. Indenting your code is a very good web design habit and ultimately makes your pages easier to maintain.

FIGURE 2.3
The use of three levels of headings shows the hierarchy of content on this sample product page.

NOTE

On many web pages nowadays, graphical images of ornately rendered letters and logos are often used in place of the ordinary text headings discussed in this chapter. However, using text headings is one of many search engine optimization (SEO) tips that you will learn about in Chapter 28, "Helping People Find Your Web Pages." Search engines look at heading tags to see how you organize your content; they give higher preference to content that you have indicated is more important (for example, a level 1 heading) versus content that you indicate is of lesser importance (lower-level headings).

CAUTION

Don't forget that anything placed in the head of a web page is not intended to be viewed on the page, whereas everything in the body of the page is intended for viewing.

Theoretically, you can also use <h4>, <h5>, and <h6> tags to make progressively less important headings, but these aren't used very often. Web browsers seldom show a noticeable difference between these headings and the <h3> headings anyway, and content usually isn't displayed in such a manner as to need six levels of headings to show the content hierarchy.

It's important to remember the difference between a *title* and a *heading*. These two words are often interchangeable in day-to-day English, but when you're talking HTML, <title> gives the entire page an identifying name that isn't displayed on the page itself; it's displayed only on the browser window's title bar. The heading tags, on the other hand, cause some text on the page to be displayed with visual emphasis. There can be only one <title> per page and it must appear within the <head> and </head> tags, whereas you can have as many <h1>, <h2>, and <h3> headings as you want, in any order that suits your fancy. However, as I mentioned before, you should use the heading tags to keep tight control over content hierarchy; do not use headings as a way to achieve a particular look because that's what CSS is for.

You'll learn to take complete control over the appearance of text on your web pages in Parts II and III of this book. Short of taking exacting control of the size, family, and color of fonts, headings provide the easiest and most popular way to draw extra attention to important text.

Validating Your Web Content

In the first chapter, I discussed ways to test your pages; one very important way to test your pages is to *validate* them. Think of it this way: It's one thing to design and draw a beautiful set of house plans, but it's quite another for an architect to stamp it as a safe structure suitable for construction. Validating your web pages is a similar process; in this case, however, the architect is an application—not a person.

In brief, validation is the process of testing your pages with a special application that searches for errors and makes sure your pages follow the strict XHTML standard. Validation is simple. In fact, the standards body responsible for developing web standards—the World Wide Web Consortium (W3C)—offers an online validation tool you can use. To validate a page, follow this URL: http://validator.w3.org/. The W3C Markup Validation Service is shown in Figure 2.4.

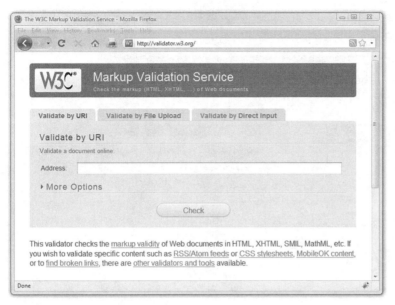

FIGURE 2.4
The W3C Markup Validation Service enables you to validate an HTML (XHTML) document to ensure it has been coded accurately.

If you've already published a page online, you can use the Validate by URI tab. Use the Validate by File Upload tab to validate files stored on your local computer file system. The Validate by Direct Input tab enables you to paste the contents of a file from your text editor. If all goes well, your page will get a passing report (see Figure 2.5).

If the W3C Markup Validation Service encounters an error in your web page, it will provide specific details (including the line numbers of the offending code). This is a great way to hunt down problems and rid your pages of buggy code. Validation not only informs you whether your pages are constructed properly, it also assists you in finding and fixing problems before you post pages for the world to see.

Peeking at Other Designers' Pages

Given the visual and sometimes audio pizzazz present in many popular web pages, you probably realize that the simple pages described in this chapter are only the tip of the HTML iceberg. Now that you know the basics, you might surprise yourself with how much of the rest you can pick up just by looking at other people's pages on the Internet. You can see the HTML for any page by right-clicking and selecting View Source in any web browser.

Don't worry if you aren't yet able to decipher what some HTML tags do or exactly how to use them yourself. You'll find out about all those things in the next few chapters. However, sneaking a preview now will show you the tags that you do know in action and give you a taste of what you'll soon be able to do with your web pages.

TIP

Some web development tools include built-in validation features you can use in lieu of the W3C Markup Validation Service. Some examples include browser extensions such as Firebug (http://getfirebug.com/) and HTML Validator (http://users.skynet.be/mgueury/mozilla/), but many other programs offer similar functionality; check your user documentation.

FIGURE 2.5
If a page passes the W3C Markup
Validation Service, you know it is
ready for prime time.

The Scoop on HTML, XML, XHTML, and HTML5

In its early days, HTML was great because it allowed scientists to share information over the Internet in an efficient and relatively structured manner. It wasn't until later that graphical web browsers were created and HTML started being used to code more than scientific papers. HTML quickly went from a tidy little markup language for researchers to an online publishing language. After it was established that HTML could be jazzed up for graphical browsing, the creators of web browsers went crazy by adding lots of nifty features to the language. Although these new features were neat at first, they compromised the original design of HTML and introduced inconsistencies when it came to how browsers displayed web pages; new features worked on only one browser or another, and you were out of luck if you happened to be running the wrong browser. HTML started to resemble a bad remodeling job of a house—a job done by too many contractors and without proper planning. As it turns out, some of the browser-specific features created during this time have now been adopted as standards whereas others have been dropped completely.

As with most revolutions, the birth of the Web was very chaotic, and the modifications to HTML reflected that chaos. Over the years, a significant effort has been made to reel in the inconsistencies of HTML and restore some order to the language. The problem with disorder in HTML is that it results in web browsers having to guess at how a page is to be displayed, which is not a good thing. Ideally, a web page designer should be able to define exactly how a page is to look and have it look the same regardless of what kind of browser or operating system someone is using. Better still, a designer should be able to define exactly what a page *means* and have that page look consistent across different browsers and platforms. This utopia is still off in the future somewhere, but a markup language called XML (Extensible Markup Language) began to play a significant role in leading us toward it.

XML is a general language used to create specific languages, such as HTML. It might sound a little strange, but it really just means that XML provides a basic structure and set of rules to which any markup language must adhere. Using XML, you can create a unique markup language to describe just about any kind of information, including web pages. Knowing that XML is a language for creating other markup languages, you could create your own version of HTML using XML. You could even create a markup language called BCCML (Bottle Cap Collection Markup Language), for example, which you could use to create and manage your extensive collection of rare bottle caps. The point is that XML lays the ground rules for organizing information in a consistent manner, and that information can be anything from web pages to bottle caps.

You might be thinking that bottle caps don't have anything to do with the Web, so why mention them? The reason is that XML is not entirely about web pages. XML is actually broader than the Web in that it can be used to represent any kind of information on any kind of computer. If you can visualize all the information whizzing around the globe among computers, mobile phones, handheld computers, televisions, and radios, you can start to understand why XML has much broader applications than just cleaning up web pages. However, one of the first applications of XML is to restore some order to the Web, which is why XML is relevant to learning HTML.

If XML describes data better than HTML, does it mean that XML is set to upstage HTML as the markup language of choice for the Web? No. XML is not a replacement for HTML; it's not even a competitor of HTML. XML's impact on HTML has to do with cleaning up HTML. HTML is a relatively unstructured language that benefits from the rules of XML. The natural merger of the two technologies resulted in HTML's adherence to the rules and structure of XML. To accomplish this merger, a new version of HTML was formulated that follows the stricter rules of XML. The new XML-compliant version of HTML is known as XHTML. Fortunately for you, you'll actually be learning XHTML throughout this book because it is really just a cleaner version of HTML.

You might have heard about HTML5, which is touted as the next web standard. It will be, but not quite yet. When it does become a web standard, it will not render XHTML useless—HTML5 is not a replacement for XHTML, but instead is a major revision of HTML 4. In other words, XHTML and HTML5 can coexist on the Web, and web browsers that currently support XHTML will also (one day) support HTML5 as well.

The goal of this book is to guide you through the basics of web publishing, using XHTML and CSS as the core languages of those pages. However, whenever possible, I will note elements of the languages that are not present in HTML5, should you want to design your content for even further sustainability. If you gain a solid understanding of web publishing and the ways in which CSS works with the overall markup language of the page (be it XHTML or HTML5), you will be in a good position if you decide you want to move from XHTML to HTML5.

Summary

This chapter introduced the basics of what web pages are and how they work, including the history and differences between HTML and XHTML. You learned that coded HTML commands are included in a text file, and that typing HTML text yourself is better than using a graphical editor to create HTML commands for you—especially when you're learning HTML.

You were introduced to the most basic and important HTML tags. By adding these coded commands to any plain-text document, you can quickly transform it into a bona fide web page. You learned that the first step in creating a web page is to put a few obligatory HTML tags at the beginning and end, including a title for the page. You then mark where paragraphs and lines end and add horizontal rules and headings if you want them. Table 2.1 summarizes all the tags introduced in this chapter.

TABLE 2.1   HTML Tags Covered in Chapter 2

Tag	Function
`<html>...</html>`	Encloses the entire HTML document.
`<head>...</head>`	Encloses the head of the HTML document. Used within the `<html>` tag pair.
`<title>...</title>`	Indicates the title of the document. Used within the `<head>` tag pair.
`<body>...</body>`	Encloses the body of the HTML document. Used within the `<html>` tag pair.
`<p>...</p>`	A paragraph; skips a line between paragraphs.
` `	A line break.
`<hr />`	A horizontal rule line.
`<h1>...</h1>`	A first-level heading.
`<h2>...</h2>`	A second-level heading.
`<h3>...</h3>`	A third-level heading.
`<h4>...</h4>`	A fourth-level heading (seldom used).
`<h5>...</h5>`	A fifth-level heading (seldom used).
`<h6>...</h6>`	A sixth-level heading (seldom used).

Finally, you learned about XML and XHTML, how they relate to HTML, and what HTML5 means in relation to what it is you're learning here.

Q&A

Q. I've created a web page, but when I open the file in my web browser, I see all the text including the HTML tags. Sometimes I even see weird gobbledygook characters at the top of the page! What did I do wrong?

A. You didn't save the file as plain text. Try saving the file again, being careful to save it as Text Only or ASCII Text. If you can't quite figure out how to get your word processor to do that, don't stress. Just type your HTML files in Notepad or TextEdit instead and everything should work just fine. (Also, always make sure that the filename of your web page ends in .html or .htm.)

Q. I've seen web pages on the Internet that don't have <html> tags at the beginning. You said pages always have to start with <html>. What's the deal?

A. Many web browsers will forgive you if you forget to include the <html> tag and will display the page correctly anyway. However, it's a very good idea to include it because some software does need it to identify the page as valid HTML. Besides, you want your pages to be bona fide XHTML pages so that they conform to the latest web standards.

Workshop

The workshop contains quiz questions and exercises to help you solidify your understanding of the material covered. Try to answer all questions before looking at the "Answers" section that follows.

Quiz

1. What four tags are required in every HTML page?

2. What HTML tags and text would you use to produce the following web content:

- ▶ A small heading with the words We are Proud to Present
- ▶ A horizontal rule across the page
- ▶ A large heading with the one word Orbit
- ▶ A medium-sized heading with the words The Geometric Juggler
- ▶ Another horizontal rule

3. What code would you use to create a complete HTML web page with the title Foo Bar, a heading at the top that reads Happy Hour at the Foo Bar, followed by the words Come on down! in regular type?

Answers

1. <html>, <head>, <title>, and <body> (along with their closing tags, </html>, </head>, </title>, and </body>).

2. Your code would look like this:

```
<h3>We are Proud to Present</h3>
<hr />
<h1>Orbit</h1>
<h2>The Geometric Juggler</h2>
<hr />
```

3. Your code would look like this:

```
<?xml version="1.0" encoding="UTF-8"?>
<!DOCTYPE html PUBLIC "-//W3C//DTD XHTML 1.1//EN"
  "http://www.w3.org/TR/xhtml11/DTD/xhtml11.dtd">

<html xmlns="http://www.w3.org/1999/xhtml" xml:lang="en">
  <head>
    <title>Foo Bar</title>
  </head>

  <body>
    <h1>Happy Hour at the Foo Bar</h1>
    <p>Come on Down!</p>
  </body>
</html>
```

Exercises

▶ Even if your main goal in reading this book is to create web content for your business, you might want to make a personal web page just for practice. Type a few paragraphs to introduce yourself to the world and use the HTML tags you've learned in this chapter to make them into a web page.

▶ Throughout the book, you'll be following along with the code examples and making pages of your own. Take a moment now to set up a basic document template containing the XML declaration, doctype declaration, and tags for the core HTML document structure. That way, you can be ready to copy and paste that information whenever you need it.

CHAPTER 3

Understanding Cascading Style Sheets

In the previous chapter, you learned the basics of HTML and XHTML, including how to set up a skeletal HTML template for all your web content. In this chapter, you will learn how to fine-tune the display of your web content using *Cascading Style Sheets (CSS)*.

The concept behind style sheets is simple: You create a style sheet document that specifies the fonts, colors, spacing, and other characteristics that establish a unique look for a website. You then link every page that should have that look to the style sheet, instead of specifying all those styles repeatedly in each separate document. Therefore, when you decide to change your official corporate typeface or color scheme, you can modify all your web pages at once just by changing one or two entries in your style sheet rather than changing them in all of your static web files. So, a *style sheet* is a grouping of formatting instructions that controls the appearance of several HTML pages at once.

Style sheets enable you to set a great number of formatting characteristics, including exacting typeface controls, letter and line spacing, and margins and page borders, just to name a few. Style sheets also enable sizes and other measurements to be specified in familiar units, such as inches, millimeters, points, and picas. You can also use style sheets to precisely position graphics and text anywhere on a web page, either at specific coordinates or relative to other items on the page.

In short, style sheets bring a sophisticated level of display to the Web. And they do so—you'll pardon the expression—with style.

WHAT YOU'LL LEARN IN THIS CHAPTER:

▶ How to create a basic style sheet

▶ How to use style classes

▶ How to use style IDs

▶ How to construct internal style sheets and inline styles

NOTE

If you have three or more web pages that share (or should share) similar formatting and fonts, you might want to create a style sheet for them as you read this chapter. Even if you choose not to create a complete style sheet, you'll find it helpful to apply styles to individual HTML elements directly within a web page.

How CSS Works

The technology behind style sheets is called CSS, which stands for Cascading Style Sheets. CSS is a language that defines style constructs such as fonts, colors, and positioning, which are used to describe how information on a web page is formatted and displayed. CSS styles can be stored directly in an HTML web page or in a separate style sheet file. Either way, style sheets contain style rules that apply styles to elements of a given type. When used externally, style sheet rules are placed in an external style sheet document with the file extension .css.

A *style rule* is a formatting instruction that can be applied to an element on a web page, such as a paragraph of text or a link. Style rules consist of one or more *style properties* and their associated values. An *internal style sheet* is placed directly within a web page, whereas an *external style sheet* exists in a separate document and is simply linked to a web page via a special tag—more on this tag in a moment.

NOTE

You might notice that I use the term *element* a fair amount in this chapter (and I will for the rest of the book, for that matter). An *element* is simply a piece of information (content) in a web page, such as an image, a paragraph, or a link. Tags are used to code elements, and you can think of an element as a tag complete with descriptive information (attributes, text, images, and so on) within the tag.

The *cascading* part of the name CSS refers to the manner in which style sheet rules are applied to elements in an HTML document. More specifically, styles in a CSS style sheet form a hierarchy in which more specific styles override more general styles. It is the responsibility of CSS to determine the precedence of style rules according to this hierarchy, which establishes a cascading effect. If that sounds a bit confusing, just think of the cascading mechanism in CSS as being similar to genetic inheritance, in which general traits are passed from parents to a child, but more specific traits are entirely unique to the child. Base style rules are applied throughout a style sheet but can be overridden by more specific style rules.

A quick example should clear things up. Take a look at the following code to see whether you can tell what's going on with the color of the text:

```
<div style="color:green">
  This text is green.
  <p style="color:blue">This text is blue.</p>
  <p>This text is still green.</p>
</div>
```

In the previous example, the color green is applied to the <div> tag via the color style property. Therefore, the text in the <div> tag is colored green. Because both <p> tags are children of the <div> tag, the green text style cascades down to them. However, the first <p> tag overrides the color style and changes it to blue. The end result is that the first line (not surrounded by a paragraph tag) is green, the first official paragraph is blue, and the second official paragraph retains the cascaded green color.

If you made it through that description on your own, congratulations. If you understood it after I explained it in the text, congratulations to you as well. Understanding CSS isn't like understanding rocket science, although many people will try to convince you that it is (so that they can charge high consultation fees, most likely!).

Like many web technologies, CSS has evolved over the years. The original version of CSS, known as *Cascading Style Sheets Level 1* (*CSS1*) was created in 1996. The later CSS 2 standard was created in 1998, and CSS 2 is still in use today. All modern web browsers support CSS 2, and you can safely use CSS 2 style sheets without too much concern. So when I talk about CSS throughout the book, I'm referring to CSS 2.

You'll find a complete reference guide to CSS at http://www.w3.org/Style/CSS/. The rest of this chapter explains how to put CSS to good use.

A Basic Style Sheet

Despite their intimidating power, style sheets can be simple to create. Consider the web pages shown in Figure 3.1 and Figure 3.2. These pages share several visual properties that could be put into a common style sheet:

▶ They use a large, bold Verdana font for the headings and a normal size and weight Verdana font for the body text.

▶ They use an image named logo.gif floating within the content and on the right side of the page.

▶ All text is black except for subheadings, which are purple.

▶ They have margins on the left side and at the top.

▶ There is vertical space between lines of text.

▶ The footnotes are centered and in small print.

FIGURE 3.1
This page uses a style sheet to fine-tune the appearance and spacing of the text and images.

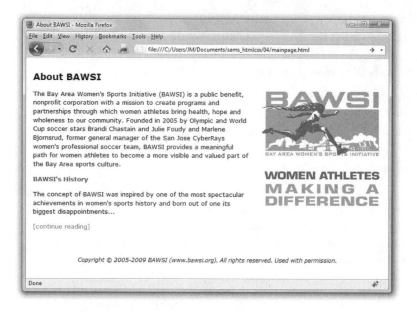

FIGURE 3.2
This page uses the same style sheet as the one shown in Figure 3.1, thus maintaining a consistent look and feel.

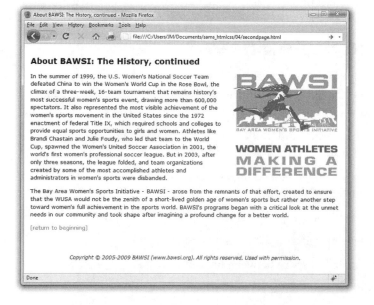

Listing 3.1 shows the code for the style sheet specifying these properties.

LISTING 3.1   A Single External Style Sheet

```
body {
  font-size: 10pt;
  font-family: Verdana, Geneva, Arial, Helvetica, sans-serif;
  color: black;
  line-height: 14pt;
  padding-left: 5pt;
  padding-right: 5pt;
  padding-top: 5pt;
}

h1 {
  font: 14pt Verdana, Geneva, Arial, Helvetica, sans-serif;
  font-weight: bold;
  line-height: 20pt;
}

p.subheader {
  font-weight: bold;
  color: #593d87;
}

img {
  padding: 3pt;
  float: right;
}

a {
  text-decoration: none;
}

a:link, a:visited {
  color: #8094d6;
}

a:hover, a:active {
  color: #FF9933;
}

div.footer {
  font-size: 9pt;
  font-style: italic;
  line-height: 12pt;
  text-align: center;
  padding-top: 30pt;
}
```

This might initially appear to be a lot of code, but if you look closely, you'll see that there isn't a lot of information on each line of code. It's fairly standard to place individual style rules on their own line to help make style sheets more readable, but that is a personal preference; you could put all the rules on one line as long as you kept using the semicolon to separate each rule (more on that in a bit). Speaking of code readability, perhaps the first thing you noticed about this style sheet code is that it doesn't look anything like normal HTML code. CSS uses a language all its own to specify style sheets.

Of course, the listing includes some familiar HTML tags. As you might guess, body, h1, p, img, a, and div in the style sheet refer to the corresponding tags in the HTML documents to which the style sheet will be applied. The curly braces after each tag name contain the specifications for how all content within that tag should appear.

In this case, the style sheet says that all body text should be rendered at a size of 10 points, in the Verdana font (if possible), with the color black, and 14 points between lines. If the user does not have the Verdana font installed, the list of fonts in the style sheet represents the order in which the browser should search for fonts to use: Geneva, then Arial, and then Helvetica. If the user has none of those fonts, the browser will use whatever default sans serif font is available. Additionally, the page should have left, right, and top margins of 5 points each.

Any text within an <h1> tag should be rendered in boldface Verdana at a size of 14 points. Moving on, any paragraph that uses only the <p> tag will inherit all the styles indicated by the body element. However, if the <p> tag uses a special class named subheader, the text will appear bold and in the color #593d87 (a purple color).

NOTE

You can specify font sizes as large as you like with style sheets, although some display devices and printers will not correctly handle fonts larger than 200 points.

The pt after each measurement in Listing 3.1 means *points* (there are 72 points in an inch). If you prefer, you can specify any style sheet measurement in inches (in), centimeters (cm), pixels (px), or widths-of-a-letter-m, which are called ems (em).

You might have noticed that each style rule in the listing ends with a semicolon (;). Semicolons are used to separate style rules from each other. It is therefore customary to end each style rule with a semicolon, so you can easily add another style rule after it.

To link this style sheet to HTML documents, include a <link /> tag in the <head> section of each document. Listing 3.2 shows the HTML code for the page shown in Figure 3.1. It contains the following <link /> tag:

```
<link rel="stylesheet" type="text/css" href="styles.css" />
```

This assumes that the style sheet is stored under the name `styles.css` in the same folder as the HTML document. As long as the web browser supports style sheets—and all modern browsers do support style sheets—the properties specified in the style sheet will apply to the content in the page without the need for any special HTML formatting code. This confirms the ultimate goal of XHTML, which is to provide a separation between the content in a web page and the specific formatting required to display that content.

LISTING 3.2   HTML Code for the Page Shown in Figure 3.1

```
<?xml version="1.0" encoding="UTF-8"?>
<!DOCTYPE html PUBLIC "-//W3C//DTD XHTML 1.1//EN"
  "http://www.w3.org/TR/xhtml11/DTD/xhtml11.dtd">

<html xmlns="http://www.w3.org/1999/xhtml" xml:lang="en">
  <head>
    <title>About BAWSI</title>
    <link rel="stylesheet" type="text/css" href="styles.css" />
  </head>
  <body>
    <h1>About BAWSI</h1>
    <p><img src="logo.gif" alt="BAWSI logo"/>The Bay Area Women's
    Sports Initiative (BAWSI) is a public benefit, nonprofit
    corporation with a mission to create programs and partnerships
    through which women athletes bring health, hope and wholeness to
    our community. Founded in 2005 by Olympic and World Cup soccer
    stars Brandi Chastain and Julie Foudy and Marlene Bjornsrud,
    former general manager of the San Jose CyberRays women's
    professional soccer team, BAWSI provides a meaningful path for
    women athletes to become a more visible and valued part of the
    Bay Area sports culture.</p>
    <p class="subheader">BAWSI's History</p>
    <p>The concept of BAWSI was inspired by one of the most
    spectacular achievements in women's sports history and born out
    of one its biggest disappointments... </p>
    <p><a href="secondpage.html">[continue reading]</a></p>
    <div class="footer">Copyright &copy; 2005-2009 BAWSI
  (www.bawsi.org). All rights reserved.  Used with permission.</div>
  </body>
</html>
```

The code in Listing 3.2 is interesting because it contains no formatting of any kind. In other words, there is nothing in the HTML code that dictates how the text and images are to be displayed—no colors, no fonts, nothing. Yet the page is carefully formatted and rendered to the screen, thanks to the link to the external style sheet, styles.css. The real benefit to this

TIP

In most web browsers, you can view the style rules in a style sheet by opening the .css file and choosing Notepad or another text editor as the helper application to view the file. (To determine the name of the .css file, look at the HTML source of any web page that links to it.) To edit your own style sheets, just use a text editor.

NOTE

Although CSS is widely supported in all modern web browsers, it hasn't always enjoyed such wide support. Additionally, not every browser's support of CSS is flawless. To find out about how major browsers compare to each other in terms of CSS support, take a look at this website: http://www.quirksmode.org/css/contents.html.

approach is that you can easily create a site with multiple pages that maintains a consistent look and feel. And you have the benefit of isolating the visual style of the page to a single document (the style sheet) so that one change impacts all pages.

▼ TRY IT YOURSELF

Create a Style Sheet of Your Own

Starting from scratch, create a new text document called mystyles.css and add some style rules for the following basic HTML tags: <body>, <p>, <h1>, and <h2>. After your style sheet has been created, make a new HTML file that contains these basic tags. Play around with different style rules and see for yourself how simple it is to change entire blocks of text in paragraphs with one simple change in a style sheet file.

A CSS Style Primer

You now have a basic knowledge of CSS style sheets and how they are based on style rules that describe the appearance of information in web pages. The next few sections of this chapter provide a quick overview of some of the most important style properties and allow you to get started using CSS in your own style sheets.

CSS includes various style properties that are used to control fonts, colors, alignment, and margins, to name just a few. The style properties in CSS can be generally grouped into two major categories:

▶ **Layout properties**—Consist of properties that affect the positioning of elements on a web page, such as margins, padding, alignment, and so on

▶ **Formatting properties**—Consist of properties that affect the visual display of elements within a website, such as the font type, size, color, and so on

Layout Properties

CSS layout properties are used to determine how content is placed on a web page. One of the most important layout properties is the display property, which describes how an element is displayed with respect to other elements. There are four possible values for the display property:

▶ **block**—The element is displayed on a new line, as in a new paragraph.

▶ **list-item**—The element is displayed on a new line with a list-item mark (bullet) next to it.

▶ **inline**—The element is displayed inline with the current paragraph.

▶ **none**—The element is not displayed; it is hidden.

It's easier to understand the display property if you visualize each element on a web page occupying a rectangular area when displayed—the display property controls the manner in which this rectangular area is displayed. For example, the block value results in the element being placed on a new line by itself, whereas the inline value places the element next to the content just before it. The display property is one of the few style properties that can be applied in most style rules. Following is an example of how to set the display property:

```
display:block;
```

You control the size of the rectangular area for an element with the width and height properties. Like many size-related CSS properties, width and height property values can be specified in several different units of measurement:

▶ **in**—Inches

▶ **cm**—Centimeters

▶ **mm**—Millimeters

▶ **px**—Pixels

▶ **pt**—Points

You can mix and match units however you choose within a style sheet, but it's generally a good idea to be consistent across a set of similar style properties. For example, you might want to stick with points for font properties or pixels for dimensions. Following is an example of setting the width of an element using pixel units:

```
width: 200px;
```

Formatting Properties

CSS formatting properties are used to control the appearance of content on a web page, as opposed to controlling the physical positioning of the content. One of the most popular formatting properties is the border property,

NOTE

The display property relies on a concept known as *relative positioning*, which means that elements are positioned relative to the location of other elements on a page. CSS also supports *absolute positioning*, which enables you to place an element at an exact location on a page independent of other elements. You'll learn more about both of these types of positioning in Part III, "Advanced Web Page Design with CSS."

which is used to establish a visible boundary around an element with a box or partial box. The following `border` properties provide a means of describing the borders of an element:

- ▶ **border-width**—The width of the border edge
- ▶ **border-color**—The color of the border edge
- ▶ **border-style**—The style of the border edge
- ▶ **border-left**—The left side of the border
- ▶ **border-right**—The right side of the border
- ▶ **border-top**—The top of the border
- ▶ **border-bottom**—The bottom of the border
- ▶ **border**—All the border sides

The `border-width` property is used to establish the width of the border edge. It is often expressed in pixels, as the following code demonstrates:

```
border-width:5px;
```

Not surprisingly, the `border-color` and `border-style` properties are used to set the border color and style. Following is an example of how these two properties are set:

```
border-color:blue;
border-style:dotted;
```

The `border-style` property can be set to any of the following values:

- ▶ **solid**—A single-line border
- ▶ **double**—A double-line border
- ▶ **dashed**—A dashed border
- ▶ **dotted**—A dotted border
- ▶ **groove**—A border with a groove appearance
- ▶ **ridge**—A border with a ridge appearance
- ▶ **inset**—A border with an inset appearance
- ▶ **outset**—A border with an outset appearance
- ▶ **none**—No border

The default value of the `border-style` property is `none`, which is why elements don't have a border unless you set the border property to a different style. The most common border styles are the `solid` and `double` styles.

The `border-left`, `border-right`, `border-top`, and `border-bottom` properties enable you to set the border for each side of an element individually. If you want a border to appear the same on all four sides, you can use the single `border` property by itself, which expects the following styles separated by a space: `border-width`, `border-style`, and `border-color`. Following is an example of using the `border` property to set a border that consists of two (double) red lines that are a total of 10 pixels in width:

```
border:10px double red;
```

Whereas the color of an element's border is set with the `border-color` property, the color of the inner region of an element is set using the `color` and `background-color` properties. The `color` property sets the color of text in an element (foreground) and the `background-color` property sets the color of the background behind the text. Following is an example of setting both color properties to predefined colors:

```
color:black;
background-color:orange;
```

You can also assign custom colors to these properties by specifying the colors in hexadecimal (covered in more detail in Chapter 8, "Working with Colors, Images, and Multimedia") or as RGB (Red, Green, Blue) decimal values, just as you do in HTML:

```
background-color:#999999;
color:rgb(0,0,255);
```

You can also control the alignment and indentation of web page content without too much trouble. This is accomplished with the `text-align` and `text-indent` properties, as the following code demonstrates:

```
text-align:center;
text-indent:12px;
```

After you have an element properly aligned and indented, you might be interested in setting its font. The following font properties are used to set the various parameters associated with fonts:

▶ **font-family**—The family of the font

▶ **font-size**—The size of the font

NOTE

The exception to the default `border-style` of none is when an image is placed within an `<a>` tag so that it serves as a linked image. In that case, a solid border is automatically set by default. That's why you often see linked images with the style `border-style:none`, which turns off the automatic border.

▶ **font-style**—The style of the font (`normal` or `italic`)

▶ **font-weight**—The weight of the font (`light`, `medium`, `bold`, and so on)

The `font-family` property specifies a prioritized list of font family names. A prioritized list is used instead of a single value to provide alternatives in case a font isn't available on a given system. The `font-size` property specifies the size of the font using a unit of measurement, usually points. Finally, the `font-style` property sets the style of the font and the `font-weight` property sets the weight of the font. Following is an example of setting these font properties:

```
font-family: Arial, sans-serif;
font-size: 36pt;
font-style: italic;
font-weight: medium;
```

Now that you know a whole lot more about style properties and how they work, refer back at Listing 3.1 and see whether it makes a bit more sense. Here's a recap of the style properties used in that style sheet, which you can use as a guide for understanding how it works:

▶ **font**—Lets you set many font properties at once. You can specify a list of font names separated by commas; if the first is not available, the next is tried, and so on. You can also include the words `bold` and/or `italic` and a font size. Each of these font properties can be specified separately with `font-family`, `font-size`, `font-weight`, and `font-style` if you prefer.

▶ **line-height**—Also known in the publishing world as *leading*. This sets the height of each line of text, usually in points.

▶ **color**—Sets the text color using the standard color names or hexadecimal color codes (see Chapter 8 for more details).

▶ **text-decoration**—Useful for turning link underlining off—simply set it to `none`. The values of `underline`, `italic`, and `line-through` are also supported. The application of styles to links is covered in more detail in Chapter 7, "Using External and Internal Links."

▶ **text-align**—Aligns text to the `left`, `right`, or `center`, along with justifying the text with a value of `justify`.

▶ **padding**—Adds padding to the left, right, top, and bottom of an element; this padding can be in measurement units or a percentage of the page width. Use `padding-left` and `padding-right` if you want to add padding to the left and right of the element independently. Use

padding-top or padding-bottom to add padding to the top or bottom of
the element, as appropriate. You'll learn more about these style properties in Chapters 9, "Working with Margins, Padding, Alignment, and
Floating," and 10, "Understanding the CSS Box Model and Positioning."

Using Style Classes

This is a "teach yourself" book, so you don't have to go to a single class to
learn how to give your pages great style, although you do need to learn
what a style class is. Whenever you want some of the text on your pages to
look different from the other text, you can create what amounts to a custom-
built HTML tag. Each type of specially formatted text you define is called a
style class. A *style class* is a custom set of formatting specifications that can be
applied to any element in a web page.

Before showing you a style class, I need to take a quick step back and clarify
some CSS terminology. First off, a CSS *style property* is a specific style that
can be assigned a value, such as color or font-size. You associate a style
property and its respective value with elements on a web page by using a
selector. A *selector* is used to identify tags on a page to which you apply
styles. Following is an example of a selector, a property, and a value all
included in a basic style rule:

```
h1 { font: 36pt Courier; }
```

In this code, h1 is the selector, font is the style property, and 36pt Courier
is the value. The selector is important because it means that the font setting
will be applied to all h1 elements in the web page. But maybe you want to
differentiate between some of the h1 elements—what then? The answer lies
in style classes.

Suppose you want two different kinds of <h1> headings for use in your documents. You would create a style class for each one by putting the following
CSS code in a style sheet:

```
h1.silly { font: 36pt Comic Sans; }
h1.serious { font: 36pt Arial; }
```

Notice that these selectors include a period (.) after h1, followed by a
descriptive class name. To choose between the two style classes, use the
class attribute, like this:

```
<h1 class="silly">Marvin's Munchies Inc. </h1>
<p>Text about Marvin's Munchies goes here. </p>
```

Or you could use this:

```
<h1 class="serious">MMI Investor Information</h1>
<p>Text for business investors goes here.</p>
```

When referencing a style class in HTML code, simply specify the class name in the `class` attribute of an element. In the previous example, the words `Marvin's Munchies Inc.` would appear in a 36-point Comic Sans font, assuming that you included a `<link />` to the style sheet at the top of the web page and assuming that the user has the Comic Sans font installed. The words `MMI Investor Information` would appear in the 36-point Arial font instead. You can see another example of classes in action in Listing 3.2; look for the `subheader` `<p>` class and the `footer` `<div>` class.

What if you want to create a style class that could be applied to any element, rather than just headings or some other particular tag? You can associate a style class with the `<div>` tag, as in Listing 3.2, which is used to enclose any text in a block that is somewhat similar to a paragraph of text; the `<div>` tag is another useful container element.

You can essentially create your own custom HTML tag by using the `div` selector followed by a period (`.`) followed by any style class name you make up and any style specifications you choose. That tag can control any number of font, spacing, and margin settings all at once. Wherever you want to apply your custom tag in a page, use a `<div>` tag with the `class` attribute followed by the class name you created.

For example, the style sheet in Listing 3.1 includes the following style class specification:

```
div.footer {
  font-size: 9pt;
  font-style: italic;
  line-height: 12pt;
  text-align: center;
  padding-top: 30pt;
}
```

This style class is applied in Listing 3.2 with the following tag:

```
<div class="footer">
```

Everything between that tag and the closing `</div>` tag in Listing 3.2 appears in 9-point, centered, italic text with 12-point vertical line spacing and 30 points of padding at the top of the element.

What makes style classes so valuable is how they isolate style code from web pages, effectively allowing you to focus your HTML code on the actual

---

TIP

You might have noticed a change in the coding style when multiple properties are included in a style rule. For style rules with a single style, you'll commonly see the property placed on the same line as the rule, like this:

```
div.footer { font-size: 9pt; }
```

However, when a style rule contains multiple style properties, it's much easier to read and understand the code if you list the properties one-per-line, like this:

```
div.footer {
  font-size:9pt;
  font-style: italic;
  line-height:12pt;
  text-align: center;
  padding-top: 30pt;
}
```

content in a page, not how it is going to appear on the screen. Then you can focus on how the content is rendered to the screen by fine-tuning the style sheet. You might be surprised by how a relatively small amount of code in a style sheet can have significant effects across an entire website. This makes your pages much easier to maintain and manipulate.

Using Style IDs

When you create custom style classes, you can use those classes as many times as you would like—they are not unique. However, there will be some instances when you want to have precise control over unique elements for layout or formatting purposes (or both). In such instances, look to IDs instead of classes.

A *style ID* is a custom set of formatting specifications that can be applied only to one element in a web page. You can use IDs across a set of pages but only once per time within each page.

For example, suppose you have a title within the body of all your pages. Each page has only one title, but all the pages themselves include one instance of that title. Following is an example of a selector with an ID indicated, plus a property and a value:

```
p#title {font: 24pt Verdana, Geneva, Arial, sans-serif}
```

Notice that this selector includes a hash mark, or pound sign (#), after p, followed by a descriptive ID name. When referencing a style ID in HTML code, simply specify the ID name in the id attribute of an element, like so:

```
<p id="title">Some Title Goes Here</p>
```

Everything between the opening and closing <p> tags will appear in 24-point Verdana text—but only once on any given page. You will often see style IDs used to define specific parts of a page for layout purposes, such as a header area, footer area, main body area, and so on. These types of areas in a page will appear only once per page, so using an ID rather than a class is the appropriate choice.

Internal Style Sheets and Inline Styles

In some situations, you might want to specify styles that will be used in only one web page, in which case you can enclose a style sheet between <style> and </style> tags and include it directly in an HTML document.

Style sheets used in this manner must appear in the <head> of an HTML document. No <link /> tag is needed, and you cannot refer to that style sheet from any other page (unless you copy it into the beginning of that document, too). This kind of style sheet is known as an internal style sheet, as you learned earlier in the chapter.

Listing 3.3 shows an example of how you might specify an internal style sheet.

LISTING 3.3   A Web Page with an Internal Style Sheet

```
<?xml version="1.0" encoding="UTF-8"?>
<!DOCTYPE html PUBLIC "-//W3C//DTD XHTML 1.1//EN"
  "http://www.w3.org/TR/xhtml11/DTD/xhtml11.dtd">

<html xmlns="http://www.w3.org/1999/xhtml" xml:lang="en">
  <head>
    <title>Some Page</title>

    <style type="text/css">
      div.footer {
        font-size: 9pt;
        line-height: 12pt;
        text-align: center;
      }
    </style>
  </head>
  <body>
  ...
  <div class="footer">
  Copyright 2009 Acme Products, Inc.
  </div>
  </body>
</html>
```

In the listing code, the div.footer style class is specified in an internal style sheet that appears in the head of the page. The style class is now available for use within the body of this page. And, in fact, it is used in the body of the page to style the copyright notice.

Internal style sheets are handy if you want to create a style rule that is used multiple times within a single page. However, in some instances you might need to apply a unique style to one particular element. This calls for an inline style rule, which allows you to specify a style for only a small part of a page, such as an individual element. For example, you can create and apply a style rule within a <p>, <div>, or <span> tag via the style attribute. This type of style is known as an *inline style* because it is specified right there in the middle of the HTML code.

NOTE

<span> and </span> are *dummy* tags that do nothing in and of themselves except specify a range of content to apply any style attributes that you add. The only difference between <div> and <span> is that <div> is a block element and therefore forces a line break, whereas <span> doesn't. Therefore, you should use <span> to modify the style of any portion of text that is to appear in the middle of a sentence or paragraph without any line break.

Here's how a sample `style` attribute might look:

```
<p style="color:green">
  This text is green, but <span style="color:red">this text is
  red.</span>
  Back to green again, but...
</p>
<p>
  ...now the green is over, and we're back to the default color
  for this page.
</p>
```

This code makes use of the <span> tag to show how to apply the `color` style property in an inline style rule. In fact, both the <p> tag and the <span> tag in this example use the `color` property as an inline style. What's important to understand is that the `color:red` style property overrides the `color:green` style property for the text appearing between the <span> and </span> tags. Then in the second paragraph, neither of the color styles applies because it is a completely new paragraph that adheres to the default color of the entire page.

Validate Your Style Sheets

Just as it is important to validate your HTML or XHTML markup, it is important to validate your style sheet. A specific validation tool for CSS can be found at http://jigsaw.w3.org/ css-validator/. Just like the validation tool discussed in Chapter 2, "Understanding HTML and XHTML Connections," you can point the tool to a web address, upload a file, or paste content into the form field provided. The ultimate goal is a result such as that shown in Figure 3.3: valid!

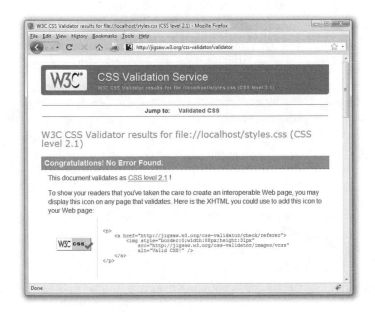

FIGURE 3.3
The W3C CSS Validator shows there are no errors in the style sheet contents of Listing 3.1.

Summary

In this chapter, you learned that a style sheet can control the appearance of many HTML pages at once. It can also give you extremely precise control over the typography, spacing, and positioning of HTML elements. You also discovered that by adding a `style` attribute to almost any HTML tag, you can control the style of any part of an HTML page without referring to a separate style sheet document.

You learned about three main approaches to including style sheets in your website: a separate style sheet file with the extension .css that is linked to in the `<head>` of your documents, a collection of style rules placed in the head of the document within the `<style>` tag, and as rules placed directly in an HTML tag via the `style` attribute.

Table 3.1 summarizes the tags discussed in this chapter. Refer to the CSS 2 style sheet standards at http://www.w3c.org for details on what options can be included after the `<style>` tag or the `style` attribute.

TABLE 3.1   HTML Tags and Attributes Covered in Chapter 3

Tag/Attributes	Function
`<style>...</style>`	Allows an internal style sheet to be included within a document. Used between `<head>` and `</head>`.
Attribute	
`type="contenttype"`	The Internet content type. (Always `"text/css"` for a CSS style sheet.)
`<link />`	Links to an external style sheet (or other document type). Used in the `<head>` section of the document.
Attribute	
`href="url"`	The address of the style sheet.
`type="contenttype"`	The Internet content type. (Always `"text/css"` for a CSS style sheet.)
`rel="stylesheet"`	The link type. (Always `"stylesheet"` for style sheets.)
`<span>...</span>`	Does nothing but provide a place to put `style` or other attributes. (Similar to `<div>...</div>` but does not cause a line break.)
Attribute	
`style="style"`	Includes inline style specifications. (Can be used in `<span>`, `<div>`, `<body>`, and most other HTML tags.)

Q&A

Q. Say I link a style sheet to my page that says all text should be blue, but there's a `<span style="font-color:red">` tag in the page somewhere. Will that text display as blue or will it display as red?

A. Red. Local inline styles always take precedence over external style sheets. Any style specifications you put between `<style>` and `</style>` tags at the top of a page will also take precedence over external style sheets (but not over inline styles later in the same page). This is the cascading effect of style sheets that I mentioned earlier in the chapter. You can think of cascading style effects as starting with an external style sheet, which is overridden by an internal style sheet, which is overridden by inline styles.

Q. Can I link more than one style sheet to a single page?

A. Sure. For example, you might have a sheet for formatting (text, fonts, colors, and so on) and another one for layout (margins, padding, alignment, and so on)—just include a `<link />` for both. Technically speaking, the CSS standard requires web browsers to give the user the option to choose between style sheets when multiple sheets are presented via multiple `<link />` tags. However, in practice, all major web browsers simply include every style sheet. The preferred technique for linking in multiple style sheets involves using the special `@import` command. Following is an example of importing multiple style sheets with `@import`:

```
@import url(styles1.css);
@import url(styles2.css);
```

Similar to the `<link />` tag, the `@import` command must be placed in the head of a web page. You learn more about this handy little command in Chapter 25, "Creating Print-Friendly Web Pages," when you learn how to create a style sheet specifically for printing web pages.

Workshop

The workshop contains quiz questions and exercises to help you solidify your understanding of the material covered. Try to answer all questions before looking at the "Answers" section that follows.

Quiz

1. What code would you use to create a style sheet to specify 30-point blue Arial headings and all other text in double-spaced, 10-point blue Times Roman (or the default browser font)?

2. If you saved the style sheet you made for Question 1 as corporate.css, how would you apply it to a web page named intro.html?

3. How many different ways are there to ensure style rules can be applied to your content?

Answers

1. Your style sheet would include the following:

```
h1 { font: 30pt blue Arial; }
body { font: 10pt blue; }
```

2. Put the following tag between the <head> and </head> tags of the intro.html document:

```
<link rel="stylesheet" type="text/css" href="corporate.css" />
```

3. Three: externally, internally, and inline.

Exercises

▶ Using the style sheet you created earlier in this chapter, add some style classes to your style sheet. To see the fruits of your labor, apply those classes to the HTML page you created as well. Use classes with your <h1> and <p> tags to get the feel for things.

▶ Develop a standard style sheet for your website and link it into all your pages. (Use internal style sheets and/or inline styles for pages that need to deviate from it.) If you work for a corporation, chances are it has already developed font and style specifications for printed materials. Get a copy of those specifications and follow them for company web pages, too.

▶ Be sure to explore the official style sheet specs at http://www.w3.org/Style/CSS/ and try some of the more esoteric style properties not covered in this chapter.

CHAPTER 4

Understanding JavaScript

The World Wide Web (WWW) began as a text-only medium—the first browsers didn't even support images within web pages. The Web has come a long way since those early days, as today's websites include a wealth of visual and interactive features in addition to useful content: graphics, sounds, animation, and video. Web scripting languages, such as JavaScript, are one of the easiest ways to spice up a web page and to interact with users in new ways.

The first part of this chapter introduces the concept of Web scripting and the JavaScript language. As the chapter moves ahead, you'll learn how to include JavaScript commands directly in your HTML documents and how your scripts will be executed when the page is viewed in a browser. You will work with a simple script, edit it, and test it in your browser, all the while learning the basic tasks involved in creating and using JavaScript scripts.

Learning Web Scripting Basics

In the world of science fiction movies (and many other movies that have no excuse), computers are often seen obeying commands in English. Although this might indeed happen in the near future, computers currently find it easier to understand languages such as BASIC, C, and Java.

You already know how to use one type of computer language: HTML. You use HTML tags to describe how you want your document formatted, and the browser obeys your commands and shows the formatted document to the user. But because HTML is a simple text markup language, it can't respond to the user, make decisions, or automate repetitive tasks. Interactive tasks such as these require a more sophisticated language: a programming language, or a *scripting* language.

Although many programming languages are complex, scripting languages are generally simple. They have a simple syntax, can perform tasks with a minimum of commands, and are easy to learn. Web scripting languages enable you to combine scripting with HTML to create interactive web pages.

Scripts and Programs

A movie or a play follows a script—a list of actions (or lines) for the actors to perform. A web script provides the same type of instructions for the web browser. A script in JavaScript can range from a single line to a full-scale application. (In either case, JavaScript scripts usually run within a browser.)

Some programming languages must be *compiled*, or translated, into machine code before they can be executed. JavaScript, on the other hand, is an *interpreted* language: The browser executes each line of script as it comes to it.

There is one main advantage to interpreted languages: Writing or changing a script is very simple. Changing a JavaScript script is as easy as changing a typical HTML document, and the change is enacted as soon as you reload the document in the browser.

Introducing JavaScript

JavaScript was developed by Netscape Communications Corporation, the maker of the Netscape web browser. JavaScript was the first web scripting language to be supported by browsers, and it is still by far the most popular.

JavaScript is almost as easy to learn as HTML, and it can be included directly in HTML documents. Here are a few of the things you can do with JavaScript:

- ► Display messages to the user as part of a web page, in the browser's status line, or in alert boxes

- ► Validate the contents of a form and make calculations (for example, an order form can automatically display a running total as you enter item quantities)

- ► Animate images or create images that change when you move the mouse over them

- ► Create ad banners that interact with the user, rather than simply displaying a graphic

NOTE

Is JavaScript a scripting language or a programming language? It depends on who you ask. We'll refer to scripting throughout this book, but feel free to include JavaScript programming on your résumé after you've finished this book.

NOTE

Interpreted languages have their disadvantages—they can't execute quickly, so they're not ideally suited for complicated work, such as graphics. Also, they require the interpreter (in JavaScript's case, usually a browser) to work.

NOTE

A bit of history: JavaScript was originally called LiveScript and was first introduced in Netscape Navigator 2.0 in 1995. It was soon renamed JavaScript to indicate a marketing relationship with Sun's Java language—although there is no other relationship, structurally or otherwise, between Java and JavaScript.

- ▶ Detect the browser in use or its features and perform advanced functions only on browsers that support them

- ▶ Detect installed plug-ins and notify the user if a plug-in is required

- ▶ Modify all or part of a web page without requiring the user to reload it

- ▶ Display or interact with data retrieved from a remote server

You can do all this and more with JavaScript, including creating entire applications. We'll explore the uses of JavaScript throughout this book.

How JavaScript Fits into a Web Page

Using the <script> tag, you can add a short script (in this case, just one line) to a web document, as shown in Listing 4.1. The <script> tag tells the browser to start treating the text as a script, and the closing </script> tag tells the browser to return to HTML mode. In most cases, you can't use JavaScript statements in an HTML document except within <script> tags. The exception is event handlers, described later in this chapter.

LISTING 4.1   A Simple HTML Document with a Simple Script

```
<?xml version="1.0" encoding="UTF-8"?>
<!DOCTYPE html PUBLIC "-//W3C//DTD XHTML 1.1//EN"
  "http://www.w3.org/TR/xhtml11/DTD/xhtml11.dtd">

<html xmlns="http://www.w3.org/1999/xhtml" xml:lang="en">
  <head>
    <title>The American Eggplant Society</title>
  </head>

  <body>
    <h1>The American Eggplant Society</h1>
    <p>Welcome to our site. Unfortunately, it is still
       under construction.</p>
    <p>We last worked on it on this date:
    <script type="text/javascript">
    <!-- Hide the script from old browsers
    document.write(document.lastModified);
    // Stop hiding the script -->
    </script>
    </p>
  </body>
</html>
```

JavaScript's `document.write` statement, which you'll learn more about later, sends output as part of the web document. In this case, it displays the modification date of the document, as shown in Figure 4.1.

FIGURE 4.1
Using `document.write` to display a last-modified date.

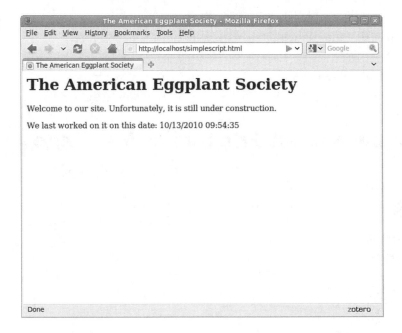

In this example, we placed the script within the body of the HTML document. There are actually four different places where you might use scripts:

▶ **In the body of the page**—In this case, the script's output is displayed as part of the HTML document when the browser loads the page.

▶ **In the header of the page between the** `<head>` **tags**—Scripts in the header can't create output within the HTML document, but can be referred to by other scripts. The header is often used for functions—groups of JavaScript statements that can be used as a single unit. You will learn more about functions in Chapter 14, "Getting Started with JavaScript Programming."

▶ **Within an HTML tag, such as** `<body>` **or** `<form>`—This is called an *event handler* and enables the script to work with HTML elements. When using JavaScript in event handlers, you don't need to use the `<script>` tag. You'll learn more about event handlers in Chapter 14.

▶ **In a separate file entirely**—JavaScript supports the use of files with the .js extension containing scripts; these can be included by specifying a file in the `<script>` tag.

Using Separate JavaScript Files

When you create more complicated scripts, you'll quickly find your HTML documents become large and confusing. To avoid this, you can use one or more external JavaScript files. These are files with the .js extension that contain JavaScript statements.

External scripts are supported by all modern browsers. To use an external script, you specify its filename in the <script> tag:

```
<script  type="text/javascript" src="filename.js"></script>
```

Because you'll be placing the JavaScript statements in a separate file, you don't need anything between the opening and closing <script> tags—in fact, anything between them will be ignored by the browser.

You can create the .js file using a text editor. It should contain one or more JavaScript commands and only JavaScript—don't include <script> tags, other HTML tags, or HTML comments. Save the .js file in the same directory as the HTML documents that refer to it.

Understanding JavaScript Events

Many of the useful things you can do with JavaScript involve interacting with the user and that means responding to *events*—for example, a link or a button being clicked. You can define event handlers within HTML tags to tell the browser how to respond to an event. For example, Listing 4.2 defines a button that displays a message when clicked.

LISTING 4.2   A Simple Event Handler

```
<?xml version="1.0" encoding="UTF-8"?>
<!DOCTYPE html PUBLIC "-//W3C//DTD XHTML 1.1//EN"
  "http://www.w3.org/TR/xhtml11/DTD/xhtml11.dtd">

<html xmlns="http://www.w3.org/1999/xhtml" xml:lang="en">
  <head>
    <title>Event Test</title>
  </head>

  <body>
    <h1>Event Test</h1>
    <button type="button"
            onclick="alert('You clicked the button.')">
            Click Me!</button>
  </body>
</html>
```

> **TIP**
>
> External JavaScript files have a distinct advantage: You can link to the same .js file from two or more HTML documents. Because the browser stores this file in its cache, this can reduce the time it takes for your web pages to display.

In various places throughout this book, you'll learn more about JavaScript's event model and how to create simple and complex event handlers.

Exploring JavaScript's Capabilities

If you've spent any time browsing the Web, you've undoubtedly seen lots of examples of JavaScript in action. Here are some brief descriptions of typical applications for JavaScript, all of which you'll explore further, later in this book.

Improving Navigation

Some of the most common uses of JavaScript are in navigation systems for websites. You can use JavaScript to create a navigation tool—for example, a drop-down menu to select the next page to read or a submenu that pops up when you hover over a navigation link.

When it's done right, this kind of JavaScript interactivity can make a site easier to use, while remaining usable for browsers that don't support JavaScript.

Validating Forms

Form validation is another common use of JavaScript. A simple script can read values the user types into a form and can make sure they're in the right format, such as with ZIP Codes or phone numbers. This allows users to notice common errors and fix them without waiting for a response from the web server. You'll learn how to work with form data in Chapter 26, "Working with Web-Based Forms."

Special Effects

One of the earliest and most annoying uses of JavaScript was to create attention-getting special effects—for example, scrolling a message in the browser's status line or flashing the background color of a page.

These techniques have fortunately fallen out of style, but thanks to the W3C DOM and the latest browsers, some more impressive effects are possible with JavaScript—for example, creating objects that can be dragged and dropped on a page or creating fading transitions between images in a slideshow.

Remote Scripting (AJAX)

For a long time, the biggest limitation of JavaScript was that there was no way for it to communicate with a web server. For example, you could use it to verify that a phone number had the right number of digits, but not to look up the user's location in a database based on the number.

Now that some of JavaScript's advanced features are supported by most browsers, this is no longer the case. Your scripts can get data from a server without loading a page or send data back to be saved. These features are collectively known as AJAX (Asynchronous JavaScript And XML), or *remote scripting*. You'll learn how to develop AJAX scripts in Chapter 24, "AJAX: Remote Scripting."

You've seen AJAX in action if you've used Google's Gmail mail application or recent versions of Yahoo! Mail or Microsoft Hotmail. All of these use remote scripting to present you with a responsive user interface that works with a server in the background.

Displaying Time with JavaScript

One common and easy use for JavaScript is to display dates and times. Because JavaScript runs on the browser, the times it displays will be in the user's current time zone. However, you can also use JavaScript to calculate "universal" (UTC) time.

As a basic introduction to JavaScript, you will now create a simple script that displays the current time and the UTC time within a web page, starting with the next section.

Beginning the Script

Your script, like most JavaScript programs, begins with the HTML `<script>` tag. As you learned earlier in this chapter, you use the `<script>` and `</script>` tags to enclose a script within the HTML document.

To begin creating the script, open your favorite text editor and type the beginning and ending `<script>` tags as shown.

```
<script type="text/javascript"></script>
```

NOTE

UTC stands for Universal Time Coordinated, and is the atomic time standard based on the old GMT (Greenwich Mean Time) standard. This is the time at the Prime Meridian, which runs through Greenwich, London, England.

CAUTION

Remember to include only valid JavaScript statements between the starting and ending `<script>` tags. If the browser finds anything but valid JavaScript statements within the `<script>` tags, it will display a JavaScript error message.

Adding JavaScript Statements

Your script now needs to determine the local and UTC times, and then display them to the browser. Fortunately, all the hard parts, such as converting between date formats, are built in to the JavaScript interpreter.

Storing Data in Variables

To begin the script, you will use a *variable* to store the current date. You will learn more about variables in Chapter 16, "Using JavaScript Variables, Strings, and Arrays." A *variable* is a container that can hold a value—a number, some text, or in this case, a date.

To start writing the script, add the following line after the first `<script>` tag. Be sure to use the same combination of capital and lowercase letters in your version because JavaScript commands and variable names are case sensitive.

```
now = new Date();
```

This statement creates a variable called `now` and stores the current date and time in it. This statement and the others you will use in this script use JavaScript's built-in `Date` object, which enables you to conveniently handle dates and times. You'll learn more about working with dates in Chapter 17, "Using JavaScript Functions and Objects."

Calculating the Results

Internally, JavaScript stores dates as the number of milliseconds since January 1, 1970. Fortunately, JavaScript includes a number of functions to convert dates and times in various ways, so you don't have to figure out how to convert milliseconds to day, date, and time.

To continue your script, add the following two statements before the final `</script>` tag:

```
localtime = now.toString();
utctime = now.toGMTString();
```

These statements create two new variables: `localtime`, containing the current time and date in a nice readable format, and `utctime`, containing the UTC equivalent.

NOTE

Notice the semicolon at the end of the previous statement. This tells the browser that it has reached the end of a statement. Semicolons are optional, but using them helps you avoid some common errors. We'll use them throughout this book for clarity.

NOTE

The `localtime` and `utctime` variables store a piece of text, such as January 1, 2001 12:00 PM. In programming parlance, a piece of text is called a *string*.

Creating Output

You now have two variables—`localtime` and `utctime`—which contain the results we want from our script. Of course, these variables don't do us much good unless we can see them. JavaScript includes a number of ways to display information, and one of the simplest is the `document.write` statement.

The `document.write` statement displays a text string, a number, or anything else you throw at it. Because your JavaScript program will be used within a web page, the output will be displayed as part of the page. To display the result, add these statements before the final `</script>` tag:

```
document.write("<strong>Local time:</strong> " + localtime + "<br/>");
document.write("<strong>UTC time:</strong> " + utctime);
```

These statements tell the browser to add some text to the web page containing your script. The output will include some brief strings introducing the results and the contents of the `localtime` and `utctime` variables.

Notice the HTML tags, such as `<strong>`, within the quotation marks—because JavaScript's output appears within a web page, it needs to be formatted using HTML. The `<br/>` tag in the first line ensures that the two times will be displayed on separate lines.

Adding the Script to a Web Page

You should now have a complete script that calculates a result and displays it. Your listing should match Listing 4.3.

LISTING 4.3   The Complete Date and Time Script

```
<script type="text/javascript">
now = new Date();
localtime = now.toString();
utctime = now.toGMTString();
document.write("<strong>Local time:</strong> " + localtime + "<br/>");
document.write("<strong>UTC time:</strong> " + utctime);
</script>
```

To use your script, you'll need to add it to an HTML document. If you use the general template you've seen in the chapters so far, you should end up with something like Listing 4.4.

NOTE

Notice the plus signs (+) used between the text and variables in Listing 4.3. In this case, it tells the browser to combine the values into one string of text. If you use the plus sign between two numbers, they are added together.

NOTE

Notepad and other Windows text editors might try to be helpful and add the .txt extension to your script. Be sure your saved file has the correct extension.

LISTING 4.4　The Date and Time Script in an HTML Document

```
<?xml version="1.0" encoding="UTF-8"?>
<!DOCTYPE html PUBLIC "-//W3C//DTD XHTML 1.1//EN"
  "http://www.w3.org/TR/xhtml11/DTD/xhtml11.dtd">

<html xmlns="http://www.w3.org/1999/xhtml" xml:lang="en">
  <head>
    <title>Displaying Times and Dates</title>
  </head>

  <body>
    <h1>Current Date and Time</h1>
    <script type="text/javascript">
     now = new Date();
     localtime = now.toString();
     utctime = now.toGMTString();
     document.write("<strong>Local time:</strong> "
          + localtime + "<br/>");
    document.write("<strong>UTC time:</strong> " + utctime);
    </script>
  </body>
</html>
```

Now that you have a complete HTML document, save it with the .htm or .html extension.

Testing the Script

To test your script, you simply need to load the HTML document you created in a web browser. If you typed the script correctly, your browser should display the result of the script, as shown in Figure 4.2. (Of course, your result won't be the same as mine, but it should be the same as the setting of your computer's clock.)

A note about Internet Explorer 6.0 and above: Depending on your security settings, the script might not execute, and a yellow highlighted bar on the top of the browser might display a security warning. In this case, click the yellow bar and select Allow Blocked Content to allow your script to run. (This happens because the default security settings allow JavaScript in online documents, but not in local files.)

Modifying the Script

Although the current script does indeed display the current date and time, its display isn't nearly as attractive as the clock on your wall or desk. To remedy that, you can use some additional JavaScript features and a bit of HTML to display a large clock.

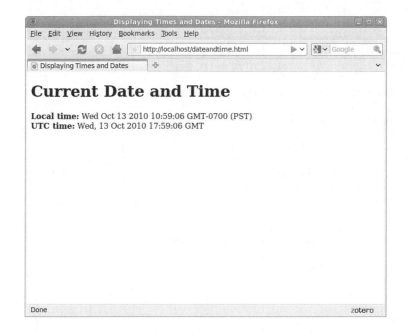

FIGURE 4.2
Firefox displays the results of the
Date and Time script.

To display a large clock, we need the hours, minutes, and seconds in separate
variables. Once again, JavaScript has built-in functions to do most of the
work:

```
hours = now.getHours();
mins = now.getMinutes();
secs = now.getSeconds();
```

These statements load the hours, mins, and secs variables with the components of the time using JavaScript's built-in date functions.

After the hours, minutes, and seconds are in separate variables, you can
create document.write statements to display them:

```
document.write("<h1>");
document.write(hours + ":" + mins + ":" + secs);
document.write("</h1>");
```

The first statement displays an HTML <h1> header tag to display the clock
in a large typeface. The second statement displays the hours, mins, and secs
variables, separated by colons, and the third adds the closing </h1> tag.

You can add the preceding statements to the original date and time script
to add the large clock display. Listing 4.5 shows the complete modified
version of the script.

LISTING 4.5   The Date and Time Script with Large Clock Display

```
<?xml version="1.0" encoding="UTF-8"?>
<!DOCTYPE html PUBLIC "-//W3C//DTD XHTML 1.1//EN"
  "http://www.w3.org/TR/xhtml11/DTD/xhtml11.dtd">

<html xmlns="http://www.w3.org/1999/xhtml" xml:lang="en">
  <head>
    <title>Displaying Times and Dates</title>
  </head>

  <body>
    <h1>Current Date and Time</h1>
    <script type="text/javascript">
     now = new Date();
     localtime = now.toString();
     utctime = now.toGMTString();
     document.write("<strong>Local time:</strong> "
         + localtime + "<br/>");
     document.write("<strong>UTC time:</strong> " + utctime);
     hours = now.getHours();
     mins = now.getMinutes();
     secs = now.getSeconds();
     document.write("<h1>");
     document.write(hours + ":" + mins + ":" + secs);
     document.write("</h1>");
    </script>
  </body>
</html>
```

Now that you have modified the script, save the HTML file and open the modified file in your browser. If you left the browser running, you can simply use the Reload button to load the new version of the script. Try it and verify that the same time is displayed in both the upper portion of the window and the new large clock. Figure 4.3 shows the results.

Dealing with JavaScript Errors

As you develop more complex JavaScript applications, you're going to run into errors from time to time. JavaScript errors are usually caused by mistyped JavaScript statements.

To see an example of a JavaScript error message, modify the statement you added in the previous section. We'll use a common error: omitting one of the parentheses. Change the last `document.write` statement in Listing 4.5 to read:

```
document.write("</h1>";
```

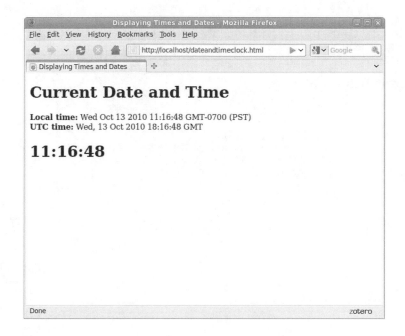

FIGURE 4.3
Firefox displays the modified Date
and Time script.

NOTE

The time formatting produced
by this script isn't perfect;
hours after noon are in 24-hour
time, and there are no leading
zeroes, so 12:04 is displayed
as 12:4. See Chapter 17 for
solutions to these issues.

Save your HTML document again and load the document into the browser.
Depending on the browser version you're using, one of two things will
happen: Either an error message will be displayed, or the script will simply
fail to execute.

If an error message is displayed, you're halfway to fixing the problem by
adding the missing parenthesis. If no error was displayed, you should configure your browser to display error messages so that you can diagnose
future problems:

- ▶ In Firefox, you can also select Tools, JavaScript Console from the
  menu. The console is shown in Figure 4.4, displaying the error message you created in this example.

- ▶ In Chrome, select Tools, JavaScript Console from the Customizations
  (Options) menu. A console will display in the bottom of the browser
  window.

- ▶ In Internet Explorer, select Tools, Internet Options. On the Advanced
  page, uncheck the Disable Script Debugging box and check the
  Display a Notification About Every Script Error box. (If this is disabled, a yellow icon in the status bar will still notify you of errors.)

The error we get in this case is `missing ) after argument list` (Firefox) or
`Expected ')'` (Internet Explorer), which turns out to be exactly the problem.
Be warned, however, that error messages aren't always this enlightening.

FIGURE 4.4
Firefox's JavaScript Console
displays an error message.

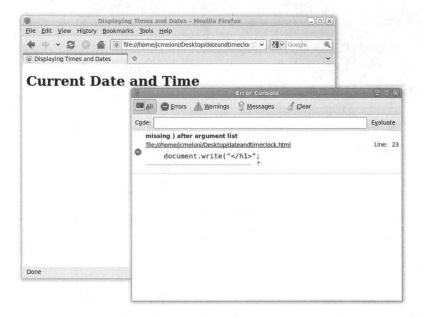

Although Internet Explorer displays error dialog boxes for each error, Firefox's JavaScript Console displays a single list of errors and enables you to test commands. For this reason, you might find it useful to install Firefox for debugging and testing JavaScript, even if Internet Explorer is your primary browser.

Summary

During this chapter, you've learned what web scripting is and what JavaScript is. You've also learned how to insert a script into an HTML document or refer to an external JavaScript file, what sorts of things JavaScript can do, and how JavaScript differs from other web languages. You also wrote a simple JavaScript program and tested it using a web browser. You discovered how to modify and test scripts and what happens when a JavaScript program runs into an error.

In the process of writing this script, you have used some of JavaScript's basic features: variables, the `document.write` statement, and functions for working with dates and times.

Now that you've learned a bit of JavaScript syntax, you're ready to continue on to learn all manner and sorts of things about web development before settling in to write interactive websites using client-side scripting.

Q&A

Q. Do I need to test my JavaScript on more than one browser?

A. In an ideal world, any script you write that follows the standards for JavaScript will work in all browsers, and 93% of the time (give or take) that's true in the real world. But browsers do have their quirks, and you should test your scripts on Internet Explorer and Firefox at a minimum.

Q. If I plan to learn PHP or some other server-side programming language anyway, will I have any use for JavaScript?

A. Certainly. JavaScript is the ideal language for many parts of a web-based application, such as form validation. Although PHP and other server-side languages have their uses, they can't interact directly with the user on the client-side.

Q. When I try to run my script, the browser displays the actual script in the browser window instead of executing it. What did I do wrong?

A. This is most likely caused by one of three errors. First, you might be missing the beginning or ending `<script>` tags. Check them, and verify that the first reads `<script type="text/javascript">`. Second, your file might have been saved with a .txt extension, causing the browser to treat it as a text file. Rename it to .htm or .html to fix the problem. Third, make sure your browser supports JavaScript and that it is not disabled in the Preferences dialog.

Q. Why are the `<strong>` and `<br />` tags allowed in the statements to print the time? I thought HTML tags weren't allowed within the `<script>` tags.

A. Because this particular tag is inside quotation marks, it's considered a valid part of the script. The script's output, including any HTML tags, is interpreted and displayed by the browser. You can use other HTML tags within quotation marks to add formatting, such as the `<h1>` tags we added for the large clock display.

Workshop

The workshop contains quiz questions and exercises to help you solidify your understanding of the material covered. Try to answer all questions before looking at the "Answers" section that follows.

Quiz

1. When a user views a page containing a JavaScript program, which machine actually executes the script?

    a. The user's machine running a web browser

    b. The web server

    c. A central machine deep within Netscape's corporate offices

2. What software do you use to create and edit JavaScript programs?

    a. A browser

    b. A text editor

    c. A pencil and a piece of paper

3. What are variables used for in JavaScript programs?

    a. Storing numbers, dates, or other values

    b. Varying randomly

    c. Causing high school algebra flashbacks

4. What should appear at the very end of a JavaScript script embedded in an HTML file?

    a. The `<script type="text/javascript">` tag

    b. The `</script>` tag

    c. The `END` statement

Answers

1. a. JavaScript programs execute on the web browser. (There is actually a server-side version of JavaScript, but that's another story.)

2. b. Any text editor can be used to create scripts. You can also use a word processor if you're careful to save the document as a text file with the .html or .htm extension.

3. a. Variables are used to store numbers, dates, or other values.

4. b. Your script should end with the `</script>` tag.

Exercises

▶ Add a millisecond field to the large clock. You can use the `getMilliseconds` function, which works just like `getSeconds` but returns milliseconds.

▶ Modify the script to display the time, including milliseconds, twice. Notice whether any time passes between the two time displays when you load the page.

CHAPTER 5
Working with Fonts, Text Blocks, and Lists

In the early days of the Web, text was displayed in only one font and in one size. However, a combination of HTML and CSS now makes it possible to control the appearance of text (font type, size, or color) and how it is aligned and displayed on a web page. In this chapter, you'll learn how to change the visual display of the font—its font family, size, and weight— and how to incorporate boldface, italics, superscripts, subscripts, and strikethrough text into your pages. You will also learn how to change type-faces and font sizes. Then, after becoming conversant in these textual aspects, you'll learn the basics of text alignment and some advanced text tips and tricks, such as the use of lists. Because lists are so common, HTML provides tags that automatically indent text and add numbers, bullets, or other symbols in front of each listed item. You'll learn how to format different types of lists, which are part of the many ways to display content in your website.

WHAT YOU'LL LEARN IN THIS CHAPTER:

► How to use boldface, italics, and special text formatting
► How to tweak the font
► How to use special characters
► How to align text on a page
► How to use the three types of HTML lists
► How to place lists within lists

NOTE

When viewing other designers' web content, you might notice methods of marking up text that are different than those taught in this book. The old way of formatting text includes the use of the `<b></b>` tag pair to indicate when a word should be bolded, the `<i></i>` tag pair to indicate when a word should be in italics, and the use of a `<font></font>` tag pair to specify font family, size, and other attributes. However, there is no reason to learn it because it is being phased out of HTML, and CSS is considerably more powerful.

You can make the most of learning how to style text throughout this chapter if you have some sample text that you can use to display different fonts and colors and that can also be indented, centered, or otherwise manipulated. It doesn't really matter what type of text you use because there are so many different stylistic possibilities to try that they would never appear all on the same web page anyway (unless you wanted to drive your visitors batty). Take this opportunity just to get a feel for how text-level changes can affect the appearance of your content.

▶ If the text you'll be using is from a word processing or database program, be sure to save it to a new file in plain-text or ASCII format. You can then add the appropriate HTML tags and style attributes to format it as you go through this chapter.

▶ Any text will do, but try to find (or type) some text you want to put onto a web page. The text from a company brochure or from your résumé might be a good choice.

▶ Any type of outline, bullet points from a presentation, numbered steps, glossary, or list of textual information from a database will serve as good material to work with.

▶ Before you use the code introduced in this chapter to format the body text, add the set of skeleton HTML tags you've used in previous chapters (the `<html>`, `<head>`, `<title>`, and `<body>` tags).

Boldface, Italics, and Special Text Formatting

Way back in the age of the typewriter, we were content with a plain-text display and with using an occasional underline to show emphasis. Today, **boldface** and *italic* text have become de rigueur in all paper communication. Naturally, you can add bold and italic text to your web content as well. There are several tags and style rules that make text formatting possible.

The old school approach to adding bold and italic formatting to text involves the `<b></b>` and `<i></i>` tag pairs. For boldface text, put the `<b>` tag at the beginning of the text and `</b>` at the end. Similarly, you can make any text italic by enclosing it between `<i>` and `</i>` tags. Although this approach still works fine in browsers and is supported by XHTML, it isn't as flexible or powerful as the CSS style rules for text formatting.

Although you'll learn much more about CSS style rules in Part III, "Advanced Web Page Design with CSS," it's worth a little foreshadowing just so that you understand the text formatting options. The `font-weight` style rule enables you to set the weight, or boldness, of a font using a style rule. Standard settings for `font-weight` include `normal`, `bold`, `bolder`, and `lighter` (with `normal` being the default). Italic text is controlled via the `font-style` rule, which can be set to `normal`, `italic`, or `oblique`. Style rules can be specified together if you want to apply more than one, as the following example demonstrates:

```
<p style="font-weight:bold; font-style:italic">This paragraph is bold and
italic!</p>
```

In this example, both style rules are specified in the `style` attribute of the `<p>` tag. The key to using multiple style rules is that they must be separated by a semicolon (`;`).

You aren't limited to using font styles in paragraphs, however. The following code shows how to italicize text in a bulleted list:

```
<ul>
  <li style="font-style:italic">Important Stuff</li>
  <li style="font-style:italic">Critical Information</li>
  <li style="font-style:italic">Highly Sensitive Material</li>
  <li>Nothing All That Useful</li>
</ul>
```

You can also use the `font-weight` style rule within headings, but a heavier font usually doesn't have an effect on headings because they are already bold by default.

Although using CSS enables you to apply richer formatting, there are a few other HTML tags that are good for adding special formatting to text when you don't necessarily need to be as specific as CSS allows you to be. Following are some of these tags. Listing 5.1 and Figure 5.1 demonstrate each tag in action.

- ▶ **`<small></small>`**—Small text
- ▶ **`<big></big>`**—Big text; not present in HTML5 because text size is better controlled by CSS
- ▶ **`<sup></sup>`**—Superscript text
- ▶ **`<sub></sub>`**—Subscript text
- ▶ **`<em></em>`** or **`<i></i>`**—Emphasized (italic) text
- ▶ **`<strong></strong>`** or **`<b></b>`**—Strong (boldface) text

CAUTION

There used to be a <u> tag for creating underlined text, but there are a couple of reasons not to use it now. First off, users expect underlined text to be a link, so they might get confused if you underline text that isn't a link. Second, the <u> tag is *deprecated*, which means that it has been phased out of the HTML/XHTML language, as has the <strike> tag. Both tags are still supported in web browsers and likely will be for quite a while, but using CSS is the preferred approach to creating underlined and strikethrough text. In HTML5, deleted text can be surrounded by the <strike> <strike> tag pair, which will render as text with a strikethrough.

▶ **<tt></tt>**—Monospaced text (typewriter font) not present in HTML5 because font appearance is better controlled by CSS

▶ **<pre></pre>**—Monospaced text, preserving spaces and line breaks

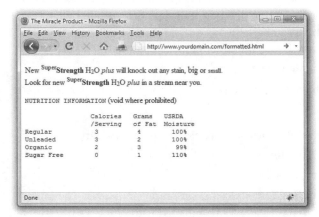

FIGURE 5.1
Here's what the character formatting from Listing 5.1 looks like.

LISTING 5.1   Special Formatting Tags

```
<?xml version="1.0" encoding="UTF-8"?>
<!DOCTYPE html PUBLIC "-//W3C//DTD XHTML 1.1//EN"
  "http://www.w3.org/TR/xhtml11/DTD/xhtml11.dtd">

<html xmlns="http://www.w3.org/1999/xhtml" xml:lang="en">
  <head>
    <title>The Miracle Product</title>
  </head>

  <body>
    <p>
      New <sup>Super</sup><strong>Strength</strong> H<sub>2</sub>O
      <em>plus</em> will knock out any stain, <big>big</big> or
      <small>small</small>.<br /> Look for new
      <sup>Super</sup><b>Strength</b> H<sub>2</sub>O <i>plus</i>
      in a stream near you.
    </p>
    <p>
      <tt>NUTRITION INFORMATION</tt> (void where prohibited)
    </p>
    <pre>
              Calories   Grams    USRDA
              /Serving   of Fat   Moisture
Regular          3         4       100%
Unleaded         3         2       100%
```

LISTING 5.1   Continued

```
Organic        2        3        99%
Sugar Free     0        1        110%
    </pre>
  </body>
</html>
```

The `<tt>` tag usually changes the typeface to Courier New, a monospaced font. (*Monospaced* means that all the letters and spaces are the same width.) However, web browsers let users change the monospaced `<tt>` font to the typeface of their choice (look on the Options menu of your browser). The monospaced font might not even be monospaced for some users, although the vast majority of users stick with the standard fonts that their browsers show by default.

The `<pre>` tag causes text to appear in the monospaced font, but it also does something else unique and useful. As you learned in Chapter 2, "Understanding HTML and XHTML Connections," multiple spaces and line breaks are normally ignored in HTML files, but `<pre>` causes exact spacing and line breaks to be preserved. For example, without `<pre>`, the text at the end of Figure 5.1 would look like the following:

```
calories grams usrda /serving of fat moisture regular
3 4 100% unleaded 3 2 100% organic 2 3 99% sugar free 0 1 110%
```

Even if you added `<br />` tags at the end of every line, the columns wouldn't line up properly. However, when you put `<pre>` at the beginning and `</pre>` at the end, the columns line up properly because the exact spaces are kept—no `<br />` tags are needed. The `<pre>` tag gives you a quick and easy way to preserve the alignment of any monospaced text files you might want to transfer to a web page with minimum effort.

CSS provides you with more robust methods for lining up text (and doing anything with text, actually), and you'll learn more about them throughout Part III.

Tweaking the Font

The `<big>`, `<small>`, and `<tt>` tags give you some rudimentary control over the size and appearance of the text on your pages. However, there might be times when you'd just like a bit more control over the size and appearance of your text. Before I get into the appropriate way to tinker with the font in XHTML code, let's briefly look at how things were done

NOTE

You'll learn more about controlling the color of the text on your
pages in Chapter 8, "Working
with Colors, Images, and
Multimedia." That chapter also
shows you how to create your
own custom colors and how to
control the color of text links.

prior to CSS because you might still find examples of this method when
you look at the source code for other websites. Remember, just because
these older methods are in use doesn't mean you should follow suit.

Before style sheets entered the picture, the now phased-out <font> tag was
used to control the fonts in web page text. For example, the following
HTML will change the size and color of some text on a page:

```
<font size="5" color="purple">this text will be big and purple.</font>
```

As you can see, the size and color attributes of the <font> tag made it possible to alter the font of the text without too much effort. Although this
approach worked fine, it was replaced with a far superior approach to font
formatting, thanks to CSS style rules. Following are a few of the main style
rules used to control fonts:

- **font-family**—Sets the family (typeface) of the font
- **font-size**—Sets the size of the font
- **color**—Sets the color of the font

The font-family style rule enables you to set the typeface used to display
text. You can and usually should specify more than one value for this style
(separated by commas) so that if the first font isn't available on a user's
system, the browser can try an alternative. You've already seen this in previous chapters.

Providing alternative font families is important because each user potentially has a different set of fonts installed, at least beyond a core set of common basic fonts (Arial, Times New Roman, and so forth). By providing a
list of alternative fonts, you have a better chance of your pages gracefully
falling back on a known font when your ideal font isn't found. Following
is an example of the font-family style used to set the typeface for a paragraph of text:

```
<p style="font-family:arial, sans-serif, 'times roman'">
```

There are several interesting things about this example. First, arial is specified as the primary font. Capitalization does not affect the font family, so
arial is no different from Arial or ARIAL. Another interesting thing about
this code is how single quotes are used around the Times Roman font name
because it has a space in it. However, because 'times roman' appears after
the generic specification of sans-serif, it is unlikely that 'times roman'
would be used. Because sans-serif is in the second position, it says to the
browser "if Arial is not on this machine, use the default sans-serif font."

The `font-size` and `color` style rules are also commonly used to control the size and color of fonts. The `font-size` style can be set to a predefined size (such as `small`, `medium`, or `large`) or you can set it to a specific point size (such as `12pt` or `14pt`). The `color` style can be set to a predefined color (such as `white`, `black`, `blue`, `red`, or `green`), or you can set it to a specific hexadecimal color (such as `#FFB499`). Following is the previous paragraph example with the font size and color specified:

```
<p style="font-family:arial, sans-serif, 'times roman'; font-size:14pt;
color:green">
```

The sample web content in Listing 5.2 and shown in Figure 5.2 uses some font style rules to create the beginning of a basic online résumé

LISTING 5.2   Using Font Style Rules to Create a Basic Résumé

```
<?xml version="1.0" encoding="UTF-8"?>
<!DOCTYPE html PUBLIC "-//W3C//DTD XHTML 1.1//EN"
  "http://www.w3.org/TR/xhtml11/DTD/xhtml11.dtd">

<html xmlns="http://www.w3.org/1999/xhtml" xml:lang="en">
  <head>
    <title>R&eacute;sum&eacute; for Jane Doe</title>

    <style type="text/css">
      body {
        font-family: Verdana, sans-serif;
        font-size: 12px;
      }

      h1 {
        font-family:Georgia, serif;
        font-size:28px;
        text-align:center;
      }

      p.contactinfo {
        font-size:14px;
        text-align:center;
      }

      p.categorylabel {
        font-size:12px;
        font-weight:bold;
        text-transform:uppercase;
      }

      div.indented {
        margin-left: 25px;
      }
    </style>
```

NOTE

You'll learn about hexadecimal colors in Chapter 8. For now, just understand that the `color` style rule enables you to specify exact colors beyond just using `green`, `blue`, `orange`, and so forth.

LISTING 5.2   Continued

```
    </head>
    <body>
        <h1>Jane Doe</h1>
        <p class="contactinfo">1234 Main Street, Sometown,
        CA 93829<br/>
        tel: 555-555-1212, e-mail: jane@doe.com</p>

        <p class="categorylabel">Summary of Qualifications</p>
        <ul>
        <li>Highly skilled and dedicated professional offering a
        solid background in whatever it is you need.</li>
        <li>Provide comprehensive direction for whatever it is
        that will get me a job.</li>
        <li>Computer proficient in a wide range of industry-related
        computer programs and equipment. Any industry.</li>
        </ul>

        <p class="categorylabel">Professional Experience</p>
        <div class="indented">
                <p><span style="font-weight:bold;">Operations Manager,
                Super Awesome Company, Some City, CA [Sept 2002 -
                present]</span></p>
                <ul>
                <li>Direct all departmental operations</li>
                <li>Coordinate work with internal and external
                resources</li>
                <li>Generally in charge of everything</li>
                </ul>
            <p><span style="font-weight:bold;">Project Manager,
                Less Awesome Company, Some City, CA [May 2000 - Sept
                2002]</span></p>
                <ul>
                <li>Direct all departmental operations</li>
                <li>Coordinate work with internal and external
                resources</li>
                <li>Generally in charge of everything</li>
                </ul>
        </div>

        <p class="categorylabel">Education</p>
        <ul>
        <li>MBA, MyState University, May 2002</li>
        <li>B.A, Business Administration, MyState University,
        May 2000</li>
        </ul>

        <p class="categorylabel">References</p>
        <ul>
        <li>Available upon request.</li>
        </ul>
    </body>
</html>
```

Using CSS, which organizes sets of styles into classes—as you learned in Chapter 3, "Understanding Cascading Style Sheets"—you can see how text formatting is applied to different areas of this content. If you look closely at the definition of the `div.indented` class, you will see the use of the `margin-left` style. This style, which you will learn more about in Part III, applies a certain amount of space (25 pixels, in this example) to the left of the element. That space accounts for the indentation shown in Figure 5.2.

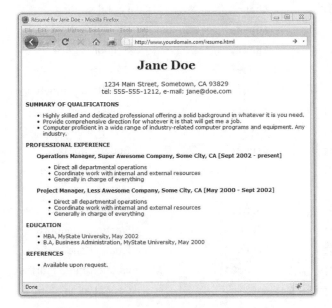

FIGURE 5.2
Here's what the code used in Listing 5.2 looks like.

Working with Special Characters

Most fonts now include special characters for European languages, such as the accented *é* in *Café*. There are also a few mathematical symbols and special punctuation marks, such as the circular bullet •.

You can insert these special characters at any point in an HTML document using the appropriate codes, as shown in Table 5.1. You'll find an even more extensive list of codes for multiple character sets at http://www.webstandards.org/learn/reference/named_entities.html.

For example, the word *café* could be written using either of the following methods:

```
caf&eacute;
caf&#233;
```

TIP

Looking for the copyright © and registered trademark ® symbols? Those codes are © and ®, respectively.

To create an unregistered trademark ™ symbol, use ™.

TABLE 5.1   Commonly Used English Language Special Characters

Character	Numeric Code	Code Name	Description
"	&#34;	&quot;	Quotation mark
&	&#38;	&amp;	Ampersand
<	&#60;	&lt;	Less than
>	&#62;	&gt;	Greater than
¢	&#162;	&cent;	Cent sign
£	&#163;	&pound;	Pound sterling
¦	&#166;	¦ or &brkbar;	Broken vertical bar
§	&#167;	&sect;	Section sign
©	&#169;	&copy;	Copyright
®	&#174;	&reg;	Registered trademark
°	&#176;	&deg;	Degree sign
±	&#177;	&plusmn;	Plus or minus
²	&#178;	&sup2;	Superscript two
³	&#179;	&sup3;	Superscript three
·	&#183;	&middot;	Middle dot
¹	&#185;	&sup1;	Superscript one
¼	&#188;	&frac14;	Fraction one-fourth
½	&#189;	&frac12;	Fraction one-half
¾	&#190;	&frac34;	Fraction three-fourths
Æ	&#198;	&AElig;	Capital AE ligature
æ	&#230;	&aelig;	Small ae ligature
É	&#201;	&Eacute;	Accented capital E
é	&#233;	&eacute;	Accented small e
×	&#215;	&times;	Multiplication sign
÷	&#247;	&divide;	Division sign

Although you can specify character entities by number, each symbol also has a mnemonic name that is often easier to remember.

HTML/XHTML uses a special code known as a *character entity* to represent special characters such as © and ®. Character entities are always specified starting with & and ending with ;. Table 5.1 lists the most commonly used character entities, although HTML supports many more.

Table 5.1 includes codes for the angle brackets, quotation, and ampersand. You must use those codes if you want these symbols to appear on your pages; otherwise, the web browser interprets them as HTML commands.

In Listing 5.3 and Figure 5.3, several of the symbols from Table 5.1 are shown in use.

LISTING 5.3   Special Character Codes

```
<?xml version="1.0" encoding="UTF-8"?>
<!DOCTYPE html PUBLIC "-//W3C//DTD XHTML 1.1//EN"
  "http://www.w3.org/TR/xhtml11/DTD/xhtml11.dtd">

<html xmlns="http://www.w3.org/1999/xhtml" xml:lang="en">
  <head>
    <title>Punctuation Lines</title>
  </head>

  <body>
    <p>
      Q: What should you do when a British banker picks a fight
      with you?<br />
      A: &pound; some &cent;&cent; into him.
      <hr />
      Q: What do you call it when a judge takes part of a law
      off the books?<br />
      A: &sect; violence.
      <hr />
      Q: What did the football coach get from the locker room
      vending machine in the middle of the game?<br />
      A: A &frac14; back at &frac12; time.
      <hr />
      Q: How hot did it get when the police detective interrogated
      the mathematician?<br />
      A: x&sup3;&deg;
      <hr />
      Q: What does a punctilious plagiarist do?<br />
      A: &copy;
      <hr />
    </p>
  </body>
</html>
```

FIGURE 5.3
This is how the HTML page in
Listing 5.3 looks in most web
browsers.

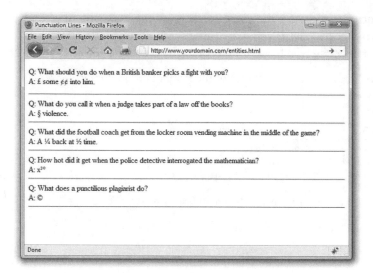

Aligning Text on a Page

Now that you've seen how to change the appearance of your content at the text level, it's time to take it a step further and modify the blocks of text that appear on the page. It's easy to take for granted the fact that most paragraphs are automatically aligned to the left when you're reading information on the Web. However, there certainly are situations in which you might choose to align content to the right or even the center of a page. HTML gives you the option to align a single HTML block-level element, such as text contained within a <p></p> or <div></div> tag pair. Before we get into the details of aligning block elements, however, let's briefly note how attributes work.

Using Attributes

Attributes are used to provide additional information related to an HTML tag. *Attributes* are special code words used inside an HTML tag to control exactly what the tag does. They are very important in even the simplest bit of web content, so it's important that you are comfortable using them.

Attributes invoke the use of styles, classes, or IDs that are applied to particular tags. If you define a particular class or ID in a style sheet—as you learned in Chapter 3, "Understanding Cascading Style Sheets" then you can invoke that class or ID using class="someclass" or id="someid" within the tag itself. When the browser renders the content for display, it will look to the style sheet to determine exactly how the content will appear according to the associated style definitions. Similarly, you can use the `style` attribute to include style information for a particular element without connecting the element to an actual style sheet. For example, when you begin a paragraph with the `<p>` tag, you can specify whether the text in that particular paragraph should be aligned to the left margin, the right margin, or to the center of the page by setting the style attribute. If you want to associate that particular paragraph with an existing class or ID, you set the `class` or `id` attribute.

In the following example, each paragraph could be left-aligned:

```
<p style="text-align: left;">Text goes here.</p>
<p class="leftAlignStyle">Text goes here.</p>
<p id="firstLeftAlign">Text goes here.</p>
```

In the first paragraph, the style appears directly in the `style` attribute. In the second paragraph, the paragraph will be left-aligned if the style sheet entry for the `leftAlignStyle` class includes the `text-align` statement. Similarly, the third paragraph will be left-aligned if the style sheet entry for the `firstLeftAlign` class includes the text-align statement.

In the previous example, you might have noticed the use of lowercase for tags, attributes, and styles. The exacting XHTML standard requires tags and attributes to be lowercase; the XHTML standard also requires quotation marks around attribute values.

For example, the following code will be rendered by most popular web browsers:

```
<P STYLE=TEXT-ALIGN:CENTER>
```

However, this code does not conform to XHTML standards because the tag is uppercase, the `style` attribute and its value (`text-align:center`) is uppercase, and the value isn't in quotation marks. If you want to stay compatible with the latest standards and software, you should always use the following instead:

```
<p style="text-align:center">
```

Aligning Block-Level Elements

To align a block-level element such as `<p>` to the right margin without creating a separate class or ID in a style sheet, simply place `style="text-align:right"` inside the `<p>` tag at the beginning of the paragraph. Similarly, to center the element, use `<p style="text-align:center">`. To align a paragraph to the left, use `<p style="text-align:left">`.

> **NOTE**
>
> Every attribute and style rule in HTML has a default value that is assumed when you don't set the attribute yourself. In the case of the `text-align` style rule of the `<p>` tag, the default value is `left`, so using the bare-bones `<p>` tag has the same effect as using `<p style="text-align:left">`. Learning the default values for common style rules is an important part of becoming a good web page developer.

The text-align part of the style attribute is referred to as a *style rule*, which means that it is setting a particular style aspect of an HTML element. There are many style rules you can use to carefully control the formatting of web content.

The text-align style rule is not reserved for just the <p> tag. In fact, you can use the text-align style rule with any block-level element, which includes <h1>, <h2>, the other heading tags, and the <div> tag, among others. The <div> tag is especially handy because it can encompass other block-level elements and thus enable you to control the alignment of large portions of your web content all at once. The div in the <div> tag is for *division*.

Listing 5.4 demonstrates the style attribute and text-align style rule with both the <p> and the <div> tags. The results are shown in Figure 5.4. You'll learn many more advanced uses of the <div> tag in Part III.

LISTING 5.4   The text-align Style Rule Used with the style Attribute

```
<?xml version="1.0" encoding="UTF-8"?>
<!DOCTYPE html PUBLIC "-//W3C//DTD XHTML 1.1//EN"
  "http://www.w3.org/TR/xhtml11/DTD/xhtml11.dtd">

<html xmlns="http://www.w3.org/1999/xhtml" xml:lang="en">
  <head>
    <title>Bohemia</title>
  </head>

  <body>
    <div style="text-align:center">
      <h1>Bohemia</h1>
      <h2>by Dorothy Parker</h2>
    </div>
    <p style="text-align:left">
      Authors and actors and artists and such<br />
      Never know nothing, and never know much.<br />
      Sculptors and singers and those of their kidney<br />
      Tell their affairs from Seattle to Sydney.
    </p>
    <p style="text-align:center">
      Playwrights and poets and such horses' necks<br />
      Start off from anywhere, end up at sex.<br />
      Diarists, critics, and similar roe<br />
      Never say nothing, and never say no.
    </p>
    <p style="text-align:right">
      People Who Do Things exceed my endurance;<br />
      God, for a man that solicits insurance!
    </p>
  </body>
</html>
```

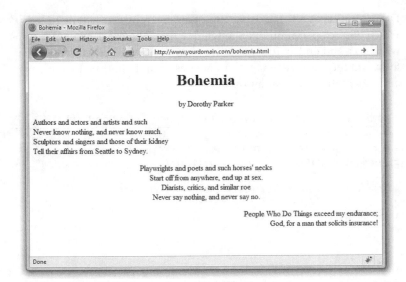

FIGURE 5.4
The results of using the text alignment in Listing 5.4.

The use of `<div style="text-align:center">` ensures that the content area, including the two headings, are centered. However, the text alignment of the individual paragraphs within the `<div>` override the setting and ensure that the text of the first paragraph is left-aligned, the second paragraph is centered, and the third paragraph is right-aligned.

The Three Types of HTML Lists

For clarity, it's often useful to present information on a web page as a list of items. There are three basic types of HTML lists. All three are shown in Figure 5.5, and Listing 5.5 reveals the HTML used to construct them.

- ▶ **Ordered list**—An indented list that has numbers or letters before each list item. The ordered list begins with the `<ol>` tag and ends with a closing `</ol>` tag. List items are enclosed in the `<li></li>` tag pair, and line breaks appear automatically at each opening `<li>` tag. The entire list is indented.

- ▶ **Unordered list**—An indented list that has a bullet or other symbol before each list item. The unordered list begins with the `<ul>` tag and closes with `</ul>`. Like the ordered list, its list items are enclosed in the `<li></li>` tag pair. A line break and symbol appear at each opening `<li>` tag, and the entire list is indented.

▶ **Definition list**—A list of terms and their meanings. This type of list, which has no special number, letter, or symbol before each item, begins with <dl> and ends with </dl>. The <dt></dt> tag pair encloses each term and the <dd></dd> tag pair encloses each definition. Line breaks and indentations appear automatically.

LISTING 5.5   Unordered Lists, Ordered Lists, and Definition Lists

```
<?xml version="1.0" encoding="UTF-8"?>
<!DOCTYPE html PUBLIC "-//W3C//DTD XHTML 1.1//EN"
  "http://www.w3.org/TR/xhtml11/DTD/xhtml11.dtd">

<html xmlns="http://www.w3.org/1999/xhtml" xml:lang="en">
  <head>
    <title>How to Be Proper</title>
  </head>

  <body>
    <h1>How to Be Proper</h1>
    <h2>Basic Etiquette for a Gentlemen Greeting a Lady Aquaintance</h2>
    <ul>
      <li>Wait for her acknowledging bow before tipping your hat.</li>
      <li>Use the hand farthest from her to raise the hat.</li>
      <li>Walk with her if she expresses a wish to converse; Never
      make a lady stand talking in the street.</li>
      <li>When walking, the lady must always have the wall.</li>
    </ul>
    <h2>Recourse for a Lady Toward Unpleasant Men Who Persist in Bowing</h2>
    <ol>
      <li>A simple stare of iciness should suffice in most instances.</li>
      <li>A cold bow discourages familiarity without offering insult.</li>
      <li>As a last resort: "Sir, I have not the honour of your
      aquaintance."</li>
    </ol>
    <h2>Proper Address of Royalty</h2>
    <dl>
      <dt>Your Majesty</dt>
      <dd>To the king or queen.</dd>
      <dt>Your Royal Highness</dt>
      <dd>To the monarch's spouse, children, and siblings.</dd>
      <dt>Your Highness</dt>
      <dd>To nephews, nieces, and cousins of the sovereign.</dd>
    </dl>
  </body>
</html>
```

FIGURE 5.5
The three basic types of HTML lists.

NOTE

Remember that different web browsers can display web content quite differently. The HTML standard doesn't specify exactly how web browsers should format lists, so users with older web browsers might not see exactly the same indentation you see. You can use CSS to gain precise control over list items, which you will learn about later in this chapter.

Placing Lists Within Lists

Although definition lists are officially supposed to be used for defining terms, many web page authors use them anywhere they'd like to see some indentation. In practice, you can indent any text simply by putting `<dl><dd>` at the beginning of it and `</dd></dl>` at the end and skipping over the `<dt></dt>` tag pair. However, a better approach to indenting text is to use the `<blockquote></blockquote>` tag pair, which indents content without the presumption of a definition and allows for much more clear styling. With one set of attributes, you can set the width, height, background color, border type and color of your element area, and other visual effects.

Because of the level of control over the display of your items that you have when using CSS, there is no need to use *nested* lists to achieve the visual appearance of indentation. Reserve your use of nested lists for when the content warrants it. In other words, use nested lists to show a hierarchy of information, such as in Listing 5.6.

Ordered and unordered lists can be nested inside one another, down to as many levels as you want. In Listing 5.6, a complex indented outline is constructed from several unordered lists. You'll notice in Figure 5.6 that Firefox automatically uses a different type of bullet for each of the first three levels of indentation, making the list very easy to read. This is common in modern browsers.

NOTE

Nesting refers to a tag that appears entirely within another tag. Nested tags are also referred to as *child tags* of the (parent) tag that contains them. It is a common (but not required) coding practice to indent nested tags so that you can easily see their relationship to the parent tag.

LISTING 5.6   Using Lists to Build Outlines

```
<?xml version="1.0" encoding="UTF-8"?>
<!DOCTYPE html PUBLIC "-//W3C//DTD XHTML 1.1//EN"
  "http://www.w3.org/TR/xhtml11/DTD/xhtml11.dtd">

<html xmlns="http://www.w3.org/1999/xhtml" xml:lang="en">
  <head>
    <title>Vertebrates</title>
  </head>

  <body>
    <h1>Vertebrates</h1>
    <ul>
      <li><span style="font-weight:bold">Fish</span>
        <ul>
          <li>Barramundi</li>
          <li>Kissing Gourami</li>
          <li>Mummichog</li>
        </ul>
      </li>
      <li><span style="font-weight:bold">Amphibians</span>
      <ul>
          <li>Anura
            <ul>
              <li>Goliath Frog</li>
              <li>Poison Dart Frog</li>
              <li>Purple Frog</li>
            </ul>
          </li>
          <li>Caudata
            <ul>
              <li>Hellbender</li>
              <li>Mudpuppy</li>
            </ul>
          </li>
        </ul>
      </li>
      <li><span style="font-weight:bold">Reptiles</span>
        <ul>
          <li>Nile Crocodile</li>
          <li>King Cobra</li>
          <li>Common Snapping Turtle</li>
        </ul>
      </li>
    </ul>
  </body>
</html>
```

As shown in Figure 5.6, a web browser will normally use a solid disc for the first-level bullet, a hollow circle for the second-level bullet, and a solid square for all deeper levels. However, you can explicitly choose which type of bullet to use for any level by using `<ul style="list-style-type:disc">`, `<ul style="list-style-type:circle">`, or `<ul style="list-style-type:square">` instead of `<ul>`.

FIGURE 5.6
In Firefox, multilevel unordered lists are neatly indented and bulleted for improved readability.

You can even change the bullet for any single point within an unordered list by using the `list-style-type` style rule in the `<li>` tag. For example, the following codes displays a hollow circle in front of the words extra and super and a solid square in front of the word special:

```
<ul style="list-style-type:circle">
  <li>extra</li>
  <li>super</li>
  <li style="list-style-type:square">special</li>
</ul>
```

The `list-style-type` style rule also works with ordered lists, but instead of choosing a type of bullet, you choose the type of numbers or letters to place in front of each item. Listing 5.7 shows how to use Roman numerals (`list-style-type:upper-roman`), capital letters (`list-style-type:upper-alpha`), lowercase letters (`list-style-type:lower-alpha`), and ordinary numbers in a multilevel list. Figure 5.7 shows the resulting outline, which is nicely formatted.

Although Listing 5.7 uses the `list-style-type` style rule only with the `<ol>` tag, you can also use it for specific `<li>` tags within a list (although it's hard to imagine a situation in which you would want to do this). You can also explicitly specify ordinary numbering with `list-style-type:decimal`, and you can make lowercase Roman numerals with `list-style-type:lower-roman`.

LISTING 5.7   Using the `list-style-type` Style Rule with the `style` Attribute in Multitiered Lists

```
<?xml version="1.0" encoding="UTF-8"?>
<!DOCTYPE html PUBLIC "-//W3C//DTD XHTML 1.1//EN"
  "http://www.w3.org/TR/xhtml11/DTD/xhtml11.dtd">

<html xmlns="http://www.w3.org/1999/xhtml" xml:lang="en">
  <head>
    <title>Advice from the Golf Guru</title>
  </head>

  <body>
    <h1>How to Win at Golf</h1>
    <ol style="list-style-type:upper-roman">
      <li>Training
        <ol>
          <li>Mental prep
            <ol style="list-style-type:upper-alpha">
              <li>Watch golf on TV religiously</li>
              <li>Get that computer game with Tiger whatsisname</li>
              <li>Rent "personal victory" subliminal tapes</li>
            </ol>
          </li>
          <li>Equipment
            <ol style="list-style-type:upper-alpha">
              <li>Make sure your putter has a pro autograph on it</li>
              <li>Pick up a bargain bag of tees-n-balls at Costco</li>
            </ol>
          </li>
          <li>Diet
            <ol style="list-style-type:upper-alpha">
              <li>Avoid junk food
                <ol style="list-style-type:lower-alpha">
                  <li>No hotdogs</li>
                </ol>
              </li>
              <li>Drink  wine and mixed drinks only, no beer</li>
            </ol>
          </li>
        </ol>
```

LISTING 5.7   Continued

```
      </li>
      <li>Pre-game
        <ol>
          <li>Dress
            <ol style="list-style-type:upper-alpha">
              <li>Put on shorts, even if it's freezing</li>
              <li>Buy a new hat if you lost last time</li>
            </ol>
          </li>
          <li>Location and Scheduling
            <ol style="list-style-type:upper-alpha">
              <li>Select a course where your spouse or boss
                  won't find you</li>
              <li>To save on fees, play where your buddy works</li>
            </ol>
          </li>
          <li>Opponent
            <ol style="list-style-type:upper-alpha">
              <li>Look for: overconfidence, inexperience</li>
              <li>Buy opponent as many pre-game drinks as possible</li>
            </ol>
          </li>
        </ol>
      </li>
      <li>On the Course
        <ol>
          <li>Tee off first, then develop severe hayfever</li>
          <li>Drive cart over opponent's ball to degrade
              aerodynamics</li>
          <li>Say "fore" just before ball makes contact
              with opponent</li>
          <li>Always replace divots when putting</li>
          <li>Water cooler holes are a good time to correct
              any errors in ball
          placement</li>
        </ol>
      </li>
    </ol>
  </body>
</html>
```

FIGURE 5.7
A well-formatted outline can
make almost any plan look more
plausible.

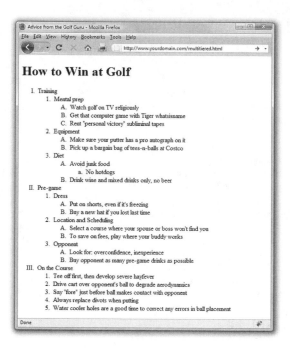

Summary

In this chapter, you learned how to make text appear as boldface or italic
and how to code superscripts, subscripts, special symbols, and accented letters. You saw how to make the text line up properly in preformatted pas-
sages of monospaced text and how to control the size, color, and typeface of
any section of text on a web page. You also learned that attributes are used
to specify options and special behavior of many HTML tags and how to use
the `style` attribute with CSS style rules to align text. You also discovered
how to create and combine three basic types of HTML lists: ordered lists,
unordered lists, and definition lists. Lists can be placed within other lists to
create outlines and other complex arrangements of text.

Table 5.2 summarizes the tags and attributes discussed in this chapter.
Don't feel like you have to memorize all these tags, by the way!

TABLE 5.2   HTML Tags and Attributes Covered in Chapter 5

Tag/Attribute	Function
`<em>...</em>`	Emphasis (usually italic).
`<strong>...</strong>`	Stronger emphasis (usually bold).
`<b>...</b>`	Boldface text.

TABLE 5.2   Continued

Tag/Attribute	Function
`<i>...</i>`	Italic text.
`<tt>...</tt>`	Typewriter (monospaced) font.
`<pre>...</pre>`	Preformatted text (exact line endings and spacing will be preserved—usually rendered in a monospaced font).
`<big>...</big>`	Text is slightly larger than normal.
`<small>...</small>`	Text is slightly smaller than normal.
`<sub>...</sub>`	Subscript.
`<sup>...</sup>`	Superscript.
`<div>...</div>`	A region of text to be formatted.
`<dl>...</dl>`	A definition list.
`<dt>...</dt>`	A definition term, as part of a definition list.
`<dd>...</dd>`	The corresponding definition to a definition term, as part of a definition list.
`<ol>...</ol>`	An ordered (numbered) list.
`<ul>...</ul>`	An unordered (bulleted) list.
`<li>...</li>`	A list item for use with `<ol>` or `<ul>`.

Attributes

`style="font-family:typeface"`	The typeface (family) of the font, which is the name of a font, such as Arial. (Can also be used with `<p>`, `<h1>`, `<h2>`, `<h3>`, and so on.)
`style="font-size:size"`	The size of the font, which can be set to `small`, `medium`, or `large`, as well as `x-small`, `x-large`, and so on. Can also be set to a specific point size (such as 12 pt).
`style="color:color"`	Changes the color of the text.
`style="text-➥align:alignment"`	Align text to center, left, or right. (Can also be used with `<p>`, `<h1>`, `<h2>`, `<h3>`, and so on.)
`style="list-➥style-type:➥numtype"`	The type of numerals used to label the list. Possible values are `decimal`, `lower-roman`, `upper-roman`, `lower-alpha`, `upper-alpha`, and `none`.
`style="list-style-➥type:bullettype"`	The bullet dingbat used to mark list items. Possible values are `disc`, `circle`, `square`, and `none`.
`style="list-style-➥type:type"`	The type of bullet or number used to label this item. Possible values are `disc`, `circle`, `square`, `decimal`, `lower-roman`, `upper-roman`, `lower-alpha`, `upper-alpha`, and `none`.

Q&A

Q. **How do I find out the exact name for a font I have on my computer?**

A. On a Windows or Macintosh computer, open the Control Panel and click the Fonts folder—the fonts on your system are listed. (Vista users might have to switch to "Classic View" in your Control Panel.) When specifying fonts in the `font-family` style rule, use the exact spelling of font names. Font names are not case-sensitive, however.

Q. **How do I put Kanji, Arabic, Chinese, and other non-European characters on my pages?**

A. First of all, users who need to read these characters on your pages must have the appropriate language fonts installed. They must also have selected that language character set and its associated font for their web browsers. You can use the Character Map program in Windows (or a similar program in other operating systems) to get the numerical codes for each character in any language font. To find Character Map, click Start, All Programs, Accessories, and then System Tools. If the character you want has a code of 214, use Ö to place it on a web page. If you cannot find the Character Map program, use your operating system's built-in Help function to find the specific location.

The best way to include a short message in an Asian language (such as `We Speak Tamil-Call Us!`) is to include it as a graphics image. That way every user will see it, even if they use English as their primary language for web browsing. But even to use a language font in a graphic, you will likely have to download a specific language pack for your operating system. Again, check your system's Help function for specific instructions.

Q. **I've seen web pages that use three-dimensional little balls or other special graphics for bullets. How do they do that?**

A. That trick is a little bit beyond what this chapter covers. You'll learn how to do it yourself in Chapter 8.

Q. **How do I "full justify" text so that both the left and right margins are flush?**

A. You can use `text-align:justify` in your style declaration.

Workshop

The workshop contains quiz questions and activities to help you solidify your understanding of the material covered. Try to answer all questions before looking at the "Answers" section that follows.

Quiz

1. How would you create a paragraph in which the first three words are bold, using styles rather than the <b> or <strong> tags?

2. How would you represent the chemical formula for water?

3. How do you display "© 2010, Webwonks Inc." on a web page?

4. How would you center everything on an entire page?

5. What would you use to create a definition list to show that the word *glunch* means "a look of disdain, anger, or displeasure" and that the word *glumpy* means "sullen, morose, or sulky"?

Answers

1. You would use the following:

   ```
   <p><span style="font-weight: bold">First three words</span> are
   bold.</p>
   ```

2. You would use H₂O.

3. You would use either of the following:

   ```
   &copy; 2010, Webwonks Inc.
   &#169; 2010, Webwonks Inc.
   ```

4. If you thought about putting a <div style="text-align:center"> immediately after the <body> tag at the top of the page, and </div> just before the </body> tag at the end of the page, then you're correct. However, the text-align style is also supported directly in the <body> tag, which means you can forego the <div> tag and place the style="text-align:center" style directly in the <body> tag. Presto, the entire page is centered!

5. You would use the following:

   ```
   <dl>
   <dt>glunch</dt><dd>a look of disdain, anger, or displeasure</dd>
   <dt>glumpy</dt><dd>sullen, morose, or sulky</dd>
   </dl>
   ```

Exercises

▶ Apply the font-level style attributes you learned about in this chapter to various block-level elements such as `<p>`, `<div>`, `<ul>`, and `<li>` items. Try nesting your elements to get a feel for how styles do or do not cascade through the content hierarchy.

▶ Use the text alignment style attributes to place blocks of text in various places on your web page. Try nesting your paragraphs and divisions (`<p>` and `<div>`) to get a feel for how styles do or do not cascade through the content hierarchy.

▶ Try producing an ordered list outlining the information you'd like to put on your web pages. This will give you practice formatting HTML lists and also give you a head start on thinking about the issues covered in later chapters of this book.

CHAPTER 6

Using Tables to Display Information

In this chapter, you learn how to build HTML tables you can use to control the spacing, layout, and appearance of tabular data in your web content. Although you can achieve similar results using CSS, there are definitely times when a table is the best way to present information, and you'll find that tables are useful for arranging information into rows and columns. I will also explain how designers have used tables for page layout in the past and how that isn't always the best idea. Before we begin, just remember a table is simply an orderly arrangement of content into vertical columns and horizontal rows.

Creating a Simple Table

A table consists of rows of information with individual cells inside. To make tables, you have to start with a <table> tag. Of course, you end your tables with the </table> tag. If you want the table to have a border, use a border attribute to specify the width of the border in pixels. A border size of 0 or none (or leaving the border attribute out entirely) will make the border invisible, which is handy if you find yourself using a table as a page layout tool (not recommended).

With the <table> tag in place, the next thing you need is the <tr> tag. The <tr> tag creates a table row, which contains one or more cells of information before the closing </tr>. To create these individual cells, use the <td> tag (<td> stands for table data). Place the table information between the <td> and </td> tags. A *cell* is a rectangular region that can contain any text, images, and HTML tags. Each row in a table consists of at least one cell. Multiple cells within a row form columns in a table.

WHAT YOU'LL LEARN IN THIS CHAPTER:

▶ How to create simple tables

▶ How to control the size of tables

▶ How to align content and span rows and columns within tables

TIP

As you read this chapter, think about how arranging text into tables could benefit your web content. The following are some specific ideas to keep in mind:

▶ The most obvious application of tables is to organize tabular information, such as a multicolumn list of names and numbers.

▶ Whenever you need multiple columns of text or images, tables are the answer.

TIP

Some style properties enable you to take much more control over table borders. For example, you can set the border width (border-width), style (border-style), and color (border-color). These properties work fine, but you have to apply them to each table element, which can be cumbersome even if you use classes for your table row or table cell elements.

There is one more basic tag involved in building tables. The <th> tag works exactly like a <td> tag except <th> indicates that the cell is part of the heading of the table. Most web browsers render the text in <th> cells as centered and boldface.

You can create as many cells as you want, but each row in a table should have the same number of columns as the other rows. The HTML code shown in Listing 6.1 creates a simple table using only the four table tags I've mentioned thus far. Figure 6.1 shows the resulting page as viewed in a web browser.

LISTING 6.1   Creating Tables with the <table>, <tr>, <td>, and <th> Tags

```
<?xml version="1.0" encoding="UTF-8"?>
<!DOCTYPE html PUBLIC "-//W3C//DTD XHTML 1.1//EN"
  "http://www.w3.org/TR/xhtml11/DTD/xhtml11.dtd">

<html xmlns="http://www.w3.org/1999/xhtml" xml:lang="en">
  <head>
    <title>Baseball Standings</title>
  </head>

  <body>
  <h1>Baseball Standings</h1>
    <table>
      <tr>
        <th>Team</th>
        <th>W</th>
    <th>L</th>
        <th>GB</th>
      </tr>
      <tr>
        <td>Los Angeles Dodgers</td>
        <td>62</td>
        <td>38</td>
        <td>—</td>
      </tr>
      <tr>
        <td>San Francisco Giants</td>
        <td>54</td>
        <td>46</td>
        <td>8.0</td>
      </tr>
      <tr>
        <td>Colorado Rockies</td>
        <td>54</td>
        <td>46</td>
        <td>8.0</td>
      </tr>
```

LISTING 6.1   Continued

```
      <tr>
        <td>Arizona Diamondbacks</td>
        <td>43</td>
        <td>58</td>
        <td>19.5</td>
      </tr>
      <tr>
        <td>San Diego Padres</td>
        <td>39</td>
        <td>62</td>
        <td>23.5</td>
      </tr>
    </table>
  </body>
</html>
```

TIP

HTML ignores extra spaces between words and tags. However, you might find your HTML tables easier to read (and less prone to time-wasting errors) if you use spaces to indent <tr> and <td> tags, as I did in Listing 6.1.

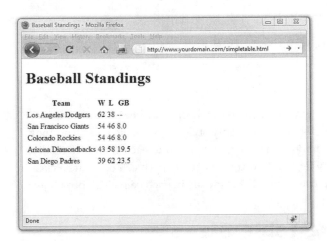

FIGURE 6.1
The HTML code in Listing 6.1 creates a table with six rows and four columns.

The table in the example contains baseball standings, which are perfect for arranging in rows and columns—if not a little plain. You'll learn to jazz things up a bit during this chapter. The headings in the table show the Team, Wins (W), Losses (L), and Games Behind (GB) in the standings.

Although we did not apply any styles to the HTML in Listing 6.1, you can use any text style in a table cell. However, styles or HTML tags used in one cell don't carry over to other cells, and tags from outside the table don't apply within the table. For example, consider the following table:

```
<p style="font-weight:bold">
  <table>
    <tr>
      <td style="font-style:italic">hello</td>
      <td>there</td>
    </tr>
  </table>
</p>
```

In this example, the <p> tag is used around a table to demonstrate how tables are immune to outside tags. The word there would be neither bold-face nor italic because neither the font-weight:bold style outside the table nor the font-style:italic style from the previous cell affects it. In this example, the word hello is in italics, however.

To boldface the words hello and there, change the table code to this:

```
<table style="font-weight:bold">
  <tr>
    <td style="font-style:italic">hello</td>
    <td>there</td>
  </tr>
</table>
```

In this example, both words are in bold and the word hello is italicized as well. Of course, you don't have to apply styles at the table level. The font-weight:bold style could just as easily be applied to each cell individually; you could repeat style="font-weight:bold" in each cell or create a class in your style sheet and use class="classname" in each cell—it's your choice.

Controlling Table Sizes

When a table width is not specified, the size of a table and its individual cells automatically expand to fit the data you place into it. However, you can choose to control the exact size of the entire table by using width and/or height styles in the <table> tag. You can also control the size of each cell by putting width and height styles in the individual <td> tags. The width and height styles can be specified as either pixels or percentages. For example, the following code creates a table 500 pixels wide and 400 pixels high:

```
<table style="width:500px; height:400px">
```

To make the first cell of the table 20% of the total table width and the second cell 80% of the table width, type the following:

NOTE

There are actually width and height HTML attributes that were deprecated in the move to XHTML, and you might still see them when you look at another designer's code. These attributes still work in web browsers, but you should use the width and height style properties instead because they represent the appropriate use of XHTML.

```
<table style="width:100%">
  <tr>
    <td style="width:20%">skinny cell</td>
    <td style="width:80%">fat cell</td>
  </tr>
</table>
```

Notice that the table is sized to 100%, which ensures the table fills the entire width of the browser window. When you use percentages instead of fixed pixel sizes, the table will resize automatically to fit any size browser window while maintaining the aesthetic balance you're after. In this case, the two cells within the table are automatically resized to 20% and 80% of the total table width, respectively.

In Listing 6.2, the simple table from Listing 6.1 is expanded to show specific control over table cell widths.

LISTING 6.2   Specifying Table Cell Widths

```
<?xml version="1.0" encoding="UTF-8"?>
<!DOCTYPE html PUBLIC "-//W3C//DTD XHTML 1.1//EN"
  "http://www.w3.org/TR/xhtml11/DTD/xhtml11.dtd">

<html xmlns="http://www.w3.org/1999/xhtml" xml:lang="en">
  <head>
    <title>Baseball Standings</title>
  </head>

  <body>
  <h1>Baseball Standings</h1>
    <table>
      <tr>
        <th style="width:35px;"></th>
        <th style="width:175px;">Team</th>
        <th style="width:25px;">W</th>
        <th style="width:25px;">L</th>
        <th style="width:25px;">GB</th>
      </tr>
      <tr>
        <td><img src="losangeles.gif" alt="Los Angeles
          Dodgers" /></td>
        <td>Los Angeles Dodgers</td>
        <td>62</td>
        <td>38</td>
        <td>—</td>
      </tr>
      <tr>
        <td><img src="sanfrancisco.gif" alt="San Francisco
          Giants" /></td>
        <td>San Francisco Giants</td>
        <td>54</td>
```

LISTING 6.2   Continued

```
          <td>46</td>
          <td>8.0</td>
        </tr>
        <tr>
          <td><img src="colorado.gif" alt="Colorado
              Rockies" /></td>
          <td>Colorado Rockies</td>
          <td>54</td>
          <td>46</td>
          <td>8.0</td>
        </tr>
        <tr>
          <td><img src="arizona.gif" alt="Arizona
              Diamondbacks" /></td>
          <td>Arizona Diamondbacks</td>
          <td>43</td>
          <td>58</td>
          <td>19.5</td>
        </tr>
        <tr>
          <td><img src="sandiego.gif" alt="San Diego Padres" /></td>
          <td>San Diego Padres</td>
          <td>39</td>
          <td>62</td>
          <td>23.5</td>
        </tr>
      </table>
    </body>
</html>
```

You can see the consistent column widths in Figure 6.2.

FIGURE 6.2
The HTML code in Listing 6.2 creates a table with six rows and five
columns, with specific widths used
for each column.

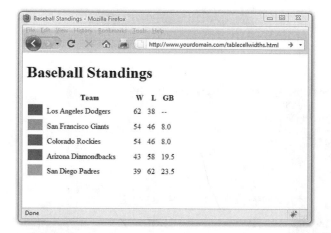

There are two differences between the code from Listing 6.1 and the code used in Listing 6.2. First, an additional column has been added in Listing 6.2; this column does not have a heading, but the `<th></th>` tag pair is still present in the first table row. In rows two through six, this additional column contains an image (the `<img />` tag). The second difference in Listing 6.2 is the addition of a specific width style for each `<th>` element in the first row. The first column is defined as 35px wide, the second 175px wide, and the third, fourth, and fifth columns are each 25px wide.

Also note that these widths are not repeated in the `<td>` elements in subsequent rows. Technically you must define only the widths in the first row; the remaining rows will follow suit because they are all part of the same table. However, if you used another formatting style (such as a style to change font size or color), that style must be repeated for each element that should have those display properties.

Alignment and Spanning Within Tables

By default, anything you place inside a table cell is aligned to the left and vertically centered. Figures 6.1 and 6.2 show this default alignment. However, you can align the contents of table cells both horizontally and vertically with the `text-align` and `vertical-align` style properties.

You can apply these alignment attributes to any `<tr>`, `<td>`, or `<th>` tag. Alignment attributes assigned to a `<tr>` tag apply to all cells in that row. Depending on the size of your table, you can save yourself a considerable amount of time and effort by applying these attributes at the `<tr>` level and not in each `<td>` or `<th>` tag.

The HTML code in Listing 6.3 uses a combination of text alignment styles to apply a default alignment to a row, but it is overridden in a few individual cells. Figure 6.3 shows the result of the code in Listing 6.3.

Following are some of the more commonly used `vertical-align` style property values: `top`, `middle`, `bottom`, `text-top`, `text-bottom`, and `baseline` (for text). These property values give you plenty of flexibility in aligning table data vertically.

LISTING 6.3   Alignment, Cell Spacing, Borders, and Background Colors in Tables

```
<?xml version="1.0" encoding="UTF-8"?>
<!DOCTYPE html PUBLIC "-//W3C//DTD XHTML 1.1//EN"
  "http://www.w3.org/TR/xhtml11/DTD/xhtml11.dtd">

<html xmlns="http://www.w3.org/1999/xhtml" xml:lang="en">
  <head>
    <title>Things to Fear</title>
  </head>

  <body>
    <h1>Things to Fear</h1>
    <table border="2" cellpadding="4" cellspacing="2"
    width="100%">
      <tr style="background-color:red;color:white">
        <th colspan="2">Description</th>
        <th>Size</th>
        <th>Weight</th>
        <th>Speed</th>
      </tr>
      <tr style="vertical-align:top">
        <td><img src="handgun.gif" alt=".38 Special"/></td>
        <td style="font-size: 14px;font-weight:bold;
        vertical-align:middle;text-align:center">.38 Special</td>
        <td>Five-inch barrel.</td>
        <td>Twenty ounces.</td>
        <td>Six rounds in four seconds.</td>
      </tr>
      <tr style="vertical-align:top">
        <td><img src="rhino.gif" alt="Rhinoceros" /></td>
        <td style="font-size: 14px;font-weight:bold;
        vertical-align:middle;text-align:center">Rhinoceros</td>
        <td>Twelve feet, horn to tail.</td>
        <td>Up to two tons.</td>
        <td>Thirty-five miles per hour in bursts.</td>
      </tr>
      <tr style="vertical-align:top">
        <td><img src="axeman.gif" alt="Broad Axe" /></td>
        <td style="font-size: 14px;font-weight:bold;
        vertical-align:middle;text-align:center">Broad Axe</td>
        <td>Thirty-inch blade.</td>
        <td>Twelve pounds.</td>
        <td>Sixty miles per hour on impact.</td>
      </tr>
    </table>
  </body>
</html>
```

FIGURE 6.3
The code in Listing 6.3 shows the use of the colspan attribute and alignment styles.

At the top of Figure 6.3, a single cell (Description) spans two columns. This is accomplished with the colspan attribute in the <th> tag for that cell. As you might guess, you can also use the rowspan attribute to create a cell that spans more than one row.

Spanning is the process of forcing a cell to stretch across more than one row or column of a table. The colspan attribute causes a cell to span across multiple columns; rowspan has the same effect on rows.

Additionally, text styles are used in the second cell within the Description column to create bold text that is both vertically aligned to the middle and horizontally aligned to the center of the cell.

There are a few tricks in Listing 6.3 that I haven't explained yet. You can give an entire table—and each individual row or cell in a table—its own background, distinct from any background you might use on the web page itself. You can do this by placing the background-color or background-image style in the <table>, <tr>, <td>, or <th> tag exactly as you would in the <body> tag (see Chapter 8, "Working with Colors, Images, and Multimedia"). To give an entire table a yellow background, for example, you would use <table style="background-color:yellow"> or the equivalent <table style="background-color:#FFFF00">. In Listing 6.3, only the top row has a background color; it uses <tr style="background-color:red;color:white"> to apply a red background across the cells in that row. Additionally, the color style ensures that the text in that row is white.

TIP

Keeping the structure of rows and columns organized in your mind can be the most difficult part of creating tables with cells that span multiple columns or rows. The tiniest error can often throw the whole thing into disarray. You'll save yourself time and frustration by sketching your tables on paper before you start writing the HTML to implement them.

NOTE

You will often see alternating row colors in a table. For instance, one row might have a grey background and the next row might have a white background. Alternating row colors helps users read the content of your table more clearly, especially if the table is quite large.

NOTE

Although the `cellpadding` and `cellspacing` attributes are still allowed in XHTML, a CSS equivalent for them exists in the form of the `padding` and `border-spacing` style properties.

Similar to the `background-color` style property is the `background-image` property (not shown in this example), which is used to set an image for a table background. If you wanted to set the image `leaves.gif` as the background for a table, you would use `<table style="background-image:url(leaves.gif)">`. Notice that the image file is placed within parentheses and preceded by the word `url`, which indicates that you are describing where the image file is located.

Tweaking tables goes beyond just using style properties. As shown in Listing 6.3, you can control the space around the borders of a table with the `cellpadding` and `cellspacing` attributes. The `cellspacing` attribute sets the amount of space (in pixels) between table borders and between table cells themselves. The `cellpadding` attribute sets the amount of space around the edges of information in the cells, also in pixels. Setting the `cellpadding` value to `0` causes all the information in the table to align as closely as possible to the table borders, possibly even touching the borders. The `cellpadding` and `cellspacing` attributes give you good overall control of the table's appearance.

Page Layout with Tables

At the beginning of this chapter, I indicated that designers have used tables for page layout and to display tabular information. You will still find many examples of table-based layouts if you peek at another designer's source code. This method of design grew out of the old (mid-1990s to early 2000s) inconsistencies in browser support for CSS. All browsers supported tables and in generally the same way, so web designers latched on to the table-based method of content creation to achieve the same visual page display across all browsers. However, now that support for CSS is relatively similar across all major browsers, designers can follow the long-standing standards-based recommendation *not* to use tables for page layout.

The World Wide Web Consortium (W3C), the standards body that oversees the future of the Web, promotes style sheets as the proper way to lay out pages (instead of using tables). Style sheets are ultimately much more powerful than tables, which is why the bulk of this book teaches you how to use style sheets for page layout.

The main reasons for avoiding using tables for layout include the following:

▶ **Mixing presentation with content**—One of the goals of CSS and standards-compliant web design is to separate the presentation layer from the content layer.

▶ **Creating unnecessarily difficult redesigns**—To change a table-based layout, you would have to change the table-based layout on every single page of your site (unless it is part of a complicated, dynamically driven site, in which case you would have to undo all the dynamic pieces and remake them).

▶ **Accessibility issues**—Screen reading software looks to tables for content and will often try to read your layout table as a content table.

▶ **Rendering on mobile devices**—Table layouts are often not flexible enough to scale downward to small screens (see Chapter 12, "Creating Fixed or Liquid Layouts").

These are but a few of the issues in table-based web design. For a closer look at some of these issues, see the popular presentation "Why Tables for Layout Is Stupid" at http://www.hotdesign.com/seybold/everything.html.

Summary

In this brief chapter, you learned to arrange text and images into organized arrangements of rows and columns called tables. You learned the three basic tags for creating tables and many optional attributes and styles for controlling the alignment, spacing, and appearance of tables. You also discovered that tables can be used together and nested within one another for an even wider variety of layout options.

Table 6.1 summarizes the tags and attributes covered in this chapter.

TABLE 6.1   HTML Tags and Attributes Covered in Chapter 6

Tag/Attribute	Function
`<table>...</table>`	Creates a table that can contain any number of rows (`<tr>` tags).
Attributes	
`border="width"`	Indicates the width in pixels of the table borders. Using `border="0"` or omitting the `border` attribute makes borders invisible.
`cellspacing=` `➥"spacing"`	The amount of space between the cells in the table, in pixels.
`cellpadding=` `➥"padding"`	The amount of space between the edges of the cell and its contents, in pixels.
`style=` `➥"width:width"`	The width of the table on the page, either in exact pixel values or as a percentage of the page width.

TABLE 6.1   Continued

Tag/Attribute	Function
style= ➥"height:height"	The height of the table on the page, either in exact pixel values or as a percentage of the page height.
style="background- ➥color:color"	Background color of the table and individual table cells that don't already have a background color.
style= ➥"backgroundimage: ➥url(imageurl)"	A background image to display within the table and individual table cells that don't already have a background image. (If a background color is also specified, the color will show through transparent areas of the image.)

Attributes

`<tr>...</tr>`	Defines a table row containing one or more cells (`<td>` tags).

Attributes

style="text-align: alignment"	The horizontal alignment of the contents of the cells within this row. Possible values are `left`, `right`, and `center`.
style="vertical- align:alignment"	The vertical alignment of the contents of the cells within this row. Commonly used values include `top`, `middle`, and `bottom`.
style="background- color:color"	Background color of all cells in the row that do not already have a background color.
style= "backgroundimage: url(imageurl)"	Background image to display within all cells in the row that do not already have their own background image.
`<td>...</td>`	Defines a table data cell.
`<th>...</th>`	Defines a table heading cell. (Accepts all the same attributes and styles as `<td>`.)

Attributes

style="text- align:alignment"	The horizontal alignment of the contents of the cell. Possible values are `left`, `right`, and `center`.
style="vertical- align:alignment"	The vertical alignment of the contents of the cell. Commonly used values are `top`, `middle`, and `bottom`.
rowspan="numrows"	The number of rows this cell will span.
colspan="numcols"	The number of columns this cell will span.
style="width:width"	The width of this column of cells, in exact pixel values or as a percentage of the table width.

TABLE 6.1   Continued

Attributes

`style=` `"height:height"`	The height of this row of cells, in exact pixel values or as a percentage of the table height.
`style="background-` `color:color"`	Background color of the cell.

`style=`
`"backgroundimage:`
`url(imageurl)"`
	Background image to display within the cell.

Q&A

Q. I made a big table and when I load the page, nothing appears on the page for a long time. Why the wait?

A. Complex tables can take a while to appear on the screen. The web browser has to figure out the size of everything in the table before it can display any part of it. You can speed things up a bit by always including `width` and `height` attributes for every graphics image within a table. Using `width` attributes in the `<table>` and `<td>` tags also helps.

Q. Can I put a table within a table?

A. Yes, you can nest tables within other table cells. However, nested tables—especially large ones—take time to load and render properly. Before you create a nested table, think about the content you are placing on the page and ask yourself if it could be displayed using CSS. You might not know all the answers until you finish this book, but here's a hint: In most cases, the answer will be yes.

Workshop

The workshop contains quiz questions and exercises to help you solidify your understanding of the material covered. Try to answer all questions before looking at the "Answers" section that follows.

Quiz

1. How would you create a simple two-row, two-column table with a standard border?

2. Expanding on question 1, how would you add 30 pixels of space between the table border and the cells?

3. Continuing with the table you've built in questions 1 and 2, how would you make the top-left cell green, the top-right cell red, the bottom-left cell yellow, and the bottom-right cell blue?

Answers

1. Use the following HTML:

```
<table border="1">
  <tr>
    <td>Top left...</td>
    <td>Top right...</td>
  </tr>
  <tr>
    <td>Bottom left...</td>
    <td>Bottom right...</td>
  </tr>
</table>
```

2. Add `cellspacing="30"` to the `<table>` tag.

3. Add `style="background-color:green"` to the top left `<td>` tag, add `style="background-color:red"` to the top right `<td>` tag, add `style="background-color:yellow"` to the bottom left `<td>` tag, and add `style="background-color:blue"` to the bottom right `<td>` tag.

Exercises

▶ Do you have any pages that have information visitors might be interested in viewing as lists or tables? Use a table to present some tabular information. Make sure each column has its own heading (or perhaps its own graphic). Play around with the various types of alignment and spacing that you have learned in this chapter.

▶ You will often see alternating row colors in a table, with one row having a grey background and the next a white background. The goal of alternating colors in table rows is so that the individual rows are easier to discern when looking quickly at the table full of data. Create a table with alternating row colors and text colors (if necessary). Although the lesson on colors comes in Chapter 8, you have enough information in this lesson to begin trying out the process.

Using External and Internal Links

So far, you have learned how to use HTML tags to create some basic web pages. However, at this point, those pieces of content are islands unto themselves, with no connection to anything else (although it is true that in Chapter 3, "Understanding Cascading Style Sheets," I sneaked a few page links into the examples). To turn your work into real web content, you need to connect it to the rest of the Web—or at least to your other pages within your own personal or corporate sites.

This chapter shows you how to create hypertext links to content within your own document and how to link to other external documents. Additionally, you will learn how to style hypertext links so that they display in the color and decoration that you desire—not necessarily the default blue underlined display.

Using Web Addresses

The simplest way to store web content for an individual website is to place the files all in the same folder together. When files are stored together like this, you can link to them by simply providing the name of the file in the `href` attribute of the <a> tag.

An *attribute* is an extra piece of information associated with a tag that provides further details about the tag. For example, the `href` attribute of the <a> tag identifies the address of the page to which you are linking.

After you have more than a few pages, or when you start to have an organization structure to the content in your site, you should put your files into directories (or *folders*, if you will) whose names reflect the content within them. For example, all your images could be in an "images" directory, corporate information could be in an "about" directory, and so on.

WHAT YOU'LL LEARN IN THIS CHAPTER:

▶ How to use anchor links
▶ How to link between pages on your own site
▶ How to link to external content
▶ How to link to an email address
▶ How to use window targeting with your links
▶ How to style your links with CSS

NOTE

Before we begin, you might want a refresher on the basics of where to put files on your server and how to manage files within a set of directories. This information is important to know when creating links in web content. Refer back to Chapter 1, "Publishing Web Content," specifically the section titled "Understanding Where to Place Files on the Web Server."

CAUTION

The / forward slash is always used to separate directories in HTML. Don't use the \ backslash (which is normally used in Windows) to separate your directories. Remember, everything in the Web moves forward, so use forward slashes.

Regardless of how you organize your documents within your own web server, you can use relative addresses, which include only enough information to find one page from another.

A *relative address* describes the path from one web page to another, instead of a full (or *absolute*) Internet address.

If you recall from Chapter 1, the document root of your web server is the directory designated as the top-level directory for your web content. In web addresses, that document root is represented by the forward slash (/). All subsequent levels of directories are separated by the same type of forward slash. For example:

```
/directory/subdirectory/subsubdirectory/
```

Suppose you are creating a page named zoo.html in your document root and you want to include a link to pages named african.html and asian.html in the elephants subdirectory. The links would look like the following:

```
<a href="/elephants/african.html">Learn about African elephants.</a>
<a href="/elephants/asian.html">Learn about Asian elephants.</a>
```

These specific addresses are actually called *relative-root addresses* in that they are relative addresses that lack the entire domain name, but they are specifically relative to the document root specified by the forward slash.

Using a regular relative address, you can skip the initial forward slash. This type of address allows the links to become relative to whatever directory they are in—it could be the document root or it could be another directory one or more levels down from the document root:

```
<a href="elephants/african.html">Learn about African elephants.</a>
<a href="elephants/asian.html">Learn about Asian elephants.</a>
```

Your african.html and asian.html documents in the elephants subdirectory could link back to the main zoo.html page in either of these ways:

```
<a href="http://www.yourdomain.com/zoo.html">Return to the zoo.</a>
<a href="/zoo.html">Return to the zoo.</a>
<a href="../zoo.html">Return to the zoo.</a>
```

The first link is an absolute link. With an absolute link there is *absolutely* no doubt where the link should go because the full URL is provided—domain name included.

The second link is a relative-root link. It is relative to the domain you are currently browsing and therefore does not require the protocol type (for example, http://) and the domain name (for example, www.yourdomain. com), but the initial forward slash is provided to show that the address begins at the document root.

In the third link, the *double dot* (..) is a special command that indicates the folder that contains the current folder—in other words, the *parent folder*. Anytime you see the double dot, just think to yourself "go up a level" in the directory structure.

If you use relative addressing consistently throughout your web pages, you can move the pages to another folder, disk drive, or web server without changing the links.

Relative addresses can span quite complex directory structures if necessary. Chapter 27, "Organizing and Managing a Website," offers more detailed advice for organizing and linking large numbers of web pages.

TIP

The general rule surrounding relative addressing (elephants/ african.html) versus absolute addressing (http://www.takeme 2thezoo.com/elephants/african .html) is that you should use relative addressing when linking to files that are stored together, such as files that are all part of the same website. Absolute addressing should be used when you're linking to files somewhere else—another computer, another disk drive, or, more commonly, another website on the Internet.

TRY IT YOURSELF ▼

Creating a Simple Site Architecture

Hopefully, by now, you've created a page or two of your own while working through the chapters. Follow these steps to add a few more pages and link them together:

1. Use a home page as a main entrance and as a central hub to which all of your other pages are connected. If you created a page about yourself or your business, use that page as your home page. You also might like to create a new page now for this purpose.

2. On the home page, put a list of links to the other HTML files you've created (or placeholders for the HTML files you plan to create soon). Be sure that the exact spelling of the filename, including any capitalization, is correct in every link.

3. On every other page besides the home page, include a link at the bottom (or top) leading back to your home page. That makes it simple and easy to navigate around your site.

4. You might also want to include a list of links to related or interesting sites, either on your home page or on a separate links page. People often include a list of their friends' personal pages on their own home page. Businesses, however, should be careful not to lead potential customers away to other sites too quickly—there's no guarantee they'll remember to use relative addressing for links between your own pages and absolute addressing for links to other sites.

Linking Within a Page Using Anchors

The <a> *tag*—the tag responsible for hyperlinks on the Web—got its name from the word "anchor," and means a link serves as a designation for a spot in a web page. In examples shown throughout this book so far, you've learned how to use the <a> tag to link to somewhere else, but that's only half of its usefulness. Let's get started working with anchor links that link to content within the same page.

Identifying Locations in a Page with Anchors

The <a> tag can be used to mark a spot on a page as an anchor, enabling you to create a link that points to that exact spot. Listing 7.1, which is presented a bit later in this chapter, demonstrates a link to an anchor within a page. To see how such links are made, let's take a quick peek ahead at the first <a> tag in the listing:

```
<a id="top"></a>
```

NOTE

Instead of using id, older versions of HTML used name. Newer versions of HTML and XHTML have done away with the name attribute and instead use id.

The <a> tag normally uses the href attribute to specify a hyperlinked target. The <a href> is what you click and <a id> is where you go when you click there. In this example, the <a> tag is still specifying a target but no actual link is created. Instead, the <a> tag gives a name to the specific point on the page where the tag occurs. The </a> tag must be included and a unique name must be assigned to the id attribute, but no text between <a> and </a> is necessary.

Linking to Anchor Locations

Listing 7.1 shows a site with various anchor points placed throughout a single page. Take a look at the last <a> tag in Listing 7.1 to see an example:

```
<a href="#top">Return to Index.</a>
```

The # symbol means that the word top refers to a named anchor point within the current document, rather than to a separate page. When a user clicks Return to Index, the web browser displays the part of the page starting with the <a id="top"> tag.

LISTING 7.1   Setting Anchor Points by Using the `<a>` Tag with an `id` Attribute

```
<?xml version="1.0" encoding="UTF-8"?>
<!DOCTYPE html PUBLIC "-//W3C//DTD XHTML 1.1//EN"
 "http://www.w3.org/TR/xhtml11/DTD/xhtml11.dtd">

<html xmlns="http://www.w3.org/1999/xhtml" xml:lang="en">
 <head>
  <title>Alphabetical Shakespeare</title>
 </head>

 <body>
  <h1><a id="top"></a>First Lines of Shakespearean Sonnets</h1>
  <p>Don't you just hate when you go a-courting, and you're down
   on one knee about to rattle off a totally romantic Shakespearean
   sonnet, and zap! You space it. <em>"Um... It was, uh... I think it
   started with a B..."</em></p>
  <p>Well, appearest thou no longer the dork. Simply refer to this page,
   click on the first letter of the sonnet you want, and get an instant
   reminder of the first line to get you started. <em>"Beshrew that
   heart that makes my heart to groan..."</em></p>
  <h2 style="text-align:center">Alphabetical Index</h2>
  <h3 style="text-align:center">
  <a href="#A">A</a> <a href="#B">B</a> <a href="#C">C</a>
  <a href="#D">D</a> <a href="#E">E</a> <a href="#F">F</a>
  <a href="#G">G</a> <a href="#H">H</a> <a href="#I">I</a>
  <a href="#J">J</a> <a href="#K">K</a> <a href="#L">L</a>
  <a href="#M">M</a> <a href="#N">N</a> <a href="#O">O</a>
  <a href="#P">P</a> <a href="#Q">Q</a> <a href="#R">R</a>
  <a href="#S">S</a> <a href="#T">T</a> <a href="#U">U</a>
  <a href="#V">V</a> <a href="#W">W</a> <a href="#X">X</a>
  <a href="#Y">Y</a> <a href="#Z">Z</a>
  </h3>
  <hr />
  <h3><a id="A"></a>A</h3>
  <ul>
  <li>A woman's face with nature's own hand painted,</li>
  <li>Accuse me thus, that I have scanted all, </li>
  <li>Against my love shall be as I am now</li>
  <li>Against that time (if ever that time come) </li>
  <li>Ah wherefore with infection should he live, </li>
  <li>Alack what poverty my muse brings forth, </li>
  <li>Alas 'tis true, I have gone here and there, </li>
  <li>As a decrepit father takes delight, </li>
  <li>As an unperfect actor on the stage, </li>
  <li>As fast as thou shalt wane so fast thou grow'st, </li>
  </ul>
  <p><a href="#top"><em>Return to Index.</em></a></p>
  <hr />
  <!-- continue with the alphabet -->
  <h3><a id="Z"></a>Z</h3>
  <p>(No sonnets start with Z.)</p>
  <p><a href="#top"><em>Return to Index.</em></a></p>
 </body>
</html>
```

NOTE

Near the end of Listing 7.1 you will see a line that reads:

`<!-- continue with the alphabet -->`

This text (an HTML comment) will appear in your source code, but will not be displayed by the browser. You can learn more about commenting your code in Chapter 27.

CAUTION

Anchor names specified via the id attribute in the `<a>` tag must start with an alphanumeric character. So, if you want to simply number the IDs of anchors, be sure to start them with text (as in photo1, photo2, and so on) instead of just 1, 2, and so on. Purely numeric anchor IDs will work in browsers, but they don't qualify as valid XHTML code.

Each of the `<a href>` links in Listing 7.1 makes an underlined link leading to a corresponding `<a id>` anchor—or it would if I had filled in all the text. Only A and Z will work in this example because only the A and Z links have corresponding text to link to, but feel free to fill in the rest on your own! Clicking the letter Z under Alphabetical Index in Figure 7.1, for example, takes you to the part of the page shown in Figure 7.2.

FIGURE 7.1
The `<a id>` tags in Listing 7.1 don't appear at all on the web page. The `<a href>` tags appear as underlined links.

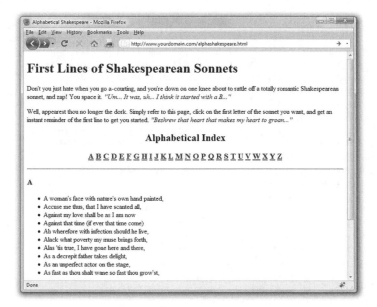

FIGURE 7.2
Clicking the letter Z on the page shown in Figure 7.1 takes you to the appropriate section of the same page.

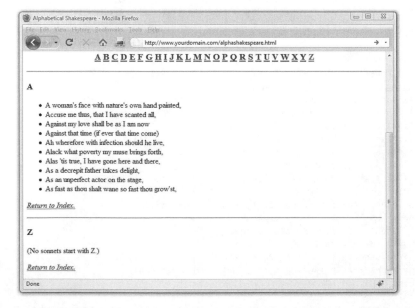

Having mastered the concept of linking to sections of text within a single page, you can now learn to link together other pieces of web content.

Linking Between Your Own Web Content

As you learned earlier in this chapter, you do not need to include http:// before each address specified in the `href` attribute when linking to content within your domain (or on the same computer, if you are viewing your site locally). When you create a link from one file to another file within the same domain or on the same computer, you don't need to specify a complete Internet address. In fact, if the two files are stored in the same folder, you can simply use the name of the HTML file by itself:

```
<a href="pagetwo.html">Go to Page 2.</a>
```

As an example, Listing 7.2 and Figure 7.3 show a quiz page with a link to the answers page shown in Listing 7.3 and Figure 7.4. The answers page contains a link back to the quiz page. Because the page in Listing 7.2 links to another page in the same directory, the filename can be used in place of a complete address.

LISTING 7.2   The `historyanswers.html` file

```
<?xml version="1.0" encoding="UTF-8"?>
<!DOCTYPE html PUBLIC "-//W3C//DTD XHTML 1.1//EN"
 "http://www.w3.org/TR/xhtml11/DTD/xhtml11.dtd">

<html xmlns="http://www.w3.org/1999/xhtml" xml:lang="en">
 <head>
  <title>History Quiz</title>
 </head>

 <body>
  <h1>History Quiz</h1>
  <p>Complete the following rhymes. (Example: William the Conqueror
  Played cruel tricks on the Saxons in... ten sixty-six.)</p>
  <ol>
  <li>Columbus sailed the ocean blue in...</li>
  <li>The Spanish Armada met its fate in...</li>
  <li>London burnt like rotten sticks in...</li>
  </ol>
  <p style="text-align: center;font-weight: bold;">
  <a href="historyanswers.html">Check Your Answers!</a>
  </p>
 </body>
</html>
```

FIGURE 7.3
This is the `historyquiz.html` file
listed in Listing 7.2 and referred
to by the link in Listing 7.3.

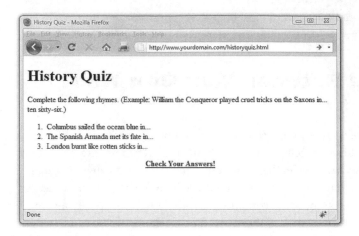

LISTING 7.3   The `historyanswers.html` File That `historyquiz.html`
Links To

```
<?xml version="1.0" encoding="UTF-8"?>
<!DOCTYPE html PUBLIC "-//W3C//DTD XHTML 1.1//EN"
 "http://www.w3.org/TR/xhtml11/DTD/xhtml11.dtd">

<html xmlns="http://www.w3.org/1999/xhtml" xml:lang="en">
 <head>
  <title>History Quiz Answers</title>
 </head>

 <body>
  <h1>History Quiz Answers</h1>
  <ol>
  <li>...fourteen hundred and ninety-two.</li>
  <li>...fifteen hundred and eighty eight.</li>
  <li>...sixteen hundred and sixty-six.</li>
  </ol>
  <p style="text-align: center;font-weight: bold;">
  <a href="historyquiz.html">Return to the Questions</a>
  </p>
 </body>
</html>
```

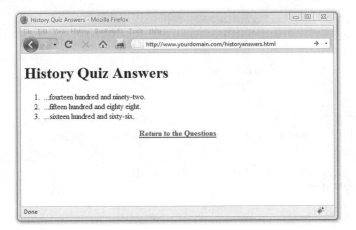

FIGURE 7.4
The `Check Your Answers!` link in Figure 7.3 takes you to this answers page. The `Return to the Questions` link takes you back to what's shown in Figure 7.3.

Using filenames instead of complete Internet addresses saves you a lot of typing. More important, the links between your pages will work properly no matter where the group of pages is stored. You can test the links while the files are still on your computer's hard drive. You can then move them to a web server, a CD-ROM, a DVD, or a memory card, and all the links will still work correctly. There is nothing magic about this simplified approach to identifying web pages—it all has to do with web page addressing, as you've already learned.

Linking to External Web Content

The only difference between linking to pages within your own site and linking to external web content is that when linking outside your site, you need to include the full address to that bit of content. The full address includes the http:// before the domain name, and then the full pathname to the file (for example, an HTML file, image file, multimedia file, and so on).

For example, to include a link to Google from within one of your own web pages, you would use this type of absolute addressing in your `<a>` link:

```
<a href="http://www.google.com/">Go to Google</a>
```

You can apply what you learned in previous sections to creating links to named anchors on other pages. Linked anchors are not limited to the same page. You can link to a named anchor on another page by including the address or filename followed by # and the anchor name. For example, the

CAUTION

As you might know, you can leave out the http:// at the front of any address when typing it into most web browsers. However, you cannot leave that part out when you type an Internet address into an `<a href>` link on a web page.

following link would take you to an anchor named `photos` within the african.html page inside the elephants directory on the domain www.takeme2thezoo.com.

```
<a href="http://www.takemetothezoo.com/elephants/african.html#photos">
Check out the African Elephant Photos!</a>
```

If you are linking from another page already on the www.takemetothezoo.com domain (because you are, in fact, the site maintainer), your link might simply be as follows:

```
<a href="/elephants/african.html#photos">Check out the
    African Elephant Photos!</a>
```

The http:// and the domain name would not be necessary in that instance, as you have already learned.

Linking to an Email Address

In addition to linking between pages and between parts of a single page, the <a> tag allows you to link to email addresses. This is the simplest way to enable your web page visitors to talk back to you. Of course, you could just provide visitors with your email address and trust them to type it into whatever email programs they use, but that increases the likelihood for errors. By providing a clickable link to your email address, you can make it almost completely effortless for them to send you messages and eliminate the chance for typos.

An HTML link to an email address looks like the following:

```
<a href="mailto:yourusername@yourdomain.com">Send me an
    email message.</a>
```

The words `Send me an email message` will appear just like any other <a> link.

If you want people to see your actual email address (so that they can make note of it or send a message using a different email program), include it both in the `href` attribute and as part of the message between the <a> and </a> tags, like this:

```
<a href="mailto:you@yourdomain.com">you@yourdomain.com</a>
```

In most web browsers, when someone clicks the link, she gets a window into which she can type a message that is immediately sent to you—whatever email program the person uses to send and receive email will automatically be used. You can provide some additional information in the link so that the subject and body of the message also have default values. You do this by adding `subject` and `body` variables to the `mailto` link. You separate the variables from the email address with a question mark (?), the value from the variable with an equal sign (=), and then separate each of the variable and value pairs with an ampersand (&). You don't have to understand the variable/value terminology at this point. Here is an example of specifying a subject and body for the preceding email example:

```
<a href="mailto:author@somedomain.com?subject=Book Question&body=
When is the next edition coming out?">author@somedomain.com</a>
```

When a user clicks this link, an email message is created with `author@somedomain.com` as the recipient, `Book Question` as the subject of the message, and `When is the next edition coming out?` as the message body.

Before you run off and start plastering your email address all over your web pages, I have to give you a little warning and then let you in on a handy trick. You're no doubt familiar with spammers that build up databases of email addresses and then bombard them with junk mail advertisements. One way spammers harvest email addresses is by using programs that automatically search web pages for `mailto` links.

Fortunately, there is a little trick that will thwart the vast majority of spammers. This trick involves using character entities to encode your email address, which confuses scraper programs that attempt to harvest your email address from your web pages. As an example, take the email address, `jcmeloni@gmail.com`. If you replace the letters in the address with their character entity equivalents, most email harvesting programs will be thrown off. Lowercase ASCII character entities begin at a for letter a and increase through the alphabet in order. For example, letter j is &#106, c is &#99, and so on. Replacing all the characters with their ASCII attributes produces the following:

```
<a href="mailto:&#106;&#099;&#109;&#101;&#108;&#111;&#110;&#105;
&#064;&#103;&#109;&#097;&#105;&#108;&#046;&#099;&#111;&#109;">Send
me an email message.</a>
```

Because the browser interprets the character encoding as, well, characters, the end result is the same from the browser's perspective. However, automated email harvesting programs search the raw HTML code for pages, which in this case is showing a fairly jumbled-looking email address. If you don't want to figure out the character encoding for your own address, just type **email address encoder** in your search engine and you will find some services online that will produce an encoded string for you.

TIP

If you want to specify only an email message subject and not the body, you can just leave off the ampersand and the body variable, equal sign, and value text string as follows:

```
<a href="mailto:
author@somedomain.com?
subject=
Book Question>
author@somedomain.com</a>
```

TIP

It is customary to put an email link to the web page author at the bottom of every web page. Not only does this make it easy for others to contact you, it gives them a way to tell you about any problems with the page that your testing might have missed. Just don't forget to use the email address character entity trick so that your address flies under the radar of spammers.

Opening a Link in a New Browser Window

Now that you have a handle on how to create addresses for links—both internal (within your site) and external (to other sites)—there is one additional method of linking: forcing the user to open links in new windows.

You've no doubt heard of *pop-up windows*, which are browser windows—typically advertising products or services—that are opened and displayed automatically without the user's approval. However, the concept of opening another window or targeting another location does serve a valid purpose in some instances. For example, you might want to present information in a smaller secondary browser window but still allow the user to see the information in the main window. This is often the case when clicking on a link to an animated demo, movie clip, or other multimedia element. You could also want to target a new browser window when you are linking to content off-site.

However, opening a new browser window on behalf of your user—especially when it's a full-size new window—goes against some principles of usability and accessibility. When people opened new windows, typically it happened through the use of the target attribute of the <a> tag. The target attribute has been removed from the <a> tag in the strict XHTML 1.1 specification.

There are valid ways to achieve the same result while still adhering to principles of usability and accessibility, but these methods require a little JavaScript and other advanced techniques. You will learn about these methods as we move into the JavaScript portion of this book, which will also cover standards-compliant and accessible ways to invoke new windows with your external links.

Using CSS to Style Hyperlinks

The default display of a text-based hyperlink on a web page is underlined blue text. You might also have noticed that links you have previously visited appear as underlined purple text—that color is also a default. If you've spent any time at all on the Web, you will also have noticed that not all links are blue or purple—and for that, I think, we are all thankful. Using a little CSS and knowledge of the various pseudoclasses for the <a> link, you can make your links look however you want.

A *pseudoclass* is a class that describes styles for elements that apply to certain circumstances, such as various states of user interaction with that element.

For example, the common pseudoclasses for the <a> tag are link, visited, hover, and active. You can remember them with the mnemonic "Love-Hate"—LV (love) HA (hate), if you choose.

▶ a:link describes the style of a hyperlink that has not been visited previously.

▶ a:visited describes the style of a hyperlink that has been visited previously and is present in the browser's memory.

▶ a:hover describes the style of a hyperlink as a user's mouse hovers over it (and before it has been clicked).

▶ a:active describes the style of a hyperlink that is in the act of being clicked, but has not yet been released.

For example, let's say you want to produce a link with the following styles:

▶ A font that is bold and Verdana (and not underlined, meaning it has no text decoration)

▶ A base color that is light blue

▶ A color of red when users hover over it or when they are clicking it

▶ A color of gray after users have visited it

Your style sheet entries might look like the following:

```
a {
    font-family: Verdana, sans-serif;
    font-weight: bold;
    text-decoration: none;
}
a:link {
    color: #6479A0;
}
a:visited {
    color: #CCCCCC;
}
a:hover {
    color: #E03A3E;
}
a:active {
    color: #E03A3E;
}
```

NOTE

The colors in this example are indicated by their hexadecimal values, which you will learn about in Chapter 8.

Because the sample link will be Verdana bold (and not underlined) regardless of the state it is in, those three property and value pairs can reside in the rule for the a selector. However, because each pseudoclass must have a specific color associated with it, we use a rule for each pseudoclass as shown in the code example. The pseudoclass inherits the style of the parent rule, unless the rule for the pseudoclass specifically overrides that rule. In other words, all the pseudoclasses in the previous example will be Verdana bold (and not underlined). If, however, we had used the following rule for the hover pseudoclass, the text would display in Comic Sans when users hovered over it (if, in fact, the user has the Comic Sans font installed):

```
a:hover {
    font-family: "Comic Sans MS";
    color: #E03A3E;
}
```

Additionally, because the active and hover pseudoclasses use the same font color, you can combine style rules for them:

```
a:hover, a:active {
    color: #E03A3E;
}
```

Listing 7.4 puts these code snippets together to produce a page using styled pseudoclasses; the results of this code can be seen in Figure 7.5.

LISTING 7.4   Using Styles to Display Link Pseudoclasses

```
<?xml version="1.0" encoding="UTF-8"?>
<!DOCTYPE html PUBLIC "-//W3C//DTD XHTML 1.1//EN"
 "http://www.w3.org/TR/xhtml11/DTD/xhtml11.dtd">

<html xmlns="http://www.w3.org/1999/xhtml" xml:lang="en">
 <head>
  <title>Sample Link Style</title>

  <style type="text/css">
   a {
    font-family: Verdana, sans-serif;
    font-weight: bold;
    text-decoration: none;
   }
   a:link {
    color: #6479A0;
   }
   a:visited {
    color: #CCCCCC;
   }
   a:hover, a:active {
    color: #FF0000;
   }
  </style>
 </head>
```

LISTING 7.4   Continued

```
<body>
        <h1>Sample Link Style</h1>
        <p><a href="simplelinkstyle.html">The first time you see me,
        I should be a light blue, bold, non-underlined link in
        the Verdana font</a>.</p>
</body>
</html>
```

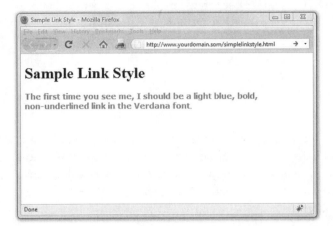

FIGURE 7.5
A link can use particular styles to control the visual display.

If you view the example in your web browser, indeed the link should be a light blue, bold, non-underlined Verdana font. If you hover over the link, or click the link without releasing it, it should turn red. If you click and release the link, the page will simply reload because the link points to the file with the same name. However, at that point the link will be in your browser's memory and thus will be displayed as a visited link—and it will appear gray instead of blue.

You can use CSS to apply a wide range of text-related changes to your links. You can change fonts, sizes, weights, decoration, and so on. Sometimes you might want several different sets of link styles in your style sheet. In that case, you can create classes; you aren't limited to working with only one set of styles for the <a> tag. The following example is a set of style sheet rules for a footerlink class for links I might want to place in the footer area of my website:

```
a.footerlink {
    font-family: Verdana, sans-serif;
    font-weight: bold;
    font-size: 75%;
    text-decoration: none;
```

```
}
a.footerlink:link, a.footerlink:visited {
   color: #6479A0;
}
a.footerlink:hover, a.footerlink:active {
   color: #E03A3E;
}
```

As you can see in the example that follows, the class name (`footerlink`) appears after the selector name (a), separated by a dot, and before the pseudoclass name (`hover`), separated by a colon:

```
selector.class:pseudoclass
a.footerlink:hover
```

Summary

The <a> tag is what makes hypertext "hyper." With it, you can create links between pages and links to specific anchor points on any page. This chapter focused on creating and styling simple links to other pages using either relative or absolute addressing to identify the pages.

You learned that when you're creating links to other people's pages, it's important to include the full Internet address of each page in an <a href> tag. For links between your own pages, include just the filenames and enough directory information to get from one page to another.

You discovered how to create named anchor points within a page and how to create links to a specific anchor. You also learned how to link to your email address so that users can easily send you messages. You even learned how to protect your email address from spammers. Finally, you learned methods for controlling the display of your links using CSS.

Table 7.1 summarizes the <a> tag discussed in this chapter.

TABLE 7.1   HTML Tags and Attributes Covered in Chapter 7

Tag/Attribute	Function
<a>...</a>	With the `href` attribute, this creates a link to another document or anchor; with the `id` attribute, this creates an anchor that can be linked to.
Attributes	
href="address"	The address of the document or anchor point to link to.
id="name"	The name for this anchor point in the document.

Q&A

Q. **What happens if I link to a page on the Internet, and then the person who owns that page deletes or moves it?**

A. That depends on how the maintainer of that external page has set up his web server. Usually, you will see a `page not found` message or something to that effect when you click a link that has been moved or deleted. You can still click the Back button to return to your page. As a site maintainer, you can periodically run link-checking programs to ensure your internal and external links are valid. An example of this is the Link Checker service at http://validator.w3.org/checklink.

Q. **One of the internal links on my website works fine on my computer, but when I put the pages on the Internet, the link doesn't work anymore. What's up?**

A. These are the most likely culprits:

> ▶ **Capitalization problems**—On Windows computers, linking to a file named MyFile.html with `<a href="myfile.html">` will work. On most web servers, the link must be `<a href="MyFile.html">` (or you must change the name of the file to MyFile.html). To make matters worse, some text editors and file transfer programs actually change the capitalization without telling you! The best solution is to stick with all-lowercase filenames for web pages.

> ▶ **Spaces in filenames**—Most web servers don't allow filenames with spaces. For example, you should never name a web page my page.html. Instead, name it mypage.html or even my_page.html (using an underscore instead of a space).

> ▶ **Local absolute addresses**—If, for some reason, you link to a file using a local absolute address, such as C:\mywebsite\news.html, the link won't work when you place the file on the Internet. You should never use local absolute addresses; when this occurs, it is usually an accident caused by a temporary link that was created to test part of a page. So, be careful to remove any test links before publishing a page on the Web.

Q. **Can I put both `href` and `id` in the same `<a>` tag? Would I want to for any reason?**

A. You can, and it might save you some typing if you have a named anchor point and a link right next to each other. It's generally better, however, to use `<a href>` and `<a id>` separately to avoid confusion because they play very different roles in an HTML document.

Q. **What happens if I accidentally misspell the name of an anchor or forget to put the `#` in front of it?**

A. If you link to an anchor name that doesn't exist within a page or misspell the anchor name, the link goes to the top of that page.

Workshop

The workshop contains quiz questions and exercises to help you solidify your understanding of the material covered. Try to answer all questions before looking at the "Answers" section that follows.

Quiz

1. Your best friend from elementary school finds you on the Internet and says he wants to trade home page links. How do you put a link to his site at www.supercheapsuits.com/~billybob/ on one of your pages?

2. What HTML would you use to make it possible for someone clicking the words "About the Authors" at the top of a page to skip down to a list of credits somewhere else on the page?

3. If your email address is bon@soir.com, how would you make the text "goodnight greeting" into a link that people can click to compose and send you an email message?

Answers

1. Put the following on your page:

   ```
   <a href="http://www.supercheapsuits.com/~billybob/">Billy
      Bob's site</a>
   ```

2. Type this at the top of the page:

   ```
   <a href="#credits">About the Authors</a>
   ```

   Type this at the beginning of the credits section:

   ```
   <a id="credits"></a>
   ```

3. Type the following on your web page:

   ```
   Send me a <a href="mailto:bon@soir.com">goodnight greeting</a>!
   ```

Exercises

▶ Create an HTML file consisting of a formatted list of your favorite websites. You might already have these sites bookmarked in your web browser, in which case you can visit them to find the exact URL in the browser's address bar.

▶ If you have created any pages for a website, look through them and consider whether there are any places in the text where you'd like to make it easy for people to contact you. Include a link in that place to your email address. You can never provide too many opportunities for people to contact you and tell you what they need or what they think about your products—especially if you're running a business.

CHAPTER 8
Working with Colors, Images, and Multimedia

This list might look long, but each of these tasks is short and sweet, and will help you move your web development experience from the white background/black text examples so far in this book to more interesting (or at least colorful) examples. But that's not to say that dark text on a light background is bad—in fact, it's the most common color combination you'll find online.

Although paying attention to color schemes and producing a visually appealing website is important, you don't have to be an artist by trade to put high-impact graphics on your web pages. More importantly, you don't need to spend hundreds or thousands of dollars on software, either. This chapter will help you get started with creating some of the images you can use in your website. Although the sample figures in this chapter use a popular and free graphics program for Windows, Mac, and Linux users (GNU Image Manipulation Program, or GIMP), you can apply the knowledge learned in this chapter to any major Windows or Macintosh graphics application—although the menus and options will look slightly different.

After you learn to create the graphics themselves, you'll learn how to integrate your graphics using HTML and CSS. At the end of the chapter you'll learn a bit about integrating additional media, or multimedia, into your website.

Best Practices for Choosing Colors

I can't tell you exactly which colors to use in your website, but I can help you understand the considerations you should make when selecting those colors on your own. The colors you use can greatly influence your visitors; if you are running an e-commerce site, you will want to use colors that entice your users to view your catalog and eventually purchase something. To that end, you want to make sure colors are used judiciously and with respect. You might wonder how respect enters into the mix when talking about colors, but remember the World Wide Web is an international community and interpretations differ; for instance, pink is a very popular color in Japan, but very unpopular in Eastern European countries. Similarly, green is the color of money in the United States, but the vast majority of other countries have multi-colored paper bills such that "the color of money" isn't a single color at all and thus the metaphor would be of no value to them.

Besides using colors that are culturally sensitive, other best practices include the following:

- ▶ Use a natural palette of colors. This doesn't mean you should use earth tones, but instead refers to using colors that one would naturally see on a casual stroll around town—avoid ultrabright colors that can cause eye strain.

- ▶ Use a small color palette. You don't need to use 15 different colors to achieve your goals. In fact, if your page includes text and images in 15 different colors, you might reevaluate the message you're attempting to send. Focus on three or four main colors with a few complimentary colors, at the most.

- ▶ Consider your demographics. You are likely not able to control your demographics and thus have to find a middle ground that accommodates everyone. The colors enjoyed by younger people are not necessarily those appreciated by older people, just as there are color biases between men and women and people from different geographic regions and cultures.

With just these few tips in mind, it might seem as if your color options are limited. Not so—it simply means you should think about the decisions you're making before you make them. A search for **color theory** in the search engine of your choice should give you more food for thought, as will the use of the color wheel.

The *color wheel* is a chart that shows the organization of colors in a circular manner. The method of display is an attempt to help you visualize the relationships between primary, secondary, and complementary colors. Color schemes are developed from working with the color wheel; understanding color schemes can help you determine the color palette to use consistently throughout your website. For example, knowing something about color relationships will hopefully enable you to avoid using orange text on a light blue background, or bright blue text on a brown background.

Some common color schemes in web design are as follows:

- **Analogous**—Colors that are adjacent to each other on the color wheel, such as yellow and green. One color is the dominant color and its analogous friend is used to enrich the display.

- **Complementary**—Colors that are opposite from each other on the color wheel, such as a warm color (red) and a cool color (green).

- **Triadic**—Three colors that are equally spaced around the color wheel. The triadic scheme provides balance while still allowing rich color use.

There are entire books and courses devoted to understanding color theory, so continuing the discussion in this book would indeed be a tangent. However, if you intend to work in web design and development, you will be served well by a solid understanding of the basics of color theory. Spend some time reading about it—an online search will provide a wealth of information.

Additionally, spend some hands-on time with the color wheel. The Color Scheme Generator at http://colorschemedesigner.com/ enables you to start with a base color and produce monochromatic, complementary, triadic, tetradic, analogic, and accented analogic color schemes.

Understanding Web Colors

Specifying a background color other than white for a web page is easier than you probably realize. For example, to specify blue as the background color for a page, put `style="background-color:blue"` inside the `<body>` tag or in the style sheet rule for the body element. Of course, you can use many colors other than blue. In fact, there are 16 colors listed in the W3C standards: aqua, black, blue, fuchsia, gray, green, lime, maroon, navy, olive, purple, red, silver, teal, white, and yellow.

Obviously there are many more colors displayed on the Web than just those 16. In fact, there are 140 color names that you can use with assurance that all browsers will display these colors similarly. Here's a partial list of the 140 descriptive color names: azure, bisque, cornflowerblue, darksalmon, firebrick, honeydew, lemonchiffon, papayawhip, peachpuff, saddlebrown, thistle, tomato, wheat, and whitesmoke.

NOTE

For a complete list of the 140 descriptive color names, their hexadecimal codes, and an example of the color as displayed by your browser, visit http://www.w3schools.com/HTML/html_colornames.asp.

TIP

It's worth pointing out that color names are not case-sensitive. So, Black, black, and BLACK are all black, although most web designers stick with lower-case or mixed case (if they use color names at all, as most designers will use the hexadecimal notation for a more nuanced approach to color use).

But names are subjective—for instance, if you look at the color chart of 140 cross-browser color names, you will not be able to distinguish between fuchsia and magenta. You will then realize that the associated hexadecimal color values for those two terms, fuchsia and magenta, are exactly the same: #FF00FF. You'll learn about hexadecimal color values in the next section, but for now, know that if you want to be standards-compliant and use more than the 16 color names the W3C standards dictate, you should use the hexadecimal color codes whenever possible.

There are, in fact, 16 million colors made possible with hexadecimal color codes. However, most modern computer displays can display "only" 16,384. But 16,384 is still a lot more than 140, or 16.

You should be aware that not all computer monitors display colors in the same hues. What might appear as a beautiful light blue background color on your monitor might be more of a purple hue on another user's monitor. Neutral, earth-tone colors (such as medium gray, tan, and ivory) can produce even more unpredictable results on many computer monitors. These colors might even seem to change color on one monitor depending on lighting conditions in the room or the time of day.

In addition to changing the background of your pages to a color other than white, you can change the color of text links, including various properties of links (such as the color for when a user hovers over a link versus when the user clicks a link—as you learned in previous chapters). You can also set the background color of container elements (such as paragraphs, divs, blockquotes, and table cells), and you can use colors to specify the borders around those elements. You'll see some examples of colors and container elements later in this chapter.

There are plenty of very bad websites, some created by earnest people with no trace of irony whatsoever. However, "The World's Worst Website" shown in Figure 8.1 was purposefully created to show some of the more egregious sins of website design, especially with its use of colors. A screenshot does not do it justice—visit and experience the site for yourself at http://www.angelfire.com/super/badwebs/main.htm.

If you search for **bad website examples** in your search engine, you will find many sites that collect examples of bad design and explain just why such a site should be in a Hall of Shame rather than a Hall of Fame. Many sites are considered bad because of their visual displays, and that display begins with color selection. Therefore, understanding colors, as well as the nuances of their specification and use, is a crucial step to creating a good website.

FIGURE 8.1
A partial screenshot of "The
World's Worst Website."

Using Hexadecimal Values for Colors

To remain standards-compliant, as well as to retain precise control over the colors in your website, you can reference colors by their hexadecimal value. The *hexadecimal value* of a color is an indication of how much red, green, and blue light should be mixed into each color. It works a little bit like Play-Doh—just mix in the amounts of red, blue, and green you want to get the appropriate color.

The hexadecimal color format is *#rrggbb,* in which *rr, gg,* and *bb* are two-digit hexadecimal values for the red (rr), green (gg), and blue (bb) components of the color. If you're not familiar with hexadecimal numbers, don't sweat it. Just remember that FF is the maximum and 00 is the minimum. Use one of the following codes for each component:

- ▶ FF means full brightness.
- ▶ CC means 80% brightness.
- ▶ 99 means 60% brightness.
- ▶ 66 means 40% brightness.
- ▶ 33 means 20% brightness.
- ▶ 00 means none of this color component.

For example, bright red is #FF0000, dark green is #003300, bluish-purple is #660099, and medium-gray is #999999. To make a page with a red background and dark green text, the HTML code would look like the following:

```
<body style="background-color:#FF0000; color:#003300">
```

Although only six examples of two-digit hexadecimal values are shown here, there are actually 225 combinations of two-digit hexadecimal values— 0 through 9 and A through F, paired up. For example, F0 is a possible hex value (decimal value 240), 62 is a possible hex value (decimal value 98), and so on.

As previously discussed, the rr, gg, and bb in the #rrggbb hexadecimal color code format stand for the red, green, and blue components of the color. Each of those components has a decimal value ranging from 0 (no color) to 255 (full color).

So, white (or #FFFFFF) translates to a red value of 255, a green value of 255, and a blue value of 255. Similarly, black (#000000) translates to a red value of 0, a green value of 0, and a blue value of 0. True red is #FF0000 (all red, no green, and no blue), true green is #00FF00 (no red, all green, no blue), and true blue is #0000FF (no red, no green, and all blue). All other hexadecimal notations translate to some variation of the 255 possible values for each of the three colors. The cross-browser compatible color name cornflowerblue is associated with the hexadecimal notation #6495ED—a red value of 40, a green value of 149, and a blue value of 237 (almost all of the available blue values).

When picking colors, either through a graphics program or by finding something online that you like, you might see the color notion in hexadecimal or decimal. If you type **hexadecimal color converter** in your search engine, you will find numerous options to help you convert color values into something you can use in your style sheets.

Using CSS to Set Background, Text, and Border Colors

When using CSS, there are three instances in which color values can be used: when specifying the background color, the text color, or the border color of elements. Previous chapters contained examples of specifying colors without going in great detail about color notion or color theory. For example, in Chapter 7, "Using External and Internal Links," you learned about using colors for various link states.

Figure 8.2 shows an example of color usage that could easily go into a web design Hall of Shame. I can't imagine ever using these combinations of colors and styles in a serious website, but it serves here as an example of how color style *could* be applied to various elements.

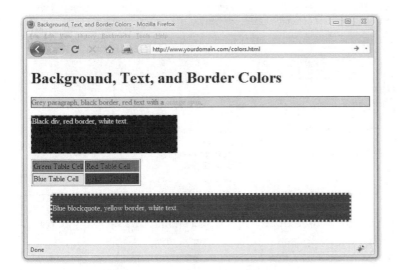

FIGURE 8.2
Background, text, and border colors can all be set using CSS.

Listing 8.1 shows the XHTML and CSS styles used to produce Figure 8.2.

LISTING 8.1   Using Styles to Produce Background, Text, and Border Colors

```
<?xml version="1.0" encoding="UTF-8"?>
<!DOCTYPE html PUBLIC "-//W3C//DTD XHTML 1.1//EN"
  "http://www.w3.org/TR/xhtml11/DTD/xhtml11.dtd">

<html xmlns="http://www.w3.org/1999/xhtml" xml:lang="en">
  <head>
    <title>Background, Text, and Border Colors</title>
  </head>

  <body>
      <h1>Background, Text, and Border Colors</h1>

      <p style="background-color:#CCCCCC;
      border:1px solid #000000; color:#FF0000">
      Grey paragraph, black border, red text with a
      <span style="color:#FFA500">orange span</span>.</p>

      <div style="width:300px; height:75px; margin-bottom: 12px;
      background-color:#000000; border:2px dashed #FF0000;
```

LISTING 8.1   Continued

```
      color: #FFFFFF">
      Black div, red border, white text. </div>

      <table border="1">
      <tr>
      <td style="background-color: #00FF00">Green Table Cell</td>
      <td style="background-color: #FF0000">Red Table Cell</td>
      </tr>
      <tr>
      <td style="background-color: #FFFF00">Blue Table Cell</td>
      <td style="background-color: #0000FF">Yellow Table Cell</td>
      </tr>
      </table>

      <blockquote style="background-color:#0000FF;
      border:4px dotted #FFFF00; color:#FFFFFF"><p>Blue blockquote,
      yellow border, white text.</p></blockquote>
  </body>
</html>
```

Looking at the styles used in Listing 8.1, you should be able to figure out almost everything except some of the border styles. In CSS, borders can't be designated as a color without also having a width and type; in the first example shown in Listing 8.1, the border width is 1px, and the border type is solid. In the second example shown in Listing 8.1, the border width is 2px, and the border type is dashed. In the fourth example shown in Listing 8.1, the border width is 4px, and the border type is dotted.

When picking colors for your website, remember that a little bit goes a long way—if you really like a bright and spectacular color, use it as an accent color and not throughout the primary design elements. For readability, remember that light backgrounds with dark text are much easier to read than dark backgrounds with light text.

Finally, consider the not-insignificant portion of your audience that might be color blind. For accessibility, you might consider using the Colorblind Web Page Filter tool at http://colorfilter.wickline.org/ to see what your site will look like to a person with color blindness.

Choosing Graphics Software

Selecting an overall color scheme for your website is one thing; creating or editing images to go into those templates are quite another—and beyond the scope of this book (or a single book, for that matter). However, in the

NOTE

Adobe Photoshop is without a doubt the cream of the crop when it comes to image-editing programs. However, it is expensive and quite complex if you don't have experience working with computer graphics. For more information on Adobe's products, visit the Adobe website at http://www.adobe.com/. If you are in the market for one of their products, you can download a free evaluation version from their site.

sections that follow, you'll learn a few of the basic actions that anyone maintaining a website should quickly master.

You can use almost any graphics program to create and edit images for your website, from the simple paint program that typically comes free with your computer's operating system to an expensive professional program such as Adobe Photoshop. Similarly, if you have a digital camera or scanner attached to your computer, it probably came with some graphics software capable of creating web page graphics. There are also several free image editors available for download—or even online as a web application—that deal just with the manipulation of photographic elements.

If you already have software you think might be good for creating web graphics, try using it to do everything described in these next sections. If your software can't do some of the tasks covered here, it probably won't be a good tool for web graphics. In that case, download and install GIMP from http://www.gimp.org. This fully functional graphics program is completely free and is used to perform the actions shown in this chapter.

If GIMP doesn't suit you, consider downloading the evaluation version of Adobe Photoshop or Corel DRAW. For photo manipulation only, there are many free options, all with helpful features. Google's Picasa, which is available free at http://picasa.google.com/, is one such option. Picnik (http://www.picnik.com/) is another. Both of these programs are suited for editing images rather than creating them from scratch, and Picasa is also oriented toward organizing your digital photograph collection. As such, these types of programs are not necessarily going to help you design a banner or button image for your site. However, these programs can help you work with some supplementary images, and they are powerful enough that they are worth checking out.

The Least You Need to Know About Graphics

Two forces are always at odds when you post graphics and multimedia on the Internet. The users' eyes and ears want all your content to be as detailed and accurate as possible, and they also want that information displayed immediately. Intricate, colorful graphics mean big file sizes, which increase the transfer time even over a fast connection. How do you maximize the quality of your presentation while minimizing file size? To make these choices, you need to understand how color and resolution work together to create a subjective sense of quality.

Using Another Site's Material

One of the best ways to save time creating the graphics and media files for web pages is, of course, to avoid creating them altogether. Grabbing a graphic from any web page is as simple as right-clicking it (or clicking and holding the button on a Macintosh mouse) and selecting Save Image As or Save Picture As (depending on your browser). Extracting a background image from a page is just as easy: Right-click it and select Save Background As.

However, you should never use images without the explicit permission of the owner, either by asking them or by looking for a Creative Commons license. To take images without explicit permission is a copyright violation (and is also distasteful). To learn more about copyrights, visit http://www.utsystem.edu/OGC/IntellectualProperty/cprtindx.htm.

You might also want to consider royalty-free clip art, which doesn't require you to get copyright permission. A good source of clip art online is Microsoft's Office Online Clip Art and Media website, which is located at http://office.microsoft.com/clipart/. Barry's Clipart Server is another popular clip art destination, and it's located at http://www.barrysclipart.com/.

NOTE

There are several types of image resolution, including pixel, spatial, spectral, temporal, and radiometric. You could spend hours just learning about each type; and if you were taking a graphics design class, you might do just that. For now, however, all you need to remember is that large images take longer to download and also use a lot of space in your display. Display size and storage or transfer size are factors you should take into consideration when designing your website.

The resolution of an image is the number of individual dots, or *pixels*, that make up an image. Large, high-resolution images generally take longer to transfer and display than small, low-resolution images. Resolution is usually specified as the width times the height of the image, expressed in pixels; a 300×200 image, for example, is 300 pixels wide and 200 pixels high.

You might be surprised to find that resolution isn't the most significant factor determining an image file's storage size (and transfer time). This is because images used on web pages are always stored and transferred in compressed form. Image compression is the mathematical manipulation that images are put through to squeeze out repetitive patterns. The mathematics of image compression is complex, but the basic idea is that repeating patterns or large areas of the same color can be squeezed out when the image is stored on a disk. This makes the image file much smaller and allows it to be transferred faster over the Internet. The web browser then restores the original appearance of the image when the image is displayed.

In the sections that follow, you'll learn how to create graphics with big visual impact but small file sizes. The techniques you'll use to accomplish this depend on the contents and purpose of each image. There are as many uses for web graphics as there are web pages, but four types of graphics are by far the most common:

- ▸ Photos of people, products, or places
- ▸ Graphical banners and logos
- ▸ Buttons or icons to indicate actions and provide links
- ▸ Background textures for container elements

Preparing Photographic Images

TIP

If you don't have a scanner or digital camera, almost all film developers offer a service that transfers photos from 35mm film to a CD-ROM or DVD-ROM for a modest fee. You can then copy the files from the CD-ROM or DVD-ROM to your hard drive, and then use your graphics program to open and modify the image files.

To put photos on your web pages, you need to convert your print-based photos to digital images or create photos digitally by using a digital camera. You might need to use the custom software that comes with your scanner or camera to save pictures onto your hard drive, or you can just drag and drop files from your camera to your hard drive. If you are using a scanner to create digital versions of your print photos, you can control just about any scanner directly from the graphics program of your choice—see the software documentation for details.

After you transfer the digital image files to your computer, you can use your graphics program to crop, resize, color-correct, and compress to get them ready for use in your website.

Cropping an Image

Because you want web page graphics to be as compact as possible, you'll usually need to crop your digital photos. When you *crop* a photo, you select the area you want to display, and you crop away the rest.

The GIMP toolbox offers quick access to the crop tool and its possible attributes. Find an image file—either a digital image you have taken with your camera and stored on your hard drive or an image you have found online. After opening the image in GIMP, perform the following steps to crop it in GIMP:

1. In the GIMP toolbox, click the crop tool (see Figure 8.3). Depending on the tool you select, there might be additional attributes you can select. For example, Figure 8.3 shows the attributes for the cropping tool (such as the aspect ratio, position, size, and so on).

TRY IT YOURSELF ▼

Cropping in GIMP

FIGURE 8.3
Select the crop tool from the toolbox.

▼ TRY IT YOURSELF

Cropping in GIMP
continued

FIGURE 8.4
Select the area of the image
that you want to display.

2. In the image you want to crop, draw a box around the selection by clicking the upper-left corner of the portion of the image you want to keep
and holding the left mouse button while you drag down to the lower-
right corner (see Figure 8.4).

3. Click one of the corners of the selection to apply the cropping.

Your graphics program will likely have a different method than the one shown, but
the concept is the same: select the area to keep, and then crop out the rest.

TIP

Your graphics software will likely
have an omnipresent size display somewhere in the image
window itself. In GIMP, the current image size can be seen in
the top of the window. Other
programs might show it in the
lower-right or lower-left corner.
You might also see the magnifi-
cation ratio in the window and
the ability to change it (by
zooming in or zooming out).

Even after your image has been cropped, it might be larger than it needs to
be for a web page. Depending on the design of a specific web page, you
might want to limit large images to no more than 800×600 pixels (if it is
shown on a page by itself, such as an item catalog) or even 640×480 pixels
or smaller. When shown alongside text, images tend to be in the 250 to 350
pixel range for width, so there's just enough room for the text as well. In
some cases, you might want to also provide a thumbnail version of the
image that links to a larger version, in which case you'll probably stick
closer to 100 pixels in the larger dimension for the thumbnail.

Resizing an Image

The exact tool necessary to change an image's size will depend on the program you are using. In GIMP, go to the Image menu and click Scale Image to open the Scale Image dialog box (see Figure 8.5).

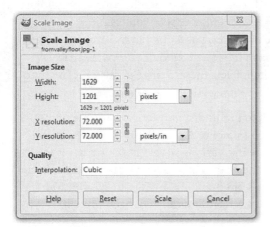

FIGURE 8.5
Use the Scale Image dialog box to change the size of an image.

You'll almost always want to resize using the existing aspect ratio, meaning that when you enter the width you'd like the image to be, the height will be calculated automatically (and vice versa) to keep the image from squishing out of shape. In GIMP, the aspect ratio is locked by default, as indicated by the chain link displayed next to the Width and Height options shown in Figure 8.5. Clicking once on the chain will unlock it, enabling you to specify pixel widths and heights of your own choosing—squished or not.

In most, if not all, graphics programs, you can also resize the image based on percentages instead of providing specific pixel dimensions. For example, if my image started out as 1629×1487, and I didn't want to do the math to determine the values necessary to show it as half that width, I could simply select Percent (in this instance from the drop-down next to the pixel display shown in Figure 8.5) and change the default setting (100) to 50. The image width would then become 815 pixels wide by 744 high—and no math was necessary on my part.

Tweaking Image Colors

If you are editing photographic images rather than creating your own graphics, you might need to use some color-correction tools to get the

NOTE

As with many of the features in GIMP, the Scale Image dialog box appears in front of the window containing the image being resized. This placement enables you to make changes in the dialog box, apply them, and see the results immediately.

photo just right. Like many image editing programs, GIMP offers several options for adjusting an image's brightness, contrast, and color balance, as well as a filter to reduce the dreaded red-eye. To remove red-eye using GIMP, go to Filters, click Enhance, and then click Red Eye Removal.

Most of these options are pretty intuitive. If you want the image to be brighter, adjust the brightness. If you want more red in your image, adjust the color balance. In GIMP, the Colors menu gives you access to numerous tools. As with the Scale Image dialog box described in the previous section, each tool displays a dialog box in the foreground of your workspace. As you adjust the colors, the image reflects those changes. This preview function is a feature included in most image editing software.

Figure 8.6 shows the Adjust Hue/Lightness/Saturation tool, one of the many tools provided on the Colors menu. As shown in the figure, many color-related changes occur by using various sliders in dialog boxes to adjust the values you are working with. The Preview feature enables you to see what you are doing as you are doing it. The Reset Color button returns the image to its original state without any changes applied.

FIGURE 8.6
The Adjust Hue/Lightness/
Saturation tool is one of many
slider-based color modification
tools available in GIMP.

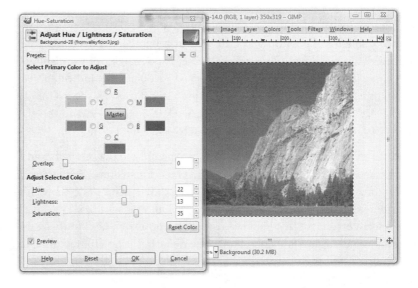

Because of the numerous tools available to you and the preview function available with each tool, a little playful experimentation is the best way to find out what each tool does.

Controlling JPEG Compression

Photographic images on the Web work best when saved in the JPEG file format rather than GIF; JPEG enables you to retain the number of colors in the file while still keeping the overall file size to a manageable level. When you're finished adjusting the size and appearance of your photo, select File, Save As and choose JPEG as the file type. Your graphics program will likely provide you with another dialog box through which you can control various JPEG options, such as compression.

Figure 8.7 shows the Save as JPEG dialog box you'll see when you save a JPEG in GIMP. You can see here that you can control the compression ratio for saving JPEG files by adjusting the Quality slider between 1 (low quality, small file size) and 100 (high quality, large file size).

FIGURE 8.7
GIMP enables you to reduce file size while still retaining image quality by saving in the JPEG format.

You might want to experiment a bit to see how various JPEG compression levels affect the quality of your images, but 85% quality (or 15% compression) is generally a good compromise between file size (and therefore download speed) and quality for most photographic images.

Creating Banners and Buttons

Graphics that you create from scratch, such as banners and buttons, require you to make considerations uniquely different from photographs.

TIP

For many years, designing for
800×600 screen resolution has
been the norm. Still keep that
low number in mind, as many
people do not open applications in full-screen mode.
However, designing for a baseline 1,024×768 screen resolution is not a bad idea.

The first decision you need to make when you produce a banner or button
is how big it should be. Most people accessing the web now have a computer with a screen that is at least 1024×768 pixels in resolution, if not considerably larger. For example, my screen is currently set at 1440×900 pixels.
You should generally plan your graphics so that they will always fit within
smaller screens (1024×768), with room to spare for scrollbars and margins.
The crucial size constraint is the horizontal width of your pages because
scrolling a page horizontally is a huge hassle and a source of confusion for
web users. Vertically scrolling a page is much more acceptable, so it's okay
if your pages are taller than the minimum screen sizes.

Assuming that you target a minimum resolution of 800×600 pixels, full-sized
banners and title graphics should be no more than 770 pixels wide by 430
pixels tall, which is the maximum viewable area of the page after you've
accounted for scrollbars, toolbars, and other parts of the browser window.
Within a page, normal photos and artwork should be from 100 to 300 pixels
in each dimension, and smaller buttons and icons should be 20 to 100 pixels
tall and wide. Obviously, if you design for the 1024×768 resolution, you have
more screen "real estate" to work with, but the size guidelines for banners,
buttons, and other supplementary graphics are still in effect.

To create a new image in GIMP, go to File and choose New. The Create a
New Image dialog box displays (see Figure 8.8). If you aren't sure how big
the image needs to be, just accept the default size of a 640×480. Or you can
choose one of the other pre-determined sizes in the Template drop-down,
such as Web banner common 468×60 or Web banner huge 728×90. Those
two settings are indeed considered "common" and "huge" for website
banners. Otherwise, enter the width and height of the new image.

For the image's background color, you should usually choose white to
match the background that most web browsers use for web pages
(although as you learned in the previous chapter, that color can be
changed). When you know that you'll be creating a page with a background other than white, you can choose a different background color for
your image. Or you might want to create an image with no background at
all, in which case you'll select Transparency as the background color. When
an image's background is transparent, the web page behind the image is
allowed to show through those areas of the image. In GIMP, select the
background color for your new image by opening the Advanced Options
in the Create a New Image dialog box.

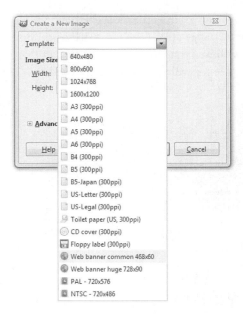

FIGURE 8.8
You need to decide on the size of an image before you start working on it.

When you enter the width and height of the image in pixels and click OK, you are faced with a blank canvas—an intimidating sight if you're as art-phobic as most of us! However, because there are so many image creation tutorials (not to mention entire books) available to lead you through the process, I am comfortable leaving you to your own creative devices. This section is all about introducing you to the things you want to keep in mind when creating graphics for use in your sites. This section does not neces-sarily teach you exactly how to do it because being comfortable with the tool *you* choose is the first step to mastering them.

Reducing the Number of Colors in an Image

One of the most effective ways to reduce the size of, and therefore the download time for, an image is to reduce the number of colors used in the image. This can drastically reduce the visual quality of some photographic images, but it works great for most banners, buttons, and other icons.

You'll be glad to know that there is a special file format for images with a limited number of colors; it's called the Graphics Interchange Format (GIF). When you save an image as a GIF, you might be prompted to flatten layers or reduce the number of colors by converting to an indexed image,

TIP

Dithering is a technique used by image-editing programs to simulate a color that isn't in the color palette with alternating pixels of two similar colors. For example, a dithered pink color would consist of alternating pixels of red and white pixels, which would give the general impression of pink. Dithering can make images look better in some cases, but it should usually be avoided for web page graphics. Why? It substantially increases the information complexity of an image, and that usually results in much larger file sizes and slower downloads.

as those are requirements for GIFs, as shown in Figure 8.9. The dialog box will simply ask you to confirm these changes that the save process will do for you—do not concern yourself with understanding these options at this time, but read your software's help file regarding layers and indexed colors for a full understanding.

FIGURE 8.9
When saving an image as a GIF, you might be prompted to convert it to an indexed color palette.

Remember, the GIF image format is designed for images that contain areas of solid colors, such as web page titles and other illustrated graphics; the GIF format is not ideal for photographs.

PNG (pronounced "ping") is another useful file format that is supported in all major web browsers. Although the GIF image format enables you to specify a single transparent color, which means that the background of the web page will show through those areas of an image, the PNG format takes things a step further by enabling you to specify varying degrees of transparency.

Working with Transparent Images

You might have seen websites that use background colors or images in their container elements, but also have images present in the foreground that allow the background to show through parts of the foreground graphics. In these cases, the images in the foreground have portions which are transparent, so that the images themselves—which are always on a rectangular canvas—do not show the areas of the canvas in which the design does not occur. You'll often want to use these types of partially transparent images to make graphics look good over any background color or background image you might have in place.

To make part of an image transparent, the image must be saved in the GIF or PNG file format. As mentioned previously in this chapter, most graphics programs that support the GIF format enable you to specify one color to be transparent, whereas PNG images allow for a range of transparency. Largely because of this transparency range, the PNG format is superior to GIF. All the latest web browsers already support PNG images. For more information on the PNG image format, visit http://www.libpng.org/pub/png/pngintro.html.

The process of creating a transparent image depends on the type of image you are creating (GIF or PNG) and the graphics software you are using to create it. For instructions, look in your graphics program's help files or type **transparent images with** *[your program here]* into your search engine.

Creating Tiled Backgrounds

Any GIF or JPEG image can be used as a background tile within a container element. However, before you go off and create a tiled background, especially a highly patterned tiled background, ask yourself what that tiled background adds to the overall look and feel of your website, and—more importantly—ask yourself if the text of the site can be read easily when placed over that pattern.

Think about the websites you frequent every day and consider the fact that few use tiled, patterned backgrounds on their entire page. If you restrict your browsing to websites for companies, products, sports teams, or other sites in which information (primarily text) is privileged, the number of sites with tiled, patterned backgrounds will decrease even further. Although the Web affords everyone the right of individuality in design, if you are creating a site for your business, you might want to avoid a highly patterned background with contrasting colored text.

If you do use a tiled, patterned background image for your entire site, remember that tiled images look best when you can't tell they're tiled images. In other words, you know you have a good image when the top edge of a background tile matches seamlessly with the bottom edge, and the left edge matches with the right.

Figures 8.10 and 8.11 show background tiles in use, both with seamless background, but with varying degrees of effectiveness.

FIGURE 8.10
This is an example of a seamless background image whereby you can tell the background is tiled because you can see six identical shapes.

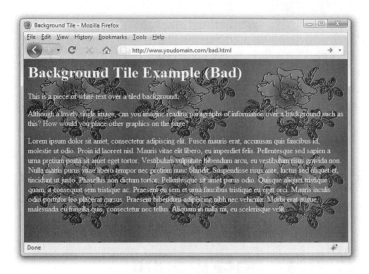

FIGURE 8.11
This is also an example of a seamless background image, only you can't tell that it is tiled.

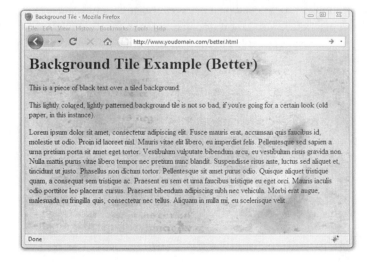

TIP

If you really want to use a background tile but you just cannot seem to get the pattern you want, you can check out some of the hundreds of sites on the Internet offering public-domain background images that are free or inexpensive, yet professionally designed.

Further on in this chapter, you'll learn how to place background images within your container elements. Despite my warnings in this section, there are actually times when background images can be powerful weapons in your design arsenal—just not when used as entire page backgrounds.

Creating Animated Web Graphics

The GIF image format enables you to create animated images that can be used to add some motion that will spice up any web page. Animated GIF images also transfer much faster than most of the video or multimedia files that are often used for similar effect. With GIMP, you can create animated GIFs by creating multiple layers within an image, and then modifying the Animated GIF options when saving the file. Additionally, if you have a series of images you want to animate, you can use the free, web-based GIF animation service at Gickr (http://www.gickr.com/).

The first step in creating a GIF animation is to create a series of images to be displayed one after the other—or a series of layers, depending on your particular software program. Each of these images is called a *frame*. By the way, this use of the word *frame* has nothing whatsoever to do with the *frames* you'll learn about in Chapter 20, "Using Windows and Frames." Instead, think of the frames like how movies or cartoons are put together—the images that you see on the screen are made up of many individual frames with slight differences in their appearance. After you have your frames in mind, the process of tying them together is relatively simple—it's the planning stage that's the most difficult. Take some time to sketch out the frames in storyboard fashion, especially if you plan to have more than just a few frames. After you know how your frames are going to fit together, use the Gickr service mentioned earlier in this section, or read the documentation for your graphics software to learn its particular process for pulling it all together.

You should get two or three images ready now so that you can try putting them on your own pages as you follow along the rest of this chapter. If you have some image files already saved in the GIF, PNG, or JPEG format (the filenames will end in .gif, .png, or .jpg), use those. It's also fine to use any graphics you created while reading the preceding section.

Search engines (such as Google) can become a gold mine of images by leading you to sites related to your own theme. Search engines can also help you discover the oodles of sites specifically dedicated to providing free and cheap access to reusable media collections. Also, don't forget Microsoft's massive clip art library at the Office Online Clip Art and Media website, located at http://office.microsoft.com/clipart/. Other valuable sources include Google Images (http://images.google.com/) and Flickr (http://www.flickr.com)—look for images using Creative Commons licenses that allow for free use with attribution.

Placing Images on a Web Page

To put an image on a web page, first move the image file into the same folder as the HTML file or in a directory named `images` for easy organization.

Insert the following HTML tag at the point in the text where you want the image to appear. Use the name of your image file instead of *myimage.gif*:

```
<img src="myimage.gif" alt="My Image" />
```

If your image file were in the images directory below the document root, you would use the following:

```
<img src="/images/myimage.gif" alt="My Image" />
```

Both the src and the alt attributes of the <img /> tag are required in XHTML web pages. The src attribute identifies the image file, and the alt attribute enables you to specify descriptive text about the image, the latter of which is intended to serve as an alternative to the image in the event that a user is unable to view the image. You'll read more on the alt attribute later, in the section "Describing Images with Text."

As an example of how to use the <img /> tag, Listing 8.2 inserts an image at the top of the page, before a paragraph of text. Whenever a web browser displays the HTML file in Listing 8.2, it automatically retrieves and displays the image file, as shown in Figure 8.12.

LISTING 8.2   Using the <img /> Tag to Place Images on a Web Page

```
<?xml version="1.0" encoding="UTF-8"?>
<!DOCTYPE html PUBLIC "-//W3C//DTD XHTML 1.1//EN"
 "http://www.w3.org/TR/xhtml11/DTD/xhtml11.dtd">


<html xmlns="http://www.w3.org/1999/xhtml" xml:lang="en">
 <head>
  <title>A Spectacular Yosemite View</title>
 </head>

 <body>
  <h1>A Spectacular Yosemite View</h1>
  <p><img src="hd.jpg" alt="Half Dome" /></p>
  <p><strong>Half Dome</strong> is a granite dome in Yosemite National
➥Park,
   located in northeastern Mariposa County, California, at the eastern
   end of Yosemite Valley. The granite crest rises more than 4,737 ft
   (1,444 m) above the valley floor.</p>
  <p>This particular view is of Half Dome as seen from Washburn
Point.</p>
 </body>
</html>
```

FIGURE 8.12
When a web browser displays the HTML code shown in Listing 8.2, it renders the hd.jpg image.

If you guessed that img stands for *image*, you're right. And src stands for *source*, which is a reference to the location of the image file. As discussed at the beginning of this book, an image is always stored in a file separate from the text, even though it appears to be part of the same page when viewed in a browser.

Just as with the <a href> tag used for hyperlinks, you can specify any complete Internet address in the src attribute of the <img /> tag. Alternatively, if an image is located in the same folder as the HTML file, you can specify just the filename. You can also use relative addresses, such as /images/birdy.jpg or ../smiley.gif.

Describing Images with Text

Each <img /> tag in Listing 8.2 includes a short text message, such as alt="Half Dome". The alt stands for *alternate text*, which is the message that appears in place of the image itself if it does not load. An image might not load if its address is incorrect, if the user has turned off automatic image downloading in her web browser preferences, or if the Internet connection is very slow and the data has yet to transfer. Figure 8.13 shows an example of alt text used in place of an image.

NOTE

Theoretically, you can include an image from any website within your own pages. In those cases, the image is retrieved from the other page's web server whenever your page is displayed. You could do this, but you shouldn't! Not only is it bad manners because you are using the other person's bandwidth for your own personal gain, it also can make your pages display more slowly. You also have no way of controlling when the image might be changed or deleted.

If you are granted permission to republish an image from another web page, always transfer a copy of that image to your computer and use a local file reference, such as <img src= "myimage.jpg" /> instead of <img src="http://www. otherserver.com/theirimage. jpg" />. This advice is not applicable, however, when you host your images—such as photographs—at a service specifically meant as an image repository, such as Flickr (http:// www.flickr.com/). Services like Flickr provide you with a URL for each image, and each URL includes Flickr's domain in the address.

FIGURE 8.13
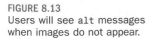

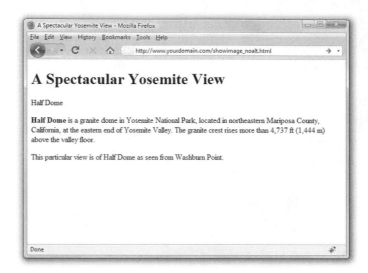

Even when graphics have fully loaded and are visible in the web browser, the alt message typically appears in a little box (known as a *tool tip*) whenever the mouse pointer passes over an image. The alt message also helps any user who is visually impaired (or is using a voice-based interface to read the web page).

You must include a suitable alt attribute in every <img /> tag on your web page, keeping in mind the variety of situations in which people might see that message. A brief description of the image is usually best, but web page authors sometimes put short advertising messages or subtle humor in their alt messages; too much humor and not enough information is frowned upon, however. For small or unimportant images, it's tempting to omit the alt message altogether, but it is a required attribute of the <img /> tag. This doesn't mean your page won't display properly, but it does mean you'll be in violation of the latest XHTML standards. I recommend assigning an empty text message to alt if you absolutely don't need it (alt=""), which is sometimes the case with small or decorative images.

The title attribute is not required by the <img /> tag, but it functions similarly to the alt attribute; in fact, the title attribute supersedes the alt attribute for tool tips if both attributes are present. Knowing this, the best approach for describing images via text is to use both the alt attribute and the title attribute to provide relevant notation or helpful hints about the image that you think might be useful when viewed as a tool tip or via screen reader software.

Specifying Image Height and Width

Because text moves over the Internet much faster than graphics, most web browsers display the text on a page before they display images. This gives users something to read while they're waiting to see the pictures, which makes the whole page seem to load faster.

You can make sure that everything on your page appears as quickly as possible and in the right places by explicitly stating each image's height and width. That way, a web browser can immediately and accurately make room for each image as it lays out the page and while it waits for the images to finish transferring.

For each image you want to include in your site, you can use your graphics program to determine its exact height and width in pixels. You might also be able to find these image properties by using system tools. For example, in Windows, you can see an image's height and width by right-clicking on the image, selecting Properties, and then selecting Details. After you know the height and width of an image, you can include its dimensions in the `<img />` tag, like this:

```
<img src="myimage.gif" alt="Fancy Picture" width="200" height="100" />
```

TIP

The height and width specified for an image doesn't have to match the image's actual height and width. A web browser will try to squish or stretch the image to display whatever size you specify. However, this is generally a bad idea because browsers aren't particularly good at resizing images. If you want an image to display smaller, you're definitely better off resizing it in an image editor.

Aligning Images

Just as you can align text on a page, you can align images on the page using special attributes. Not only can you align images horizontally, you also can align them vertically with respect to text and other images that surround them.

Horizontal Image Alignment

As discussed in Chapter 5, "Working with Fonts, Text Blocks, and Lists," you can use `<div style="text-align:center">`, `<div style="text-align:right">` and `<div style="text-align:left">` to align an element to the center, to the right margin, or to the left margin. These style settings affect both text and images and can be used within the `<p>` tag as well.

Like text, images are normally lined up with the left margin unless a `style="text-align:center"` or `style="text-align:right"` setting indicates that they should be centered or right-justified. In other words, `left` is the default value of the `text-align` style property.

NOTE

The float style property is actually more powerful than described here and, in fact, applies to more than just images. You can use the float style property creatively to arrive at some interesting page layouts, as you'll learn later in the book.

NOTE

Notice the addition of padding in the style attribute for both <img/> tags used in Listing 8.3. This padding provides some breathing room between the image and the text—6 pixels on all four sides of the image. You will learn more about padding in Chapter 9, "Working with Margins, Padding, Alignment, and Floating."

You can also wrap text around images by using the float style property directly within the <img /> tag.

In Listing 8.3, <img style="float:left" /> aligns the first image to the left and wraps text around the right side of it, as you might expect. Similarly, <img style="float:right" /> aligns the second image to the right and wraps text around the left side of it. Figure 8.14 shows how these images align on a web page. There is no concept of floating an image to the center because there would be no way to determine how to wrap text on each side of it.

LISTING 8.3   Using text-align Styles to Align Images on a Web Page

```
<?xml version="1.0" encoding="UTF-8"?>
<!DOCTYPE html PUBLIC "-//W3C//DTD XHTML 1.1//EN"
 "http://www.w3.org/TR/xhtml11/DTD/xhtml11.dtd">

<html xmlns="http://www.w3.org/1999/xhtml" xml:lang="en">
 <head>
  <title>More Spectacular Yosemite Views</title>
 </head>

<body>
 <h1>More Spectacular Yosemite Views</h1>
 <p><img src="elcap_sm.jpg" alt="El Capitan" width="100"
 height="75" style="float:left; padding: 6px;"/><strong>El
 Capitan</strong> is a 3,000-foot (910 m) vertical rock formation
 in Yosemite National Park, located on the north side of Yosemite
 Valley, near its western end. The granite monolith is one of the
 world's favorite challenges for rock climbers. The formation was
 named "El Capitan" by the Mariposa Battalion when it explored the
 valley in 1851.</p>
 <p><img src="tunnelview_sm.jpg" alt="Tunnel View" width="100"
 height="80" style="float:right; padding: 6px;"/><strong>Tunnel
 View</strong> is a viewpoint on State Route 41 located directly east
 of the Wawona Tunnel as one enters Yosemite Valley from the south.
 The view looks east into Yosemite Valley including the southwest face
 of El Capitan, Half Dome, and Bridalveil Falls. This is, to many, the
 first views of the popular attractions in Yosemite.</p>
 </body>
</html>
```

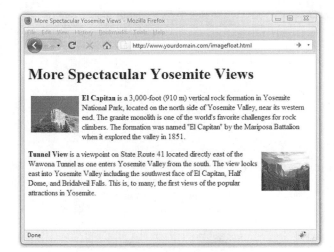

FIGURE 8.14
Showing the image alignment from Listing 8.3.

Vertical Image Alignment

Sometimes, you might want to insert a small image in the middle of a line of text; or you might like to put a single line of text next to an image as a caption. In either case, it would be handy to have some control over how the text and images line up vertically. Should the bottom of the image line up with the bottom of the letters, or should the text and images all be arranged so that their middles line up? You can choose between these and several other options:

NOTE

The vertical-align style property also supports values of top and bottom, which can be used to align images with the overall top or bottom of a line of elements regardless of any text on the line.

▶ To line up the top of an image with the top of the tallest image or letter on the same line, use `<img style="vertical-align:text-top" />`.

▶ To line up the bottom of an image with the bottom of the text, use `<img style="vertical-align:text-bottom" />`.

▶ To line up the middle of an image with the overall vertical center of everything on the line, use `<img style="vertical-align:middle" />`.

▶ To line up the bottom of an image with the baseline of the text, use `<img style="vertical-align:baseline" />`.

All four of these options are used in Listing 8.4 and displayed in Figure 8.15. Four thumbnail images are now listed vertically down the page, along with descriptive text next to each image. Various settings for the vertical-align style property are used to align each image and its relevant text.

TIP

If you don't include any align attribute in an <img /> tag, the bottom of the image will line up with the baseline of any text next to it. That means you never actually have to type style="vertical-align: baseline" because it is assumed by default. However, if you specify a margin for an image and intend for the alignment to be a bit more exacting with the text, you might want to explicitly set the vertical-align attribute to text-bottom. Take a look at the last image shown in Figure 8.15 to see an example of the text appearing slightly below the image due to the image margin—this is a result of the baseline setting for vertical-align.

LISTING 8.4   Using vertical-align Styles to Align Text with Images

```
<?xml version="1.0" encoding="UTF-8"?>
<!DOCTYPE html PUBLIC "-//W3C//DTD XHTML 1.1//EN"
 "http://www.w3.org/TR/xhtml11/DTD/xhtml11.dtd">

<html xmlns="http://www.w3.org/1999/xhtml" xml:lang="en">
 <head>
  <title>Small But Mighty Spectacular Yosemite Views</title>
 </head>

<body>
 <h1>Small But Mighty Yosemite Views</h1>
 <p><img src="elcap_sm.jpg" alt="El Capitan" width="100"
 height="75" style="vertical-align:text-top;"/><strong>El
 Capitan</strong> is a 3,000-foot (910 m) vertical rock formation
 in Yosemite National Park.</p>
 <p><img src="tunnelview_sm.jpg" alt="Tunnel View" width="100"
 height="80" style="vertical-align:text-bottom;"/><strong>Tunnel
 View</strong> looks east into Yosemite Valley.</p>
 <p><img src="upperyosefalls_sm.jpg" alt="Upper Yosemite Falls"
 width="87" height="100" style="vertical-align:middle;"/><strong>Upper
 Yosemite Falls</strong> are 1,430 ft and are among the twenty highest
 waterfalls in the world. </p>
 <p><img src="hangingrock_sm.jpg" alt="Hanging Rock" width="100"
 height="75" style="vertical-align:baseline;"/><strong>Hanging
 Rock</strong>, off Glacier Point, used to be a popular spot for people
 to, well, hang from. Crazy people.</p>
 </body>
</html>
```

FIGURE 8.15
Showing the vertical image alignment options used in Listing 8.4.

Turning Images into Links

You probably noticed in Figure 8.12 that the image on the page is quite large, which is fine in this particular example but isn't ideal when you're trying to present multiple images. It makes more sense in this case to create smaller image thumbnails that link to larger versions of each image. Then, you can arrange the thumbnails on the page so that visitors can easily see all the content, even if they see only a smaller version of the actual (larger) image. Thumbnails are one of the many ways you can use image links to spice up your pages.

To turn any image into a clickable link to another page or image, you can use the `<a href>` tag that you used previously to make text links. Listing 8.5 contains the code for a modification of Listing 8.3—which already used thumbnails—to provide links to larger versions of the images. To ensure that the user knows to click the thumbnails, the image and some helper text is enclosed in a `<div>`, as shown in Figure 8.16.

LISTING 8.5   Using Thumbnails for Effective Image Links

```
<?xml version="1.0" encoding="UTF-8"?>
<!DOCTYPE html PUBLIC "-//W3C//DTD XHTML 1.1//EN"
 "http://www.w3.org/TR/xhtml11/DTD/xhtml11.dtd">

<html xmlns="http://www.w3.org/1999/xhtml" xml:lang="en">
 <head>
  <title>More Spectacular Yosemite Views</title>
   <style type="text/css">
   div.imageleft {
    float:left;
    clear: all;
    text-align:center;
    font-size:9px;
    font-style:italic;
   }
   div.imageright {
    float:right;
    clear: all;
    text-align:center;
    font-size:9px;
    font-style:italic;
   }
   img {
    padding: 6px;
    border: none;
   }
   </style>
 </head>
 <body>
```

LISTING 8.5   Continued

```
<h1>More Spectacular Yosemite Views</h1>
<p><div class="imageleft">
<a href="http://www.flickr.com/photos/nofancyname/614253439/"><img
src="elcap_sm.jpg" alt="El Capitan" width="100" height="75"/></a>
<br/>click image to enlarge</div><strong>El Capitan</strong>
is a 3,000-foot (910 m) vertical rock formation in Yosemite National
Park, located on the north side of Yosemite Valley, near its western
end. The granite monolith is one of the world's favorite challenges
for rock climbers. The formation was named "El Capitan" by the
Mariposa Battalion when it explored the valley in 1851.</p>
<p><div class="imageright">
<a href="http://www.flickr.com/photos/nofancyname/614287355/"><img
src="tunnelview_sm.jpg" alt="Tunnel View" width="100" height="80"/></a>
<br/>click image to enlarge</div><strong>Tunnel View</strong> is a
viewpoint on State Route 41 located directly east of the Wawona Tunnel
as one enters Yosemite Valley from the south. The view looks east into
Yosemite Valley including the southwest face of El Capitan, Half Dome,
and Bridalveil Falls. This is, to many, the first views of the popular
attractions in Yosemite.</p>
</body>
</html>
```

FIGURE 8.16
Using thumbnails as links improves the layout of a page that uses large images.

The code in Listing 8.5 uses additional styles that will be explained in more detail in later chapters, but you should be able to figure out the basics:

▶ The <a> tags link these particular images to larger versions, which in this case are stored on an external server (at Flickr).

▶ The <div> tags, and their styles, are used to align those sets of graphics and caption text (and also include some padding).

Unless instructed otherwise, web browsers display a colored rectangle around the edge of each image link. Like text links, the rectangle usually appears blue for links that haven't been visited recently or purple for links that have been visited recently—unless you specify different colored links in your style sheet. Because you seldom, if ever, want this unsightly line around your linked images, you should usually include `style="border:none"` in any `<img />` tag within a link. In this instance, the `border:none` style is made part of the style sheet entry for the `img` element because we use the same styles twice.

When you click one of the thumbnail images on the sample page shown, the link is opened in the browser, as shown in Figure 8.17.

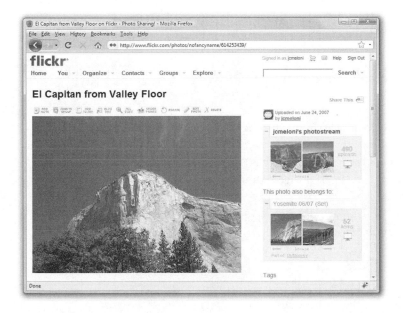

FIGURE 8.17
Clicking a linked thumbnail image opens the target of the link.

Using Background Images

As you learned earlier in this chapter, you can use background images to act as a sort of wallpaper in a container element, so that the text or other images appear on top of this underlying design.

The basic style properties that work together to create a background are as follows:

▶ **background-color**—Specifies the background color of the element. Although not image-related, it is part of the set of background-related properties.

▶ **background-image**—Specifies the image to use as the background of the element using the following syntax: `url('imagename.gif')`.

▶ **background-repeat**—Specifies how the image should repeat, both horizontally and vertically. By default (without specifying anything), background images will repeat both horizontally and vertically. Other options are `repeat` (same as default), `repeat-x` (horizontal), `repeat-y` (vertical), and `no-repeat` (only one appearance of the graphic).

▶ **background-position**—Specifies where the image should be initially placed relative to its container. Options include `top-left`, `top-center`, `top-right`, `center-left`, `center-center`, `center-right`, `bottom-left`, `bottom-center`, `bottom-right`, and specific pixel and percentage placements.

When specifying a background image, you can put all of these specifications together into one property, like so:

```
body {
    background: #ffffff url('imagename.gif') no-repeat top right;
}
```

In the previous style sheet entry, the body element of the web page will be white and include a graphic named imagename.gif on the top right. Another use for the `background` property is the creation of custom bullets for your unordered lists. To use images as bullets, first define the style for the `<ul>` tag as follows:

```
ul {
  list-style-type: none;
  padding-left: 0;
  margin-left: 0;
}
```

Next, change the declaration for the `<li>` tag to:

```
li {
  background: url(mybullet.gif) left center no-repeat
}
```

Make sure that `mybullet.gif` (or whatever you name your graphic) is on the web server and accessible; in that case, all unordered list items will show your custom image rather than the standard-filled disc bullet.

We will return to the specific use of background properties in Part III, "Advanced Web Page Design with CSS," when using CSS for overall page layouts.

Using Imagemaps

Sometimes you might want to use an image as navigation, but beyond the simple button-based or link-based navigation that you often see in websites. For example, perhaps you have a website with medical information, and you want to show an image of the human body that links to pages that provide information about various body parts. Or, you have a website that provides a world map users can click to access information about countries. You can divide an image into regions that link to different documents, depending on where users click within that image. This is called an *imagemap*, and any image can be made into an imagemap.

Why Imagemaps Aren't Always Necessary

The first thing you should know about imagemaps is that you probably won't need to use them except in very special cases. It's almost always easier and more efficient to use several ordinary images that are placed directly next to one another and provide a separate link for each image.

For example, see Figure 8.18. This is a web page that shows 12 different corporate logos; this example is a common type of web page in the business world, one in which you give a little free advertisement to your partners. You *could* present these logos as one large image and create an imagemap that provides links to each of the 12 companies. Users could click each logo in the image to visit each company's site. Or, you could display the images on the page as in this example and use 12 separate images—one for each company—with each image including a link to that particular company.

An imagemap is the best choice for an image that has numerous parts, is oddly arranged, or the design of the image itself might be too complicated to divide into separate images. Figure 8.19 shows an image that is best suited as an imagemap.

Mapping Regions Within an Image

To create any type of imagemap, you need to figure out the numerical pixel coordinates of each region within the image that you want to turn into a clickable link. These clickable links are also known as *areas*. Your graphics program might provide you with an easy way to find these coordinates. Or you might want to use a standalone imagemapping tool such as Mapedit (http://www.boutell.com/mapedit/) or the online imagemap maker at http://www.image-maps.com/. In addition to helping you map the coordinates, these tools also provide the HTML code necessary to make the maps work.

FIGURE 8.18
Web page with 12 different logos; this could be presented as a single imagemap or divided into 12 separate pieces.

FIGURE 8.19
An image that wouldn't take well to being sliced up—better make it an imagemap.

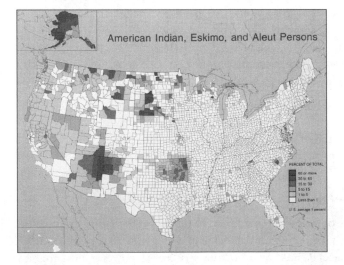

Using an imagemapping tool is often as simple as using your mouse to draw a rectangle (or a custom shape) around the area you want to be a link. Figure 8.20 shows the result of one of these rectangular selections as well as the interface for adding the URL and the title or alternate text for this link. Several pieces of information are necessary to creating the HTML for your imagemap: coordinates, target URL, title of link, and alternative text for the link.

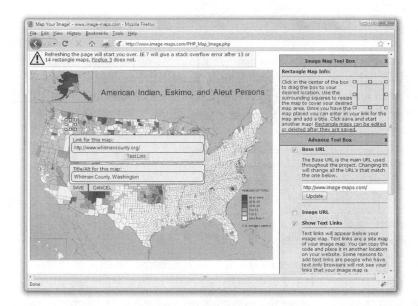

FIGURE 8.20
Using an imagemapping tool to create linked areas of a single graphic.

Creating Your Own Imagemap

You're more likely to remember how to make imagemaps if you get an image of your own and turn it into an imagemap as you continue with this chapter:

► For starters, it's easiest to choose a fairly large image that is visually divided into roughly rectangular regions.

► If you don't have a suitable image handy, use your favorite graphics program to make one. Perhaps use a single photograph showing several people and use each person as an area of the imagemap.

► Try a few different imagemapping tools to determine which you like best. Start with standalone software such as MapEdit (http://www.boutell.com/mapedit/) and move to the online imagemap maker at http://www.image-maps.com/. There are others; use the search engine of your choice to find variations on the imagemap software theme.

Creating the HTML for an Imagemap

If you use an imagemap generator, you will already have the HTML necessary for creating the imagemap. However, it is a good idea to understand the parts of the code so that you can check it for accuracy. The following HTML code is required to start any imagemap:

```
<map name="mapname">
```

Keep in mind that you can use whatever name you want for the name of the <map> tag, although it helps if you make it as descriptive as possible. Next, you'll need an <area /> tag for each region of the image. Following is an example of a single <area /> tag that is used in the mapping-a-map imagemap example:

```
<area shape="rect" coords="100,136,116,152"
    href="http://www.whitmancounty.org/"
    alt="Whitman County, WA"
    title="Whitman County, WA" />
```

This <area /> tag has five attributes, which you will use with every area you describe in an imagemap:

- ▸ shape indicates whether the region is a rectangle (shape="rect"), a circle (shape="circle"), or an irregular polygon (shape="poly").

- ▸ coords gives the exact pixel coordinates for the region. For rectangles, give the x,y coordinates of the upper-left corner followed by the x,y coordinates of the lower-right corner. For circles, give the x,y center point followed by the radius in pixels. For polygons, list the x,y coordinates of all the corners in a connect-the-dots order.

- ▸ href specifies the page to which the region links. You can use any address or filename that you would use in an ordinary <a href> link tag.

- ▸ alt enables you to provide a piece of text that is associated with the shape. Most browsers (Firefox excluded) display this text in a small box when a user hovers his mouse over the shape. This text adds a subtle but important visual cue to users who might not otherwise realize that they are looking at an imagemap. Firefox correctly uses the title attribute in addition to the alt attribute to provide a visual cue, which is why, as noted previously in this chapter, you should use both attributes.

Each distinct clickable region in an imagemap must be described as a single area, which means a typical imagemap consists of a list of areas. After coding the <area /> tags, you are done defining the imagemap, so wrap things up with a closing </map> tag.

The last step in creating an imagemap is wiring it to the actual map image. The map image is placed on the page using an ordinary <img /> tag. However, there is an extra usemap attribute that is coded like this:

```
<img src="map.png" usemap="#countymap"
  style="border:none; width:650px; height:509px"
  alt="Native Peoples Census Map" />
```

When specifying the value of the usemap attribute, use the name you put in the id of the <map> tag (and don't forget the # symbol). Also include the style attribute to specify the height and width of the image and to turn off the border around the imagemap, which you might or might not elect to keep in imagemaps of your own.

Listing 8.6 shows the complete code for a sample web page containing the map graphic, its imagemap, and a few mapped areas.

LISTING 8.6   Defining the Regions of an Imagemap with <map> and <area /> Tags

```
<?xml version="1.0" encoding="UTF-8"?>
<!DOCTYPE html PUBLIC "-//W3C//DTD XHTML 1.0 Transitional//EN"
  "http://www.w3.org/TR/xhtml1/DTD/xhtml1-transitional.dtd">

<html xmlns="http://www.w3.org/1999/xhtml" xml:lang="en">
 <head>
  <title>Testing an Imagemap</title>
 </head>

 <body>
  <h1>Testing an Imagemap</h1>
    <p style="text-align:center">Click on a logo to go to the
    county's web site.<br/>
    <img src="map.png" usemap="#countymap"
    style="border:none; width:650px;height:509px"
    alt="Native Peoples Census Map" /></p>

    <map name="countymap" id="countymap">
    <area shape="rect" coords="100,136,116,152"
     href="http://www.whitmancounty.org/"
     alt="Whitman County, WA" title="Whitman County, WA" />
    <area shape="rect" coords="29,271,42,283"
     href="http://www.sccgov.org/" alt="Santa Clara County, CA"
     title="Santa Clara County, CA" />
    <area shape="rect" coords="535,216,548,228"
     href="http://visitingmifflincounty.com/"
     alt="Mifflin County, PA" title="Mifflin County, PA" />
    </map>
  </body>
</html>
```

NOTE

If you're a stickler for details, you might have noticed—check out the first few lines of code—that this web page is coded as an XHTML 1.0 document, as opposed to the XHTML 1.1 used with most of the other examples in the book. This is done because some browsers (Internet Explorer, for one) are lagging in their support of a single XHTML 1.1 change in how imagemaps are used. This change is specific to the usemap attribute, which in XHTML 1.1 doesn't require the # symbol in front of the map name. In fact, the # symbol isn't allowed at all in XHTML 1.1. The # symbol is, however, allowed in XHTML 1.0, so to satisfy current web browsers and still provide you with a valid web page; this particular example uses XHTML 1.0.

Figure 8.21 shows the imagemap in action. Notice in the bottom of your browser window that your browser (in this example, Firefox) displays the link address for whatever area the mouse is hovering over. Additionally, when you hover the mouse over an area, the alt or title text for that area—in this example, Whitman County—is displayed on the imagemap.

FIGURE 8.21
The imagemap defined in Listing 8.6 as it displays on the web page.

NOTE

There is a method of producing mapped images that relies solely on CSS and not the HTML <map> tag. You will learn more about this in Chapter 11, "Using CSS to Do More with Lists, Text, and Navigation."

Integrating Multimedia into Your Website

Now that you've learned how to work with static images, the natural next step is to work with multimedia. The term *multimedia* encompasses everything we see and hear on a web page: audio, video, and animation, as well as static images and text. In this section, you won't learn how to create any particular audio, video, or animation, but you will learn how to include such files in your site, through either linking or embedding the content.

Remember, though, that not every user has devices that will play your media type, nor do all users have broadband Internet connections which allow these large files to transfer quickly. Always warn your visitors that the links they click will take them to multimedia files and offer them the choice to view or listen to the content—don't force the files upon them.

Creating multimedia of any kind can be a challenging and complicated task. If you're planning to create your own content from scratch, you'll need far more than this book to become the next crackerjack multimedia developer. After you have some content, however, this section will show you how to place your new creations into your web pages.

For those of us who are artistically challenged, several alternative ways to obtain useful multimedia assets are available. Aside from the obvious (such as hiring an artist), here are a few suggestions:

▶ Much of the material on the Internet is free. Of course, it's still a good idea to double-check with the author or current owner of the content; you don't want to be sued for copyright infringement. In addition, various offices of the U.S. government generate content which, by law, belongs to all Americans. (For example, any NASA footage found online is free for your use.)

▶ Many search engines (google.com, yahoo.com, bing.com, and so on) have specific search capabilities for finding multimedia files. As long as you are careful about copyright issues, this can be an easy way to find multimedia related to a specific topic. A simple search for **sample Flash animations**, **sample QuickTime movie**, or **sample audio files** will produce more results than you can handle.

▶ If you are creatively inclined, determine the medium you like most— for some of you it might be video production, others may enjoy audio production, and still others might want to dabble in animation. After you have determined a starting point, look into the various types of software which will enable you to create such artistic masterpieces. Many companies provide multimedia software, such as Adobe (http://www.adobe.com/) and Apple (http://www.apple.com/).

Linking to Multimedia Files

The simplest and most reliable option for incorporating a video or audio file into your website is to simply link it in with <a href>, exactly as you would link to another HTML file.

For example, the following line could be used to offer a MOV video of a hockey game:

```
<a href="hockey.mov">View the hockey video clip.</a>
```

NOTE

Regardless of the specific media types shown in this chapter, the procedures shown for incorporating multimedia into your web pages will be similar no matter which media format you choose.

NOTE

In case you're unfamiliar with *helper applications* (*helper apps* for short), they are the external programs that a web browser calls on to display any type of file it can't handle on its own. Generally, the helper application associated with a file type is called on whenever a web browser can't display that type of file on its own.

Plug-ins are a special sort of helper application installed directly into a web browser and they enable you to view multimedia content directly within the browser window.

NOTE

If your browser has no support for QuickTime, you can download the QuickTime player free from Apple at http://www. apple.com/quicktime/. Even if you do have QuickTime installed, some browsers might still play QuickTime movies differently based on whether a plug-in is installed. For example, on my Windows computer, Internet Explorer and Firefox both play QuickTime movies directly in the browser window via a plug-in, whereas Opera launches QuickTime as a helper application.

When the user clicks the words View the hockey video clip., the hockey.mov QuickTime video file is transferred to her computer from your web server. Whichever helper application or plug-in she has installed automatically starts as soon as the file has finished downloading. If no compatible helper or plug-in can be found, the web browser will offer her a chance to download the appropriate plug-in or save the video on her hard drive for later viewing.

The click action results in the browser either playing the video with the help of a plug-in (if one is found that can play the clip) or deferring to a suitable helper application.

If you change the link from pond.wmv (Windows Media) to pond.mov (QuickTime), your browser handles the link differently. Instead of launching another program, the QuickTime plug-in enables you to view the movie clip directly in the browser window.

As you might have guessed, this approach of using a simple link to play multimedia files offers the best backward compatibility because the browser bears all the responsibility of figuring out how to play a multimedia clip. The downside to this is that you don't have much control over how a clip is played, and you definitely can't play a clip directly in the context of a page.

Embedding Multimedia Files

XHTML contains a standard <object> tag that is the preferred way to embed multimedia of any kind in a web page. This tag is used instead of the old <embed /> tag that you might still see in some HTML source code.

Embedding a multimedia file into a page produces a set of software controls that allow the file to be played directly—no secondary window is necessary, and there's no need to navigate away from the page you are on. Following is code to embed the pond video using the <object> tag by itself:

```
<object classid="CLSID:6BF52A52-394A-11d3-B153-00C04F79FAA6"
 width="320" height="305">
 <param name="type" value="video/x-ms-wmv" />
 <param name="URL" value="pond.wmv" />
 <param name="uiMode" value="full" />
 <param name="autoStart" value="false" />
</object>
```

This code isn't too terribly complicated when you consider that it literally embeds a video directly into your web page (see Figure 8.22). The messiest part of the code is the classid attribute of the <object> tag, which is set to a long alphanumeric code. This code is the global ID for Windows Media Player, which means that you're telling the `<object>` tag to embed Windows Media Player on the page to play the video clip. You can just copy and paste this code into your own web pages.

NOTE

It's important to note that Windows Media Player is a sophisticated enough media player that it automatically *streams* multimedia files, which means that it begins playing them after loading only the first few seconds of content. The idea is that the rest of the content is loaded in the background while you're watching or listening to earlier portions. The result is that visitors don't have to wait through long download times when viewing or listening to your multimedia clips.

FIGURE 8.22
The `<object>` tag enables you to embed a video clip on a web page while specifying which media player is to play it.

The width and height attributes of the `<object>` tag determine the size of the embedded Windows Media Player window. Some browsers will automatically size the embedded player to fit the content if you leave these attributes off, whereas others won't show anything at all. Play it safe by setting them to a size that suits the multimedia content being played.

There are four `<param>` tags within the `<object>` tag that are responsible for additional details about how the clip is to be played. Each tag has two attributes, `name` and `value`, which are responsible for associating data (`value`) with a particular setting (`name`). In this example, the URL for the media clip is set to `pond.wmv`. The third parameter, `uiMode`, determines which buttons and user interface options are made available by Windows Media Player—`full` indicates that all user interface features are enabled, such as the control buttons and volume slider. Finally, the `autoStart` parameter is set to `false` so that the video clip does not automatically start playing when the page is opened in a browser.

The type parameter is perhaps the trickiest. It identifies the type of media being displayed, which in this case is a Windows Media Video (WMV) file. This media type must be specified as one of the standard Internet MIME types.

A *MIME type* is an identifier for uniquely identifying different types of media objects on the Internet. MIME stands for Multipurpose Internet Mail Extensions, and this name comes from the fact that MIME types were originally used to identify email attachments. These MIME types should be used in the type attribute of the <object> tag to identify what kind of multimedia object is being referenced in the data attribute.

Following are the MIME types for several popular sound and video formats you might want to use in your web pages:

- ▶ **WAV Audio**—audio/x-wav
- ▶ **AU Audio**—audio/basic
- ▶ **MP3 Audio**—audio/mpeg
- ▶ **MIDI Audio**—audio/midi
- ▶ **WMA Audio**—audio/x-ms-wma
- ▶ **RealAudio**—audio/x-pn-realaudio-plugin
- ▶ **AVI**—video/x-msvideo
- ▶ **WMV**—video/x-ms-wmv
- ▶ **MPEG Video**—video/mpeg
- ▶ **QuickTime**—video/quicktime

Listing 8.7 shows the relevant code for the pond web page, where you can see the <object> tag as it appears in context.

LISTING 8.7   Using an <object> Tag to Directly Embed a WMV Video Clip

```
<?xml version="1.0" encoding="UTF-8"?>
<!DOCTYPE html PUBLIC "-//W3C//DTD XHTML 1.1//EN"
 "http://www.w3.org/TR/xhtml11/DTD/xhtml11.dtd">

<html xmlns="http://www.w3.org/1999/xhtml" xml:lang="en">
 <head>
  <title>Fun in the Pond</title>
 </head>

 <body>
```

LISTING 8.7   Continued

```
<h1>Fun in the Pond</h1>
<div style="float:left; padding:3px">
  <object classid="CLSID:6BF52A52-394A-11d3-B153-00C04F79FAA6"
  width="320" height="305">
  <param name="type" value="video/x-ms-wmv" />
  <param name="URL" value="pond.wmv" />
  <param name="uiMode" value="full" />
  <param name="autoStart" value="false" />
  <embed width="320" height="305" type="video/x-ms-wmv"
  src="pond.wmv" controls="All" loop="false" autostart="false"
  pluginspage="http://www.microsoft.com/windows/windowsmedia/" />
  </object>
  </div>
  <p>Michael's backyard pond is not only a fun hobby but also
  an ongoing home improvement project that is both creative and
  relaxing.</p>
  <p>He has numerous fish in the pond, all Koi from various places
  as far as Japan, Israel, and Australia. Although they don't bark,
  purr, or fetch anything other than food, these fish are his pets,
  and good ones at that.</p>
  </body>
</html>
```

NOTE

Because the <embed /> tag is not supported in XHTML, it will prevent your pages from validating. Unfortunately, there really is no workaround for this problem—we'll just have to wait for browsers to fully support the <object> tag by itself or move to the <embed /> element of HTML5.

You might notice that there's some extra code that didn't appear in the earlier <object> tag example. Unfortunately, as discussed earlier in the section, not all web browsers are entirely consistent in their support of the <object> tag. For this reason, it is necessary to include an <embed /> tag within the <object> tag to account for browser inconsistencies. This isn't an ideal solution, but it's all we have while browser vendors continue to lag behind prevailing standards. If you pay close attention, you'll notice that the <embed /> tag contains all the same information as the <object> tag.

The <object> tag is a bit more complex than what is revealed here. However, you don't need to know how to use the more advanced facets of the <object> tag just to play multimedia content. In other words, it isn't important for you to become a multimedia guru to share some multimedia clips on your web pages.

Additional Tips for Using Multimedia

Before you add video, audio, or animations to your website, first ask yourself if you really should. When you use these types of multimedia, be sure to do so for a reason. Gratuitous sound and video, just like gratuitous images, can detract from your overall message. Then again, if your message is "Look at the videos I have made" or "Listen to my music and

NOTE

Video files aren't the only media files you can include within your website using the <object> and <embed /> tags. Adding any multimedia file will follow the same process. To determine exactly which classid and codebase attributes to use, as well as additional parameters (in the <param /> tags), use your search engine to look up something like **object embed *mediatype***, where ***mediatype*** is Real Audio, QuickTime, Flash, or whatever you want.

download some songs," then multimedia absolutely must play a role in your website.

Here are a few additional tips to keep in mind:

► Don't include multimedia in a page and set it to automatically play when the page loads. Always give users the option to start (and stop) your sound or video.

► When possible, give users a choice of multimedia players. Don't limit yourself to multimedia content playable by only one type of player on only one operating system.

► Multimedia files are larger than the typical graphics and text files, which means you need to have the space on your web server to store them, as well as the bandwidth allotment to transfer them to whomever requests them via your website.

► If your site is entirely audio or video and offers very little by way of text or graphics, understand that a certain segment of your audience won't see or hear what you want to present because of the limitations of their system or bandwidth. Provide these users with additional options to get your information.

► Leverage free online video hosting services, such as YouTube (http://www.youtube.com/). Not only does YouTube provide storage for your video clips, it will provide you with the code necessary to embed the video in your own web page. For example, Figure 8.23 shows the YouTube page for the cutest puppy in the world. If you copy and paste the text from the Embed area shown in the figure, you would get the following:

```
<object width="425" height="344">
<param name="movie" value="http://www.youtube.com/v/yPxiHd2BOpo
&rel=0&color1=0xb1b1b1&color2=0xcfcfcf&feature=player_profilepage
&fs=1"></param>
<param name="allowFullScreen" value="true"></param>
<param name="allowScriptAccess" value="always"></param>
<embed
src="http://www.youtube.com/v/yPxiHd2BOpo&rel=0&color1=0xb1b1b1
&color2=0xcfcfcf&feature=player_profilepage&fs=1"
type="application/x-shockwave-flash" allowfullscreen="true"
allowScriptAccess="always" width="425" height="344"></embed>
</object>
```

You could then insert the code into your web page.

FIGURE 8.23
YouTube provides storage of your video files as well as links and <object> code for use in your own pages.

Summary

In this chapter, you learned a few best practices for thinking about color use, and how to use the color wheel to help you find colors that will complement your text. Additionally, you learned about hexadecimal notion for colors—that all colors are expressed in notations related to the amount of red, green, and blue in them—and how hexadecimal notation enables you to apply nuanced colors to your elements. More importantly, you learned about the three color-related style properties that can be used to apply color to container backgrounds, borders, and text using CSS.

You also learned the basics of preparing graphics for use on web pages. If nothing else, you learned that this is a very complex topic, and you learned just enough in this chapter to whet your appetite. The examples in this chapter used the popular (and free!) GIMP software package, but feel free to use the graphics software that best suits your needs. Among the actions you learned were how to crop, resize, and tweak image colors, and you also learned about the different file formats. There are many considerations you must keep in mind when including graphics in your site, including graphic size and resolution and how to use transparency, animated GIFs, and tiled backgrounds.

After you have created or edited some images, you can place them in your web page, which you also learned how to do through the <img /> tag. You learned how to include a short text message that appears in place of the image as it loads and also appears whenever users move the mouse pointer over the image. You also discovered how to control the horizontal and vertical alignment of each image and how to wrap text around the left or right of an image.

You learned how to use images as links—either by using the <a> tag around the images or by creating imagemaps. You also learned a little bit about how to use images in the background of container elements.

Finally, you learned how to embed video and sound into a web page. You discovered how to use a simple link to a multimedia file, which is the most broadly supported but least flexible option for playing media content. You then learned how to use the <object> tag to embed a media player directly in a web page. Not only that, you discovered that for maximum browser compatibility, it helps to assist the <object> tag with the <embed /> tag. The <object> and <embed /> tags can be used to include a vast array of media types, including WAV, MP3, RealAudio, and MIDI files—not to mention AVI, WMV, and QuickTime videos, to name just a few.

Table 8.1 summarizes the tags and attributes covered in this chapter.

TABLE 8.1   Tags and Attributes Covered in Chapter 8

Tag	Function
<img />	Places an image file within the page.
<map>...</map>	A client-side imagemap referenced by <img usemap="..." />. Includes one or more <area /> tags.
<area />	Defines a clickable link within a client-side imagemap.
<embed />	Embeds a multimedia file to be read or displayed by a plug-in application; this tag is technically deprecated but still useful due to browsers not fully supporting the <object> tag yet.
<object>...</object>	Inserts images, videos, Java applets, ActiveX controls, or other objects into a document.
<param>...</param>	Runtime settings for an object, such as the width and height of the area it occupies on a page.

Attribute/Style	Function
style="background-color:color"	Sets the background color of an element (such as <body>, <p>, <div>, <blockquote>, and other containers).
style="color:color"	Sets the color of text within an element.
style="border:size type color "	Sets the color of the four borders around an element. Border colors cannot be used without also specifying the width and type of the border.

TABLE 8.1　Continued

Attribute/Style	Function
`src="address"`	The address or filename of the image.
`alt="altdescription"`	An alternative description of the image that is displayed in place of the image, primarily for users who can't view the image itself.
`title="title"`	A text message that is displayed as an image title, typically in a small pop-up box (tool tip) over the image.
`width="width"`	The width of the image (in pixels).
`height="height"`	The height of the image (in pixels).
`style="border:attributes"`	Gets rid of the border around the image if the image is serving as a link.
`style="vertical-align:alignment"`	Aligns the image vertically to `text-top`, `top`, `text-bottom`, `bottom`, `middle`, or `baseline`.
`style="float:float"`	Floats the image to one side so text can wrap around it. Possible values are `left`, `right`, and `none` (default).
`usemap="name"`	The name of an imagemap specification for client-side image mapping. Used with `<map>` and `<area />`.
`shape="value"`	Within the `<area />` tag, specifies the shape of the clickable area. Valid options for this attribute are `rect`, `poly`, and `circle`.
`coords="values"`	Within the `<area />` tag, specifies the coordinates of the clickable region within an image. Its meaning and setting vary according to the type of area.
`href="linkurl"`	Within the `<area />` tag, specifies the URL that should be loaded when the area is clicked.
`name="name"`	A named parameter property.
`value="value"`	The value associated with a named parameter property.
`width="width"`	The width of the embedded object in pixels.
`height="height"`	The height of the embedded object in pixels.
`type="mimetype"`	The MIME type of the multimedia content.
`src="mediaurl"`	The URL of the file to embed.
`controls="controls"`	The configuration of the user input controls for the media player; use `all` to enable all controls.
`loop="loop"`	Play the media clip once or loop it repeatedly; set to `true` or `false`.
`autostart="autostart"`	Play the media clip upon opening the page; set to `true` or `false`.
`pluginspage="pluginurl"`	The URL of the plug-in required to play the media clip.

Q&A

Q. **Instead of learning all this stuff myself, shouldn't I just hire a graphic artist to design my pages?**

A. This is a difficult question to answer, and it's not because I have a conflict of interest here—I work for a web development and design agency, so it's in my best interest to recommend agencies. But an agency isn't always the best solution. Hiring a graphic designer takes time and money. Additionally, there are many graphic artists who do not produce work suitable for the Web—they are specifically print-based artists, and the print world is quite different than the online world. Also, hiring an individual who deems himself a graphic designer to create a website might not play to the strengths of that particular graphic designer. In other words, he might be good at designing the graphical elements of a website, but he might *not* be good as a content architect or at working with HTML and CSS. If your site is simply a personal site, a professional design might not be where you want to spend your money. But if your site is intended to promote a business, a product, a school, or anything else whereby your image is integral to your success, it's worth your while (and money) to consult with web design professional.

Q. **I've produced graphics for printing on paper. Are web page graphics any different?**

A. Yes. In fact, many of the rules for print graphics are reversed on the Web. Web page graphics have to be low resolution, whereas print graphics should be as high resolution as possible. White washes out black on computer screens, whereas black bleeds into white on paper. Also, someone might stop a web page from loading when only half the graphics have been downloaded. Try to avoid falling into old habits if you've done a lot of print graphics design.

Q. **I used the `<img />` tag just as you advised, but when I view the page, all I see is a little box with some shapes in it. What's wrong?**

A. The broken image icon you're seeing can mean one of two things: Either the web browser couldn't find the image file or the image isn't saved in a format the browser recognizes. To solve these problems, first check to make sure that the image is where it is supposed to be. If it is, then open the image in your graphics editor and save it again as a GIF, JPG, or PNG format.

Q. **What happens if I overlap areas on an imagemap?**

A. You are allowed to overlap areas on an imagemap. Just keep in mind that when determining which link to follow, one area will have precedence over the other area. Precedence is assigned according to which areas are listed first in the imagemap. For example, the first area in the map has precedence over the second area, which means that a click in the overlapping portion of the areas will link to the first area. If you have an area within an imagemap that doesn't link to anything (known as a *dead area*), you can use this overlap trick to deliberately prevent this area from linking to anything. To do this, just place the dead area before other areas so that the dead area overlaps them, and then set its `href` attribute to `""`.

Q. **I hear a lot about streaming video and audio. What does that mean?**

A. In the past, video and audio files took minutes and sometimes hours to retrieve through most modems, which severely limited the inclusion of video and audio on web pages. The goal that everyone is moving toward is streaming video or audio, which plays while the data is being received. In other words, you don't have to completely download the clip before you can start to watch it or listen to it.

Streaming playback is now widely supported through most media players, in both standalone versions and plug-ins. When you embed a media object using the `<object>` tag, the underlying media player automatically streams the media clip if streaming is supported in the player.

Workshop

The workshop contains quiz questions and exercises to help you solidify your understanding of the material covered. Try to answer all questions before looking at the "Answers" section that follows.

Quiz

1. How would you give a web page a black background and make all text bright green? Based on what you've learned in this chapter, would you even want to use that color combination?

2. You have a scanned picture of a horse that you need to put on a web page. How big should you make it? In what file format should you save it?

3. How would you insert an elephant.jpg image file at the top of a web page?

4. How would you make the word *Elephant* display whenever the actual elephant.jpg image couldn't be displayed by a web browser?

Answers

1. Put the following at the beginning of the web page or use a style rule for the body element:

```
<body style="background-color:#000000; color:#00FF00">
```

2. Depending on how important the image is to your page, you should make it as small as 100×40 pixels or as large as 300×120 pixels. The JPEG format, with about 85% compression, would be best. Of course, you could also provide a thumbnail link to a larger image that is viewed by itself.

3. Copy the image file into the same directory folder as the HTML text file. Immediately after the <body> tag in the HTML text file, type <p><img src="elephant.jpg" alt="" /></p>.

4. Use the following HTML:

```
<img src="elephant.jpg" alt="elephant" />
```

Exercises

▶ Select a base color that you like—perhaps a lovely blue or an earthy tone—and use the Color Scheme Generator at http://colorscheme-designer.com/ to come up with a set of colors that you can use in a website. I recommend the tetrad or accented analogic scheme types.

▶ After you have a set of colors—or a few options for sets of colors—create a basic HTML page with a <h1> element, a paragraph of text, and perhaps some list items. Use the color-related styles you've learned about in this chapter to change the background color of the page and the text of the various block-level elements, to see how these sets of colors might work together. See how they interact and determine which colors are best used for containers and which are best used for plain text, header text, and link text.

▶ Before you start designing graphics for an important business site, try spicing up your own personal home page. This will give you a chance to learn GIMP (or give you a chance to use your graphics software) so that you'll know what you're doing when you tackle the task at work.

▶ Practicing any of the image placement methods in this chapter will go a long way toward helping you determine the role that images can, and will, play in the websites you design. Using a few sample images, practice using the float style to place images and text in relation to one another. Remember the possible values for float are left, right, and none (default).

CHAPTER 9

Working with Margins, Padding, Alignment, and Floating

Now that you've learned some of the basics of creating web content, in this chapter you'll learn the nitty-gritty of using CSS to enhance that content. Throughout the previous chapter, you have learned how to use basic CSS for display purposes (such as font sizes and colors). In the chapters that follow, you'll dive in to using CSS to control aspects of your entire web page and not just individual pieces of text or graphics.

Before tackling page layout, however, it is important to understand four particular CSS properties individually before putting them all together:

▶ **The `margin` and `padding` properties**—For adding space around elements

▶ **The `align` and `float` properties**—Used to place your elements in relation to others

The examples provided during this chapter are not the most stylish examples of web content ever created, but they are not intended to be. Instead, the examples clearly show just how XHTML and CSS are working together. After you master CSS through this and other chapters, you'll be able to create web-based masterpieces such as the one shown in Figure 9.1, an example at CSS Zen Garden.

The sites at CSS Zen Garden probably do not look like the typical e-commerce or social networking sites that you visit on a regular basis. Instead, these sites showcase the artistic possibilities that can unfold using CSS. Make no mistake, these sites take careful thought and planning, but the potential designs are limitless.

WHAT YOU'LL LEARN IN THIS CHAPTER:

▶ How to add margins around elements

▶ How to add padding within elements

▶ How to keep everything aligned

▶ How to use the `float` property

FIGURE 9.1
This is one of many examples in
the CSS Zen Garden of XHTML and
CSS at work.

NOTE

Sites in the CSS Zen Garden
(http://www.csszengarden.
com/) show the types of design
that can be accomplished
through using standards-
compliant CSS. All of the user-
submitted entries in the Garden
use exactly the same HTML file,
but artists are free to modify
the CSS file to create their own
visual display. The example
shown in Figure 9.1 is by
Andy Clarke of Stuff and
Nonsense (http://www.
stuffandnonsense.co.uk/).

Using Margins

Style sheet *margins* enable you to add empty space around the *outside* of the
rectangular area for an element on a web page. It is important to remember
that the `margin` property works with space outside of the element.

Following are the style properties for setting margins:

- ▶ `margin-top`—Sets the top margin

- ▶ `margin-right`—Sets the right margin

- ▶ `margin-bottom`—Sets the bottom margin

- ▶ `margin-left`—Sets the left margin

- ▶ `margin`—Sets the top, right, bottom, and left margins as a single
  property

You can specify margins using any of the individual margin properties or
using the single `margin` property. Margins can be specified as auto, meaning the browser itself sets the margin in specific lengths (pixels, points,
ems) or in percentages. If you decide to set a margin as a percentage, keep
in mind that the percentage is calculated based on the size of the entire

page, not the size of the element. So, if you set the margin-left property to 25%, the left margin of the element will end up being 25% of the width of the entire page.

The code in Listing 9.1 produces four rectangles on the page, each 250 pixels wide, 100 pixels high, and with a 5-pixel solid black border (see Figure 9.2). Each rectangle—or <div>, in this case—has a different background color. We want the margin around each <div> to be 15 pixels on all sides, so we can use the following:

```
margin-top:15px;
margin-right:15px;
margin-bottom:15px;
margin-left:15px;
```

You could also write that in shorthand, using the margin property:

```
margin:15px 15px 15px 15px;
```

When you use the margin property (or padding, or border) and you want all four values to be the same, you can simplify this even further and use:

```
margin:15px;
```

When using shorthand for setting margins, padding or borders, there are actually three approaches, which vary based on how many values you use when setting the property:

- **One value**—The size of all the margins
- **Two values**—The size of the top/bottom margins and the left/right margins (in that order)
- **Four values**—The size of the top, right, bottom, and left margins (in that order)

You might find it easier to stick to either using one value or all four values, but that's certainly not a requirement.

LISTING 9.1   Simple Code to Produce Four Colored <div>s with Borders and Margins

```
<?xml version="1.0" encoding="UTF-8"?>
<!DOCTYPE html PUBLIC "-//W3C//DTD XHTML 1.1//EN"
  "http://www.w3.org/TR/xhtml11/DTD/xhtml11.dtd">

<html xmlns="http://www.w3.org/1999/xhtml" xml:lang="en">
  <head>
  <title>Color Blocks</title>
```

NOTE

You can remember the short-hand order at least two different ways. First, if you think of an element as a rectangle, start at the top and work your way clockwise around the sides: top side, right side, bottom side, left side. Or you can use a first-letter mnemonic device and remember "TRBL," pronounced "trouble," which also represents a possible state of being should you forget the order of the margin properties.

Also note that the TRBL order is valid for padding properties and border properties as well.

LISTING 9.1   Continued

```
<style type="text/css">
    div {
        width:250px;
        height:100px;
        border:5px solid #000000;
        color:black;
        font-weight:bold;
        text-align:center;
    }

    div#d1 {
        background-color:red;
        margin:15px;
    }

    div#d2 {
        background-color:green;
        margin:15px;
    }

    div#d3 {
        background-color:blue;
    }

    div#d4 {
        background-color:yellow;
        margin:15px;
    }
</style>
</head>

<body>
    <div id="d1">DIV #1</div>
    <div id="d2">DIV #2</div>
    <div id="d3">DIV #3</div>
    <div id="d4">DIV #4</div>
</body>
</html>
```

You can see the output of Listing 9.1 in Figure 9.2.

Next, working with just the margin property in the style sheet entries in Listing 9.1, let's shift the margins around. In this example, you can't really see the right-side margin on any of these <div> elements because there's nothing to the right of them and they are not aligned to the right. With that in mind, let's set margin-right to 0px in all of these. Beyond that, the next set of goals is to produce the following:

▶ No margin around the first color block.

▶ A left-side margin of 15 pixels, a top margin of 5 pixels, and no bottom margin around the second color block.

▶ A left-side margin of 75 pixels and no top margin or bottom margins around the third color block.

▶ A left-side margin of 250 pixels and a top margin of 25 pixels around the fourth color block.

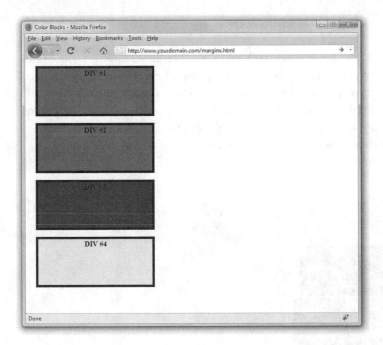

FIGURE 9.2
The basic color blocks sample page shows four color blocks, each with equal margins.

This seems like it would be straightforward—no margin is being set around the first block. Except we want a margin at the top of the second block, so really there will be a visible margin between the first and second blocks, even if we are not specifying a margin for the first block.

The new style sheet entries for the four named `<div>`s would now look like this:

```
div#d1 {
  background-color:red;
  margin:0px;
}

div#d2 {
```

```
    background-color:green;
    margin:5px 0px 0px 15px;
}

div#d3 {
    background-color:blue;
    margin:0px 0px 0px 75px;
}

div#d4 {
    background-color:yellow;
    margin:25px 0px 0px 250px;
}
```

The result of the previous code changes (see Figure 9.3) seems random but is actually quite useful for pointing out a few other important points. For example, when you recall that one of the goals was to produce no margin at all around the first color block, you might expect the border of the color block to be flush with the browser window. But, as shown in Figure 9.3, there is a clear space between the content of the page and the frame of the browser window.

FIGURE 9.3
Modifications to the color blocks sample page display some different margins.

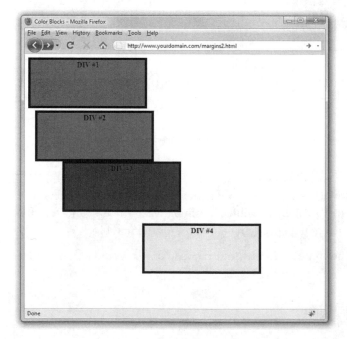

If we were working on element placement—which we will get to in the
next chapter—this would cause a problem in your layout. To ensure that
your placements and margins are counted from a position flush with the
browser, you will need to address the margin of the <body> element itself.
In this case, you would add the following to your style sheet:

```
body {
  margin:0px;
}
```

Another "gotcha" to remember is that if you have two bordered elements
stacked on top of each other but with no margin between them, the point
at which they touch will appear to have a double border. You might then
consider making the top element's border-bottom half the width and also
make the bottom element's border-top half the width. If you do this, the
borders will appear to be the same width as the other sides when stacked
on top of each other.

Also, you might have thought that by using a left-side margin of 250 pixels—
the width of the <div>s—the fourth color block would begin where the third
color block ended. That is not the case, however, because the third color block
has a margin-left of 75 pixels. In order for them to even be close to lining
up, the margin-left value for the fourth div would have to be 325 pixels.

Changing the styles to those shown in the code that follows produces the
spacing shown in Figure 9.4.

```
body {
  margin:0px;
}
div {
  width:250px;
  height:100px;
  color:black;
  font-weight:bold;
  text-align:center;
}
div#d1 {
  border:5px solid #000000;
  background-color:red;
  margin:0px;
}
div#d2 {
  border-width:6px 6px 3px 6px;
  border-style:solid;
  border-color:#000000;
  background-color:green;
  margin:10px 0px 0px 15px;
```

```
}
div#d3 {
  border-width:3px 6px 6px 6px;
  border-style:solid;
  border-color:#000000;
  background-color:blue;
  margin:0px 0px 0px 15px;
}
div#d4 {
  border:5px solid #000000;
  background-color:yellow;
  margin:0px 0px 0px 265px;
}
```

These changes give the <body> element a zero margin, thus ensuring that a margin-left value of 25 pixels truly is 25 pixels from the edge of the browser frame. It also shows the second and third color blocks stacked on top of each other, but with modifications to the border element so that a double border does not appear. Additionally, the fourth color block begins where the third color block ends.

FIGURE 9.4
A third modification to the color blocks pulls items into closer relation with each other.

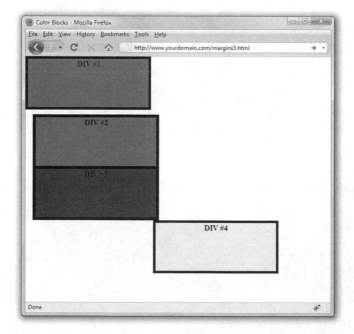

As you can see in Figure 9.4, there is some overlap between the right edge of the third color block and the left edge of the fourth color block. Why is that the case, if the color blocks are 250 pixels wide, the third color block

has a `margin-left` value of 15 pixels, and the fourth color block is supposed to have a 265 pixel margin to its left? Well, it does have that 265
pixel margin, but that margin size is not enough because we also have to
factor in the 6 pixels of border. If we change the `margin` property for the
fourth color block to reflect the following code, the third and fourth blocks
line up according to plan (see Figure 9.5):

```
margin:0px 0px 0px 276px;
```

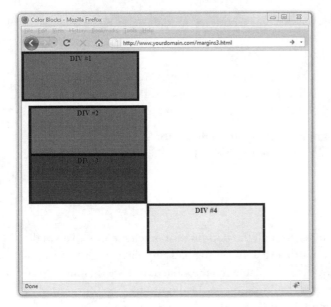

FIGURE 9.5
Changing the margin to allow for
11 pixels of border width.

As shown in these examples, margin specifications are incredibly useful for element placement, but you must use caution when setting these specifications.

Padding Elements

Padding is similar to margins in that it adds extra space to elements, but the
big difference is where that space is located. If you recall, margins are added
to the outside of elements. On the other hand, padding adds space *inside* the
rectangular area of an element. As an example, if you create a style rule for
an element that establishes a width of 50 pixels and a height of 30 pixels,
and then sets the padding of the rule to 5 pixels, the remaining content area
will be 40 pixels by 20 pixels. Also, because the padding of an element
appears within the element's content area, it will assume the same style as
the content of the element, including the background color.

You specify the padding of a style rule using one of the `padding` properties, which work very much like the `margin` properties. The following padding properties are available for use in setting the padding of style rules:

- **`padding-top`**—Sets the top padding

- **`padding-right`**—Sets the right padding

- **`padding-bottom`**—Sets the bottom padding

- **`padding-left`**—Sets the left padding

- **`padding`**—Sets the top, right, bottom, and left padding as a single property

As with margins, you can set the padding of style rules using individual padding properties or the single `padding` property. Padding can also be expressed using either a unit of measurement or a percentage.

Following is an example of how you might set the left and right padding for a style rule so that there are 10 pixels of padding on each side of an element's content:

```
padding-left:10px;
padding-right:10px;
```

As with margins, you can set all the padding for an element with a single property (the `padding` property). To set the padding property, you can use the same three approaches available for the `margin` property. Following is an example of how you would set the vertical padding (top/bottom) to 12 pixels and the horizontal padding (left/right) to 8 pixels for a style rule:

```
padding:12px 8px;
```

Following is more explicit code that performs the same task by specifying all the padding values:

```
padding:12px 8px 12px 8px;
```

In all the previous figures, you'll note that the text `DIV #1`, `DIV #2`, and so on appears at the top of the colored block, with just a little space between the border and the text. That amount of space hasn't been specified by any padding value, but it appears as a sort of default within the element. But if you want specific control over your element padding, Listing 9.2 shows some examples. All of the color blocks are 250 pixels wide, 100 pixels high, have a 5-pixel solid black border, and 25 pixels of margin (see Figure 9.6). The fun stuff happens within the padding values for each individual `<div>`.

LISTING 9.2   Simple Code to Produce Four Colored <div>s with Borders,
Margins, and Padding

```
<?xml version="1.0" encoding="UTF-8"?>
<!DOCTYPE html PUBLIC "-//W3C//DTD XHTML 1.1//EN"
  "http://www.w3.org/TR/xhtml11/DTD/xhtml11.dtd">

<html xmlns="http://www.w3.org/1999/xhtml" xml:lang="en">
  <head>
    <title>Color Blocks</title>
    <style type="text/css">
      body {
          margin:0px;
      }
      div {
          width:250px;
          height:100px;
          border:5px solid #000000;
          color:black;
          font-weight:bold;
          margin:25px;
      }

      div#d1 {
          background-color:red;
          text-align:center;
          padding:15px;
      }

      div#d2 {
          background-color:green;
          text-align:right;
          padding:25px 50px 6px 6px;
      }

      div#d3 {
          background-color:blue;
          text-align:left;
          padding:6px 6px 6px 50px;
      }

      div#d4 {
          background-color:yellow;
          text-align:center;
          padding:50px;
      }
    </style>
  </head>

  <body>
    <div id="d1">DIV #1</div>
    <div id="d2">DIV #2</div>
```

LISTING 9.2   Continued

```
      <div id="d3">DIV #3</div>
      <div id="d4">DIV #4</div>
   </body>
</html>
```

FIGURE 9.6
The basic color blocks sample
page shows four color blocks with
variable padding.

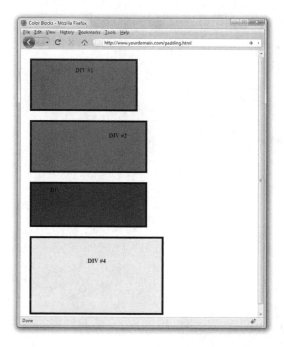

You should immediately recognize that something is amiss in this example.
The color blocks are all supposed to be 250 pixels wide and 100 pixels
high. The color blocks in Figure 9.6 are not uniform because despite our
efforts to control the size of the <div>, the padding applied later overrides
that initial size declaration.

If you place the text in a <p> element and give that element a white background (see Figure 9.7), you can see where the padding is in relation to the
text. When there just isn't room to use all the padding that is defined, the
surrounding element has to make adjustments. You will learn about this
effect in detail in Chapter 10, "Understanding the CSS Box Model and
Positioning."

The greatest number of "tweaks" or "nudges" you make in your web
design with CSS will have to do with margins and padding. Just remember: margins outside the element, padding inside it.

FIGURE 9.7
Showing the padding in relation to
the text.

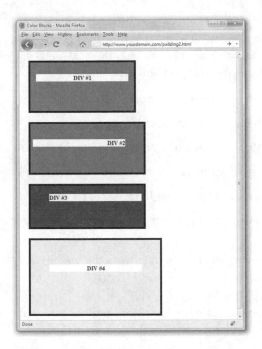

Keeping Everything Aligned

Knowing that content on a web page doesn't always fill the entire width of
the rectangular area in which it is displayed, it is often helpful to control
the alignment of the content. Even if text within a rectangular area extends
to multiple lines, alignment still enters the picture because you might want
the text left-justified, right-justified, or centered. There are two style properties that enable you to control the alignment of elements: `text-align`
and `vertical-align`.

You saw examples of these style properties in action—aligning images—in
Chapter 8, "Working with Colors, Images, and Multimedia," but it doesn't
hurt to mention these properties again here because alignment plays a role
in overall page design as well.

As a refresher, using `text-align` aligns an element horizontally within its
bounding area, and it can be set to `left`, `right`, `center`, or `justify`.

The `vertical-align` property is similar to `text-align` except that it is
used to align elements vertically. The `vertical-align` property specifies
how an element is aligned with its parent, or in some cases, the current
line of elements on the page. Current line refers to the vertical placement
of elements that appear within the same parent element—in other words,

inline elements. If several inline elements appear on the same line, you can set their vertical alignments the same to align them vertically. A good example would be a row of images that appear one after the next—the `vertical-align` property enables you to align them vertically.

Following are common values for use with the `vertical-align` property:

- ▶ **top**—Aligns the top of an element with the current line
- ▶ **middle**—Aligns the middle of an element with the middle of its parent
- ▶ **bottom**—Aligns the bottom of an element with the current line
- ▶ **text-top**—Aligns the top of an element with the top of its parent
- ▶ **baseline**—Aligns the baseline of an element with the baseline of its parent
- ▶ **text-bottom**—Aligns the bottom of an element with the bottom of its parent

Alignment works in conjunction with margins, padding, and—as you will learn in the next section—the `float` property to enable you to maintain control over your design.

Understanding the `Float` Property

Understanding the `float` property is fundamental to understanding CSS-based layout and design; it is one of the last pieces in the puzzle of how all these elements fit together. Briefly stated, the `float` property allows elements to be moved around in the design such that other elements can wrap around them. You will often find `float` used in conjunction with images (as you saw in Chapter 8), but you can—and many designers do—float all sorts of elements in their layout.

Elements float horizontally, not vertically, so all you have to concern yourself with are two possible values: `right` and `left`. When used, an element that floats will float as far right or as far left (depending on the value of `float`) as the containing element will allow it. For example, if you have three `<div>`s float values of left, they will all line up to the left of the containing body element. If you have your `<div>`s within another `<div>`, they will line up to the left of *that* element, even if that element itself is floated to the right.

Floating is best understood by seeing a few examples, so let's move on to Listing 9.3. This listing simply defines three rectangular `<div>`s and floats them next to each other (floating to the left).

LISTING 9.3   Using float to Place <div>s

```
<?xml version="1.0" encoding="UTF-8"?>
<!DOCTYPE html PUBLIC "-//W3C//DTD XHTML 1.1//EN"
  "http://www.w3.org/TR/xhtml11/DTD/xhtml11.dtd">

<html xmlns="http://www.w3.org/1999/xhtml" xml:lang="en">
  <head>
    <title>Color Blocks</title>
    <style type="text/css">
      body {
          margin:0px;
      }
      div {
          width:250px;
          height:100px;
          border:5px solid #000000;
          color:black;
          font-weight:bold;
          margin:25px;
      }

      div#d1 {
          background-color:red;
          float:left;
      }

      div#d2 {
          background-color:green;
          float:left;
      }

      div#d3 {
          background-color:blue;
          float:left;
      }
    </style>
  </head>

  <body>
    <div id="d1">DIV #1</div>
    <div id="d2">DIV #2</div>
    <div id="d3">DIV #3</div>
  </body>
</html>
```

The resulting page is shown in Figure 9.8, and already you can see a problem—
these three color blocks were supposed to be floated next to each other. Well,
actually they are floated next to each other, except the browser window is not
wide enough to display these three 250-pixel-wide blocks with 25 pixels of
margin between them. Because they are floating, the third one simply floats to
the next line.

FIGURE 9.8
Using `float` to place the color
blocks.

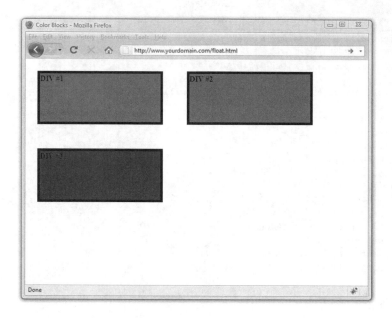

You can imagine this could be a problem in a specifically designed visual lay-out, so pay attention to your margins, padding, alignment, and floating while also testing within a target browser window size. Granted, the browser window shown in Figure 9.8 is a small one—to make this point about floating elements moving to the next line when there is no room for them to fit where they should. In other words, if you open the same HTML file with a larger browser window, you might not see the issue—this is why you should also check your sites at different resolutions to see if a fix is needed. The fix here is to adjust the margins and other size-related properties of your `<div>`s.

Figure 9.9 shows another interesting possibility when using the `float` proper-ty. The only changes made to the code from Listing 9.3 involved making the color blocks only 100-pixels wide, reducing the margins to 10px, and changing the `float` alignment of the second color block to right (instead of left).

However, something very interesting happened. The second color block now appears visually as the third color block because it is flush right. The second color block has a `float` value of `right`, so it has floated all the way to the right. The first and third color blocks are floating as left as possible, regardless of the way in which the `<div>` code appears in the HTML, which is as follows:

```
<div id="d1">DIV #1</div>
<div id="d2">DIV #2</div>
<div id="d3">DIV #3</div>
```

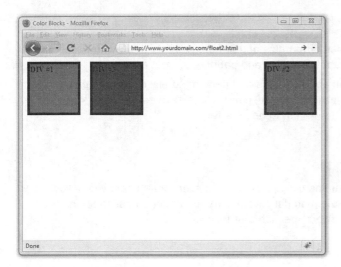

FIGURE 9.9
Using float to place the color blocks.

Floating takes a lot of practice to get used to, especially when there are additional elements in your page and not just a few colored blocks. For example, what happens when you add a basic paragraph into the mix? All elements placed after the floating element will float around that element. To avoid that, use the `clear` property.

The `clear` property has five possible values: `left`, `right`, `both`, `none`, and `inherit`. The most common values are `left`, `right`, and `both`. Specifying `clear:left` ensures there are no other floating elements allowed to the left, `clear:right` ensures there are no other floating elements to the right, and so on. Floating and clearing is a learn-by-doing process, so look for more situations in the Workshop section later in this chapter.

Summary

This chapter introduced you to some of the most fundamental style properties in CSS-based design: `margin`, `padding`, and `float`. You learned how the `margin` property controls space around the outside of elements and how the `padding` property works with space within the elements.

After a refresher on the `text-align` and `vertical-align` properties you learned about in a previous lesson, you learned about the `float` property. The `float` property allows for specific placement of elements and additional content around those elements.

Q&A

Q. **The examples of margins and padding all had to do with boxes and text. Can I apply margins and padding to images as well?**

A. Yes, you can apply margins and padding to any block-level element, such as a `<p>`, a `<div>`, an `<img/>`, lists such as `<ul>` and `<ol>`, and list items (`<li>`)—just to name a few.

Workshop

The workshop contains quiz questions and exercises to help you solidify your understanding of the material covered. Try to answer all questions before looking at the "Answers" section that follows.

Quiz

1. To place two `<div>` elements next to each other, but with a 30-pixel margin between them, what entry or entries can you use in the style sheet?

2. Which CSS style property and value is used to ensure that content does not appear to the left of a floating element?

3. What style sheet entry is used to place text within a `<div>` to appear 12 pixels from the top of the element?

Answers

1. You can use several. The first `<div>` uses a style property of `margin-right:15px` and the second `<div>` uses a style property of `margin-left:15px`. Or you can assign the full 30 pixels to either `<div>` using `margin-right` or `margin-left` as appropriate.

2. In this instance, use `clear:left`.

3. `padding-top:12px`

Exercises

▶ Fully understanding margins, padding, alignment, and floating takes practice. Using the color blocks code or `<div>`s of your own, practice all manner and sorts of spacing and floating before moving on to the next chapter. The next chapter discusses the CSS box model as a whole, which encompasses the individual items discussed in this chapter.

▶ While you're at it, practice applying margins and padding to every block-level element you've learned so far. Get used to putting images within blocks of text and putting margins around the images so that the text does not run right up to the edge of the graphic.

CHAPTER 10

Understanding the CSS Box Model and Positioning

In the previous chapter, I mentioned the CSS Box Model a few times—this chapter begins with a discussion of the box model and explains how the information you learned in the previous chapter helps you understand this model. By learning the box model, you won't tear your hair out when you create a design, and then realize the elements don't line up or that they seem a little "off." You'll know that in almost all cases, something—the margin, the padding, or the border—just needs a little tweaking for it to work out.

You'll also learn more about CSS positioning, including stacking elements on top of each in a three-dimensional way (rather than a vertical way). Finally, you'll learn about controlling the flow of text around elements using the float property.

WHAT YOU'LL LEARN IN THIS CHAPTER:

▶ How to conceptualize the CSS box model
▶ How to position your elements
▶ How to control the way elements stack up
▶ How to manage the flow of text

The CSS Box Model

Every element in HTML is considered a "box," whether it is a paragraph, a <div>, an image, or so on. Boxes have consistent properties, whether we see them or not, and whether they are specified at all in the style sheet or not. They're always present, and as designers, we have to keep their presence in mind when creating a layout.

Figure 10.1 is a diagram of the box model. The box model describes the way in which every HTML block-level element has the potential for a border, padding, and margin and how the border, padding, and margin are applied. In other words, all elements have some padding between the content and the border of the element. Additionally, the border might or might not be visible, but there is space for it, just as there is a margin between the border of the element and any other content outside of the element.

FIGURE 10.1
Every element in HTML is represented by the CSS box model.

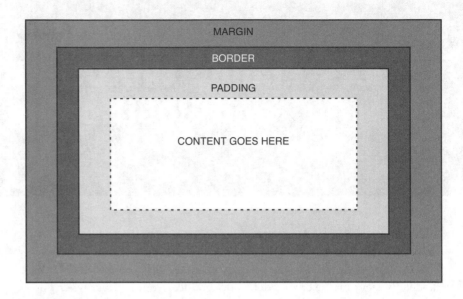

Here's yet another explanation of the box model, going from the outside
inward:

▶ The *margin* is the area outside of the element. It never has color; it is
  always transparent.

▶ The *border* extends around the element, on the outer edge of any
  padding. The border can be of several types, widths, and colors.

▶ The *padding* exists around the content and inherits the background
  color of the content area.

▶ The *content* is surrounded by padding.

Here's where the tricky part comes in: To know the true height and width of
an element, you have to take all the elements of the box model into account.
If you remember the example from the previous chapter when, despite
specifically indicating a <div> should be 250 pixels wide and 100 pixels high,
that <div> had to grow larger to accommodate the padding in use.

You already know how to set the width and height of an element using the
width and height properties. The following example shows how to define
a <div> that is 250 pixels wide, 100 pixels high, has a red background, and
has a black single pixel border:

```
div {
  width: 250px;
  height: 100px;
```

```
    background-color: #ff0000;
    border: 1px solid #000000;
}
```

This simple <div> is shown in Figure 10.2.

FIGURE 10.2
This is a simple <div>.

If we define a second element with these same properties, but also add margin and padding properties of a certain size, we begin to see how the size of the element changes. This is because of the box model.

The second <div> will be defined as follows, just adding 10 pixels of margin and 10 pixels of padding to the element:

```
div#d2 {
    width: 250px;
    height: 100px;
    background-color: #ff0000;
    border: 5px solid #000000;
    margin: 10px;
    padding: 10px;
}
```

The second <div>, shown in Figure 10.3, is defined as the same height and width as the first one, but the overall height and width of the entire box surrounding the element itself is much larger when margins and padding are put in play.

FIGURE 10.3
This is supposed to be another simple <div> but the box model affects the size of the second <div>.

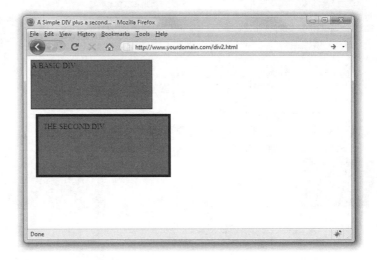

The total *width* of an element is the sum of the following:

```
width + padding-left + padding-right + border-left + border-right +
margin-left + margin-right
```

The total *height* of an element is the sum of the following:

```
height + padding-top + padding-bottom + border-top + border-bottom +
margin-top + margin-bottom
```

Therefore, the second <div> has an actual width of 300 (250 + 10 + 10 + 5 + 5 + 10 + 10) and an actual height of 150 (100 + 10 + 10 + 5 + 5 + 10 + 10).

By now you can begin to see how the box model will affect your design. Let's say you have only 250 pixels of horizontal space, but you like 10 pixels of margin, 10 pixels of padding, and 5 pixels of border on all sides. To accommodate what you like with what you have room to display, you must specify the width of your <div> as only 200 pixels, so that 200 + 10 + 10 + 5 + 5 + 10 + 10 would add up to that 250 pixels of available horizontal space.

Not only is it important to understand the concept behind the box model, but the mathematics of the model are important as well. In dynamically driven sites or sites in which the client-side display is driven by user interactions (such as through JavaScript events), your server-side or client-side code may draw and re-draw container elements on the fly. In other words, your code will produce the numbers, but you have to provide the boundaries.

Now that you've been schooled in the way of the box model, keep it in mind throughout the rest of the work you do in this book and in your web

NOTE

Throughout this book you've been drilled in the use of the DOCTYPE declaration—all sample code includes a DOCTYPE. Continue this practice not only so that your code validates, but because there is a very specific issue with Internet Explorer and the CSS box model: If a DOCTYPE is not defined, Internet Explorer manipulates the height and width of your elements in a way you did not intend. This causes browser incompatibility issues with your layout, so just remember to include a DOCTYPE.

design. Among other things, it will affect element positioning and content flow, which are the two topics we will tackle next.

The Whole Scoop on Positioning

Relative positioning is the default type of positioning used by HTML. You can think of relative positioning as being akin to laying out checkers on a checkerboard: The checkers are arranged from left to right, and when you get to the edge of the board, you move on to the next row. Elements that are styled with the `block` value for the `display` style property are automatically placed on a new row, whereas `inline` elements are placed on the same row immediately next to the element preceding them. As an example, `<p>` and `<div>` tags are considered block elements, whereas the `<span>` tag is considered an inline element.

The other type of positioning supported by CSS is known as *absolute positioning* because it enables you to set the exact position of HTML content on a page. Although absolute positioning gives you the freedom to spell out exactly where an element is to appear, the position is still relative to any parent elements that appear on the page. In other words, absolute positioning enables you to specify the exact location of an element's rectangular area with respect to its parent's area, which is very different from relative positioning.

With the freedom of placing elements anywhere you want on a page, you can run into the problem of overlap, which is when an element takes up space used by another element. There is nothing stopping you from specifying the absolute locations of elements so they overlap. In this case, CSS relies on the z-index of each element to determine which element is on the top and which is on the bottom. You'll learn more about the z-index of elements later in the chapter. For now, let's look at exactly how you control whether a style rule uses relative or absolute positioning.

The type of positioning (relative or absolute) used by a particular style rule is determined by the `position` property, which is capable of having one of the following two values: `relative` or `absolute`. After specifying the type of positioning, you then provide the specific position using the following properties:

- ▶ **left**—The left position offset
- ▶ **right**—The right position offset
- ▶ **top**—The top position offset
- ▶ **bottom**—The bottom position offset

You might think that these position properties make sense only for absolute positioning, but they actually apply to both types of positioning. Under relative positioning, the position of an element is specified as an off-set relative to the original position of the element. So, if you set the `left` property of an element to 25px, the left side of the element will be shifted over 25 pixels from its original (relative) position. An absolute position, on the other hand, is specified relative to the parent of the element to which the style is applied. So, if you set the `left` property of an element to 25px under absolute positioning, the left side of the element will appear 25 pixels to the right of the parent element's left edge. On the other hand, using the `right` property with the same value would position the element so that its *right* side is 25 pixels to the right of the parent's *right* edge.

Let's return to the color blocks example to show how positioning works. In Listing 10.1, the four color blocks have relative positioning specified. As you can see in Figure 10.4, the blocks are positioned vertically.

FIGURE 10.4
The color blocks are positioned vertically with one on top of the other.

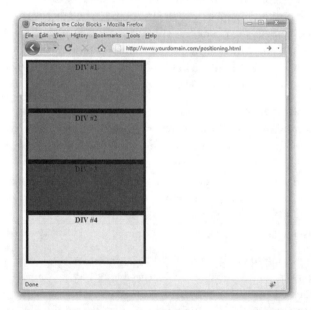

LISTING 10.1   Showing Relative Positioning with Four Color Blocks

```
<?xml version="1.0" encoding="UTF-8"?>
<!DOCTYPE html PUBLIC "-//W3C//DTD XHTML 1.1//EN"
 "http://www.w3.org/TR/xhtml11/DTD/xhtml11.dtd"">

<html xmlns="http://www.w3.org/1999/xhtml" xml:lang="en">
 <head>
  <title>Positioning the Color Blocks</title>
```

LISTING 10.1   Continued

```
<style type="text/css">
div {
  position:relative;
  width:250px;
  height:100px;
  border:5px solid #000;
  color:black;
  font-weight:bold;
  text-align:center;
  }
  div#d1 {
  background-color:red;
  }

  div#d2 {
  background-color:green;
  }

  div#d3 {
  background-color:blue;
  }

  div#d4 {
  background-color:yellow;
  }
  </style>

</head>
<body>
  <div id="d1">DIV #1</div>
  <div id="d2">DIV #2</div>
  <div id="d3">DIV #3</div>
  <div id="d4">DIV #4</div>
</body>
</html>
```

The style sheet entry for the <div> element itself sets the position style property for the <div> element to relative. Because the remaining style rules are inherited from the <div> style rule, they inherit its relative positioning. In fact, the only difference between the other style rules is that they have different background colors.

Notice in Figure 10.4 that the <div> elements are displayed one after the next, which is what you would expect with relative positioning. But to make things more interesting, which is what we're here to do, you can change the positioning to absolute and explicitly specify the placement of the colors. In Listing 10.2, the style sheet entries are changed to use absolute positioning to arrange the color blocks.

LISTING 10.2   Using Absolute Positioning of the Color Blocks

```
<?xml version="1.0" encoding="UTF-8"?>
<!DOCTYPE html PUBLIC "-//W3C//DTD XHTML 1.1//EN"
 "http://www.w3.org/TR/xhtml11/DTD/xhtml11.dtd">

<html xmlns="http://www.w3.org/1999/xhtml" xml:lang="en">
 <head>
  <title>Positioning the Color Blocks</title>
    <style type="text/css">
    div {
     position:absolute;
     width:250px;
     height:100px;
     border:5px solid #000;
     color:black;
     font-weight:bold;
     text-align:center;
    }
    div#d1 {
     background-color:red;
     left:0px;
     toppx;
    }
    div#d2 {
     background-color:green;
     left:75px;
     top:25px;
    }
    div#d3 {
     background-color:blue;
     left:150px;
     top:50px;
    }
    div#d4 {
     background-color:yellow;
     left:225px;
     top:75px;
    }
    </style>
 </head>
<body>
 <div id="d1">DIV #1</div>
 <div id="d2">DIV #2</div>
     <div id="d3">DIV #3</div>
 <div id="d4">DIV #4</div>
</body>
</html>
```

This style sheet sets the position property to absolute, which is necessary for the style sheet to use absolute positioning. Additionally, the left and top properties are set for each of the inherited <div> style rules. However, the position of each of these rules is set so that the elements are displayed overlapping each other, as shown in Figure 10.5.

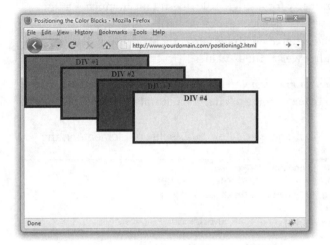

FIGURE 10.5
The color blocks are displayed using absolute positioning.

Now we're talking layout! Figure 10.5 shows how absolute positioning enables you to place elements exactly where you want them. It also reveals how easy it is to arrange elements so that they overlap each other. You might be curious as to how a web browser knows which elements to draw on top when they overlap. The next section covers how you can control stacking order.

Controlling the Way Things Stack Up

There are situations in which you'd like to carefully control the manner in which elements overlap each other on a web page. The z-index style property enables you to set the order of elements with respect to how they stack on top of each other. Although the name *z-index* might sound a little strange, it refers to the notion of a third dimension (Z) that points into the computer screen, in addition to the two dimensions that go across (X) and down (Y) the screen. Another way to think of the z-index is the relative position of a single magazine within a stack of magazines. A magazine near the top of the stack has a higher z-index than a magazine lower in the stack. Similarly, an overlapped element with a higher z-index is displayed on top of an element with a lower z-index.

The z-index property is used to set a numeric value that indicates the relative z-index of a style rule. The number assigned to z-index has meaning only with respect to other style rules in a style sheet, which means that setting the z-index property for a single rule doesn't mean much. On the other hand, if you set z-index for several style rules that apply to overlapped elements, the elements with higher z-index values will appear on top of elements with lower z-index values.

Listing 10.3 contains another version of the color blocks style sheet and HTML that uses z-index settings to alter the natural overlap of elements.

LISTING 10.3   Using z-index to Alter the Display of Elements in the Color Blocks Sample

```
<?xml version="1.0" encoding="UTF-8"?>
<!DOCTYPE html PUBLIC "-//W3C//DTD XHTML 1.1//EN"
 "http://www.w3.org/TR/xhtml11/DTD/xhtml11.dtd">

<html xmlns="http://www.w3.org/1999/xhtml" xml:lang="en">
 <head>
  <title>Positioning the Color Blocks</title>
   <style type="text/css">
   div {
     position:absolute;
     width:250px;
     height:100px;
     border:5px solid #000;
     color:black;
     font-weight:bold;
     text-align:center;
   }
   div#d1 {
     background-color:red;
     left:0px;
     top:0px;
     z-index:0;
   }
   div#d2 {
     background-color:green;
     left:75px;
     top:25px;
     z-index:3;
   }
   div#d3 {
     background-color:blue;
     left:150px;
     top:50px;
     z-index:2;
   }
   div#d4 {
```

LISTING 10.3 Continued

```
      background-color:yellow;
      left:225px;
      top:75px;
      z-index:1;
    }
  </style>
</head>
<body>
 <div id="d1">DIV #1</div>
 <div id="d2">DIV #2</div>
 <div id="d3">DIV #3</div>
 <div id="d4">DIV #4</div>
</body>
</html>
```

The only change in this code from what you saw in Listing 10.2 is the addition of the z-index property in each of the numbered div style classes. Notice that the first numbered div has a z-index setting of 0, which should make it the lowest element in terms of the z-index, whereas the second div has the highest z-index. Figure 10.6 shows the color blocks page as displayed with this style sheet, which clearly shows how the z-index affects the displayed content and makes it possible to carefully control the overlap of elements.

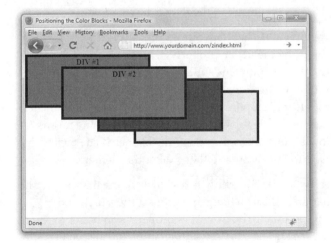

FIGURE 10.6
Using z-index to alter the display of the color blocks.

Although the examples show color blocks that are simple <div> elements, the z-index style property can affect any HTML content, including images.

Managing the Flow of Text

Now that you've seen some examples of placing elements relative to other elements or placing them absolutely, it's time to revisit the flow of content around elements. The conceptual *current line* is an invisible line used to place elements on a page. This line has to do with the flow of elements on a page; it comes into play as elements are arranged next to each other across and down the page. Part of the flow of elements is the flow of text on a page. When you mix text with other elements (such as images), it's important to control how the text flows around those other elements.

You've already seen two of these style properties in Chapter 9, "Working with Margins, Padding, Alignment, and Floating." Following are some style properties that provide you with control over text flow:

- ▶ `float`—Determines how text flows around an element
- ▶ `clear`—Stops the flow of text around an element
- ▶ `overflow`—Controls the overflow of text when an element is too small to contain all the text

The `float` property is used to control how text flows around an element. It can be set to either `left` or `right`. These values determine where to position an element with respect to flowing text. So, setting an image's `float` property to `left` positions the image to the left of flowing text.

As you learned in the previous chapter, you can prevent text from flowing next to an element by using the `clear` property, which can be set to `none`, `left`, `right`, or `both`. The default value for the clear property is `none`, indicating that text is to flow with no special considerations for the element. The `left` value causes text to stop flowing around an element until the left side of the page is free of the element. Likewise, the `right` value means that text is not to flow around the right side of the element. The `both` value indicates that text isn't to flow around either side of the element.

The `overflow` property handles overflow text, which is text that doesn't fit within its rectangular area; this can happen if you set the `width` and `height` of an element too small. The `overflow` property can be set to `visible`, `hidden`, or `scroll`. The `visible` setting automatically enlarges the element so that the overflow text will fit within it; this is the default setting for the property. The `hidden` value leaves the element the same size, allowing the overflow text to remain hidden from view. Perhaps the most interesting value is `scroll`, which adds scrollbars to the element so that you can move around and see the text.

Summary

This chapter began with an important discussion about the CSS box model and how to calculate the width and height of elements when taking margins, padding, and borders into consideration. The chapter continued by tackling absolute positioning of elements, and then you learned about positioning using `z-index`. You also discovered a few nifty little style properties that enable you to control the flow of text on a page.

This chapter was brief, but chock full of fundamental information about controlling the design of your site. It is worth re-reading and working through the examples so that you have a good foundation for your work.

Q&A

Q. **How would I determine when to use relative positioning and when to use absolute positioning?**

A. Although there are no set guidelines regarding the use of relative versus absolute positioning, the general idea is that absolute positioning is required only when you want to exert a finer degree of control over how content is positioned. This has to do with the fact that absolute positioning enables you to position content down to the exact pixel, whereas relative positioning is much less predictable in terms of how it positions content. This isn't to say that relative positioning can't do a good job of positioning elements on a page; it just means that absolute positioning is more exact. Of course, this also makes absolute positioning potentially more susceptible to changes in screen size, which you can't really control.

Q. **If I don't specify the z-index of two elements that overlap each other, how do I know which element will appear on top?**

A. If the z-index property isn't set for overlapping elements, the element appearing later in the web page will appear on top. The easy way to remember this is to think of a web browser drawing each element on a page as it reads it from the HTML document; elements read later in the document are drawn on top of those that were read earlier.

Workshop

The workshop contains quiz questions and exercises to help you solidify your understanding of the material covered. Try to answer all questions before looking at the "Answers" section that follows.

Quiz

1. What's the difference between relative positioning and absolute positioning?

2. Which CSS style property controls the manner in which elements overlap each other?

3. What HTML code could you use to display the words "Where would you like to" starting exactly at the upper-left corner of the browser window and displays the words "GO TODAY?" in large type exactly 80 pixels down and 20 pixels to the left of the corner?

Answers

1. In relative positioning, content is displayed according to the flow of a page, with each element physically appearing after the element preceding it in the HTML code. Absolute positioning, on the other hand, allows you to set the exact position of content on a page.

2. The z-index style property is used to control the manner in which elements overlap each other.

3. You could use the following:

```
<span style="position:absolute;left:0px;top:0px">
Where would you like to</span>
<h1 style="position:absolute;left:80px;top:20px">GO TODAY?</h1>
```

Exercises

▶ Practice working with the intricacies of the CSS box model by creating a series of elements with different margins, padding, and borders and see how these properties affect their height and width.

▶ Find a group of images that you like and use absolute positioning and maybe even some z-index values to arrange them in a sort of gallery. Try to place your images so they form a design (such as a square, triangle, or circle).

CHAPTER 11

Using CSS to Do More with Lists, Text, and Navigation

In Chapter 5, "Working with Fonts, Text Blocks, and Lists," you were introduced to three types of HTML lists, and in Chapter 9, "Working with Margins, Padding, Alignment, and Floating," you learned about margins, padding, and alignment of elements. In this chapter, you will learn how margins, padding, and alignment styles can be applied to different types of HTML lists, helping you produce some powerful design elements purely in HTML and CSS.

Specifically, you will learn how to modify the appearance of list elements—beyond the use of the `list-style-type` property that you learned in Chapter 5—and how to use a CSS-styled list to replace the client-side image maps you learned about in Chapter 8, "Working with Colors, Images, and Multimedia." You will put into practice many of the CSS styles you've learned thus far, and the knowledge you will gain in this chapter will lead directly into using lists for more than just simply presenting a bulleted or numbered set of items. You will learn a few of the many ways to use lists as vertical or horizontal navigation, including how to use lists to create drop-down menus.

The methods explained in this chapter represent a very small subset of the numerous and varied navigation methods you can create using lists. However, the concepts are all similar; different results come from your own creativity and application of these basic concepts. To help you get your creative juices flowing, I will provide pointers to other examples of CSS-based navigation at the end of this chapter.

WHAT YOU'LL LEARN IN THIS CHAPTER:

▶ How the CSS box model affects lists

▶ How to customize the list item indicator

▶ How to use list items and CSS to create an image map

▶ How navigation lists differ from regular lists

▶ How to create vertical navigation with CSS

▶ How to create horizontal navigation with CSS

HTML List Refresher

As you learned in Chapter 5, there are three basic types of HTML lists. Each presents content in a slightly different way based on its type and the context:

▶ The *ordered list* is an indented list that displays numbers or letters before each list item. The ordered list is surrounded by <ol> and </ol> tags and list items are enclosed in the <li></li> tag pair. This list type is often used to display numbered steps or levels of content.

▶ The *unordered list* is an indented list that displays a bullet or other symbol before each list item. The unordered list is surrounded by <ul> and </ul> tags, and list items are enclosed in the <li></li> tag pair. This list type is often used to provide a visual cue to show that brief, yet specific, bits of information will follow.

▶ A *definition list* is often used to display terms and their meanings, thereby providing information hierarchy within the context of the list itself—much like the ordered list but without the numbering. The definition list is surrounded by <dl> and </dl> tags with <dt> and </dt> tags enclosing the term, and <dd> and </dd> tags enclosing the definitions.

When the content warrants it, you can nest your ordered and unordered — or place lists within other lists. Nested lists produce a content hierarchy, so reserve their use for when your content actually has a hierarchy you want to display (such as content outlines or tables of content). Or, as you will learn later in this chapter, you can use nested lists when your site navigation contains sub-navigational elements.

NOTE

Some older browsers handle margins and padding differently, especially around lists and list items. However, at the time of writing, the HTML and CSS in this and other chapters in this book are displayed identically in current versions of the major web browsers (Apple Safari, Google Chrome, Microsoft Internet Explorer, Mozilla Firefox, and Opera). Of course, you should still review your web content in all browsers before you publish it online, but the need for "hacking" style sheets to accommodate the rendering idiosyncrasies of browsers is fading away.

How the CSS Box Model Affects Lists

Specific list-related styles include list-style-image (for placement of an image as a list-item marker), list-style-position (indicating where to place the list-item marker), and list-style-type (the type of list-item marker itself). But although these styles control the structure of the list and list items, you can use margin, padding, color, and background-color styles to achieve even more specific displays with your lists.

In Chapter 9, you learned that every element has some padding between the content and the border of the element; you also learned there is a margin between the border of the element and any other content. This is true for lists, and when you are styling lists, you must remember that a "list" is actually made up of two elements: the parent list element type (<ul> or <ol>) and the individual list items themselves. Each of these elements has margins and padding that can be affected by a style sheet.

The examples in this chapter show you how different CSS styles affect the visual display of HTML lists and list items. Keep these basic differences in mind as you practice working with lists in this chapter, and you will be able to use lists to achieve advanced visual effects within site navigation.

Listing 11.1 creates a basic list containing three items. In this listing, the unordered list itself (the <ul>) is given a blue background, a black border, and a specific width of 100 pixels, as shown in Figure 11.1. The list items (the individual <li>) have a gray background and a yellow border. The list item text and indicators (the bullet) are black.

LISTING 11.1   Creating a Basic List with Color and Border Styles

```
<?xml version="1.0" encoding="UTF-8"?>
<!DOCTYPE html PUBLIC "-//W3C//DTD XHTML 1.1//EN"
  "http://www.w3.org/TR/xhtml11/DTD/xhtml11.dtd">

<html xmlns="http://www.w3.org/1999/xhtml" xml:lang="en">
  <head>
    <title>List Test</title>
    <style type="text/css">
      ul {
          background-color: #6666ff;
          border: 1px solid #000000;
          width:100px;
      }
      li {
          background-color: #cccccc;
          border: 1px solid #ffff00;
      }
    </style>
  </head>

  <body>
    <h1>List Test</h1>
    <ul>
      <li>Item #1</li>
      <li>Item #2</li>
      <li>Item #3</li>
    </ul>
  </body>
</html>
```

NOTE

You can test the default padding-left value as displayed by different browsers by creating a simple test file such as that shown in Listing 11.1. Then, add padding-left: 40px; to the declaration for the ul selector in the style sheet. If you reload the page and the display does not change, then you know that your test browser uses 40 pixels as a default value for padding-left.

FIGURE 11.1
Styling the list and list items with colors and borders.

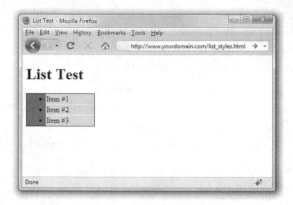

As shown in Figure 11.1, the `<ul>` creates a box in which the individual list items are placed. In this example, the entirety of the box has a blue background. But also note that the individual list items—in this example, they use a gray background and a yellow border—do not extend to the left edge of the box created by the `<ul>`.

This is because browsers automatically add a certain amount of padding to the left side of the `<ul>`. Browsers don't add padding to the margin, as that would appear around the outside of the box. They add padding inside the box and only on the left side. That padding value is approximately 40 pixels.

The default left-side padding value remains the same regardless of the type of list. If you add the following line to the style sheet, creating a list with no item indicators, you will find the padding remains the same (see Figure 11.2):

```
list-style-type: none;
```

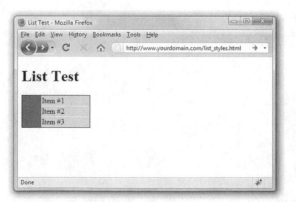

When you are creating a page layout that includes lists of any type, play around with padding to place the items "just so" on the page. Similarly, just because there is no default margin associated with lists doesn't mean you can't assign some to the display; adding `margin` values to the declaration for the `ul` selector will provide additional layout control.

But remember, so far we've worked with only the list definition itself; we haven't worked with the application of styles to the individual list items. In Figures 11.1 and 11.2, the gray background and yellow border of the list item shows no default padding or margin. Figure 11.3 shows the different effects created by applying padding or margin values to list items rather than the overall list "box" itself.

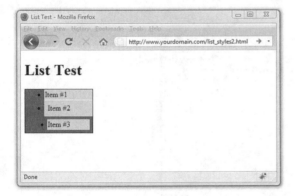

FIGURE 11.3
Different values affect the padding and margins on list items.

The first list item is the base item with no padding or margin applied to it. However, the second list item uses `style="padding: 6px;"`, and you can see the six pixels of padding on all sides (between the content and the yellow border surrounding the element). Note that the placement of the bullet remains the same as the first list item. The third list item uses `style="margin: 6px;"` to apply six pixels of margin around the list item; this margin allows the blue background of the `<ul>` to show through.

Placing List Item Indicators

All this talk of margins and padding raises other issues: the control of list item indicators (when used) and how text should wrap around them (or not). The default value of the `list-style-position` property is "outside"— this placement means the bullets, numbers, or other indicators are kept to the left of the text, outside of the box created by the `<li></li>` tag pair.

When text wraps within the list item, it wraps within that box and remains flush left with the left border of element.

But when the value of list-style-position is "inside," the indicators are inside the box created by the <li></li> tag pair. Not only are the list item indicators then indented further (they essentially become part of the text), the text wraps beneath each item indicator.

An example of both outside and inside list-style-positions is shown in Figure 11.4. The only changes between Listing 11.1 and the code used to produce the example shown in Figure 11.4 (not including the filler text added to "Item #2" and "Item #3") is that the second list item contains style="list-style-position: outside;", and the third list item contains style="list-style-position: inside;".

FIGURE 11.4
The difference between outside and inside values for list-style-position.

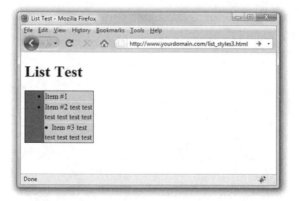

The additional filler text used for the second list item shows how the text wraps when the width of the list is defined as a value that is too narrow to display all on one line. The same result would have been achieved without using style="list-style-position: outside;" because that is the default value of list-style-position without any explicit statement in the code.

However, you can clearly see the difference when the "inside" position is used. In the third list item, the bullet and the text are both within the gray area bordered by yellow—the list item itself. Margins and padding affect list items differently when the value of list-style-position is inside (see Figure 11.5).

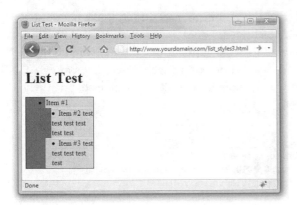

FIGURE 11.5
Margin and padding changes the display of items using the inside `list-style-position`.

In Figure 11.5, both the second and third list items have a `list-style-position` value of `inside`. However, the second list item has a `margin-left` value of 12 pixels, and the third list item has a `padding-left` value of 12 pixels. Although both content blocks (list indicator plus the text) show text wrapped around the bullet, and the placement of these blocks within the gray area defining the list item is the same, the affected area is the list item within the list itself.

As you would expect, the list item with the `margin-left` value of 12 pixels displays 12 pixels of red showing through the transparent margin surrounding the list item. Similarly, the list item with the `padding-left` value of 12 pixels displays 12 pixels of gray background (of the list item) before the content begins. Padding is within the element; margin is outside the element.

By understanding the way margins and padding affect both list items and the list in which they appear, you should be able to create navigation elements in your website that are pure CSS and do not rely on external images. Later in this chapter, you will learn how to create both vertical and horizontal navigation menus as well as menu drop-downs.

Creating Image Maps with List Items and CSS

In Chapter 8, you learned how to create client-side image maps using the `<map/>` tag in HTML. Image maps enable you to define an area of an image and assign a link to that area (rather than having to slice an image into pieces, apply links to individual pieces, and stitch the image back together in HTML). However, you can also create an image map purely out of valid XHTML and CSS.

NOTE

For links to several tutorials geared toward creating XHTML and CSS image maps, visit http://designreviver.com/tutorials/css-image-map-techniques-and-tutorials/. The levels of interactivity in these tutorials differ, and some might introduce client-side coding outside of the scope of this book, but the explanations are thorough.

The code in Listing 11.2 produces an image map similar to the one shown in Figure 11.6. (The code in Listing 11.2 does not produce the red borders shown in the figure. The borders were added to the figure to highlight the defined areas.) When the code is rendered in a web browser, it simply looks like a web page with an image placed in it. The actions happen when your mouse hovers over a "hot" area.

LISTING 11.2   Creating an Image Map Using CSS

```
<?xml version="1.0" encoding="UTF-8"?>
<!DOCTYPE html PUBLIC "-//W3C//DTD XHTML 1.1//EN"
  "http://www.w3.org/TR/xhtml11/DTD/xhtml11.dtd">

<html xmlns="http://www.w3.org/1999/xhtml" xml:lang="en">
  <head>
    <title>CSS Image Map Example</title>
    <style type="text/css">
    #theImg {
       width:500px;
       height:375px;
       background:url(tea_shipment.jpg) no-repeat;
       position:relative;
       border: 1px solid #000000;
    }
    #theImg ul {
       margin:0px;
       padding:0px;
       list-style:none;
    }
    #theImg a {
       position:absolute;
       text-indent: -1000em;
    }
    #theImg a:hover {
       border: 1px solid #ffffff;
    }
    #ss a {
       top:0px;
       left:5px;
       width:80px;
       height:225px;
    }
    #gn a {
       top:226px;
       left:15px;
       width:70px;
       height:110px;
    }
    #ib a {
       top:225px;
       left:85px;
```

LISTING 11.2   Continued

```
        width:60px;
        height:90px;
    }
    #iTEA1 a {
        top:100px;
        left:320px;
        width:178px;
        height:125px;
    }
    #iTEA2 a {
        top:225px;
        left:375px;
        width:123px;
        height:115px;
    }
    </style>
  </head>
<body>
    <div id="theImg">
    <ul>
    <li id="ss"><a href="[some URL]"
        title="Sugarshots">Sugarshots</a></li>
    <li id="gn"><a href="[some URL]"
        title="Golden Needle">Golden Needle</a></li>
    <li id="ib"><a href="[some URL]"
        title="Irish Breakfast">Irish Breakfast</a></li>
    <li id="iTEA1"><a href="[some URL]"
        title="IngenuiTEA">IngenuiTEA</a></li>
    <li id="iTEA2"><a href="[some URL]"
        title="IngenuiTEA">IngenuiTEA</a></li>
    </ul>
  </div>
  </body>
</html>
```

As shown in Listing 11.2, the style sheet has quite a few entries but the actual HTML is quite short. List items are used to create five distinct clickable areas; those "areas" are list items given a specific height and width and placed over an image that sits in the background. If the image is removed from the background of the <div> that surrounds the list, the list items still exist and are still clickable.

Let's walk through the style sheet so that you understand the pieces that make up this XHTML and CSS image map, which is—at its most basic level—just a list of links.

FIGURE 11.6
CSS enables you to define
hotspots in an image map.

The list of links is enclosed in a `<div>` named `"theImg"`. In the style sheet, this `<div>` is defined as block element that is 500 pixels wide, 375 pixels high, and with a 1-pixel solid black border. The background of this element is an image named tea_shipment.jpg that is placed in one position and does not repeat. The next bit of HTML that you see is the beginning of the unordered list (`<ul>`). In the style sheet, this unordered list is given margin and padding values of zero pixels all around and a `list-style` of `none`—list items will not be preceded by any icon.

The list item text itself never appears to the user because of this trick in the style sheet entry for all `<a>` tags within the `<div>`:

```
text-indent: -1000em;
```

By indenting the text *negative* 1000 ems, you can be assured that the text will never appear. It does exist, but it exists in a nonviewable area 1000 ems to the left of the browser window. In other words, if you raise your left hand and place it to the side of your computer monitor, `text-indent:-1000em` places the text somewhere to the left of your pinky finger. But that's what we want because we don't need to see the text link. We just need an area to be defined as a link so that the user's cursor will change as it does when rolling over any link in a website.

When the user's cursor hovers over a list item containing a link, that list item shows a one-pixel border that is solid white, thanks to this entry in the style sheet:

```
#theImg a:hover {
   border: 1px solid #ffffff;
}
```

The list items themselves are then defined and placed in specific positions based on the areas of the image that are supposed to be the clickable areas. For example, the list item with the "ss" id for "Sugarshots"—the name of the item shown in the figure—has its top-left corner placed zero pixels from the top of the <div> and five pixels in from the left edge of the <div>. This list item is 80 pixels wide and 225 pixels high. Similar style declarations are made for the "#gn", "#ib", "#iTEA1", and "#iTEA2" list items, such that the linked areas associated with those IDs appear in certain positions relative to the image.

How Navigation Lists Differ from Regular Lists

When we talk about using lists to create navigation elements, we really mean using CSS to display content in the way website visitors expect navigation to look—in short, *different* from simple bulleted or numbered lists. Although it is true that a set of navigation elements is essentially a list of links, those links are typically displayed in a way that makes it clear that users should interact with the content:

▶ The user's mouse cursor will change to indicate that the element is clickable.

▶ The area around the element changes appearance when the mouse hovers over it.

▶ The content area is visually set apart from regular text.

Older methods of creating navigation tended to rely on images—such as graphics with beveled edges and the use of contrasting colors for backgrounds and text—plus client-side programming with JavaScript to handle image-swapping based on mouse actions. But using pure CSS to create navigation from list elements produces a more usable, flexible, and search-engine friendly display that is accessible by users using all manner and sorts of devices.

Regardless of the layout of your navigational elements—horizontal or vertical—this chapter discusses two levels of navigation: primary and secondary. *Primary navigation* takes users to the introductory pages of main sections of your site; *secondary navigation* reflects those pages within a certain section.

Creating Vertical Navigation with CSS

Depending on your site architecture—both the display template you have created and the manner in which you have categorized the information in the site—you might find yourself using vertical navigation for either primary navigation or secondary navigation.

For example, suppose you have created a website for your company and the primary sections are About Us, Products, Support, and Press. Within the primary About Us section, you might have several other pages, such as Mission, History, Executive Team, and Contact Us—these other pages are the secondary navigation within the primary About Us section.

Listing 11.3 sets up a basic secondary page with vertical navigation in the side of the page and content in the middle of the page. The links in the side and the links in the content area of the page are basic HTML list elements.

This listing and the example shown in Figure 11.7 provides a starting point for showing you how CSS enables you to transform two similar HTML structures into two different visual displays (and thus two different contexts).

LISTING 11.3   Basic Page with Vertical Navigation in a List

```
<?xml version="1.0" encoding="UTF-8"?>
<!DOCTYPE html PUBLIC "-//W3C//DTD XHTML 1.1//EN"
  "http://www.w3.org/TR/xhtml11/DTD/xhtml11.dtd">

<html xmlns="http://www.w3.org/1999/xhtml" xml:lang="en">
  <head>
    <title>About Us</title>
    <style type="text/css">
      body {
          font: 12pt Verdana, Arial, Georgia, sans-serif;
      }
      #nav {
          width:150px;
          float:left;
          margin-top:12px;
          margin-right:18px;
      }
      #content {
          width:550px;
          float:left;
      }
```

LISTING 11.3   continued

```
    </style>
  </head>

  <body>
    <div id="nav">
    <ul>
      <li><a href="#">Mission</a></li>
      <li><a href="#">History</a></li>
      <li><a href="#">Executive Team</a></li>
      <li><a href="#">Contact Us</a></li>
    </ul>
    </div>
    <div id="content">
      <h1>About Us</h1>
      <p>On the introductory pages of main sections, it can be useful
      to repeat the secondary navigation and provide more context,
      such as:</p>
      <ul>
      <li><a href="#">Mission</a>: Learn more about our corporate
      mission and philanthropic efforts.</li>
      <li><a href="#">History</a>: Read about our corporate history
      and learn how we grew to become the largest widget maker
      in the country.</li>
      <li><a href="#">Executive Team</a>: Our team of executives makes
      the company run like a well-oiled machine (also useful for
      making widgets).</li>
      <li><a href="#">Contact Us</a>: Here you can find multiple
      methods for contacting us (and we really do care what you
      have to say).</li>
      </ul>
    </div>
  </body>
</html>
```

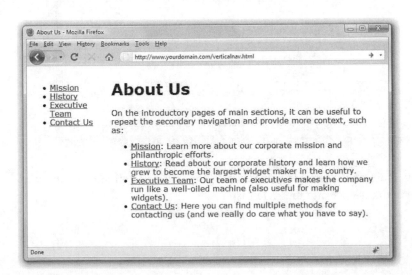

FIGURE 11.7
The starting point: unstyled list navigation.

The contents of this page are set up in two <div> elements that sit next to each other: one is given an id value of nav and the other is given an id value of content. The only styles assigned to anything in this basic page are the width, margin, and float values associated with each <div>. No styles have been applied to the list elements.

To differentiate between the links present in the list in the content area and the links present in the list in the side navigation, add the following styles to the style sheet:

```
#nav a {
   text-decoration: none;
}
#content a {
   text-decoration: none;
   font-weight: bold;
 }
```

These styles simply say that all <a> links in the <div> with the id of nav have no underline, and all <a> links in the <div> with the id of content have no underline and are bold. The difference is shown in Figure 11.8.

FIGURE 11.8
Differentiating the list elements using CSS.

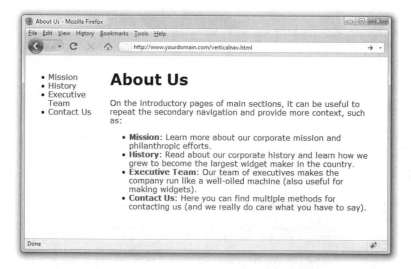

But to really make the side navigation list look like something special, you have to dig deeper into the style sheet.

Styling the Single-Level Vertical Navigation

The goal with this particular set of navigation elements is simply to present them as a block of links without bullets and with background and text colors that change depending on their link state (regular link, visited link, hovering over the link, or activated link). The first step in the process is already complete: separating the navigation from the content. We have done that by putting the navigation in a `<div>` with an `id` of `nav`.

Next, you need to modify the `<ul>` that defines the link within the `nav` `<div>`. Let's take away the list indicator and ensure that there is no extra margin or padding hanging around besides the top margin. That top margin is used to line up the top of the navigation with the top of the "About Us" header text in the content area of the page:

```
#nav ul {
   list-style: none;
   margin: 12px 0px 0px 0px;;
   padding: 0px;
}
```

Because the navigation list items themselves appear as colored areas, give each list item a bottom border so that some visual separation of the content can occur:

```
#nav li {
   border-bottom: 1px solid #ffffff;
}
```

Now on to building the rest of the list items. The idea is that when the list items simply sit there acting as links, they are a special shade of blue with bold white text (although they are a smaller font size than the body text itself). To achieve that, add the following:

```
#nav li a:link, #nav li a:visited {
   font-size: 10pt;
   font-weight: bold;
   display: block;
   padding: 3px 0px 3px 3px;
   background-color: #628794;
   color: #ffffff;
}
```

All the styles used previously should be familiar to you, except perhaps the use of `display: block;` in the style sheet entry. Setting the display property to block ensures that the entire `<li>` element is in play when a user hovers his mouse over it. Figure 11.9 shows the vertical list menu with these new styles applied to it.

FIGURE 11.9
The vertical list is starting to look
like a navigation menu.

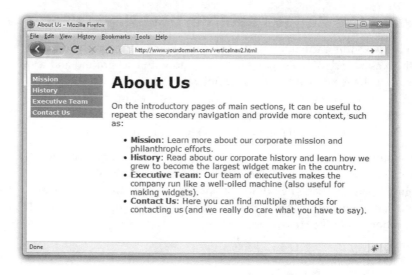

When the user's mouse hovers over a navigational list element, the idea is that some visual change takes place so the user knows the element is clickable. This is akin to how most software menus change color when a user's cursor hovers over the menu items. In this case, we'll change the background color of the list item, and we'll change the text color of the list item; they'll be different from the blue and white shown previously.

```
#nav li a:hover, #nav li a:active {
    font-size: 10pt;
    font-weight: bold;
    display: block;
    padding: 3px 0px 3px 3px;
    background-color: #6cac46;
    color: #000000;
}
```

Figure 11.10 shows the results of all the stylistic work so far. By using a few entries in a style sheet, the simple list has been transformed into a visually differentiated menu.

Styling the Multilevel Vertical Navigation

What if your site architecture calls for another level of navigation that you want your users to see at all times? That is represented by nested lists (which you learned about in previous chapters) and more style sheet entries. In this case, assume that there are four navigation elements under the Executive Team link. In the HTML, modify the list as follows:

```
<ul>
  <li><a href="#">Mission</a></li>
  <li><a href="#">History</a></li>
  <li><a href="#">Executive Team</a>
     <ul>
     <li><a href="#">&raquo; CEO</a>
     <li><a href="#">&raquo; CFO</a>
     <li><a href="#">&raquo; COO</a>
     <li><a href="#">&raquo; Other Minions</a>
     </ul>
  </li>
  <li><a href="#">Contact Us</a></li>
</ul>
```

FIGURE 11.10
The list items now change color when the mouse hovers over them.

This code produces a nested list under the Executive Team link (see Figure 11.11). The » HTML entity produces the right-pointing arrows that are displayed before the text in the new links.

The new items appear as block elements within the list, but the hierarchy of information is not visually represented. To add some sort of visual element that identifies these items as sub-navigational elements attached to the Executive Team link, modify the style sheet again to add some indentation.

But before doing that, modify some of the other style sheet entries as well. In the previous section, we added selectors such as #nav ul and #nav li, which indicate "all <ul> in the <div> called nav" and "all <li> in the <div> called nav," respectively. However, we now have two instances of <ul> and another set of <li> elements with the <div> called nav, all of which we want to appear different from the original set.

FIGURE 11.11
Creating a nested navigation list
(but one that is not yet styled
well).

To ensure both sets of list items are styled appropriately, make sure that
the style sheet selectors clearly indicate the hierarchy of the lists. To do
that, use entries such as #nav ul and #nav ul li for the first level of lists
and #nav ul ul and #nav ul ul li for the second level of lists. Listing
11.4 shows the new version of style sheet entries and HTML that produces
the menu shown in Figure 11.12.

LISTING 11.4   Multilevel Vertical Navigation in a List

```
<?xml version="1.0" encoding="UTF-8"?>
<!DOCTYPE html PUBLIC "-//W3C//DTD XHTML 1.1//EN"
  "http://www.w3.org/TR/xhtml11/DTD/xhtml11.dtd">

<html xmlns="http://www.w3.org/1999/xhtml" xml:lang="en">
  <head>
    <title>About Us</title>
    <style type="text/css">
      body {
          font: 12pt Verdana, Arial, Georgia, sans-serif;
      }
      #nav {
          width:150px;
          float:left;
          margin-top:12px;
          margin-right:18px;
      }
      #content {
          width:550px;
          float:left;
      }
      #nav a {
```

LISTING 11.4   Continued

```css
    text-decoration: none;
}
#content a {
    text-decoration: none;
    font-weight: bold;
}
#nav ul {
    list-style: none;
    margin: 12px 0px 0px 0px;
    padding: 0px;
}
#nav ul li {
    border-bottom: 1px solid #ffffff;
}
#nav ul li a:link, #nav ul li a:visited {
    font-size: 10pt;
    font-weight: bold;
    display: block;
    padding: 3px 0px 3px 3px;
    background-color: #628794;
    color: #ffffff;
}
#nav ul li a:hover, #nav ul li a:active {
    font-size: 10pt;
    font-weight: bold;
    display: block;
    padding: 3px 0px 3px 3px;
    background-color: #c6a648;
    color: #000000;
}
#nav ul ul {
    margin: 0px;
    padding: 0px;
}
#nav ul ul li {
    border-bottom: none;
}
#nav ul ul li a:link, #nav ul ul li a:visited {
    font-size: 8pt;
    font-weight: bold;
    display: block;
    padding: 3px 0px 3px 18px;
    background-color: #628794;
    color: #ffffff;
}
#nav ul ul li a:hover, #nav ul ul li a:active {
    font-size: 8pt;
    font-weight: bold;
    display: block;
    padding: 3px 0px 3px 18px;
    background-color: #c6a648;
```

LISTING 11.4   Continued

```
          color: #000000;
      }
    </style>
  </head>

  <body>
    <div id="nav">
    <ul>
      <li><a href="#">Mission</a></li>
      <li><a href="#">History</a></li>
      <li><a href="#">Executive Team</a>
          <ul>
          <li><a href="#">&raquo; CEO</a></li>
          <li><a href="#">&raquo; CFO</a></li>
          <li><a href="#">&raquo; COO</a></li>
          <li><a href="#">&raquo; Other Minions</a></li>
          </ul>
      </li>
      <li><a href="#">Contact Us</a></li>
    </ul>
    </div>
    <div id="content">
      <h1>About Us</h1>
      <p>On the introductory pages of main sections, it can be useful
      to repeat the secondary navigation and provide more context,
      such as:</p>
      <ul>
      <li><a href="#">Mission</a>: Learn more about our corporate
      mission and philanthropic efforts.</li>
      <li><a href="#">History</a>: Read about our corporate history
      and learn how we grew to become the largest widget maker
      in the country.</li>
      <li><a href="#">Executive Team</a>: Our team of executives makes
      the company run like a well-oiled machine (also useful for
      making widgets).</li>
      <li><a href="#">Contact Us</a>: Here you can find multiple
      methods for contacting us (and we really do care what you
      have to say.</li>
      </ul>
    </div>
  </body>
</html>
```

The different ways of styling vertical navigation are limited only by your own creativity. You can use colors, margins, padding, background images, and any other valid CSS to produce vertical navigation that is quite flexible and easily modified. If you type **CSS vertical navigation** in your search engine, you will find thousands of examples—and they are all based on the simple principles you've learned in this chapter.

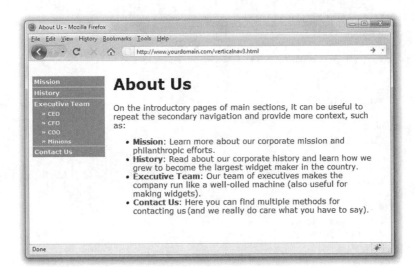

FIGURE 11.12
Creating two levels of vertical navigation using CSS.

Creating Horizontal Navigation with CSS

The lessons on navigation began with vertical navigation because the concept of converting a list into navigation is easier to grasp when the navigation still looks like a list of items that you might write vertically on a piece of paper, like a grocery list. When creating horizontal navigation, you still use HTML list elements but instead of a vertical display achieved by using the `inline` value of the `display` property for both the `<ul>` and the `<li>`, use the `block` value of the `display` property instead. It really is as simple as that.

Listing 11.5 shows a starting point for a page featuring horizontal navigation. The page contains two main `<div>` elements: one for the header and one for the content. The header `<div>` contains a logo `<div>` and a navigation `<div>` floated next to each other. The list that appears in the navigation `<div>` has a display property value of inline for both the list and the list items. You can see these elements and their placement in Figure 11.13.

LISTING 11.5   Basic Horizontal Navigation from a List

```
<?xml version="1.0" encoding="UTF-8"?>
<!DOCTYPE html PUBLIC "-//W3C//DTD XHTML 1.1//EN"
  "http://www.w3.org/TR/xhtml11/DTD/xhtml11.dtd">

<html xmlns="http://www.w3.org/1999/xhtml" xml:lang="en">
  <head>
    <title>ACME Widgets LLC</title>
```

LISTING 11.5   Continued

```
<style type="text/css">
  body {
    font: 12pt Verdana, Arial, Georgia, sans-serif;
  }
  #header {
    width: auto;
  }
  #logo {
    float:left;
  }
  #nav {
    float:left;
  }
  #nav ul {
    list-style: none;
    display: inline;
  }
  #nav li {
    display: inline;
  }
  #content {
    width: auto;
    float: left;
    clear: left;
  }
  #content a {
    text-decoration: none;
    font-weight: bold;
  }
</style>
</head>
<body>
  <div id="header">
    <div id="logo">
      <img src="acmewidgets.jpg" alt="ACME Widgets LLC" />
    </div>
    <div id="nav">
      <ul>
      <li><a href="#">About Us</a></li>
      <li><a href="#">Products</a></li>
      <li><a href="#">Support</a></li>
      <li><a href="#">Press</a></li>
      </ul>
    </div>
  </div>
  <div id="content">
    <p><strong>ACME Widgets LLC</strong> is the greatest widget-maker
    in all the land.</p>
    <p>Don't believe us? Read on...</p>
    <ul>
    <li><a href="#">About Us</a>: We are pretty great.</li>
```

LISTING 11.5   Continued

```
        <li><a href="#">Products</a>: Our products are the best.</li>
        <li><a href="#">Support</a>: It is unlikely you will need support,
        but we provide it anyway.</li>
        <li><a href="#">Press</a>: Read what others are saying (about how
        great we are).</li>
        </ul>
    </div>
  </body>
</html>
```

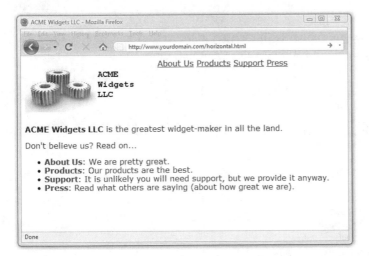

FIGURE 11.13
Creating functional—but not necessarily beautiful—horizontal navigation using inline list elements.

Modifying the display of this list occurs purely through CSS; the structure of the content within the HTML itself is already set. To achieve the desired display, use the following CSS. First, modify the <div> with the id of nav to be a particular width, display a background color and border, and use a top margin of 85 pixels (so that it displays near the bottom of the logo).

```
#nav {
    float:left;
    margin: 85px 0px 0px 0px;
    width: 400px;
    background-color: #628794;
    border: 1px solid black;
}
```

The definition for the <ul> remains the same as in Listing 11.5, except for the changes in margin and padding:

```
#nav ul {
    margin: 0px;
```

```
    padding: 0px;
    list-style: none;
    display: inline;
}
```

The definition for the `<li>` remains the same as in Listing 11.5, except it has been given a line-height value of 1.8em:

```
#nav li {
    display: inline;
    line-height: 1.8em;
}
```

The link styles are similar to those used in the vertical navigation; these entries have different padding values, but the colors and font sizes remain the same:

```
#nav ul li a:link, #nav ul li a:visited {
    font-size: 10pt;
    font-weight: bold;
    text-decoration: none;
    padding: 7px 10px 7px 10px;
    background-color: #628794;
    color: #ffffff;
}
#nav ul li a:hover, #nav ul li a:active {
    font-size: 10pt;
    font-weight: bold;
    text-decoration: none;
    padding: px 10px 7px 10px;
    background-color: #c6a648;
    color: #000000;
}
```

Putting these styles together, you produce the display shown in Figure 11.14.

When the user rolls over the navigation elements, the background and text colors change in the same way they did when the user hovered her mouse over the vertical navigation menu. Also, just as you did with the vertical navigation menu, you can use nested lists to produce drop-down functionality in your horizontal menu. Try it yourself!

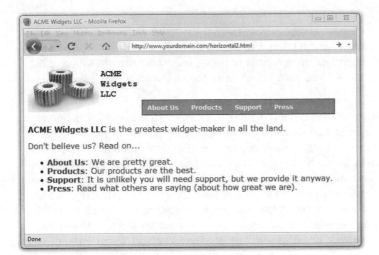

FIGURE 11.14
Creating horizontal navigation with
some style.

Summary

This chapter began with examples of how lists and list elements are affected by padding and margin styles. You first learned about the default padding associated with lists and how to control that padding. Next, you learned how to modify padding and margin values and how to place the list item indicator either inside or outside the list item so you could begin to think about how styles and lists can affect your overall site design. Finally, you learned how to leverage lists and list elements to create a pure XHTML and CSS image map, thus reducing the need for slicing up linked images or using the <map/> tag.

After learning to "think outside the (list) box," if you will, you learned how to use unordered lists to produce horizontal or vertical navigation within your website. By using CSS instead of graphics, you will have more flexibility in both the display and maintenance of your site. Throughout this chapter you learned that with a few entries in your style sheet, you can turn plain underlined text links into areas with borders, background colors, and other text styles. Additionally, you learned how to present nested lists within menus.

Q&A

Q. There are an awful lot of web pages that talk about the "box model hack" regarding margins and padding, especially around lists and list elements. Are you sure I don't have to use a hack?

A. At the beginning of this chapter, you learned that the HTML and CSS in this chapter (and others) all look the same in the current versions of the major web browsers. This is the product of several years of web developers having to do code hacks and other tricks before modern browsers began handling things according to CSS specifications rather than their own idiosyncrasies. Additionally, there is a growing movement to rid Internet users of the *very* old web browsers that necessitated most of these hacks in the first place. So, although I wouldn't necessarily advise you to design *only* for the current versions of the major web browsers, I also wouldn't recommend that you spend a ton of time implementing hacks for the older versions of browsers—which are used by less than 5% of the Internet population. You should continue to write solid code that validates and adheres to design principles, test your pages in a suite of browsers that best reflects your audience, and release your site to the world.

Q. The CSS image map seems like a lot of work. Is the `<map/>` tag so bad?

A. The `<map/>` tag isn't at all bad and is valid in both XHTML and HTML5. The determination of coordinates used in client-side image maps can be difficult, however, especially without graphics software or software intended for the creation of client-side image maps. The CSS version gives you more options for defining and displaying clickable areas, only one of which you've seen here.

Q. Can I use graphics in the navigation menus as a custom list indicator?

A. Yes. You can use graphics within the HTML text of the list item or as background images within the `<li>` element. You can style your navigation elements just as you style any other list element. The only differences between an HTML unordered list and a CSS-based horizontal or vertical navigation list is that you are calling it that, and you are using the unordered list for a specific purpose outside of the body of the text. Along with that, you then style the list to show the user that it is indeed something different—and you can do that with small graphics to accentuate your lists.

Q. Where can I find more examples of what I can do with lists?

A. The last time I checked, typing **CSS navigation** in a search engine returned approximately 44 million results. Here are a few starting places:

- ▶ A List Apart's CSS articles at http://www.alistapart.com/topics/code/
- ▶ Maxdesign's CSS Listamatic at http://css.maxdesign.com.au/listamatic/
- ▶ Vitaly Friedman's CSS Showcase at http://www.alvit.de/css-showcase/

Workshop

The workshop contains quiz questions and activities to help you solidify your understanding of the material covered. Try to answer all questions before looking at the "Answers" section that follows.

Quiz

1. What is the difference between the `inside` and `outside` `list-style-position` values? Which is the default value?

2. Does a `list-style` with a value of `none` still produce a structured list, either ordered or unordered?

3. When creating list-based navigation, how many levels of nested lists can you use?

4. When creating a navigation list of any type, can the four pseudoclasses for the a selector have the same values?

Answers

1. The `list-style-position` value of `inside` places the list item indicator inside the block created by the list item. A value of `outside` places the list item indicator outside the block. When `inside`, content wraps beneath the list item indicator. The default value is `outside`.

2. Yes. The only difference is that no list item indicator is present before the content within the list item.

3. Technically, you can nest your lists as deep as you want to. But from a usability standpoint, there is a limit to the number of levels that you would *want* to use to nest your lists. Three levels is typically the limit—more than that and you run the risk of creating a poorly organized site or simply giving the user more options than he needs to see at all times.

4. Sure, but then you run the risk of users not realizing that your beautiful menus are indeed menus (because no visual display would occur for a mouse action).

Exercises

▶ Find an image and try your hand at mapping areas using the technique shown in this chapter. Select an image that has areas where you could use hot spots or clickable areas leading to other web pages on your site or to someone else's site. Then create the HTML and CSS to define the clickable areas and the URLs to which they should lead.

▶ Using the techniques shown for a multilevel vertical list, add subnavigation items to the vertical list created at the end of the chapter.

▶ Look at the numerous examples of CSS-based navigation used in websites and find some tricky-looking actions. Using the View Source function of your web browser, look at the CSS used by these sites and try to implement something similar for yourself.

CHAPTER 12
Creating Fixed or Liquid Layouts

So far you've learned a lot about styling web content, from font sizes and colors to images, block elements, lists, and more. But what has yet to be discussed is a high-level overview of page layout. In general, there are two types of layouts—fixed and liquid—but also a layout that is a combination of the two, wherein some elements are fixed while others are liquid.

In this chapter, you'll first learn about the characteristics of these two types of layouts and see a few examples of websites that use them. At the end of the chapter, you will see a basic template that combines elements of both types of layouts. Ultimately, the type of layout you decide is up to you—it's hard to go wrong as long as your sites follow HTML and CSS standards.

WHAT YOU'LL LEARN IN THIS CHAPTER:

▶ How fixed layouts work
▶ How liquid layouts work
▶ How to create a fixed/ liquid hybrid layout

A good place for examples of liquid layouts is the WordPress Theme Gallery at http://wordpress.org/extend/themes/. WordPress is a blogging platform that is seeing increasing use as a non-blog site management tool. The theme gallery shows hundreds of examples of both fixed-width and liquid layouts which give you an idea, if not all the code, for what you could create. Even though you are not working with a WordPress blog as part of the exercises in this book, the template gallery is a place where you can see and interact with many variations on designs.

Spend some time looking at the WordPress examples and perhaps the CSS Zen Garden as well at http://www.csszengarden.com/. This will help you get a feel for the types of layouts you like without being swayed one way or the other by the content within the layout.

TRY IT YOURSELF ▼

Finding Examples of Layouts You Like

Understanding Fixed Layouts

A *fixed layout*, or fixed-width layout, is just that: a layout in which the body of the page is set to a specific width. That width is typically controlled by a master "wrapper" <div> in which all content is contained. The width property of that <div> would be set in the style attribute or in a style sheet entry if the <div> was given an ID value such as "main" or "wrapper" (although the name is up to you).

When creating a fixed-width layout, the most important decision is determining the minimum screen resolution you want to accommodate. For many years, 800×600 has been the "lowest common denominator" for web designers, resulting in a typical fixed width of approximately 760 pixels. However, since 2007, the number of people using 800×600 screen resolution has been less than 8% (and is currently approximately 4%). Given that, many web designers consider 1024×768 the current minimum screen resolution, leading to fixed-width designs anywhere between 800 and 1000 pixels wide.

A main reason for creating a fixed-width layout is so that you can have precise control over the appearance of the content area. However, if users visit your fixed-width site with smaller or much larger screen resolutions than the resolution you had in mind while you designed it, they might encounter scrollbars (if their resolution is smaller) or a large amount of empty space (if their resolution is greater).

The current ESPN.com home page provides a visual example of this issue; it has a content area fixed at 964 pixels wide. In Figure 12.1, the browser window is a shade under 800 pixels wide. On the right side of the image, important content is cut off (and at the bottom of the figure, a horizontal scrollbar displays in the browser).

However, Figure 12.2 shows how this site looks when the browser window is more than 1400 pixels wide: There is a lot of empty space (or "real estate") on both sides of the main body content.

There is another consideration when creating a fixed-width layout: whether to place the content flush-left or whether to center it. Placing the content flush-left produces extra space on the right side only; centering the content area creates extra space on both sides.

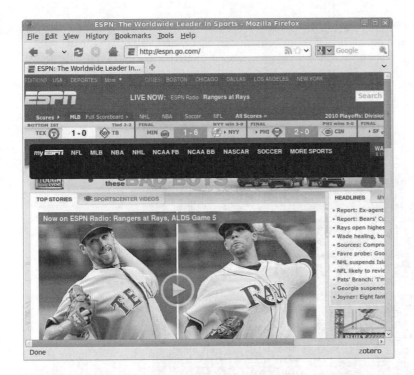

FIGURE 12.1
A fixed-width example with a smaller screen size.

FIGURE 12.2
A fixed-width example with a larger screen size.

Understanding Liquid Layouts

A *liquid layout*—also called a fluid layout—is one in which the body of the page does not use a specified width in pixels, although it might be enclosed in a master "wrapper" `<div>` that uses a percentage width. The idea behind the liquid layout is that it can be perfectly usable and still retain the overall design aesthetic even if the user has a very small or very wide screen.

Three examples of a liquid layout in action are shown in Figures 12.3, 12.4, and 12.5.

FIGURE 12.3
A liquid layout as viewed in a relatively small screen.

FIGURE 12.4
A liquid layout as viewed in a very small screen.

FIGURE 12.5
A liquid layout as viewed in a wide screen.

In Figure 12.3, the browser window is approximately 770 pixels wide. This example shows a reasonable minimum screen width before a horizontal scrollbar appears. In fact, the scrollbar does not appear until the browser is 735 pixels wide. On the other hand, Figure 12.4 shows a very small browser window (545 pixels wide).

In Figure 12.4, you can see a horizontal scrollbar; in the header area of the page content, the logo graphic is beginning to take over the text and appear on top of it. But the bulk of the page is still quite usable. The informational content on the left side of the page is still legible, and it is sharing the available space with the input form on the right side.

Figure 12.5 shows how this same page looks in a very wide screen.

In Figure 12.5, the browser window is approximately 1330 pixels wide. There is plenty of room for all of the content on the page to spread out. This liquid layout is achieved because all the design elements have a percentage width specified (instead of a fixed width). In doing so, the layout makes use of all the available browser real estate.

The liquid layout approach might seem like the best approach at first glance—after all, who wouldn't want to take advantage of all the screen real estate available to them? There is a fine line between taking advantage of space and not allowing the content to breathe, as it were. Too much content is overwhelming; not enough content in an open space is underwhelming.

The pure liquid layout can be quite impressive, but it requires a significant amount of testing to ensure that it is usable in a wide range of browsers at varying screen resolutions. You might not have the time and effort to produce such a design; in that case, a reasonable compromise is the fixed/ liquid hybrid layout.

Creating a Fixed/Liquid Hybrid Layout

A *fixed/liquid hybrid* layout is one that contains elements of both types of layouts. For example, you could have a fluid layout that includes fixed-width content areas either within the body area or as anchor elements (such as a left-side column or as a top navigation strip). You can even create a fixed content area that acts like a frame, as you'll see in Chapter 20, "Using Windows and Frames," in which the fixed content area remains fixed even as users scroll through the content.

Starting with a Basic Layout Structure

In this example, you'll learn to create a template that is liquid but with two fixed-width columns on either side of the main body area (which is a third column, if you think about it, only much wider than the others). The template will also have a delineated header and footer area. Listing 12.1 shows the basic HTML structure for this layout.

LISTING 12.1   Basic Fixed/Liquid Hybrid Layout Structure

```
<?xml version="1.0" encoding="UTF-8"?>
<!DOCTYPE html PUBLIC "-//W3C//DTD XHTML 1.1//EN"
  "http://www.w3.org/TR/xhtml11/DTD/xhtml11.dtd">

<html xmlns="http://www.w3.org/1999/xhtml" xml:lang="en">
  <head>
    <title>Sample Layout</title>
    <link href="layout.css" rel="stylesheet" type="text/css" />
  </head>

  <body>
    <div id="header">HEADER</div>
    <div id="wrapper">
      <div id="content_area">CONTENT</div>
      <div id="left_side">LEFT SIDE</div>
      <div id="right_side">RIGHT SIDE</div>
    </div>
    <div id="footer">FOOTER</div>
  </body>
</html>
```

First, note that the style sheet for this layout is linked to with the <link> tag rather than included in the template. Because a template is used for more than one page, you want to be able to control the display elements of the template in the most organized way possible. This means you need only to change the definitions of those elements in one place—the style sheet.

Next, you'll notice that the basic HTML is just that: extremely basic. And, truth be told, this basic HTML structure can be used for a fixed layout, a liquid layout, or the fixed/liquid hybrid you'll see here because all the actual styling that makes a layout fixed, liquid, or hybrid happens in the style sheet.

What you actually have with the HTML structure in Listing 12.1 is an identification of the content areas you want to include in your site. This planning is crucial to any development; you have to know what you want to include before you even think about the type of layout you are going to use, let alone the specific styles that will be applied to that layout.

At this stage, the layout.css file includes only this entry:

```
body {
    margin:0;
    padding:0;
}
```

If you look at the HTML in Listing 12.1 and say to yourself "but those <div> elements will just stack on top of each other without any styles," you are correct. As shown in Figure 12.6, there is no layout to speak of.

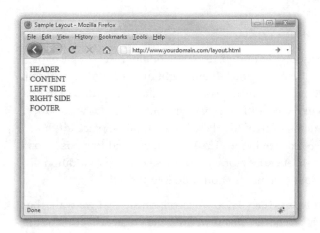

FIGURE 12.6
A basic HTML template with no styles applied to the <div> elements.

Defining Two Columns in a Fixed/Liquid Hybrid Layout

We can start with the easy things first. Because this layout is supposed to be liquid, we know that whatever we put in the header and footer areas will extend the width of the browser window regardless of how narrow or wide the window might be.

Adding the following code to the style sheet gives the header and footer area each a width of 100% and the same background color:

```
#header {
  float: left;
  width: 100%;
  background-color: #7152F4;
}
#footer {
  float: left;
  width: 100%;
  background-color: #7152F4;
}
```

Now things get a little trickier. We have to define the two fixed columns on either side of the page, plus the column in the middle. In the HTML, note that there is a <div> that surrounds all three, and it is called wrapper. This element is defined as follows:

```
#wrapper {
  float: left;
  padding-left: 200px;
  padding-right: 125px;
}
```

The use of the two padding definitions is to essentially reserve space for the two fixed-width columns on the left and right of the page. The column on the left will be 200 pixels wide, the column on the right will be 125 pixels wide, and each will have a different background color. But we also have to position the items relative to where they would be placed if the HTML remained unstyled (see Figure 12.6). This means adding position: relative to the style sheet entries for each of these columns. Additionally, we indicate that the <div> elements should float to the left.

But in the case of the left_side <div>, we also indicate that we want the right-most margin edge to be 200 pixels in from the edge. (This is in addition to the column being defined as 200 pixels wide.) We also want the margin on the left side to be a full negative margin; this will pull it into

place (as you will soon see). The right_side <div> does not include a
value for right but it does include a negative margin on the right side:

```
#left_side {
  position: relative;
  float: left;
  width: 200px;
  background-color: #52f471;
  right: 200px;
  margin-left: -100%;
}
#right_side {
  position: relative;
  float: left;
  width: 125px;
  background-color: #f452d5;
  margin-right: -125px;
}
```

At this point, let's also define the content area so that it has a white background, takes up 100% of the available area, and floats to the left relative
to its position:

```
#content_area {
  position: relative;
  float: left;
  background-color: #ffffff;
  width: 100%;
}
```

At this point, the basic layout will look something like that shown in
Figure 12.7, with the areas clearly delineated.

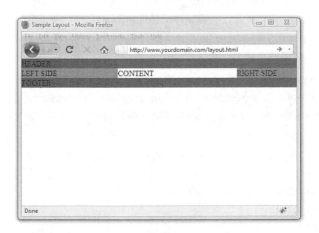

FIGURE 12.7
A basic HTML template after some
styles have been put in place.

However, there's a problem with this template if the window is resized below a certain width. Because the left column is 200 pixels wide, the right column is 125 pixels wide, and you want at least *some* text in the content area, you can imagine this page will break if the window is only 350 to 400 pixels wide. Figure 12.8 shows what happens when the window is resized just under 400 pixels wide (390, to be exact).

FIGURE 12.8
A basic HTML template resized
under 400 pixels: bad!

Setting the Minimum Width of a Layout

Although it is unlikely that users will visit your site with a browser less than 400 pixels wide, the example serves its purpose within the confines of this book's pages. You can extrapolate and apply this information broadly: Even in fixed/liquid hybrid sites, there will be a point at which your layout breaks down unless you do something about it.

That "something" is to use the min-width property. The min-width property sets the minimum width of an element, not including padding, borders, or margins. Figure 12.9 shows what happens when min-width is applied to the <body> element.

Figure 12.9 shows a wee bit of the right column after scrolling to the right, but the point is that the layout does not break when resized below a minimum width. In this case, the minimum width is 525 pixels:

```
body {
  margin: 0;
  padding: 0;
  min-width: 525px;
}
```

FIGURE 12.9
A basic HTML template resized under 400 pixels: better!

The horizontal scrollbar appears in this example because the browser window itself is less than 500 pixels wide. The scrollbar disappears when the window is slightly larger than 525 pixels wide, and it's definitely out of the picture entirely when the browser is approximately 875 pixels wide (see Figure 12.10).

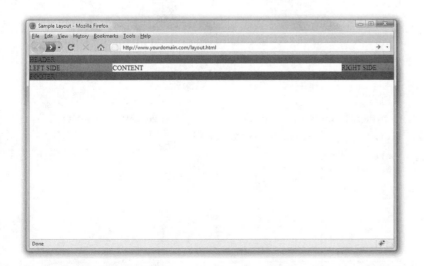

FIGURE 12.10
A basic HTML template when viewed in a browser window wider than 800 pixels.

Handling Column Height in a Fixed/Liquid Hybrid Layout

This example is all well and good except for one problem: It has no content. When content is added to the various elements, more problems arise. As shown in Figure 12.11, the columns become as tall as necessary for the content they contain.

FIGURE 12.11
Columns are only as tall as their contents.

Because you cannot count on a user's browser being a specific height, or that the content will always be the same length, you might think this poses a problem with the fixed/liquid hybrid layout. Not so. If you think a little outside the box, you can apply a few more styles that will bring all the pieces together.

First, add the following declarations in the style sheet entries for the left_side, right_side, and content_area IDs:

```
margin-bottom: -2000px;
padding-bottom: 2000px;
```

These declarations add a ridiculous amount of padding and assign a ridiculously large margin to the bottom of all three elements. You must also add position:relative to the footer ID in the style sheet so that it is visible despite this padding.

At this point, the page looks like Figure 12.12—still not what we want, but closer.

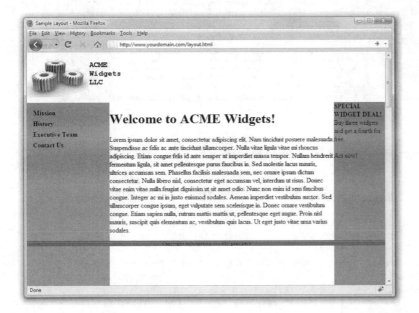

FIGURE 12.12
Color fields are now visible despite the amount of content in the columns.

To clip off all that extra color, add the following to the style sheet for the wrapper ID:

```
overflow: hidden;
```

Figure 12.13 shows the final result: a fixed-width/liquid hybrid layout with the necessary column spacing.

The full HTML code can be seen in Listing 12.2, and the final style sheet is shown in Listing 12.3.

FIGURE 12.13
Congratulations! It's a fixed-width/liquid hybrid layout.

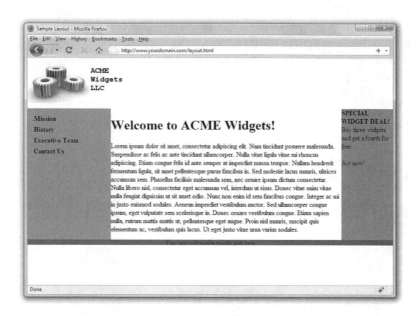

LISTING 12.2   Basic Fixed/Liquid Hybrid Layout Structure (with Content)

```
<?xml version="1.0" encoding="UTF-8"?>
<!DOCTYPE html PUBLIC "-//W3C//DTD XHTML 1.1//EN"
  "http://www.w3.org/TR/xhtml11/DTD/xhtml11.dtd">

<html xmlns="http://www.w3.org/1999/xhtml" xml:lang="en">
  <head>
    <title>Sample Layout</title>
    <link href="layout.css" rel="stylesheet" type="text/css" />
  </head>

  <body>
    <div id="header"><img src="acmewidgets.jpg" alt="ACME Widgets
      LLC"/></div>
    <div id="wrapper">
      <div id="content_area">
        <h1>Welcome to ACME Widgets!</h1>
        <p>Lorem ipsum dolor sit amet, consectetur adipiscing elit.
        Nam tincidunt posuere malesuada. Suspendisse ac felis ac ante
        tincidunt ullamcorper. Nulla vitae ligula vitae mi rhoncus
        adipiscing. Etiam congue felis id ante semper at imperdiet
        massa tempor. Nullam hendrerit fermentum ligula, sit amet
        pellentesque purus faucibus in. Sed molestie lacus mauris,
        ultrices accumsan sem. Phasellus facilisis malesuada sem, nec
        ornare ipsum dictum consectetur. Nulla libero nisl,
        consectetur eget accumsan vel, interdum ut risus. Donec
        vitae enim vitae nulla feugiat dignissim ut sit amet odio.
        Nunc non enim id sem faucibus congue. Integer ac mi in justo
        euismod sodales. Aenean imperdiet vestibulum auctor. Sed
```

LISTING 12.2   Continued

```
          ullamcorper congue ipsum, eget vulputate sem scelerisque in.
          Donec ornare vestibulum congue. Etiam sapien nulla, rutrum
          mattis mattis ut, pellentesque eget augue. Proin nisl mauris,
          suscipit quis elementum ac, vestibulum quis lacus. Ut eget
          justo vitae urna varius sodales. </p>
        </div>
        <div id="left_side">
          <ul>
          <li><a href="#">Mission</a></li>
          <li><a href="#">History</a></li>
          <li><a href="#">Executive Team</a></li>
          <li><a href="#">Contact Us</a></li>
          </ul>
        </div>
        <div id="right_side"><strong>SPECIAL WIDGET DEAL!</strong><br/>
          Buy three widgets and get a fourth for free.<br/><br/>
          Act now!
        </div>
      </div>
      <div id="footer"> Copyright information usually goes here.</div>
    </body>
</html>
```

LISTING 12.3   Full Style Sheet for Fixed/Liquid Hybrid Layout

```
body {
  margin:0;
  padding:0;
  min-width: 525px;
}
#header {
  float: left;
  width:100%;
  background-color: #ffffff;
}
#footer {
  float: left;
  width:100%;
  background-color: #7152f4;
  font-size: 8pt;
  font-weight: bold;
  text-align: center;
  position: relative;
}
#wrapper {
  float: left;
  padding-left: 200px;
  padding-right: 125px;
  overflow: hidden;
}
```

LISTING 12.3   Continued

```css
#left_side {
  position: relative;
  float: left;
  width: 200px;
  background-color: #52f471;
  right: 200px;
  margin-left: -100%;
  padding-bottom: 2000px;
  margin-bottom: -2000px;
}
#right_side {
  position: relative;
  float: left;
  width: 125px;
  background-color: #f452d5;
  margin-right: -125px;
  padding-bottom: 2000px;
  margin-bottom: -2000px;
}
#content_area {
  position: relative;
  float: left;
  background-color: #ffffff;
  width: 100%;
  padding-bottom: 2000px;
  margin-bottom: -2000px;
}
#left_side ul {
  list-style: none;
  margin: 12px 0px 0px 12px;
  padding: 0px;
}
#left_side li a:link, #nav li a:visited {
  font-size: 12pt;
  font-weight: bold;
  padding: 3px 0px 3px 3px;
  color: #000000;
  text-decoration: none;
  display: block;
}
#left_side li a:hover, #nav li a:active {
  font-size: 12pt;
  font-weight: bold;
  padding: 3px 0px 3px 3px;
  color: #ffffff;
  text-decoration: none;
  display: block;
}
```

Summary

In this chapter, you saw some practical examples of the three main types of layouts: fixed, liquid, and a fixed/liquid hybrid. In the third section of the chapter, you saw an extended example that took you through the process bit-by-bit for creating a fixed/liquid hybrid layout in which the HTML and CSS all validate properly. Remember, the most important part of creating a layout is figuring out the sections of content you think you might need to account for in the design.

Q&A

Q. I've heard about something called an *elastic layout*. How is that different from the liquid layout?

A. An *elastic layout* is a layout whose content areas resize when the user resizes the text. Elastic layouts use *ems*, which are inherently proportional to text and font size. An em is a typographical unit of measurement equal to the point size of the current font. When ems are used in an elastic layout, if a user forces the text size to increase or decrease in size by pressing Ctrl and using the mouse scroll wheel, the areas containing the text increase or decrease proportionally. Elastic layouts are very difficult to achieve and are more commonly found in portfolios rather than actual practice due to the number of hours involved in perfecting them.

Q. You've spent a lot of time talking about liquid layouts or hybrid layouts. Are they better than a purely fixed layout?

A. "Better" is a subjective term; in this book, the concern is with standards-compliant code. Most designers will tell you that liquid layouts take longer to create (and perfect), but the usability enhancements are worth it. When might the time not be worth it? If your client does not have an opinion and if they are paying you a flat rate rather than an hourly rate, then it might not be worth it. In that case, you are working only to showcase your own skills—that might be worth it to you, however.

Workshop

The workshop contains quiz questions and activities to help you solidify your understanding of the material covered. Try to answer all questions before looking at the "Answers" section that follows.

Quiz

1. Which is the best layout to use, in general: fixed, liquid, or a hybrid?

2. Can you position a fixed layout anywhere on the page?

3. What does `min-width` do?

Answers

1. This was a trick question; there is no "best" layout. It depends on your content and the needs of your audience.

2. Sure. Although most fixed layouts are flush-left or centered, you could assign a fixed position on an XY axis where you could place a `<div>` that contains all the other layout `<div>`s.

3. The `min-width` property sets the minimum width of an element, not including padding, borders, or margins.

Exercises

▶ Figure 12.13 shows the finished fixed/liquid hybrid layout, but notice there are a few areas for improvement. There isn't any space around the text in the right-side column, there aren't any margins between the body text and either column, the footer strip is a little sparse, and so on. Take some time to fix up these design elements.

▶ After you've added margin or padding as appropriate in the first exercise, spruce up this page with a horizontal navigation strip and fancier vertical navigation based on what you learned in Chapter 11, "Using CSS to Do More with Lists, Text, and Navigation."

CHAPTER 13

Understanding Dynamic Websites

The term *dynamic* means something active or something that motivates another to become active.

When talking about websites, a dynamic website is one that incorporates interactivity into its functionality and design, but also motivates a user to take an action—read more, purchase a product, and so on. In this chapter, you'll learn a little bit about the different types of interactivity that can make a site dynamic, including information about both server-side and client-side scripting (as well as some practical examples of the latter, leading to the all the remaining chapters in this book that are specifically geared toward programming with JavaScript).

You've had a brief introduction to client-side scripting in Chapter 4, "Understanding JavaScript," and you used a little of it in Chapter 11, "Using CSS to Do More with Lists, Text, and Navigation," when you used event attributes and JavaScript to change the styles of particular elements—that is called *manipulating the Document Object Model (DOM)*. You will do a bit more of that type of manipulation in this chapter before attacking the language with gusto in the following chapters.

Understanding the Different Types of Scripting

In web development, there are two different types of scripting: server-side and client-side. Server-side scripting is beyond the scope of this book, although not *too* far beyond. In fact, *Sams Teach Yourself PHP, MySQL and Apache All in One* is a natural extension of this book—in my not-so-humble opinion of it (as its author).

WHAT YOU'LL LEARN IN THIS CHAPTER:

- ▶ How to conceptualize different types of dynamic content
- ▶ Basic information about other dynamic scripting languages
- ▶ A refresher for including JavaScript in your HTML
- ▶ How to display randomized text with JavaScript
- ▶ How to change images using JavaScript and user events

NOTE

Despite its name, JavaScript is not a derivation or any other close relative to the object-oriented programming language called Java. Released by Sun Microsystems in 1995, Java is very closely related to the server-side scripting language JSP. JavaScript was created by Netscape Communications, also in 1995, and given the name to indicate a similarity in appearance to Java but not a direct connection with it.

Server-side scripting refers to scripts that run on the web server, which then sends results to your web browser. If you have ever submitted a form at a website, which includes using a search engine, you have experienced the results of a server-side script. Popular server-side scripting languages include the following (to learn more, visit the websites listed here):

- ▶ **PHP (PHP: Hypertext Preprocessor)**—http://www.php.net/
- ▶ **JSP (Java Server Pages)**—http://java.sun.com/products/jsp/
- ▶ **ASP (Active Server Pages)**—http://www.asp.net/
- ▶ **Perl**—http://www.perl.org/
- ▶ **Python**—http://www.python.org/
- ▶ **Ruby**—http://www.ruby-lang.org/

On the other hand, *client-side scripting* refers to scripts that run within your web browser; there is no interaction with a web server in order for the scripts to run. The most popular client-side scripting language, by far, is JavaScript. For several years, research has shown that more than 93% of all web browsers have JavaScript enabled.

Another client-side scripting language is Microsoft's VBScript (Visual Basic Scripting Edition). This language is only available with Microsoft Internet Explorer web browser, and therefore, it should not be used unless you are sure that users will access your site with that web browser (such as in a closed corporate environment).

Including JavaScript in HTML

Much of this chapter is a refresher from Chapter 4; I thought it would be a good idea to revisit some of the basics of JavaScript after the HTML and CSS chapters and before the heavy-duty client-side application programming begins.

If you recall, JavaScript code can live in one of two places within your files:

- ▶ In its own file with a .js extension
- ▶ Directly in your HTML files

External files are often used for script libraries (code you can reuse throughout many pages), whereas code appearing directly in the HTML files tends to achieve functionality specific to those individual pages. Regardless of where your JavaScript lives, your browser learns of its existence through the use of the <script></script> tag pair.

When you store your JavaScript in external files, it is referenced in this manner:

```
<script type="text/javascript" src="/path/to/script.js">
```

These `<script></script>` tags are typically placed between the `<head></head>` tag because it is not, strictly speaking, content that belongs in the `<body>` of the page. Instead, the `<script>` makes available a set of JavaScript functions or other information that the rest of the page can then use. However, you can also just encapsulate your JavaScript functions or code snippets with the `<script>` and place them anywhere in the page, as needed. Listing 13.1 shows an example of a JavaScript snippet placed in the `<body>` of an HTML document.

LISTING 13.1   Using JavaScript to Print Some Text

```
<?xml version="1.0" encoding="UTF-8"?>
<!DOCTYPE html PUBLIC "-//W3C//DTD XHTML 1.1//EN"
  "http://www.w3.org/TR/xhtml11/DTD/xhtml11.dtd">

<html xmlns="http://www.w3.org/1999/xhtml" xml:lang="en">
  <head>
    <title>JavaScript Example</title>
  </head>

  <body>
    <h1>JavaScript Example</h1>
    <p>This text is HTML.</p>
    <script type="text/javascript">
    <!-- Hide the script from old browsers
    document.write('<p>This text comes from JavaScript.</p>');
    // Stop hiding the script -->
    </script>
  </body>
</html>
```

Between the `<script></script>` tags is a single JavaScript command that outputs the following HTML:

```
<p>This text comes from JavaScript.</p>
```

When the browser renders this HTML page, it sees the JavaScript between the `<script></script>` tags, stops for a millisecond to execute the command, and then returns to rendering the output that now includes the HTML output from the JavaScript command. Figure 13.1 shows that this page appears as any other HTML page appears. It's an HTML page, but only a small part of the HTML comes from a JavaScript command.

FIGURE 13.1
The output of a JavaScript snippet looks like any other output.

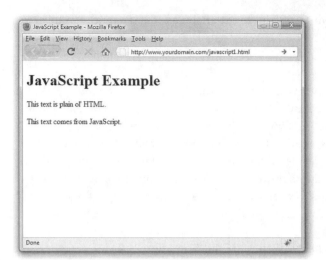

NOTE

You might have noticed these two lines in Listing 13.1:

```
    <!-- Hide the script from
old browsers
    // Stop hiding the script
-->
```

This is an HTML comment. Anything between the `<!--` start and the `-->` end will be visible in the source code, but will not be rendered by the browser. In this case, JavaScript code is surrounded by HTML comments on the off chance that your visitor is running a very old web browser or has JavaScript turned off.

Displaying Random Content

You can use JavaScript to display something different each time a page is loaded. Maybe you have a collection of text or images that you find interesting enough to include in your pages?

I'm a sucker for a good quote. If you're like me, you might find it fun to incorporate an ever-changing quote into your web pages. To create a page with a quote that changes each time the page loads, you must first gather all your quotes together, along with their respective sources. You'll then place these quotes into a JavaScript *array*, which is a special type of storage unit in programming languages that is handy for holding lists of items.

After the quotes are loaded into an array, the JavaScript used to pluck out a quote at random is fairly simple. You've already seen the snippet that will print the output into your HTML page.

Listing 13.2 contains the complete HTML and JavaScript code for a web page that displays a random quote each time it loads.

LISTING 13.2   A Random-Quote Web Page

```
<?xml version="1.0" encoding="UTF-8"?>
<!DOCTYPE html PUBLIC "-//W3C//DTD XHTML 1.1//EN"
  "http://www.w3.org/TR/xhtml11/DTD/xhtml11.dtd">

<html xmlns="http://www.w3.org/1999/xhtml" xml:lang="en">
  <head>
    <title>Quotable Quotes</title>
```

LISTING 13.2   Continued

```html
<script type="text/javascript">
  <!-- Hide the script from old browsers
  function getQuote() {
    // Create the arrays
    quotes = new Array(4);
    sources = new Array(4);

    // Initialize the arrays with quotes
    quotes[0] = "When I was a boy of 14, my father was so " +
    "ignorant...but when I got to be 21, I was astonished " +
    "at how much he had learned in 7 years.";
    sources[0] = "Mark Twain";
    quotes[1] = "Everybody is ignorant. Only on different " +
    "subjects.";
    sources[1] = "Will Rogers";
    quotes[2] = "They say such nice things about people at " +
    "their funerals that it makes me sad that I'm going to " +
    "miss mine by just a few days.";
    sources[2] = "Garrison Keilor";
    quotes[3] = "What's another word for thesaurus?";
    sources[3] = "Steven Wright";

    // Get a random index into the arrays
    i = Math.floor(Math.random() * quotes.length);

    // Write out the quote as HTML
    document.write("<dl style='background-color: lightpink'>\n");
    document.write("<dt>" + "\"<em>" + quotes[i] + "</em>\"\n");
    document.write("<dd>" + "- " + sources[i] + "\n");
    document.write("<dl>\n");
  }
  // Stop hiding the script -->
</script>
</head>

<body>
  <h1>Quotable Quotes</h1>
  <p>Following is a random quotable quote. To see a new quote just
  reload this page.</p>
  <script type="text/javascript">
    <!-- Hide the script from old browsers
    getQuote();
    // Stop hiding the script -->
  </script>
</body>
</html>
```

Although this code looks kind of long, if you look carefully, you'll see that
a lot of it consists of the four quotes available for display on the page. After
you get past the length, the code itself isn't too terribly complex.

The large number of lines between the first set of `<script></script>` tags is creating a function called `getQuote()`. After a function is defined, it can be called in other places in the same page. Note that if the function existed in an external file, the function could be called from all your pages.

If you look closely at the code, you will see some lines like this:

```
// Create the arrays
```

and

```
// Initialize the arrays with quotes
```

These are code comments. The developer uses these comments to leave notes in the code so that anyone reading it has an idea of what the code is doing in that particular place. After the first comment about creating the arrays, you can see that two arrays are created—one called `quotes` and one called `sources`—each containing four elements:

```
quotes = new Array(4);
sources = new Array(4);
```

After the second comment (about initializing the arrays with quotes), four items are added to the arrays. We'll look closely at one of them, the first quote by Mark Twain:

```
quotes[0] = "When I was a boy of 14, my father was so " +
"ignorant...but when I got to be 21, I was astonished at " +
"how much he had learned in 7 years.";
sources[0] = "Mark Twain";
```

You already know that the arrays are named quotes and sources. But the variable to which values are assigned (in this instance) are called `quotes[0]` and `sources[0]`. Because `quotes` and `sources` are arrays, the items in the array will each have their own position. When using arrays, the first item in the array is not in slot #1; it is in slot #0. In other words, you begin counting at 0 instead of 1. Therefore, the text of the first quote (a value) is assigned to `quotes[0]` (a variable). Similarly, the text of the first source is assigned to `source[0]`.

Text strings are enclosed in quotation marks. However, in JavaScript, a line break indicates an end of a command, such that the following would cause problems in the code:

```
quotes[0] = "When I was a boy of 14, my father was so
ignorant...but when I got to be 21, I was astonished at
how much he had learned in 7 years.";
```

Therefore, you see that the string is built as a series of strings enclosed in quotation marks, with a plus sign (+) connecting the strings.

The next chunk of code definitely looks the most like programming; this line gets a random number:

```
i = Math.floor(Math.random() * quotes.length);
```

But you can't just pick any random number because the purpose of the random number is to determine which of the quotes and sources should be printed—and there are only four quotes. So, this line of JavaScript does the following:

▶ Uses `Math.random()` to get a random number between 0 and 1. For example, 0.5482749 might be a result of `Math.random()`.

▶ Multiplies the random number by the length of the quotes array, which is currently 4; the length of the array is the number of elements in the array. If the random number is 0.5482749 (as shown previously), multiplying that by 4 results in 2.1930996.

▶ Uses `Math.floor()` to round the result down to the nearest whole number. In other words, 2.1930996 turns into 2.

▶ Assigns the variable i a value of 2.

The rest of the function should look familiar, with a few exceptions. First, as you learned earlier this chapter, `document.write()` is used to write HTML, which is then rendered by the browser. Next, the strings are separated to make it clear when something needs to be handled differently, such as escaping the quotation marks with a backslash when they should be printed literally (\") or when the value of a variable is substituted. The actual quote and source that is printed is the one that matches `quotes[i]` and `sources[i]`, where i is the number determined by the mathematical functions shown previously.

But the act of simply writing the function doesn't mean that any output will be created. Further on in the HTML, you can see `getQuote();` between two `<script></script>` tags; that is how the function is called. Wherever that function call is made, that is where the output of the function will be placed. In this example, the output displays below a paragraph that introduces the quotation.

Figure 13.2 shows the Quotable Quotes page as it appears when loaded in a web browser. When the page reloads, there is a one in four chance a different quote displays—it is random, after all!

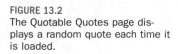

FIGURE 13.2
The Quotable Quotes page displays a random quote each time it is loaded.

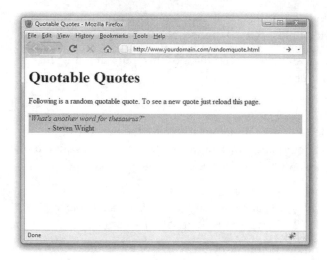

Keep in mind that you can easily modify this page to include your own quotes or other text that you want to display randomly. You can also increase the number of quotes available for display by adding more entries in the quotes and sources arrays in the code.

If you use the Quotable Quotes page as a starting point, you can easily alter the script and create your own interesting variation on the idea. And if you make mistakes along the way, so be it. The trick to getting past mistakes in script code is to be patient and carefully analyze the code you've entered. You can always remove code to simplify a script until you get it working, and then add new code one piece at a time to make sure each piece works.

Understanding the Document Object Model

Client-side interactivity using JavaScript typically takes the form of manipulating the DOM in some way. The DOM is the invisible structure of all documents—not the HTML structure or the way in which you apply levels of formatting, but a sort of overall framework or container. If this description seems vague, that's because it is; it's not a tangible object.

The overall container object is called the `document`. Any container within the document that has an ID is referenced by that ID. For example, if you have a `<div>` with an ID called `wrapper`, then in the DOM that element is referenced by the following:

```
document.wrapper
```

In Chapter 11, you changed the visibility of a specific element by changing something in the `style` object associated with it. If you wanted to access the background-color style of the `<div>` with an ID called `wrapper`, it would be referred to as:

```
document.wrapper.style.background-color
```

To change the value of that style to something else, perhaps based on an interactive user event, use the following to change the color to white:

```
document.wrapper.style.background-color="#ffffff"
```

The DOM is the framework behind your ability to refer to elements and their associated objects in this way. Obviously, this is a brief overview of something quite complicated, but at least you can now begin to grasp what this document-dot-something business is all about. To learn a lot more about the DOM, visit the World Wide Web Consortium's information about the DOM at http://www.w3.org/DOM/.

Changing Images Based on User Interaction

In Chapter 11, you were introduced to the different types of user interaction events, such as `onclick`, `onmouseover`, `onmouseout`, and so on. In that chapter, you invoked changes in text based on user interaction; in this section, you'll see an example of a visible type of interaction that is both practical and dynamic.

Figure 13.3 shows a page from an online catalog for a collectibles company. Each page in the catalog shows a large image, information about the item, and a set of smaller images at the bottom of the page. In this type of catalog, close-up images of the details of each item are important to the potential buyer, but several large images on a page becomes unwieldy from both a display and bandwidth point of view.

FIGURE 13.3
The catalog item page when first
loaded by the user.

The large image on the page is called using this `<img/>` tag:

```
<img name="product_img" src="/path/to/image.jpg" alt="photo" />
```

As you can see, this image is given a name of `product_img`. Therefore, this image exists in the DOM as `document.product_img`. This is important because a little bit of JavaScript functionality enables us to dynamically change the value of `document.product_img.src`, which is the source (`src`) of the image.

The following code snippet creates the fourth small image in the group of five images shown at the bottom of Figure 13.3. The `onmouseover` event indicates that when the user rolls over this small image, the value of `document.product_img.src`—the large image slot—is filled with the path to a matching large image.

```
<a href="#" onmouseover="javascript:document.product_img.src =
'/path/to/large4.jpg'"><img src="/path/to/small4.jpg"
width="104" height="104" style="padding: 4px; border: 0px"
alt="photo" /></a>
```

Figure 13.4 shows the same page—not reloaded by the user—whereby the slot for the large image is filled by a different image when the user rolls over a smaller image at the bottom of the page. The mouse pointer hovers over the second image from the right. As the user rolls over the small version of the interior photo, the large version of it is shown in the top area on the page.

FIGURE 13.4
The large image is replaced when the user rolls over a smaller one.

Summary

In this brief chapter, you were reminded of the differences between server-side scripting and client-side scripting, and you got a refresher for including JavaScript in your HTML files to add a little interactivity to your websites. You also learned how to use the JavaScript `document.write()` method to display random quotes upon page load. Lastly, you learned what the DOM is all about.

By applying the knowledge you've gained from previous chapters, you've learned how to use client-side scripting to make images on a web page respond to mouse movements. None of these tasks requires much in the way of programming skills, but it should inspire you to continue on throughout the book and to learn more about JavaScript to give your pages more complex interactive features.

Q&A

Q. If I want to use the random quote script from this chapter, but I want to have a library of a lot of quotes, do I have to put all the quotes in each page?

A. Yes. Each item in the array has to be there. This is where you can begin to see a bit of a tipping point between something that can be client-side and something that is better dealt with on the server side. If you have a true library of random quotations and only one is presented at any given time, it's probably best to store those items in a database table and use a little piece of server-side scripting to connect to that database, retrieve the text, and print it on the page. Alternately, you can always continue to carry all the quotes with you in JavaScript, but you should at least put that JavaScript function into a different file that can be maintained separately from the text.

Q. I've seen some online catalogs that display a large image in what looks to be a layer on top of the website content. I can see the regular website content underneath it, but the focus is on the large image. How is that done?

A. The description sounds like an effect created by a JavaScript library called Lightbox. The Lightbox library enables you to display an image, or a gallery of images, in a layer that is placed over your site content. This is a popular library used to show the details of large images or just a set of images deemed important enough to showcase "above" the content, as it were. (To install and use it, follow the instructions included with the software. You will be able to integrate it into your site using the knowledge you've gained in this book so far.)

Workshop

The workshop contains quiz questions and exercises to help you solidify your understanding of the material covered. Try to answer all questions before looking at the "Answers" section that follows.

Quiz

1. You've made a picture of a button and named it button.gif. You've also made a simple GIF animation of the button whereby it flashes green and white. You've named that GIF flashing.gif. What HTML and JavaScript code would you use to make the button flash whenever a user moves the mouse pointer over it and also link to a page named gohere.html when a user clicks the button?

2. How would you modify the code you wrote for question 1 so that the button flashes when a user moves his mouse over it and continues flashing even if he moves the mouse away from it?

3. What does the plus sign (+) mean in the following context?

```
document.write('This is a text string ' + 'that I have created.');
```

Answers

1. Your code might look something like this:

```
<a href="gohere.html"
onmouseover="javascript:document.flasher.src='flashing.gif'"
onmouseout="javascript:document.flasher.src='button.gif'">
<img src="button.gif" id="flasher" style="border-style:none" /></a>
```

2. Your code might look something like this:

```
<a href="gohere.html"
onmouseover="javascript:document.flasher.src='flashing.gif'">
<img src="button.gif" id="flasher" style="border-style:none" /></a>
```

3. The plus sign (+) is used to join two strings together.

Exercises

▶ Do you have any pages that would look flashier or be easier to understand if the navigation icons or other images changed when the mouse passed over them? If so, try creating some highlighted versions of the images and try modifying your own page using the information presented in this chapter.

▶ You can display random images—such as graphical banners or advertisements—in the same way you learned to display random content using JavaScript earlier in this chapter. Instead of printing text, just print the <img/> tag for the images you want to display.

CHAPTER 14

Getting Started with JavaScript Programming

The previous chapter reminded you of what JavaScript is, what JavaScript can do, and had you create a simple script.

In this chapter, you'll learn a few more basic concepts and script components that you'll use in just about every script you write. This will prepare you for the remaining chapters of this book, in which you'll explore specific JavaScript functions and features in greater depth.

Basic Concepts

There are a few basic concepts and terms you'll run into throughout this book. In the following sections, you'll learn about the basic building blocks of JavaScript.

Statements

Statements are the basic units of a JavaScript program. A statement is a section of code that performs a single action. For example, the following three statements are from the Date and Time example in Chapter 4, "Understanding JavaScript."

```
hours = now.getHours();
mins = now.getMinutes();
secs = now.getSeconds();
```

Although a statement is typically a single line of JavaScript, this is not a rule—it's possible to break a statement across multiple lines or to include more than one statement in a single line.

A semicolon marks the end of a statement. You can also omit the semicolon if you start a new line after the statement. If you combine statements into a single line, you must use semicolons to separate them.

NOTE

You will learn how to define, call, and return values from your own functions in Chapter 17, "Using JavaScript Functions and Objects."

Combining Tasks with Functions

In the basic scripts you've examined so far, you've seen some JavaScript statements that have a section in parentheses, like this:

```
document.write("Testing.");
```

This is an example of a *function*. Functions provide a simple way to handle a task, such as adding output to a web page. JavaScript includes a wide variety of built-in functions, which you will learn about throughout this book. A statement that uses a function, as in the preceding example, is referred to as a *function call*.

Functions take *parameters* (the expression inside the parentheses) to tell them what to do. Additionally, a function can return a value to a waiting variable. For example, the following function call prompts the user for a response and stores it in the text variable:

```
text = prompt("Enter some text.")
```

You can also create your own functions. This is useful for two main reasons: First, you can separate logical portions of your script to make it easier to understand. Second, and more importantly, you can use the function several times or with different data to avoid repeating script statements.

Variables

In Chapter 4, you learned that variables are containers that can store a number, a string of text, or another value. For example, the following statement creates a variable called fred and assigns it the value 27:

```
var fred = 27;
```

JavaScript variables can contain numbers, text strings, and other values. You'll learn more about them in Chapter 16, "Using JavaScript Variables, Strings, and Arrays."

Understanding Objects

JavaScript also supports *objects*. Like variables, objects can store data—but they can store two or more pieces of data at once.

The items of data stored in an object are called the *properties* of the object. For example, you could use objects to store information about people such as in an address book. The properties of each person object might include a name, an address, and a telephone number.

JavaScript uses periods to separate object names and property names. For example, for a person object called Bob, the properties might include `Bob.address` and `Bob.phone`.

Objects can also include *methods*. These are functions that work with the object's data. For example, our person object for the address book might include a `display()` method to display the person's information. In JavaScript terminology, the statement `Bob.display()` would display Bob's details.

Don't worry if this sounds confusing—you'll be exploring objects in much more detail later in this book. For now, you just need to know the basics. JavaScript supports three kinds of objects:

▶ *Built-in objects* are built in to the JavaScript language. You've already encountered one of these, `Date`, in Chapter 2, "Understanding HTML and XHTML Connections." Other built-in objects include `Array` and `String`, which you'll explore in Chapter 16, and `Math`, which is explained in Chapter 17.

▶ *DOM (Document Object Model) objects* represent various components of the browser and the current HTML document. For example, the `alert()` function you used earlier in this chapter is actually a method of the `window` object. You'll explore these in more detail in Chapter 15, "Working with the Document Object Model (DOM)."

▶ *Custom objects* are objects you create yourself. For example, you could create a `person` object, as mentioned earlier in this section.

Conditionals

Although event handlers notify your script when something happens, you might want to check certain conditions yourself. For example, did the user enter a valid email address?

JavaScript supports *conditional statements*, which enable you to answer questions like this. A typical conditional uses the `if` statement, as in this example:

```
if (count==1) alert("The countdown has reached 1.");
```

This compares the variable `count` with the constant 1 and displays an alert message to the user if they are the same. You will use conditional statements like this in most of your scripts.

NOTE

The `document.write` function we discussed earlier this chapter is actually the `write` method of the `document` object, which you have seen several times already.

NOTE

You'll learn more about conditionals in Chapter 18, "Controlling Flow with Conditions and Loops."

Loops

Another useful feature of JavaScript—and most other programming languages—is the capability to create *loops*, or groups of statements that repeat a certain number of times. For example, these statements display the same alert 10 times, greatly annoying the user:

```
for (i=1; i<=10; i++) {
    alert("Yes, it's yet another alert!");
}
```

The for statement is one of several statements JavaScript uses for loops. This is the sort of thing computers are supposed to be good at—performing repetitive tasks. You will use loops in many of your scripts, in much more useful ways than this example.

Event Handlers

As mentioned in Chapter 1, not all scripts are located within <script> tags. You can also use scripts as *event handlers*. Although this might sound like a complex programming term, it actually means exactly what it says: Event handlers are scripts that handle events. You learned a little bit about events in Chapter 11, "Using CSS to Do More with Lists, Text, and Navigation," but not to the extent you'll read about now.

In real life, an event is something that happens to you. For example, the things you write on your calendar are events: "Dentist appointment" or "Fred's birthday." You also encounter unscheduled events in your life: for example, a traffic ticket, an IRS audit, or an unexpected visit from relatives.

Whether events are scheduled or unscheduled, you probably have normal ways of handling them. Your event handlers might include things such as "When Fred's birthday arrives, send him a present" or "When relatives visit unexpectedly, turn out the lights and pretend nobody is home."

Event handlers in JavaScript are similar: They tell the browser what to do when a certain event occurs. The events JavaScript deals with aren't as exciting as the ones you deal with—they include such events as "When the mouse button clicks" and "When this page is finished loading." Nevertheless, they're a very useful part of JavaScript.

Many JavaScript events (such as mouse clicks, which you've seen previously) are caused by the user. Rather than doing things in a set order, your script can respond to the user's actions. Other events don't involve the user directly—for example, an event is triggered when an HTML document finishes loading.

Each event handler is associated with a particular browser object, and you can specify the event handler in the tag that defines the object. For example, images and text links have an event, `onMouseOver`, which happens when the mouse pointer moves over the object. Here is a typical HTML image tag with an event handler:

```
<img src="button.gif" onMouseOver="highlight();">
```

You specify the event handler as an attribute to the HTML tag and include the JavaScript statement to handle the event within the quotation marks. This is an ideal use for functions because function names are short and to the point and can refer to a whole series of statements.

See the Try It Yourself section at the end of this chapter for a complete example of an event handler within an HTML document.

Which Script Runs First?

You can actually have several scripts within a web document: one or more sets of `<script>` tags, external JavaScript files, and any number of event handlers. With all of these scripts, you might wonder how the browser knows which to execute first. Fortunately, this is done in a logical fashion:

▶ Sets of `<script>` tags within the `<head>` section of an HTML document are handled first, whether they include embedded code or refer to a JavaScript file. Because these scripts cannot create output in the web page, it's a good place to define functions for use later.

▶ Sets of `<script>` tags within the `<body>` section of the HTML document are executed after those in the `<head>` section, while the web page loads and displays. If there is more than one script in the body, they are executed in order.

▶ Event handlers are executed when their events happen. For example, the `onLoad` event handler is executed when the body of a web page loads. Because the `<head>` section is loaded before any events, you can define functions there and use them in event handlers.

JavaScript Syntax Rules

JavaScript is a simple language, but you do need to be careful to use its *syntax*—the rules that define how you use the language—correctly. The rest of this book covers many aspects of JavaScript syntax, but there are a few basic rules you should understand to avoid errors.

Case Sensitivity

Almost everything in JavaScript is *case sensitive*, which means you cannot use lowercase and capital letters interchangeably. Here are a few general rules:

- ▶ JavaScript keywords, such as `for` and `if`, are always lowercase.
- ▶ Built-in objects, such as `Math` and `Date`, are capitalized.
- ▶ DOM object names are usually lowercase, but their methods are often a combination of capitals and lowercase. Usually capitals are used for all but the first word, as in `toLowerCase` and `getElementById`.

When in doubt, follow the exact case used in this book or another JavaScript reference. If you use the wrong case, the browser will usually display an error message.

Variable, Object, and Function Names

When you define your own variables, objects, or functions, you can choose their names. Names can include uppercase letters, lowercase letters, numbers, and the underscore (_) character. Names must begin with a letter or underscore.

You can choose whether to use capitals or lowercase in your variable names, but remember that JavaScript is case sensitive: `score`, `Score`, and `SCORE` would be considered three different variables. Be sure to use the same name each time you refer to a variable.

Reserved Words

One more rule for variable names: They must not be *reserved words*. These include the words that make up the JavaScript language (such as `if` and `for`), DOM object names (such as `window` and `document`), and built-in object names (such as `Math` and `Date`).

Spacing

Blank space (known as *whitespace* by programmers) is ignored by JavaScript. You can include spaces and tabs within a line, or blank lines, without causing an error. Blank space often makes the script more readable.

Using Comments

JavaScript *comments* enable you to include documentation within your script. This will be useful if someone else tries to understand the script or even if you try to understand it after a long break. To include comments in a JavaScript program, begin a line with two slashes, as in this example:

```
//this is a comment.
```

You can also begin a comment with two slashes in the middle of a line, which is useful for documenting a script. In this case, everything on the line after the slashes is treated as a comment and ignored by the browser. For example,

```
a = a + 1; // add one to the value of a
```

JavaScript also supports C-style comments, which begin with /* and end with */. These comments can extend across more than one line, as the following example demonstrates:

```
/*This script includes a variety
of features, including this comment. */
```

Because JavaScript statements within a comment are ignored, C-style comments are often used for *commenting out* sections of code. If you have some lines of JavaScript that you want to temporarily take out of the picture while you debug a script, you can add /* at the beginning of the section and */ at the end.

> **CAUTION**
>
> Because these comments are part of JavaScript syntax, they are only valid inside <script> tags or within an external JavaScript file.

Best Practices for JavaScript

You should now be familiar with the basic rules for writing valid JavaScript. Along with following the rules, it's also a good idea to follow *best practices*. The following practices may not be required, but you'll save yourself and others some headaches if you follow them.

- ▶ **Use comments liberally**—These make your code easier for others to understand and also easier for you to understand when you edit them later. They are also useful for marking the major divisions of a script.

- ▶ **Use a semicolon at the end of each statement and only use one statement per line**—This will make your scripts easier to debug.

- ▶ **Use separate JavaScript files whenever possible**—This separates JavaScript from HTML and makes debugging easier and also encourages you to write modular scripts that can be reused.

▶ **Avoid being browser-specific**—As you learn more about JavaScript, you'll learn some features that only work in one browser. Avoid them unless absolutely necessary and always test your code in more than one browser.

▶ **Keep JavaScript optional**—Don't use JavaScript to perform an essential function on your site—for example, the primary navigation links. Whenever possible, users without JavaScript should be able to use your site, although it may not be quite as attractive or convenient. This strategy is known as *progressive enhancement*.

There are many more best practices involving more advanced aspects of JavaScript.

▼ TRY IT YOURSELF

Using an Event Handler

To conclude this chapter, here's a simple example of an event handler. This will demonstrate how you set up an event, which you'll use throughout this book, and how JavaScript works without `<script>` tags. Listing 14.1 shows an HTML document that includes a simple event handler.

LISTING 14.1   An HTML Document with a Simple Event Handler

```
<?xml version="1.0" encoding="UTF-8"?>
<!DOCTYPE html PUBLIC "-//W3C//DTD XHTML 1.1//EN"
  "http://www.w3.org/TR/xhtml11/DTD/xhtml11.dtd">

<html xmlns="http://www.w3.org/1999/xhtml" xml:lang="en">
  <head>
    <title>Event Handler Example</title>
  </head>

  <body>
    <h1>Event Handler Example</h1>
    <p>
    <a href="http://www.google.com/"
    onclick="alert('Aha! An Event!');">Go to Google</a>
    </p>
  </body>
</html>
```

The event handler is defined with the following `onClick` attribute within the `<a>` tag that defines a link:

```
onclick="alert('Aha! An Event!');"
```

This event handler uses the built-in `alert()` function to display a message when you click on the link. In more complex scripts, you will usually define your own function to act as an event handler. Figure 14.1 shows this example in action.

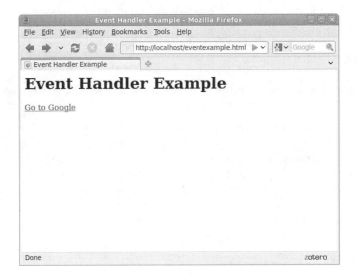

FIGURE 14.1
The browser displays an alert when you click the link.

You'll use other event handlers similar to this in the next hour, and events will be covered in more detail in Chapter 19, "Responding to Events."

Summary

During this chapter, you've been introduced to several components of JavaScript programming and syntax: functions, objects, event handlers, conditions, and loops. You also learned how to use JavaScript comments to make your script easier to read and looked at a simple example of an event handler.

TIP

Notice that after you click the OK button on the alert, the browser follows the link defined in the <a> tag. Your event handler could also stop the browser from following the link, as described in Chapter 19.

Q&A

Q. I've heard the term object-oriented applied to languages such as C++ and Java. If JavaScript supports objects, is it an object-oriented language?

A. Yes, although it might not fit some people's strict definitions. JavaScript objects do not support all the features that languages such as C++ and Java support, although the latest versions of JavaScript have added more object-oriented features.

Q. Having several scripts that execute at different times seems confusing. Why would I want to use event handlers?

A. Event handlers are the ideal way (and in JavaScript, the only way) to handle gadgets within the web page, such as buttons, check boxes, and text fields. It's actually more convenient to handle them this way. Rather than writing a script that sits and waits for a button to be pushed, you can simply create an event handler and let the browser do the waiting for you.

Workshop

The workshop contains quiz questions and exercises to help you solidify your understanding of the material covered. Try to answer all questions before looking at the "Answers" section that follows.

Quiz

1. A script that executes when the user clicks the mouse button is an example of what?

    a. An object

    b. An event handler

    c. An impossibility

2. Which of the following are capabilities of functions in JavaScript?

    a. Accept parameters

    b. Return a value

    c. Both of the above

3. Which of the following is executed first by a browser?

    a. A script in the <head> section

    b. A script in the <body> section

    c. An event handler for a button

Answers

1. b. A script that executes when the user clicks the mouse button is an event handler.

2. c. Functions can accept both parameters and return values.

3. a. Scripts defined in the <head> section of an HTML document are executed first by the browser.

Exercises

▶ Examine the Date and Time script you created in Chapter 4 and find any examples of functions and objects being used.

▶ Add JavaScript comments to the Date and Time script to make it more clear what each line does. Verify that the script still runs properly.

CHAPTER 15

Working with the Document Object Model (DOM)

The previous chapter introduced you to the basic concepts of programming in JavaScript; this chapter will help you better understand the Document Object Model (DOM), which is the framework that properties and method of JavaScript explicitly control so that you may develop rich user experiences.

Understanding the Document Object Model (DOM)

One advantage that JavaScript has over plain HTML is that these client-side scripts can manipulate the web document and its contents right there in the browser after the content has been loaded. Your script can load a new page into the browser, work with parts of the browser window and document, open new windows, and even modify text within the page dynamically.

To work with the browser and documents, JavaScript uses a hierarchy of parent and child objects called the DOM. These objects are organized into a tree-like structure and represent all the content and components of a web document.

The objects in the DOM have *properties*—variables that describe the web page or document—and *methods*—functions that enable you to work with parts of the web page.

When you refer to an object, you use the parent object name followed by the child object name or names, separated by periods. For example, JavaScript stores objects to represent images in a document as children of the document object. The following refers to the `image9` object, a child of the document object, which is a child of the window object:

```
window.document.image9
```

NOTE

The DOM is not part of JavaScript or any other programming language—rather, it's an API (application programming interface) built in to the browser.

Using window Objects

At the top of the browser object hierarchy is the window object, which represents a browser window. You've already used at least one method of the window object: method, or simply alert(), displays a message in an alert box.

There can be several window objects at a time, each representing an open browser window. Frames are also represented by window objects. You'll learn more about windows and frames in Chapter 20, "Using Windows and Frames."

The window object is the parent object for all the objects we will be looking at in this chapter. Figure 15.1 shows the window section of the DOM object hierarchy and a variety of its objects.

FIGURE 15.1
The window section of the DOM object hierarchy.

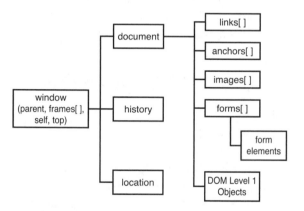

Working with the document Object

NOTE

You've already used the document.write method to display text within a web document. The examples in earlier chapters only used a single window and document, so it was unnecessary to use window. document.write—but this longer syntax would have worked equally well.

The document object represents a web document or page. Web documents are displayed within browser windows, so it shouldn't surprise you to learn that the document object is a child of the window object.

Because the window object always represents the current window (the one containing the script), you can use window.document to refer to the current document. You can also simply refer to document, which automatically refers to the current window.

If multiple windows or frames are in use, there might be several window objects, each with its own document object. To use one of these document objects, you use the name of the window and the name of the document.

In the following sections, you will look at some of the properties and methods of the document object that will be useful in your scripting.

Getting Information About the Document

Several properties of the document object include information about the current document in general:

▶ document.URL specifies the document's URL. This is a simple text field. You can't change this property. If you need to send the user to a different location, use the window.location object, which you will learn about further along.

▶ document.title lists the title of the current page, defined by the HTML <title> tag.

▶ document.referrer is the URL of the page the user was viewing prior to the current page—usually, the page with a link to the current page.

▶ document.lastModified is the date the document was last modified. This date is sent from the server along with the page.

▶ document.cookie enables you to read or set a cookie for the document.

▶ document.images returns a collection of images used in the document.

As an example of a document property, Listing 15.1 shows a short HTML document that displays its last modified date using JavaScript.

LISTING 15.1   Displaying the Last Modified Date

```
<?xml version="1.0" encoding="UTF-8"?>
<!DOCTYPE html PUBLIC "-//W3C//DTD XHTML 1.1//EN"
  "http://www.w3.org/TR/xhtml11/DTD/xhtml11.dtd">

<html xmlns="http://www.w3.org/1999/xhtml" xml:lang="en">
  <head>
    <title>Displaying the Last Modified Date</title>
  </head>
  <body>
    <h1>Displaying the Last Modified Date</h1>
    <p>This page was last modified on:</p>
    <script type="text/javascript">
       document.write(document.lastModified);
    </script>
  </body>
</html>
```

Figure 15.2 shows the output of Listing 15.1.

You might find that the
`document.lastModified` property doesn't work on your web
pages or returns the wrong
value. The date is received from
the web server, and some
servers do not maintain modification dates correctly.

Bear in mind that the newline
character is displayed as a
space by the browser, except
inside a `<pre>` container. You
will need to use the `<br/>` tag
if you want an actual line break.

You can also directly modify the
text on a web page by using
more advanced features of the
DOM, which you'll learn about
later in this chapter.

If you use JavaScript to display the value of this `document` property, you
don't have to remember to update the date each time you modify the page,
should you choose to expose this information to the user. (You could also
use the script to always print the current date instead of the last modified
date, but that would be cheating.)

Writing Text in a Document

The simplest `document` object methods are also the ones you will use most
often. In fact, you've used one of them already even in the most basic examples in this book so far. The `document.write` method prints text as part of
the HTML in a document window. An alternative statement, `document.`
`writeln`, also prints text, but it also includes a newline (`\n`) character at the
end. This is handy when you want your text to be the last thing on the line.

You can use these methods only within the body of the web page, so they
will be executed when the page loads. You can't use these methods to add
to a page that has already loaded without reloading it. You *can* write new
content for a document, however, as the next section explains.

The `document.write` method can be used within a `<script>` tag in the
body of an HTML document. You can also use it in a function, provided
you include a call to the function within the body of the document, as you
saw in Listing 15.1.

Using Links and Anchors

Another child of the document object is the link object. Actually, there can be multiple link objects in a document. Each one includes information about a link to another location or an anchor.

You can access link objects with the links array. Each member of the array is one of the link objects in the current page. A property of the array, document.links.length, indicates the number of links in the page.

Each link object (or member of the links array) has a list of properties defining the URL. The href property contains the entire URL, and other properties define portions of it. These are the same properties as the location object, defined later in this chapter.

You can refer to a property by indicating the link number and property name. For example, the following statement assigns the entire URL of the first link to the variable link1:

```
link1 = links[0].href;
```

The anchor objects are also children of the document object. Each anchor object represents an anchor in the current document—a particular location that can be jumped to directly.

Like links, you can access anchors with an array: anchors. Each element of this array is an anchor object. The document.anchors.length property gives you the number of elements in the anchors array.

Accessing Browser History

The history object is another child (property) of the window object. This object holds information about the URLs that have been visited before and after the current one, and it includes methods to go to previous or next locations.

The history object has one property you can access:

▶ history.length keeps track of the length of the history list—in other words, the number of different locations that the user has visited.

The history object has three methods you can use to move through the history list:

NOTE

The history object has current, previous, and next properties that store URLs of documents in the history list. However, for security and privacy reasons, these objects are not normally accessible by browsers.

▶ `history.go()` opens a URL from the history list. To use this method, specify a positive or negative number in parentheses. For example, `history.go(-2)` is equivalent to pressing the Back button twice.

▶ `history.back()` loads the previous URL in the history list—equivalent to pressing the Back button.

▶ `history.forward()` loads the next URL in the history list, if available. This is equivalent to pressing the Forward button.

You can use the `back` and `forward` methods of the `history` object to add your own Back and Forward buttons to a web document. The browser already has Back and Forward buttons, of course, but it's occasionally useful to include your own links that serve the same purpose.

Suppose you wanted to create a script that displays Back and Forward buttons and use these methods to navigate the browser. Here's the code that will create the Back button:

```
<input type="button" onClick="history.back();" value="Go Back">
```

The `<input>` tag defines a button labeled Go Back. The `onClick` event handler uses the `history.back()` method to go to the previous page in history. The code for the Go Forward button is similar:

```
<input type="button" onClick="history.forward();" value="Go Forward">
```

With these out of the way, you just need to build the rest of the HTML document. Listing 15.2 shows a complete HTML document, and Figure 15.3 shows a browser's display of the document. After you load this document into a browser, visit other URLs and make sure the Back and Forward buttons work as expected.

LISTING 15.2   A Web Page That Uses JavaScript to Include Back and Forward Buttons

```
<?xml version="1.0" encoding="UTF-8"?>
<!DOCTYPE html PUBLIC "-//W3C//DTD XHTML 1.1//EN"
  "http://www.w3.org/TR/xhtml11/DTD/xhtml11.dtd">

<html xmlns="http://www.w3.org/1999/xhtml" xml:lang="en">
  <head>
    <title>Using Back and Forward Buttons</title>
  </head>
  <body>
    <h1>Using Back and Forward Buttons</h1>
    <p>This page allows you to go back or forward to pages in
    the history list. These should be equivalent to the back
```

LISTING 15.2   Continued

```
and forward arrow buttons in the browser's toolbar.</p>
<p>
<input type="button"
       onclick="history.back();"
       value="Go Back" />
<input type="button"
       onclick="history.forward();"
       value="Go Forward" />
</p>
</body>
</html>
```

FIGURE 15.3
Showing custom Back and Forward buttons.

Working with the location **Object**

A third child of the window object is the location object. This object stores information about the current URL stored in the window. For example, the following statement loads a URL into the current window:

```
window.location.href="http://www.google.com";
```

The href property used in this statement contains the entire URL of the window's current location. You can also access portions of the URL with various properties of the location object. To explain these properties, consider the following URL:

http://www.google.com:80/search?q=javascript

The following properties represent parts of the URL:

- ▶ `location.protocol` is the protocol part of the URL (http: in the example).

- ▶ `location.hostname` is the host name of the URL (www.google.com in the example).

- ▶ `location.port` is the port number of the URL (80 in the example).

- ▶ `location.pathname` is the filename part of the URL (search in the example).

- ▶ `location.search` is the query portion of the URL, if any (q=javascript in the example).

Unused in this example but also accessible are

- ▶ `location.host` is the hostname of the URL plus the port number.

- ▶ `location.hash` is the anchor name used in the URL, if any (#anchor in the example) .

The `link` object, introduced earlier this chapter, also includes this list of properties for accessing portions of the URL.

The `location` object has three methods:

- ▶ `location.assign()` loads a new document when used as follows:

  `location.assign("http://www.google.com")`

- ▶ `location.reload()` reloads the current document. This is the same as the Reload button on the browser's toolbar. If you optionally include the `true` parameter, it will ignore the browser's cache and force a reload whether the document has changed or not.

- ▶ `location.replace()` replaces the current location with a new one. This is similar to setting the `location` object's properties yourself. The difference is that the `replace` method does not affect the browser's history. In other words, the Back button can't be used to go to the previous location. This is useful for splash screens or temporary pages that it would be useless to return to.

More About the DOM Structure

Previously in this chapter, you learned how some of the most important DOM objects are organized: The `window` object contains the `document`

CAUTION

Although the `location.href` property usually contains the same URL as the `document.URL` property described earlier in this chapter, you can't change the `document.URL` property. Always use `location.href` to load a new page.

object, and so on. Although these objects were the only ones available originally, the modern DOM adds objects under the document object for every element of a page.

To better understand this concept, let's look at the simple HTML document in Listing 15.3. This document has the usual <head> and <body> sections, a heading and a single paragraph of text.

LISTING 15.3   A Simple HTML Document

```
<?xml version="1.0" encoding="UTF-8"?>
<!DOCTYPE html PUBLIC "-//W3C//DTD XHTML 1.1//EN"
  "http://www.w3.org/TR/xhtml11/DTD/xhtml11.dtd">

<html xmlns="http://www.w3.org/1999/xhtml" xml:lang="en">
  <head>
    <title>A Simple HTML Document</title>
  </head>
  <body>
    <h1>This is a Level-1 Heading.</h1>
    <p>This is a simple paragraph.</p>
</body>
</html>
```

Like all HTML documents, this one is composed of various *containers* and their contents. The <html> tags form a container that includes the entire document, the <body> tags contain the body of the page, and so on.

In the DOM, each container within the page and its contents are represented by an object. The objects are organized into a tree-like structure, with the document object itself at the root of the tree, and individual elements such as the heading and paragraph of text at the leaves of the tree. Figure 15.4 shows a diagram of these relationships.

In the following sections, you will examine the structure of the DOM more closely.

Nodes

Each container or element in the document is called a *node* in the DOM. In the example in Figure 15.4, each of the objects in boxes is a node, and the lines represent the relationships between the nodes.

You will often need to refer to individual nodes in scripts. You can do this by assigning an ID or by navigating the tree using the relationships between the nodes.

NOTE

Don't worry if this tree structure confuses you; you can do almost anything by simply assigning IDs to elements and referring to them. This is the method used in some earlier examples in this book. Further on, you will look at more complicated examples that require you to understand the way objects are organized in the DOM.

FIGURE 15.4
How the DOM represents an HTML
document.

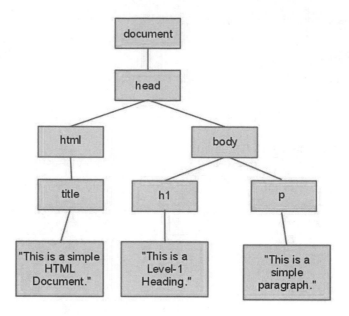

Parents and Children

As you have already learned, each JavaScript object can have a *parent*—an object that contains it—and can also have *children*—objects that it contains. The DOM uses the same terminology.

In Figure 15.4, the document object is the parent object for the remaining objects and does not have a parent itself. The html object is the parent of the head and body objects, and the h1 and p objects are children of the body object.

Text nodes work a bit differently. The actual text in the paragraph is a node in itself and is a child of the p object. Similarly, the text within the <h1> tags is a child of the h1 object.

Siblings

The DOM also uses another term for organization of objects: *siblings*. As you might expect, this refers to objects that have the same parent—in other words, objects at the same level in the DOM object tree.

In Figure 15.4, the h1 and p objects are siblings, as both are children of the body object. Similarly, the head and body objects are siblings under the html object.

Working with DOM Nodes

As you've seen, the DOM organizes objects within a web page into a tree-like structure. Each node (object) in this tree can be accessed in JavaScript. In the next sections, you will learn how you can use the properties and methods of nodes to manage them.

Basic Node Properties

You have already used the `style` property of nodes to change their style sheet values. Each node also has a number of basic properties that you can examine or set. These include the following:

- `nodeName` is the name of the node (not the ID). For nodes based on HTML tags, such as `<p>` or `<body>`, the name is the tag name: p or body. For the document node, the name is a special code: `#document`. Similarly, text nodes have the name `#text`.

- `nodeType` is an integer describing the node's type: 1 for normal HTML tags, 3 for text nodes, and 9 for the document node.

- `nodeValue` is the actual text contained within a text node. This property is not valid for other types of nodes.

- `innerHTML` is the HTML content of any node. You can assign a value including HTML tags to this property and change the DOM child objects for a node dynamically.

Node Relationship Properties

In addition to the basic properties described previously, each node has a number of properties that describe its relation to other nodes. These include the following:

- `firstChild` is the first child object for a node. For nodes that contain text, such as h1 or p, the text node containing the actual text is the first child.

- `lastChild` is the node's last child object.

- `childNodes` is an array that includes all of a node's child nodes. You can use a loop with this array to work with all the nodes under a given node.

- `previousSibling` is the sibling (node at the same level) previous to the current node.

- `nextSibling` is the sibling after the current node.

NOTE

The following sections only describe the most important properties and methods of nodes and those that are supported by current browsers. For a complete list of available properties, see the W3C's DOM specification at http://www.w3.org/TR/DOM-Level-2/.

NOTE

The `innerHTML` property is not a part of the W3C DOM specification. However, it is supported by the major browsers and is often the easiest way to change content in a page. You can also accomplish this in a more standard way by deleting and creating nodes, as described further on.

CAUTION

Remember that, like all JavaScript objects and properties, the node properties and functions described here are case sensitive. Be sure you type them exactly as shown.

Document Methods

The document node itself has several methods you might find useful. You have already used one of these, getElementById, to refer to DOM objects by their ID properties. The document node's methods include the following:

▶ getElementById(id) returns the element with the specified id attribute.

▶ getElementsByTagName(tag) returns an array of all of the elements with a specified tag name. You can use the wildcard * to return an array containing all the nodes in the document.

▶ createTextNode(text) creates a new text node containing the specified text, which you can then add to the document.

▶ createElement(tag) creates a new HTML element for the specified tag. As with createTextNode, you need to add the element to the document after creating it. You can assign content within the element by changing its child objects or the innerHTML property.

Node Methods

Each node within a page has a number of methods available. Which of these are valid depends on the node's position in the page and whether it has parent or child nodes. These include the following:

▶ appendChild(new) appends the specified new node after all of the object's existing nodes.

▶ insertBefore(new, old) inserts the specified new child node before the specified old child node, which must already exist.

▶ replaceChild(new, old) replaces the specified old child node with a new node.

▶ removeChild(node) removes a child node from the object's set of children.

▶ hasChildNodes() returns a Boolean value of true if the object has one or more child nodes or false if it has none.

▶ cloneNode() creates a copy of an existing node. If a parameter of true is supplied, the copy will also include any child nodes of the original node.

Creating Positionable Elements (Layers)

Now that you understand a little more about how the DOM is structured, you should be able to start thinking about how you can control any element in a web page, such as a paragraph or an image. For example, you can use the DOM to change the position, visibility, and other attributes of an element.

Before the W3C DOM and CSS2 standards, you could only reposition *layers*, special groups of elements defined with a proprietary tag. Although you can now position any element, it's still useful to work with groups of elements in many cases.

You can effectively create a layer, or a group of HTML objects that can be controlled as a group, using the `<div>` or `<span>` tags, which you learned about early in this book.

To create a layer with `<div>`, enclose the content of the layer between the two division tags and specify the layer's properties in the `style` attribute of the `<div>` tag. Here's a simple example:

```
<div id="layer1" style="position:absolute; left:100px; top:100px">
<p>This is the content of the layer.</p>
</div>
```

This code defines a layer with the name `layer1`. This is a moveable layer positioned 100 pixels down and 100 pixels to the right of the upper-left corner of the browser window.

You've already learned about the positioning properties and seen them in action in Parts II and III of this book. This includes setting object size (such as `height` and `width`) and position (such as `absolute` or `relative`), object visibility, and object background and borders. The remaining examples in this chapter will use HTML and CSS much like what you've already seen in this book, but will show you JavaScript-based interactions with the DOM in action.

Controlling Positioning with JavaScript

Using the code snippet from the previous section, you'll see an example of how you can control the positioning attributes of an object, using JavaScript.

NOTE

As you've learned in earlier chapters, you can specify CSS properties, such as the position property and other layer properties, in a `<style>` block, in an external style sheet, or in the `style` attribute of an HTML tag, and then control these properties using JavaScript. The code snippets shown here use properties in the `style` attribute rather than in a `<style>` block because it is a snippet of an example and not a full code listing.

Here is our sample layer (a `<div>`):

```
<div id="layer1" style="position:absolute; left:100px; top:100px">
<p>This is the content of the layer.</p>
</div>
```

To move this layer up or down within the page using JavaScript, you can change its `style.top` attribute. For example, the following statements move the layer 100 pixels down from its original position:

```
var obj = document.getElementById("layer1");
obj.style.top=200;
```

The `document.getElementById()` method returns the object corresponding to the layer's `<div>` tag, and the second statement sets the object's `top` positioning property to 200px; you can also combine these two statements:

```
document.getElementById("layer1").style.top = 200;
```

NOTE

Some CSS properties, such as `text-indent` and `border-color`, have hyphens in their names. When you use these properties in JavaScript, you combine the hyphenated sections and use a capital letter: `textIndent` and `borderColor`.

This simply sets the `style.top` property for the layer without assigning a variable to the layer's object.

Now let's create an HTML document that defines a layer and combine it with a script to allow the layer to be moved, hidden, or shown using buttons. Listing 15.4 shows the HTML document that defines the buttons and the layer. The script itself (position.js) will follow in Listing 15.5.

LISTING 15.4   The HTML Document for the Movable Layer Example

```
<?xml version="1.0" encoding="UTF-8"?>
<!DOCTYPE html PUBLIC "-//W3C//DTD XHTML 1.1//EN"
  "http://www.w3.org/TR/xhtml11/DTD/xhtml11.dtd">

<html xmlns="http://www.w3.org/1999/xhtml" xml:lang="en">
  <head>
   <title>Positioning Elements with JavaScript</title>
   <script type="text/javascript" src="position.js"></script>
   <style text="text/css">
   #buttons {
       text-align:center;
   }
   #square {
       position:absolute;
       top: 150px;
       left: 100px;
       width: 200px;
       height: 200px;
       border: 2px solid black;
       padding: 10px;
       background-color: #e0e0e0;
   }
```

LISTING 15.4   Continued

```
    </style>
  </head>
<body>
    <h1>Positioning Elements</h1>
    <form action="" name="form1">
    <div id="buttons">
    <input type="button" name="left" value="Left"
      onclick="pos(-1,0);" />
    <input type="button" name="right" value="Right"
      onclick="pos(1,0);" />
    <input type="button" name="up" value="Up"
      onclick="pos(0,-1);" />
    <input type="button" name="down" value="Down"
      onclick="pos(0,1);" />
    <input type="button" name="hide" value="Hide"
      onclick="hideSquare();" />
    <input type="button" name="show" value="Show"
      onclick="showSquare();" />
    </div>
    </form>
    <hr />
    <div id="square">
    <p>This square is an absolutely positioned
    layer that you can move using the buttons above.</p>
    </div>
</body>
</html>
```

In addition to some basic HTML, Listing 15.4 contains the following:

▶ The <script> tag in the header reads a script called position.js, which is shown in Listing 15.5.

▶ The <style> section is a brief style sheet that defines the properties for the movable layer. It sets the position property to absolute to indicate that it can be positioned at an exact location, sets the initial position in the top and left properties, and sets border and background-color properties to make the layer clearly visible.

▶ The <input> tags within the <form> section define six buttons: four to move the layer left, right, up, or down and two to control whether it is visible or hidden.

▶ The <div> section defines the layer itself. The id attribute is set to the value "square". This id is used in the style sheet to refer to the layer and will also be used in your script.

If you load it into a browser, you should see the buttons and the "square" layer, but the buttons won't do anything yet. The script in Listing 15.5 adds the ability to use the actions. When you load the code in Listing 15.4 into your browser, it should look like Figure 15.5.

FIGURE 15.5
The moveable layer is ready to be moved.

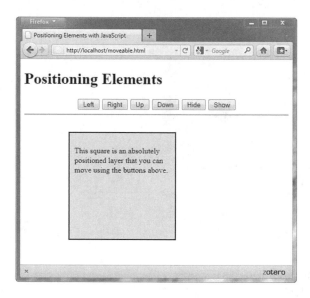

Listing 15.5 shows the JavaScript variables and functions that are called in the HTML in Listing 15.4. This code is expected (by the <script> tag) to be in a file called position.js.

LISTING 15.5   The Script for the Movable Layer Example

```
var x=100,y=150;
function pos(dx,dy) {
    if (!document.getElementById) return;
    x += 10*dx;
    y += 10*dy;
    obj = document.getElementById("square");
    obj.style.top=y + "px";
    obj.style.left=x + "px";
}
function hideSquare() {
    if (!document.getElementById) return;
    obj = document.getElementById("square");
    obj.style.display="none";
}
function showSquare() {
    if (!document.getElementById) return;
    obj = document.getElementById("square");
    obj.style.display="block";
}
```

The var statement at the beginning of the script defines two variables, x and y, that will store the current position of the layer. The pos function is called by the event handlers for all four of the movement buttons.

The parameters of the pos() function, dx and dy, tell the script how the layer should move: If dx is negative, a number will be subtracted from x, moving the layer to the left. If dx is positive, a number will be added to x, moving the layer to the right. Similarly, dy indicates whether to move up or down.

The pos() function begins by making sure the getElementById() function is supported, so it won't attempt to run in older browsers. It then multiplies dx and dy by 10 (to make the movement more obvious) and applies them to x and y. Finally, it sets the top and left properties to the new position (including the "px" to indicate the unit of measurement), thus moving the layer.

Two more functions, hideSquare() and showsquare(), hide or show the layer by setting its display property to "none" (hidden) or "block" (shown).

To use this script, save it as position.js, and then load the HTML document in Listing 15.4 into your browser. Figure 15.6 shows this script in action—well, after an action, at least. Figure 15.6 shows the script after pressing the Right button seven times and the Down button ten times.

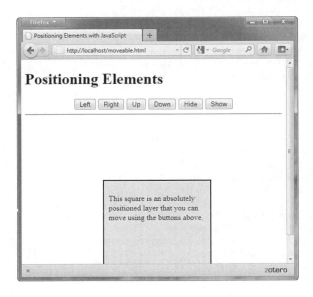

FIGURE 15.6
The moveable layer has been moved.

Hiding and Showing Objects

In the previous example, you saw some functions that could be used to hide or show the "square." In this section, we'll take a closer look at hiding and showing objects within a page.

As a refresher, objects have a `visibility` style property that specifies whether they are currently visible within the page:

```
Object.style.visibility="hidden"; // hides an object
Object.style.visibility="visible"; // shows an object
```

Using this property, you can create a script that hides or shows objects in either browser. Listing 15.6 shows the HTML document for a script that allows two headings to be shown or hidden.

LISTING 15.6   Hiding and Showing Objects

```
<?xml version="1.0" encoding="UTF-8"?>
<!DOCTYPE html PUBLIC "-//W3C//DTD XHTML 1.1//EN"
  "http://www.w3.org/TR/xhtml11/DTD/xhtml11.dtd">

<html xmlns="http://www.w3.org/1999/xhtml" xml:lang="en">
  <head>
    <title>Hiding or Showing Objects</title>
    <script type="text/javascript">
    function ShowHide() {
       if (!document.getElementById) return;
       var head1 = document.getElementById("head1");
       var head2 = document.getElementById("head2");
       var showhead1 = document.form1.head1.checked;
       var showhead2 = document.form1.head2.checked;
       head1.style.visibility=(showhead1) ? "visible" : "hidden";
       head2.style.visibility=(showhead2) ? "visible" : "hidden";
    }
    </script>
  </head>
  <body>
<h1 id="head1">This is the first heading</h1>
<h1 id="head2">This is the second heading</h1>
<p>Using the W3C DOM, you can choose whether to show or hide
the headings on this page using the checkboxes below.</p>
<form action="" name="form1">
<div>
<input type="checkbox" name="head1"
   onclick="ShowHide();" checked="checked" />
<span style="font-weight:bold">Show first heading</span><br/>
<input type="checkbox" name="head2"
   onclick="ShowHide();"checked="checked" />
<span style="font-weight:bold">Show second heading</span><br/>
</div>
</form>
</body>
</html>
```

The <h1> tags in this document define headings with the identifiers head1 and head2. The <form> section defines a form with two check boxes, one for each of the headings. When a check box is modified, the onClick method is used to call the ShowHide() function.

This function is defined within the <script> statements in the header. The function assigns the head1 and head2 variables to the objects for the headings, using the getElementById() method. Next, it assigns the showhead1 and showhead2 variables to the contents of the check boxes. Finally, the function uses the style.visibility attributes to set the visibility of the headings.

Figure 15.7 shows this example in action. In the figure, the second heading's check box has been unchecked, so only the first heading is visible.

TIP

The lines that set the visibility property might look a bit strange. The ? and : characters create *conditional expressions*, a shorthand way of handling if statements. To review conditional expressions, see Chapter 18, "Controlling Flow with Conditions and Loops."

FIGURE 15.7
The text hiding/showing example in action.

Modifying Text Within a Page

Next, you can create a simple script to modify the contents of a heading within a web page. As you learned earlier in this chapter, the nodeValue property of a text node contains its actual text, and the text node for a heading is a child of that heading. Thus, the syntax to change the text of a heading with the identifier head1 would be the following:

```
var head1 = document.getElementById("head1");
head1.firstChild.nodeValue = "New Text Here";
```

This assigns the variable head1 to the heading's object. The firstChild property returns the text node that is the only child of the heading, and its nodeValue property contains the heading text.

Using this technique, it's easy to create a page that allows the heading to be changed dynamically. Listing 15.7 shows the complete HTML document for this script.

LISTING 15.7   The Complete Text-Modifying Example

```
<?xml version="1.0" encoding="UTF-8"?>
<!DOCTYPE html PUBLIC "-//W3C//DTD XHTML 1.1//EN"
  "http://www.w3.org/TR/xhtml11/DTD/xhtml11.dtd">

<html xmlns="http://www.w3.org/1999/xhtml" xml:lang="en">
  <head>
    <title>Dynamic Text in JavaScript</title>
    <script type="text/javascript">
    function ChangeTitle() {
       if (!document.getElementById) return;
       var newtitle = document.form1.newtitle.value;
       var head1 = document.getElementById("head1");
       head1.firstChild.nodeValue=newtitle;
    }
    </script>
  </head>
  <body>
<h1 id="head1">Dynamic Text in JavaScript</h1>
<p>Using the W3C DOM, you can dynamically change the
heading at the top of this page. Enter a new title and
click the Change! button. </p>
<form action="" name="form1">
<div>
<input type="text" name="newtitle" size="40" />
<input type="button" value="Change!" onclick="ChangeTitle();" />
</div>
</form>
</body>
</html>
```

This example defines a form that enables the user to enter a new heading for the page. Pressing the button calls the ChangeTitle() function, defined in the header. This function gets the value the user entered in the form and changes the heading's value to the new text.

Figure 15.8 shows this page in action after a new title has been entered and the Change! button has been clicked.

FIGURE 15.8
The heading modification example in action.

Adding Text to a Page

Next, you can create a script that actually adds text to a page. To do this, you must first create a new text node. This statement creates a new text node with the text "this is a test":

```
var node=document.createTextNode("this is a test");
```

Next, you can add this node to the document. To do this, you use the appendChild method. The text can be added to any element that can contain text, but we will use a paragraph. The following statement adds the text node defined previously to the paragraph with the identifier p1:

```
document.getElementById("p1").appendChild(node);
```

Listing 15.8 shows the HTML document for a complete example that uses this technique, using a form to allow the user to specify text to add to the page.

LISTING 15.8   Adding Text to a Page

```
<?xml version="1.0" encoding="UTF-8"?>
<!DOCTYPE html PUBLIC "-//W3C//DTD XHTML 1.1//EN"
  "http://www.w3.org/TR/xhtml11/DTD/xhtml11.dtd">

<html xmlns="http://www.w3.org/1999/xhtml" xml:lang="en">
  <head>
    <title>Adding Text to a Page</title>
```

LISTING 15.8   Continued

```
<script type="text/javascript">
function AddText() {
    if (!document.getElementById) return;
    var sentence=document.form1.sentence.value;
    var node=document.createTextNode(" " + sentence);
    document.getElementById("p1").appendChild(node);
    document.form1.sentence.value="";
}
</script>
</head>
<body>
<h1 id="head1">Create Your Own Content</h1>
<p id="p1"> Using the W3C DOM, you can dynamically add
sentences to this paragraph. Type a sentence and click
the Add! Button.</p>
<form action="" name="form1">
<div>
<input type="text" name="sentence" size="65" />
<input type="button" value="Add!" onclick="AddText();" />
</div>
</form>
</body>
</html>
```

In this example, the <p> section defines the paragraph that will hold the added text. The <form> section defines a form with a text field called sentence, and an Add button, which calls the AddText() function. This function is defined in the header.

The AddText() function first assigns the sentence variable to the text typed in the text field. Next, it creates a new text node containing the sentence and appends the new text node to the paragraph.

Load this document into a browser to test it and try adding several sentences by typing them and clicking the Add button. Figure 15.9 shows this document after several sentences have been added to the paragraph.

FIGURE 15.9
The text addition example in
action.

Summary

In this chapter, you've learned about the DOM, JavaScript's hierarchy of web page objects. You've learned how you can use the `document` object to work with documents and used the `history` and `location` objects to control the current URL displayed in the browser.

Additionally, you learned the functions and properties you can use to manage DOM objects and used example scripts to hide and show elements within a page, modify text, and add text. You also learned how to use HTML and CSS to define a positionable layer and how you can use positioning properties dynamically with JavaScript.

This foundational knowledge of the DOM puts you in position (no pun intended) to more effectively work with JavaScript in more advanced ways, as you'll learn in the chapters that follow.

Q&A

Q. Can I avoid assigning an `id` attribute to every DOM object I want to handle with a script?

A. Yes. Although the scripts in this chapter typically use the `id` attribute for convenience, you can actually locate any object in the page by using combinations of node properties such as `firstChild` and `nextSibling`. However, keep in mind that any change you make to the HTML can change an element's place in the DOM hierarchy, so the `id` attribute is a reliable recommended way to handle this.

Q. I can use `history` and `document` instead of `window.history` and `window.document`. Can I leave out the `window` object in other cases?

A. Yes. For example, you can use `alert` instead of `window.alert` to display a message. The `window` object contains the current script, so it's treated as a default object. However, be warned that you shouldn't omit the `window` object's name when you're using frames, layers, or multiple windows or in an event handler.

Q. Can I change history entries or prevent the user from using the Back and Forward buttons?

A. You can't change the history entries. You can't prevent the use of the Back and Forward buttons, but you can use the `location.replace()` method to load a series of pages that don't appear in the history. There are a few tricks for preventing the Back button from working properly, but I don't recommend them—that's the sort of thing that gives JavaScript a bad name.

Q. What happens when my web page includes multiple HTML documents, such as when frames are used?

A. In this case, each window or frame has its own `document` object that stores the elements of the HTML document it contains.

Q. If the DOM allows any object to be dynamically changed, why does the positioning example need to use `<div>` tags to define a layer?

A. The example could just as easily move a heading or a paragraph. The `<div>` is just a convenient and standard way to group objects and to create a square object with a border.

Workshop

The workshop contains quiz questions and exercises to help you solidify your understanding of the material covered. Try to answer all questions before looking at the "Answers" section that follows.

Quiz

1. Which of the following DOM objects never has a parent node?

    a. body

    b. div

    c. document

2. Which of the following is the correct syntax to get the DOM object for a heading with the identifier head1?

    a. `document.getElementById("head1")`

    b. `document.GetElementByID("head1")`

    c. `document.getElementsById("head1")`

3. Which of the following tags can be used to create a layer?

    a. `<layer>`

    b. `<div>`

    c. `<style>`

4. Which property controls an element's left-to-right position?

    a. `left`

    b. `width`

    c. `lrpos`

5. Which of the following CSS rules would create a heading that is not currently visible in the page?

    a. `h1 {visibility: invisible;}`

    b. `h1 {display: none;}`

    c. `h1 {style: invisible;}`

Answers

1. c. The document object is the root of the DOM object tree and has no parent object.

2. a. getElementById has a lowercase *g* at the beginning and a lowercase *d* at the end, contrary to standard English grammar.

3. b. The <div> tag can be used to create positionable layers.

4. a. The left property controls an element's left-to-right position.

5. b. The none value for the display property makes it invisible. The visibility property could also be used, but its possible values are visible or hidden.

Exercises

If you want to gain more experience using the DOM features you learned in this chapter, try the following:

▶ Modify the Back and Forward example in Listing 15.2 to include a Reload button along with the Back and Forward buttons. (This button would trigger the location.reload() method.)

▶ Modify the positioning example in Listings 15.4 and 15.5 to move the square one pixel at a time rather than 10 at a time.

▶ Add a third check box to Listing 15.6 to allow the paragraph of text to be shown or hidden. You will need to add an id attribute to the <p> tag, add a check box to the form, and add the appropriate lines to the script.

CHAPTER 16

Using JavaScript Variables, Strings, and Arrays

Now that you have learned some of the fundamentals of JavaScript and the DOM, it's time to dig into more details of the JavaScript language.

In this chapter, you'll learn three tools for storing data in JavaScript: *variables*, which store numbers or text; *strings*, which are special variables for working with text; and *arrays*, which are multiple variables you can refer to by number.

Using Variables

Unless you skipped over the JavaScript-related chapters in the beginning of this book, you've already used a few variables. You probably can also figure out how to use a few more without any help. Nevertheless, there are some aspects of variables you haven't learned yet. We will now look at some of the details.

Choosing Variable Names

Variables are named containers that can store data (for example, a number, a text string, or an object). As you learned earlier in this book, each variable has a name. There are specific rules you must follow when choosing a variable name:

▶ Variable names can include letters of the alphabet, both upper- and lowercase. They can also include the digits 0–9 and the underscore (_) character.

▶ Variable names cannot include spaces or any other punctuation characters.

WHAT YOU'LL LEARN IN THIS CHAPTER:

▶ How to name and declare variables

▶ How to choose whether to use local or global variables

▶ How to assign values to variables

▶ How to convert between different data types

▶ How to use variables and literals in expressions

▶ How strings are stored in String objects

▶ How to create and use String objects

▶ How to create and use arrays of numbers and strings

NOTE

You can choose to use either friendly, easy-to-read names or completely cryptic ones. Do yourself a favor: Use longer, friendly names whenever possible. Although you might remember the difference between a, b, x, and x1 right now, you might not after a good night's sleep.

▶ The first character of the variable name must be either a letter or an underscore.

▶ Variable names are case sensitive—`totalnum`, `Totalnum`, and `TotalNum` are separate variable names.

▶ There is no official limit on the length of variable names, but they must fit within one line.

Using these rules, the following are examples of valid variable names:

```
total_number_of_fish
LastInvoiceNumber
temp1
a
_var39
```

Using Local and Global Variables

Some computer languages require you to declare a variable before you use it. JavaScript includes the var keyword, which can be used to declare a variable. You can omit var in many cases; the variable is still declared the first time you assign a value to it.

To understand where to declare a variable, you will need to understand the concept of *scope*. A variable's scope is the area of the script in which that variable can be used. There are two types of variables:

▶ *Global variables* have the entire script (and other scripts in the same HTML document) as their scope. They can be used anywhere, even within functions.

▶ *Local variables* have a single function as their scope. They can be used only within the function they are created in.

To create a global variable, you declare it in the main script, outside any functions. You can use the var keyword to declare the variable, as in this example:

```
var students = 25;
```

This statement declares a variable called `students` and assigns it a value of 25. If this statement is used outside functions, it creates a global variable. The var keyword is optional in this case, so this statement is equivalent to the previous one:

```
students = 25;
```

Before you get in the habit of omitting the var keyword, be sure you understand exactly when it's required. It's actually a good idea to always use the var keyword—you'll avoid errors and make your script easier to read, and it won't usually cause any trouble.

A local variable belongs to a particular function. Any variable you declare with the var keyword in a function is a local variable. Additionally, the variables in the function's parameter list are always local variables.

To create a local variable within a function, you must use the var keyword. This forces JavaScript to create a local variable, even if there is a global variable with the same name.

You should now understand the difference between local and global variables. If you're still a bit confused, don't worry—if you use the var keyword every time, you'll usually end up with the right type of variable.

Assigning Values to Variables

As you learned in Chapter 4, "Understanding JavaScript," you can use the equal sign to assign a value to a variable. For example, this statement assigns the value 40 to the variable lines:

```
lines = 40;
```

You can use any expression to the right of the equal sign, including other variables. You have used this syntax earlier to add one to a variable:

```
lines = lines + 1;
```

Because incrementing or decrementing variables is quite common, JavaScript includes two types of shorthand for this syntax. The first is the += operator, which enables you to create the following shorter version of the preceding example:

```
lines += 1;
```

Similarly, you can subtract a number from a variable using the -= operator:

```
lines -= 1;
```

If you still think that's too much to type, JavaScript also includes the increment and decrement operators, ++ and --. This statement adds one to the value of lines:

```
lines++;
```

Similarly, this statement subtracts one from the value of `lines`:

```
lines--;
```

You can alternately use the ++ or -- operators before a variable name, as in `++lines`. However, these are not identical. The difference is when the increment or decrement happens:

▶ If the operator is after the variable name, the increment or decrement happens *after* the current expression is evaluated.

▶ If the operator is before the variable name, the increment or decrement happens *before* the current expression is evaluated.

NOTE

These operators are strictly for your convenience. If it makes more sense to you to stick to `lines = lines + 1`, do it—your script won't suffer.

This difference is only an issue when you use the variable in an expression and increment or decrement it in the same statement. As an example, suppose you have assigned the `lines` variable the value 40. The following two statements have different effects:

```
alert(lines++);
alert(++lines);
```

The first statement displays an alert with the value 40, and then increments `lines` to 41. The second statement first increments `lines` to 41, then displays an alert with the value 41.

Understanding Expressions and Operators

TIP

Along with variables and constant values, you can also use calls to functions that return results within an expression.

An *expression* is a combination of variables and values that the JavaScript interpreter can evaluate to a single value. The characters that are used to combine these values, such as + and /, are called *operators*.

Using JavaScript Operators

You've already used some operators, such as the + sign (addition) and the `increment` and `decrement` operators. Table 16.1 lists some of the most important operators you can use in JavaScript expressions.

TABLE 16.1   Common JavaScript Operators

Operator	Description	Example
+	Concatenate (combine) strings	`message="this is" + " a test";`
+	Add	`result = 5 + 7;`
-	Subtract	`score = score - 1;`
*	Multiply	`total = quantity * price;`
/	Divide	`average = sum / 4;`
%	Modulo (remainder)	`remainder = sum % 4;`
++	Increment	`tries++;`
--	Decrement	`total--;`

Along with these, there are also many other operators used in conditional statements; you'll learn about these in Chapter 18, "Controlling Flow with Conditions and Loops."

Operator Precedence

When you use more than one operator in an expression, JavaScript uses rules of *operator precedence* to decide how to calculate the value. Table 16.1 lists the operators from lowest to highest precedence, and operators with highest precedence are evaluated first. For example, consider this statement:

```
result = 4 + 5 * 3;
```

If you try to calculate this result, there are two ways to do it. You could multiply 5 * 3 first and then add 4 (result: 19) or add 4 + 5 first and then multiply by 3 (result: 27). JavaScript solves this dilemma by following the precedence rules: Because multiplication has a higher precedence than addition, it first multiplies 5 * 3 and then adds 4, producing a result of 19.

Sometimes operator precedence doesn't produce the result you want. For example, consider this statement:

```
result = a + b + c + d / 4;
```

This is an attempt to average four numbers by adding them all together, and then dividing by four. However, because JavaScript gives division a higher precedence than addition, it will divide the d variable by 4 before adding the other numbers, producing an incorrect result.

NOTE

If you're familiar with any other programming languages, you'll find that the operators and precedence in JavaScript work, for the most part, the same way as those in C, C++, and Java, as well as web scripting languages such as PHP.

You can control precedence by using parentheses. Here's the working statement to calculate an average:

```
result = (a + b + c + d) / 4;
```

The parentheses ensure that the four variables are added first, and then the sum is divided by four.

Data Types in JavaScript

In some computer languages, you have to specify the type of data a variable will store, for example, a number or a string. In JavaScript, you don't need to specify a data type in most cases. However, you should know the types of data JavaScript can deal with.

These are the basic JavaScript data types:

- **Numbers, such as 3, 25, or 1.4142138**—JavaScript supports both integers and floating-point numbers.

- **Boolean, or logical values**—These can have one of two values: `true` or `false`. These are useful for indicating whether a certain condition is true.

- **Strings, such as "I am a jelly doughnut"**—These consist of one or more characters of text. (Strictly speaking, these are `String` objects, which you'll learn about later in this chapter.)

- **The null value, represented by the keyword `null`**—This is the value of an undefined variable. For example, the statement `document.write(fig)` will result in this value (and an error message) if the variable `fig` has not been previously used or defined.

Although JavaScript keeps track of the data type currently stored in each variable, it doesn't restrict you from changing types midstream. For example, suppose you declared a variable by assigning it a value:

```
total = 31;
```

This statement declares a variable called `total` and assigns it the value of 31. This is a numeric variable. Now suppose you changed the value of `total`:

```
total = "albatross";
```

This assigns a string value to `total`, replacing the numeric value. JavaScript will not display an error when this statement executes; it's perfectly valid, although it's probably not a very useful total.

Converting Between Data Types

JavaScript handles conversions between data types for you whenever it can. For example, you've already used statements like this:

```
document.write("The total is " + total);
```

This statement prints out a message such as `"The total is 40"`. Because the `document.write` function works with strings, the JavaScript interpreter automatically converts any nonstrings in the expression (in this case, the value of `total`) to strings before performing the function.

This works equally well with floating-point and Boolean values. However, there are some situations where it won't work. For example, the following statement will work fine if the value of `total` is `40`:

```
average = total / 3;
```

However, the `total` variable could also contain a string; in this case, the preceding statement would result in an error.

In some situations, you might end up with a string containing a number and need to convert it to a regular numeric variable. JavaScript includes two functions for this purpose:

▶ **parseInt()**—Converts a string to an integer number.

▶ **parseFloat()**—Converts a string to a floating-point number.

Both of these functions will read a number from the beginning of the string and return a numeric version. For example, these statements convert the string `"30 angry polar bears"` to a number:

```
stringvar = "30 angry polar bears";
numvar = parseInt(stringvar);
```

After these statements execute, the `numvar` variable contains the number 30. The nonnumeric portion of the string is ignored.

NOTE

These functions look for a number of the appropriate type at the beginning of the string. If a valid number is not found, the function will return the special value NaN, meaning *not a number*.

Using `String` Objects

You've already used several strings in previous chapters. Strings store a group of text characters and are named similarly to other variables. As a simple example, this statement assigns the string `This is a test` to a string variable called `test`:

```
test = "This is a test";
```

Creating a `String` Object

JavaScript stores strings as `String` objects. You usually don't need to worry about this, but it will explain some of the techniques for working with strings, which use methods (built-in functions) of the `String` object.

There are two ways to create a new `String` object. The first is the one you've already used, whereas the second uses object-oriented syntax. The following two statements create the same string:

```
test = "This is a test";
test = new String("This is a test");
```

The second statement uses the `new` keyword, which you use to create objects. This tells the browser to create a new `String` object containing the text `This is a test` and assigns it to the variable `test`.

NOTE

Although you can create a string using object-oriented syntax, the standard JavaScript syntax is simpler, and there is no difference in the strings created by these two methods.

Assigning a Value

You can assign a value to a string in the same way as any other variable. Both of the examples in the previous section assigned an initial value to the string. You can also assign a value after the string has already been created. For example, the following statement replaces the contents of the `test` variable with a new string:

```
test = "This is only a test.";
```

You can also use the concatenation operator (+) to combine the values of two strings. Listing 16.1 shows a simple example of assigning and combining the values of strings.

LISTING 16.1   Assigning Values to Strings and Combining Them

```
<?xml version="1.0" encoding="UTF-8"?>
<!DOCTYPE html PUBLIC "-//W3C//DTD XHTML 1.1//EN"
  "http://www.w3.org/TR/xhtml11/DTD/xhtml11.dtd">

<html xmlns="http://www.w3.org/1999/xhtml" xml:lang="en">
  <head>
    <title>String Text</title>
  </head>

  <body>
      <h1>String Test</h1>
    <script type="text/javascript">
     test1 = "This is a test. ";
     test2 = "This is only a test.";
     both = test1 + test2;
     alert(both);
     </script>
</body>
</html>
```

This script assigns values to two string variables, test1 and test2, and
then displays an alert with their combined value. If you load this HTML
document in a browser, your output should resemble Figure 16.1.

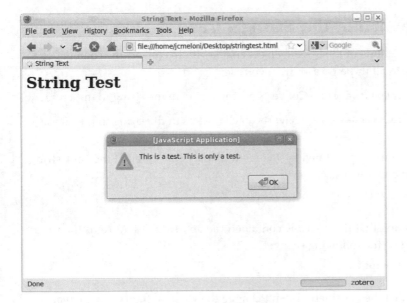

FIGURE 16.1
The output of the string example
script.

NOTE

The plus sign (+) is also used to add numbers in JavaScript. The browser knows whether to use addition or concatenation based on the types of data you use with the plus sign. If you use it between a number and a string, the number is converted to a string and concatenated.

NOTE

Remember that although test refers to a string variable, the value of test.length is a number and can be used in any numeric expression.

In addition to using the + operator to concatenate two strings, you can use the += operator to add text to a string. For example, this statement adds a period to the current contents of the string sentence:

```
sentence += ".";
```

Calculating the String's Length

From time to time, you might find it useful to know how many characters a string variable contains. You can do this with the length property of String objects, which you can use with any string. To use this property, type the string's name followed by .length.

For example, test.length refers to the length of the test string. Here is an example of this property:

```
test = "This is a test.";
document.write(test.length);
```

The first statement assigns the string This is a test to the test variable. The second statement displays the length of the string—in this case, 15 characters. The length property is a read-only property, so you cannot assign a value to it to change a string's length.

Converting the String's Case

Two methods of the String object enable you to convert the contents of a string to all uppercase or all lowercase:

▶ **toUpperCase()**—Converts all characters in the string to uppercase

▶ **toLowerCase()**—Converts all characters in the string to lowercase

NOTE

Note that the syntax for these methods is similar to the length property introduced earlier. The difference is that methods always use parentheses, whereas properties don't. The toUpperCase and toLowerCase methods do not take any parameters, but you still need to use the parentheses.

For example, the following statement displays the value of the test string variable in lowercase:

```
document.write(test.toLowerCase());
```

Assuming that this variable contained the text This Is A Test, the result would be the following string:

```
this is a test
```

Note that the statement doesn't change the value of the text variable. These methods return the upper- or lowercase version of the string, but they don't change the string itself. If you want to change the string's value, you can use a statement like this:

```
test = test.toLowerCase();
```

Working with Substrings

So far, you've worked with entire strings. JavaScript also enables you to work with *substrings*, or portions of a string. You can use the substring method to retrieve a portion of a string or the charAt method to get a single character. These are explained in the following sections.

Using Part of a String

The substring method returns a string consisting of a portion of the original string between two index values, which you must specify in parentheses. For example, the following statement displays the fourth through sixth characters of the text string:

```
document.write(text.substring(3,6));
```

At this point, you're probably wondering where the 3 and the 6 come from. There are three things you need to understand about the index parameters:

▸ Indexing starts with 0 for the first character of the string, so the fourth character is actually index 3.

▸ The second index is noninclusive. A second index of 6 includes up to index 5 (the sixth character).

▸ You can specify the two indexes in either order. The smaller one will be assumed to be the first index. In the previous example, (6,3) would have produced the same result. Of course, there is rarely a reason to use the reverse order.

As another example, suppose you defined a string called alpha to hold the alphabet:

```
alpha = "ABCDEFGHIJKLMNOPQRSTUVWXYZ";
```

The following are examples of the substring() method using this string:

▸ alpha.substring(0,4) returns ABCD.

▸ alpha.substring(10,12) returns KL.

▶ `alpha.substring(12,10)` also returns KL. Because it's smaller, 10 is used as the first index.

▶ `alpha.substring(6,7)` returns G.

▶ `alpha.substring(24,26)` returns YZ.

▶ `alpha.substring(0,26)` returns the entire alphabet.

▶ `alpha.substring(6,6)` returns the `null` value, an empty string. This is true whenever the two index values are the same.

Getting a Single Character

The `charAt` method is a simple way to grab a single character from a string. You specify the character's index, or position, in parentheses. The indexes begin at 0 for the first character. Here are a few examples using the `alpha` string:

▶ `alpha.charAt(0)` returns A.

▶ `alpha.charAt(12)` returns M.

▶ `alpha.charAt(25)` returns Z.

▶ `alpha.charAt(27)` returns an empty string because there is no character at that position.

Finding a Substring

Another use for substrings is to find a string within another string. One way to do this is with the `indexOf` method. To use this method, add `indexOf` to the string you want to search and specify the string to search for in the parentheses. This example searches for `"this"` in the `test` string:

```
loc = test.indexOf("this");
```

The value returned in the `loc` variable is an index into the string, similar to the first index in the `substring` method. The first character of the string is index `0`.

You can specify an optional second parameter to indicate the index value to begin the search. For example, this statement searches for the word `fish` in the `temp` string, starting with the 20th character:

```
location = temp.indexOf("fish",19);
```

CAUTION

As with most JavaScript methods and property names, `indexOf` is case sensitive. Make sure you type it exactly as shown here when you use it in scripts.

NOTE

One use for the second parameter is to search for multiple occurrences of a string. After finding the first occurrence, you search starting with that location for the second one, and so on.

A second method, `lastIndexOf()`, works the same way, but finds the *last* occurrence of the string. It searches the string backwards, starting with the last character. For example, this statement finds the last occurrence of `Fred` in the `names` string:

```
location = names.lastIndexOf("Fred");
```

As with `indexOf()`, you can specify a location to search from as the second parameter. In this case, the string will be searched backward starting at that location.

Using Numeric Arrays

An *array* is a numbered group of data items that you can treat as a single unit. For example, you might use an array called `scores` to store several scores for a game. Arrays can contain strings, numbers, objects, or other types of data. Each item in an array is called an *element* of the array.

Creating a Numeric Array

Unlike most other types of JavaScript variables, you typically need to declare an array before you use it. The following example creates an array with four elements:

```
scores = new Array(4);
```

To assign a value to the array, you use an index in brackets. Indexes begin with 0, so the elements of the array in this example would be numbered 0 to 3. These statements assign values to the four elements of the array:

```
scores[0] = 39;
scores[1] = 40;
scores[2] = 100;
scores[3] = 49;
```

You can also declare an array and specify values for elements at the same time. This statement creates the same `scores` array in a single line:

```
scores = new Array(39,40,100,49);
```

You can also use a shorthand syntax to declare an array and specify its contents. The following statement is an alternative way to create the `scores` array:

```
scores = [39,40,100,49];
```

TIP

Remember to use parentheses when declaring an array with the `new` keyword, as in `a=new Array(3,4,5)`, and use brackets when declaring an array without `new`, as in `a=[3,4,5]`. Otherwise, you'll run into JavaScript errors.

Understanding Array Length

Like strings, arrays have a `length` property. This tells you the number of elements in the array. If you specified the length when creating the array, this value becomes the `length` property's value. For example, these statements would print the number 30:

```
scores = new Array(30);
document.write(scores.length);
```

You can declare an array without a specific length, and change the length later by assigning values to elements or changing the `length` property. For example, these statements create a new array and assign values to two of its elements:

```
test = new Array();
test[0]=21;
test[5]=22;
```

TIP

Looking at this example, you might imagine it would be inconvenient to display all the elements of a large array. This is an ideal job for loops, which enable you to perform the same statements several times with different values. You'll learn all about loops in Chapter 18.

In this example, because the largest index number assigned so far is 5, the array has a `length` property of 6—remember, elements are numbered starting at 0.

Accessing Array Elements

You can read the contents of an array using the same notation you used when assigning values. For example, the following statements would display the values of the first three elements of the `scores` array:

```
scoredisp = "Scores: " + scores[0] + "," + scores[1] + "," + scores[2];
document.write(scoredisp);
```

Using String Arrays

So far, you've used arrays of numbers. JavaScript also enables you to use *string arrays*, or arrays of strings. This is a powerful feature that enables you to work with a large number of strings at the same time.

Creating a String Array

You declare a string array in the same way as a numeric array—in fact, JavaScript does not make a distinction between them:

```
names = new Array(30);
```

You can then assign string values to the array elements:

```
names[0] = "Henry J. Tillman";
names[1] = "Sherlock Holmes";
```

As with numeric arrays, you can also specify a string array's contents when you create it. Either of the following statements would create the same string array as the preceding example:

```
names = new Array("Henry J. Tillman", "Sherlock Holmes");
names = ["Henry J. Tillman", "Sherlock Holmes"];
```

You can use string array elements anywhere you would use a string. You can even use the string methods introduced earlier. For example, the following statement prints the first five characters of the first element of the names array, resulting in Henry:

```
document.write(names[0].substring(0,5));
```

Splitting a String

JavaScript includes a string method called split, which splits a string into its component parts. To use this method, specify the string to split and a character to divide the parts:

```
test = "John Q. Public";
parts = test.split(" ");
```

In this example, the test string contains the name John Q. Public. The split method in the second statement splits the name string at each space, resulting in three strings. These are stored in a string array called parts. After the example statements execute, the elements of parts contain the following:

- ▶ parts[0] = "John"

- ▶ parts[1] = "Q."

- ▶ parts[2] = "Public"

JavaScript also includes an array method, join, which performs the opposite function. This statement reassembles the parts array into a string:

```
fullname = parts.join(" ");
```

The value in the parentheses specifies a character to separate the parts of the array. In this case, a space is used, resulting in the final string John Q. Public. If you do not specify a character, commas are used.

Sorting a String Array

JavaScript also includes a sort method for arrays, which returns an alphabetically sorted version of the array. For example, the following statements initialize an array of four names and sort them:

```
names[0] = "Public, John Q.";
names[1] = "Doe, Jane";
names[2] = "Duck, Daisy";
names[3] = "Mouse, Mickey";
sortednames = names.sort();
```

The last statement sorts the names array and stores the result in a new array, sortednames.

Sorting a Numeric Array

NOTE

JavaScript expects the comparison function to return a negative number if a belongs before b, 0 if they are the same, or a positive number if a belongs after b. This is why a-b is all you need for the function to sort numerically.

Because the sort method sorts alphabetically, it won't work with a numeric array—at least not the way you'd expect. If an array contains the numbers 4, 10, 30, and 200, for example, it would sort them as 10, 200, 30, 4—not even close. Fortunately, there's a solution: You can specify a function in the sort method's parameters, and that function will be used to compare the numbers. The following code sorts a numeric array correctly:

```
function numcompare(a,b) {
    return a-b;
}
nums = new Array(30, 10, 200, 4);
sortednums = nums.sort(numcompare);
```

This example defines a simple function, numcompare, which subtracts the two numbers. After you specify this function in the sort method, the array is sorted in the correct numeric order: 4, 10, 30, 200.

▼ TRY IT YOURSELF

Sorting and Displaying Names

To gain more experience working with JavaScript's string and array features, you can create a script that enables the user to enter a list of names and displays the list in sorted form.

Because this will be a larger script, you will create separate HTML and JavaScript files, as described in Chapter 14, "Getting Started with JavaScript Programming." First, the sort.html file will contain the HTML structure and form fields for the script to work with. Listing 16.2 shows the HTML document.

TRY IT YOURSELF ▼

**Sorting and
Displaying Names**
continued

LISTING 16.2   The HTML Document for the Sorting Example

```
<?xml version="1.0" encoding="UTF-8"?>
<!DOCTYPE html PUBLIC "-//W3C//DTD XHTML 1.1//EN"
  "http://www.w3.org/TR/xhtml11/DTD/xhtml11.dtd">

<html xmlns="http://www.w3.org/1999/xhtml" xml:lang="en">
  <head>
    <title>Array Sorting Example</title>
   <script type="text/javascript" src="sort.js"></script>
  </head>

  <body>
     <h1>Sorting String Arrays</h1>

     <p>Enter two or more names in the field below,
     and the sorted list of names will appear in the
     text area.</p>
     <form name="theform">
     Name:
     <input type="text" name="newname" size="20" />
     <input type="button" name="addname" value="Add"
     onclick="SortNames();">
     <br/>
     <h2>Sorted Names</h2>
     <textarea cols="60" rows="10" name="sorted">
     The sorted names will appear here.
     </textarea>
     </form>
</body>
</html>
```

Because the script will be in a separate document, the <script> tag in the header of this document uses the src attribute to include a JavaScript file called sort.js. You will create this file next.

This document defines a form named theform, a text field named newname, an addname button, and a text area named sorted. Your script will use these form fields as its user interface.

Listing 16.3 provides the JavaScript necessary for the sorting process.

LISTING 16.3   The JavaScript File for the Sorting Example

```
// initialize the counter and the array
var numnames=0;
var names = new Array();
function SortNames() {
   // Get the name from the text field
```

▼ TRY IT YOURSELF

Sorting and Displaying Names

continued

LISTING 16.3   Continued

```
thename=document.theform.newname.value;
// Add the name to the array
names[numnames]=thename;
// Increment the counter
numnames++;
// Sort the array
names.sort();
document.theform.sorted.value=names.join("\n");
}
```

The script begins by defining two variables with the var keyword: numnames will be a counter that increments as each name is added, and the names array will store the names.

When you type a name into the text field and click the button, the onclick event handler calls the SortNames function. This function stores the text field value in a variable, thename, and then adds the name to the names array using numnames as the index. It then increments numnames to prepare for the next name.

The final section of the script sorts the names and displays them. First, the sort() method is used to sort the names array. Next, the join() method is used to combine the names, separate them with line breaks, and display them in the text area.

To test the script, save it as sort.js, and then load the sort.html file you created previously into a browser. You can then add some names and test the script. Figure 16.2 shows the result after sorting several names.

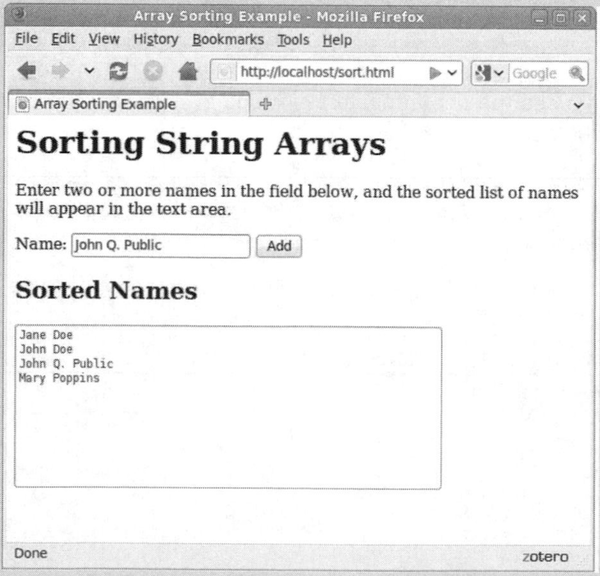

FIGURE 16.2
The output of the name-sorting example.

Summary

During this chapter, you've focused on variables and how JavaScript handles them. You've learned how to name variables, how to declare them, and the differences between local and global variables. You also explored the data types supported by JavaScript and how to convert between them.

You also learned about JavaScript's more complex variables, strings, and arrays and looked at the features that enable you to perform operations on them, such as converting strings to uppercase or sorting arrays.

In the next chapter, you'll continue your foundational JavaScript education by learning more about two additional key features: functions and objects.

Q&A

Q. What is the importance of the `var` keyword? Should I always use it to declare variables?

A. You only need to use `var` to define a local variable in a function. However, if you're unsure at all, it's always safe to use `var`. Using it consistently will help you keep your scripts organized and error free.

Q. Is there any reason I would want to use the `var` keyword to create a local variable with the same name as a global one?

A. Not on purpose. The main reason to use `var` is to avoid conflicts with global variables you might not know about. For example, you might add a global variable in the future, or you might add another script to the page that uses a similar variable name. This is more of an issue with large, complex scripts.

Q. What good are Boolean variables?

A. Often in scripts, you'll need a variable to indicate whether something has happened—for example, whether a phone number the user has entered is in the right format. Boolean variables are ideal for this; they're also useful in working with conditions, as you'll see in Chapter 18.

Q. Can I store other types of data in an array? For example, can I have an array of dates?

A. Absolutely. JavaScript enables you to store any data type in an array.

Q. What about two-dimensional arrays?

A. These are arrays with two indexes (such as columns and rows). JavaScript does not directly support this type of array, but you can use objects to achieve the same effect. You will learn more about objects in the next chapter.

Workshop

The workshop contains quiz questions and exercises to help you solidify your understanding of the material covered. Try to answer all questions before looking at the "Answers" section that follows.

Quiz

1. Which of the following is *not* a valid JavaScript variable name?

   a. `2names`

   b. `first_and_last_names`

   c. `FirstAndLast`

2. If the statement `var fig=2` appears in a function, which type of variable does it declare?

   a. A global variable

   b. A local variable

   c. A constant variable

3. If the string `test` contains the value `The eagle has landed.`, what would be the value of `test.length`?

   a. 4

   b. 21

   c. The

4. Using the same example string, which of these statements would return the word `eagle`?

   a. `test.substring(4,9)`

   b. `test.substring(5,9)`

   c. `test.substring("eagle")`

5. What will be the result of the JavaScript expression `31 + " angry polar bears"`?

   a. An error message

   b. 32

   c. "31 angry polar bears"

Answers

1. a. 2names is an invalid JavaScript variable name because it begins with a number. The others are valid, although they're probably not ideal choices for names.

2. b. Because the variable is declared in a function, it is a local variable. The var keyword ensures that a local variable is created.

3. b. The length of the string is 21 characters.

4. a. The correct statement is test.substring(4,9). Remember that the indexes start with 0 and that the second index is noninclusive.

5. c. JavaScript converts the whole expression to the string "31 angry polar bears". (No offense to polar bears, who are seldom angry and rarely seen in groups this large.)

Exercises

▶ Modify the sorting example in Listing 16.3 to convert the names to all uppercase before sorting and displaying them.

▶ Modify Listing 16.3 to display a numbered list of names in the text area.

CHAPTER 17
Using JavaScript Functions and Objects

In this chapter, you'll learn about two more key JavaScript concepts that you'll use throughout the rest of this book. First, you'll learn the details of using functions, which enable you to group any number of statements into a block. This is useful for repeating sections of code, and you can also create functions that accept parameters and return values for later use.

Whereas functions enable you to group sections of code, objects enable you to group data—you can use them to combine related data items and functions for working with the data. You'll learn how to define and use objects and their methods and will work specifically with two useful built-in objects, Math and Date.

Using Functions

The scripts you've seen so far are simple lists of instructions. The browser begins with the first statement after the <script> tag and follows each instruction in order until it reaches the closing </script> tag (or encounters an error).

Although this is a straightforward approach for short scripts, it can be confusing to read a longer script written in this fashion. To make it easier for you to organize your scripts, JavaScript supports functions, which you learned about in Chapter 14, "Getting Started with JavaScript Programming." In this section, you will learn how to define and use functions.

Defining a Function

Functions are groups of JavaScript statements that can be treated as a single unit. To use a function, you must first define it. Here is a simple example of a function definition:

WHAT YOU'LL LEARN IN THIS CHAPTER:

▶ How to define and call functions
▶ How to return values from functions
▶ How to define custom objects
▶ How to use object properties and values
▶ How to define and use object methods
▶ How to use objects to store data and related functions
▶ How to use the Math object's methods
▶ How to use with to work with objects
▶ How to use the Date object to work with dates

```
function Greet() {
    alert("Greetings.");
}
```

This snippet defines a function that displays an alert message to the user. This begins with the `function` keyword. The function's name is `Greet`. Notice the parentheses after the function's name. As you'll learn next, the space between them is not always empty.

The first and last lines of the function definition include braces ({ and }). You use these to enclose all of the statements in the function. The browser uses the braces to determine where the function begins and ends.

Between the braces, this particular function contains a single line. This uses the built-in `alert` function, which displays an alert message. The message will contain the text "Greetings."

Now, about those parentheses. The current `Greet` function always does the same thing: Each time you use it, it displays the same message. Although this avoids a bit of typing, it doesn't really provide much of an advantage.

To make your function more flexible, you can add *parameters*, also known as *arguments*. These are variables that are received by the function each time it is called. For example, you can add a parameter called `who` that tells the function the name of the person to greet. Here is the modified `Greet` function:

```
function Greet(who) {
    alert("Greetings, " + who);
}
```

Of course, to use this function, you should include it in an HTML document. Traditionally, the best place for a function definition is within the <head> section of the document. Because the statements in the <head> section are executed first, this ensures that the function is defined before it is used.

Listing 17.1 shows the `Greet` function embedded in the header section of an HTML document.

LISTING 17.1   The Greet Function in an HTML Document

```
<?xml version="1.0" encoding="UTF-8"?>
<!DOCTYPE html PUBLIC "-//W3C//DTD XHTML 1.1//EN"
  "http://www.w3.org/TR/xhtml11/DTD/xhtml11.dtd">

<html xmlns="http://www.w3.org/1999/xhtml" xml:lang="en">
  <head>
```

CAUTION

Function names are case sensitive. If you define a function such as `Greet` with a capital letter, be sure you use the identical name when you call the function. That is to say, if you define the function with the name `Greet` but you attempt to call the function using `greet`, it will not work.

LISTING 17.1 Continued

```
    <title>Functions</title>
    <script type="text/javascript">
    function Greet(who) {
        alert("Greetings, " + who);
    }
    </script>
  </head>
  <body>
    <p>This is the body of the page.</p>
</body>
</html>
```

Calling the Function

You have now defined a function and placed it in an HTML document. However, if you load Listing 17.1 into a browser, you'll notice that it does absolutely nothing. This is because the function is defined—ready to be used—but we haven't used it yet.

Making use of a function is referred to as *calling* the function. To call a function, use the function's name as a statement in a script. You will need to include the parentheses and the values for the function's parameters. For example, here's a statement that calls the Greet function:

```
Greet("Fred");
```

This tells the JavaScript interpreter to transfer control to the first statement in the Greet function. It also passes the parameter "Fred" to the function. This value will be assigned to the who variable inside the function.

Listing 17.2 shows a complete HTML document that includes the function definition and a second script in the body of the page that actually calls the function. To demonstrate the usefulness of functions, we'll call it twice to greet two different people.

LISTING 17.2 The Complete Function Example

```
<?xml version="1.0" encoding="UTF-8"?>
<!DOCTYPE html PUBLIC "-//W3C//DTD XHTML 1.1//EN"
  "http://www.w3.org/TR/xhtml11/DTD/xhtml11.dtd">

<html xmlns="http://www.w3.org/1999/xhtml" xml:lang="en">
  <head>
    <title>Functions</title>
    <script type="text/javascript">
    function Greet(who) {
```

> **TIP**
>
> Functions can have more than one parameter. To define a function with multiple parameters, list a variable name for each parameter, separated by commas. To call the function, specify values for each parameter separated by commas.

LISTING 17.2   Continued

```
        alert("Greetings, " + who);
    }
  </script>
</head>
<body>
  <h1>Function Example</h1>
  <p>Prepare to be greeted twice.</p>
  <script type="text/javascript">
  Greet("Fred");
  Greet("Ethel");
  </script>
</body>
</html>
```

This listing includes a second set of <script> tags in the body of the page. The second script includes two function calls to the Greet function, each with a different name.

Now that you have a script that actually does something, try loading it into a browser. You should see something like Figure 17.1, which shows the Greeting script when it is initially loaded in a browser.

FIGURE 17.1
The output of the Greeting example.

NOTE

Notice that the second alert message isn't displayed until you press the OK button on the first alert. This is because JavaScript processing is halted while alerts are displayed.

Returning a Value

The function you just created displays a message to the user, but functions can also return a value to the script that called them. This enables you to use functions to calculate values. As an example, you can create a function that averages four numbers.

Your function should begin with the function keyword, the function's name, and the parameters it accepts. We will use the variable names a, b, c, and d for the four numbers to average. Here is the first line of the function:

```
function Average(a,b,c,d) {
```

Next, the function needs to calculate the average of the four parameters. You can calculate this by adding them, and then dividing by the number of parameters (in this case, 4). Thus, here is the next line of the function:

```
result = (a + b + c + d) / 4;
```

This statement creates a variable called result and calculates the result by adding the four numbers, and then dividing by 4. (The parentheses are necessary to tell JavaScript to perform the addition before the division.)

To send this result back to the script that called the function, you use the return keyword. Here is the last part of the function:

```
return result;
}
```

Listing 17.3 shows the complete Average function in an HTML document. This HTML document also includes a small script in the <body> section that calls the Average function and displays the result.

LISTING 17.3   The Average Function in an HTML Document

```
<?xml version="1.0" encoding="UTF-8"?>
<!DOCTYPE html PUBLIC "-//W3C//DTD XHTML 1.1//EN"
   "http://www.w3.org/TR/xhtml11/DTD/xhtml11.dtd">

<html xmlns="http://www.w3.org/1999/xhtml" xml:lang="en">
  <head>
    <title>Function Example: Average</title>
    <script type="text/javascript">
    function Average(a,b,c,d)  {
        result = (a + b + c + d) / 4;
        return result;
    }
    </script>
  </head>
```

NOTE

I've also included the opening brace ({) on the first line of the function. This is a common style, but you can also place the brace on the next line or on a line by itself.

LISTING 17.3   Continued

```
  <body>
    <h1>Function Example: Average</h1>
    <p>The following is the result of the function call.</p>
    <script type="text/javascript">
    score = Average(3,4,5,6);
    document.write("The average is: " + score);
    </script>
</body>
</html>
```

TIP

You can also use the function call directly in an expression. For example, you could use the alert statement to display the result of the function alert(Average(1,2,3,4))

You can use a variable with the function call, as shown in this listing. This statement averages the numbers 3, 4, 5, and 6 and stores the result in a variable called score:

```
score = Average(3,4,5,6);
```

Introducing Objects

In the previous chapter, you learned how to use variables to represent different kinds of data in JavaScript. JavaScript also supports *objects*, a more complex kind of variable that can store multiple data items and functions.

Although a variable can have only one value at a time, an object can contain multiple values, as well as functions for working with the values. This enables you to group related data items and the functions that deal with them into a single object.

In this chapter, you'll learn how to define and use your own objects. You've already worked with some of them, including

> **DOM objects**—Allow your scripts to interact with web pages. You learned about these in Chapter 15, "Working with the Document Object Model (DOM)."

> **Built-in objects**—Include strings and arrays, which you learned about in Chapter 16, "Using JavaScript Variables, Strings, and Arrays."

The syntax for working with all three types of objects—DOM objects, built-in objects, and custom objects—is the same, so even if you don't end up creating your own objects, you should have a good understanding of JavaScript's object terminology and syntax.

Creating Objects

When you created an array in the previous chapter, you used the following JavaScript statement:

```
scores = new Array(4);
```

The new keyword tells the JavaScript interpreter to use a function—in this case, the built-in Array function—to create an object. You'll create a function for a custom object later in this chapter.

Object Properties and Values

Each object has one or more *properties*—essentially, variables that will be stored within the object. For example, in Chapter 15, you learned that the location.href property gives you the URL of the current document. The href property is one of the properties of the location object in the DOM.

You've also used the length property of String objects, as in the following example from the previous chapter:

```
test = "This is a test.";
document.write(test.length);
```

Like variables, each object property has a *value*. To read a property's value, you simply include the object name and property name, separated by a period, in any expression, as in test.length previously. You can change a property's value using the = operator, just like a variable. The following example sends the browser to a new URL by changing the location.href property:

```
location.href="http://www.google.com/";
```

NOTE

An object can also be a property of another object. This is referred to as a *child object*.

Understanding Methods

Along with properties, each object can have one or more *methods*. These are functions that work with the object's data. For example, the following JavaScript statement reloads the current document, as you learned in Chapter 15:

```
location.reload();
```

When you use reload(), you're using a method of the location object. Like normal functions, methods can accept arguments in parentheses and can return values.

Using Objects to Simplify Scripting

Although JavaScript's variables and arrays are versatile ways to store data, sometimes you need a more complicated structure. For example, suppose you are creating a script to work with a business card database that contains names, addresses, and phone numbers for a variety of people.

If you were using regular variables, you would need several separate variables for each person in the database: a name variable, an address variable, and so on. This would be very confusing.

Arrays would improve things slightly. You could have a names array, an addresses array, and a phone number array. Each person in the database would have an entry in each array. This would be more convenient, but still not perfect.

With objects, you can make the variables that store the database as logical as business cards. Each person is represented by a Card object, which has properties for name, address, and phone number. You can even add methods to the object to display or work with the information.

In the following sections, you'll use JavaScript to actually create the Card object and its properties and methods. Later in this chapter, you'll use the Card object in a script to display information for several members of the database.

Defining an Object

The first step in creating an object is to name it and its properties. We've already decided to call the object a Card object. Each object will have the following properties:

- ▶ name
- ▶ address
- ▶ workphone
- ▶ homephone

The first step in using this object in a JavaScript program is to create a function to make new Card objects. This function is called the *constructor* for an object. Here is the constructor function for the Card object:

```
function Card(name,address,work,home) {
    this.name = name;
```

```
    this.address = address;
    this.workphone = work;
    this.homephone = home;
}
```

The constructor is a simple function that accepts parameters to initialize a new object and assigns them to the corresponding properties. This function accepts several parameters from the statement that calls the function, and then assigns them as properties of an object. Because the function is called `Card`, the object is the `Card` object.

Notice the `this` keyword. You'll use it any time you create an object definition. Use `this` to refer to the current object—the one that is being created by the function.

Defining an Object Method

Next, you will create a method to work with the `Card` object. Because all `Card` objects will have the same properties, it might be handy to have a function that prints out the properties in a neat format. Let's call this function `PrintCard`.

Your `PrintCard` function will be used as a method for `Card` objects, so you don't need to ask for parameters. Instead, you can use the `this` keyword again to refer to the current object's properties. Here is a function definition for the `PrintCard()` function:

```
function PrintCard() {
    line1 = "Name: " + this.name + "<br/>\n";
    line2 = "Address: " + this.address + "<br/>\n";
    line3 = "Work Phone: " + this.workphone + "<br/>\n";
    line4 = "Home Phone: " + this.homephone + "<hr/>\n";
    document.write(line1, line2, line3, line4);
}
```

This function simply reads the properties from the current object (`this`), prints each one with a caption, and skips to a new line.

You now have a function that prints a card, but it isn't officially a method of the `Card` object. The last thing you need to do is make `PrintCard` part of the function definition for `Card` objects. Here is the modified function definition:

```
function Card(name,address,work,home) {
    this.name = name;
    this.address = address;
    this.workphone = work;
    this.homephone = home;
    this.PrintCard = PrintCard;
}
```

TIP

The previous example uses lowercase names such as workphone for properties, and an uppercase name (PrintCard) for the method. You can use any case for property and method names, but this is one way to make it clear that PrintCard is a method rather than an ordinary property.

The added statement looks just like another property definition, but it refers to the PrintCard function. This will work so long as the PrintCard function is defined with its own function definition. Methods are essentially properties that define a function rather than a simple value.

Creating an Object Instance

Now let's use the object definition and method you just created. To use an object definition, you create a new object. This is done with the new keyword. This is the same keyword you've already used to create Date and Array objects.

The following statement creates a new Card object called tom:

```
tom = new Card("Tom Jones", "123 Elm Street", "555-1234", "555-9876");
```

As you can see, creating an object is easy. All you do is call the Card() function (the object definition) and give it the required attributes, in the same order as the definition.

After this statement executes, a new object is created to hold Tom's information. This is called an *instance* of the Card object. Just as there can be several string variables in a program, there can be several instances of an object you define.

Rather than specify all the information for a card with the new keyword, you can assign them after the fact. For example, the following script creates an empty Card object called holmes, and then assigns its properties:

```
holmes = new Card();
holmes.name = "Sherlock Holmes";
holmes.address = "221B Baker Street";
holmes.workphone = "555-2345";
holmes.homephone = "555-3456";
```

After you've created an instance of the Card object using either of these methods, you can use the PrintCard() method to display its information. For example, this statement displays the properties of the tom card:

```
tom.PrintCard();
```

Extending Built-in Objects

JavaScript includes a feature that enables you to extend the definitions of built-in objects. For example, if you think the String object doesn't quite fit your needs, you can extend it, adding a new property or method. This might be very useful if you were creating a large script that used many strings.

You can add both properties and methods to an existing object by using the prototype keyword. (A *prototype* is another name for an object's definition, or constructor function.) The prototype keyword enables you to change the definition of an object outside its constructor function.

As an example, let's add a method to the String object definition. You will create a method called heading, which converts a string into an HTML heading. The following statement defines a string called title:

```
title = "Fred's Home Page";
```

This statement would output the contents of the title string as an HTML level 1 header:

```
document.write(title.heading(1));
```

Listing 17.4 adds a heading method to the String object definition that will display the string as a heading, and then displays three headings using the method.

LISTING 17.4   Adding a Method to the String Object

```
<?xml version="1.0" encoding="UTF-8"?>
<!DOCTYPE html PUBLIC "-//W3C//DTD XHTML 1.1//EN"
  "http://www.w3.org/TR/xhtml11/DTD/xhtml11.dtd">

<html xmlns="http://www.w3.org/1999/xhtml" xml:lang="en">
  <head>
    <title>Test of Heading Method</title>
  </head>
  <body>
    <script type="text/javascript">
    function addhead (level) {
       html = "h" + level;
       text = this.toString();
       start = "<" + html + ">";
       stop = "</" + html + ">";
       return start + text + stop;
    }
    String.prototype.heading = addhead;
    document.write ("This is a heading 1".heading(1));
    document.write ("This is a heading 2".heading(2));
    document.write ("This is a heading 3".heading(3));
    </script>
</body>
</html>
```

First, you define the `addhead()` function, which will serve as the new string method. It accepts a number to specify the heading level. The `start` and `stop` variables are used to store the HTML "begin header" and "end header" tags, such as `<h1>` and `</h1>`.

After the function is defined, use the `prototype` keyword to add it as a method of the `String` object. You can then use this method on any `String` object or, in fact, any JavaScript string. This is demonstrated by the last three statements, which display quoted text strings as level 1, 2, and 3 headers.

▼ TRY IT YOURSELF

Storing Data in Objects

Now you've created a new object to store business cards and a method to print them out. As a final demonstration of objects, properties, functions, and methods, you will now use this object in a web page to display data for several cards.

Your script will need to include the function definition for `PrintCard`, along with the function definition for the `Card` object. You will then create three cards and print them out in the body of the document. We will use separate HTML and JavaScript files for this example. Listing 17.5 shows the complete script.

LISTING 17.5   A Sample Script That Uses the `Card` Object

```
// define the functions
function PrintCard() {
line1 = "<strong>Name: </strong>" + this.name + "<br/>\n";
line2 = "<strong>Address: </strong>" + this.address + "<br/>\n";
line3 = "<strong>Work Phone: </strong>" + this.workphone + "<br/>\n";
line4 = "<strong>Home Phone: </strong>" + this.homephone + "<hr/>\n";
document.write(line1, line2, line3, line4);
}
function Card(name,address,work,home) {
    this.name = name;
    this.address = address;
    this.workphone = work;
    this.homephone = home;
    this.PrintCard = PrintCard;
}
// Create the objects
sue = new Card("Sue Suthers", "123 Elm Street", "555-1234", "555-9876");
phred = new Card("Phred Madsen", "233 Oak Lane", "555-2222", "555-4444");
henry = new Card("Henry Tillman", "233 Walnut Circle", "555-1299",
        "555-1344");
// And print them
sue.PrintCard();
phred.PrintCard();
henry.PrintCard();
```

Notice that the `PrintCard()` function has been modified slightly to make things look good with the captions in boldface. To use this script, save it as `cardtest.js`. Next, you'll need to include the script in a simple HTML document. Listing 17.6 shows the HTML document for this example.

LISTING 17.6 The HTML File for the `Card` Object Example

```
<?xml version="1.0" encoding="UTF-8"?>
<!DOCTYPE html PUBLIC "-//W3C//DTD XHTML 1.1//EN"
  "http://www.w3.org/TR/xhtml11/DTD/xhtml11.dtd">

<html xmlns="http://www.w3.org/1999/xhtml" xml:lang="en">
  <head>
    <title>JavaScript Business Cards</title>
  </head>
  <body>
    <h1>JavaScript Business Cards</h1>
    <p>Script begins here.</p>
    <hr/>
    <script type="text/javascript" src="cardtest.js" > </script>
<p>End of script.</p>
</body>
</html>
```

To test the script, save the HTML document in the same directory as the `cardtest.js` file you created earlier, and then load the HTML document into a browser. The browser's display of this example is shown in Figure 17.2.

TRY IT YOURSELF ▼

Storing Data in Objects
continued

FIGURE 17.2
Displaying the output of the business card example.

NOTE

This example isn't a very sophisticated database because you have to include the data for each person in the HTML document. However, an object like this could be used to store a database record retrieved from a database server with thousands of records.

Using the Math **Object**

The Math object is a built-in JavaScript object that includes math constants and functions. You don't need to create a Math object; it exists automatically in any JavaScript program. The Math object's properties represent mathematical constants, and its methods are mathematical functions.

Rounding and Truncating

Three of the most useful methods of the Math object enable you to round decimal values up and down:

- ▶ Math.ceil() rounds a number up to the next integer.

- ▶ Math.floor() rounds a number down to the next integer.

- ▶ Math.round() rounds a number to the nearest integer.

All of these take the number to be rounded as their single parameter. You might notice one thing missing: the capability to round to a decimal place, such as for dollar amounts. Fortunately, you can easily simulate this. Here is a simple function that rounds numbers to two decimal places:

```
function round(num) {
   return Math.round(num * 100) / 100;
}
```

This function multiplies the value by 100 to move the decimal, and then rounds the number to the nearest integer. Finally, the value is divided by 100 to restore the decimal to its original position.

Generating Random Numbers

One of the most commonly used methods of the Math object is the Math.random() method, which generates a random number. This method doesn't require any parameters. The number it returns is a random decimal number between zero and one.

You'll usually want a random number between one and a value. You can do this with a general-purpose random number function. The following is a function that generates random numbers between one and the parameter you send it:

```
function rand(num) {
   return Math.floor(Math.random() * num) + 1;
}
```

This function multiplies a random number by the value specified in the num parameter, and then converts it to an integer between one and the number by using the Math.floor() method.

Other Math Functions

The Math object includes many functions beyond those you've looked at here. For example, Math.sin() and Math.cos() calculate sines and cosines. The Math object also includes properties for various mathematical constants, such as Math.PI.

Working with Math Functions

The Math.random method generates a random number between 0 and 1. However, it's difficult for a computer to generate a truly random number. (It's also hard for a human being to do so—that's why dice were invented.)

Today's computers do reasonably well at generating random numbers, but just how good is JavaScript's Math.random function? One way to test it is to generate many random numbers and calculate the average of all of them.

In theory, the average should be somewhere near .5, halfway between 0 and 1. The more random values you generate, the closer the average should get to this middle ground.

As an example of the use of the Math object's methods, you can create a script that tests JavaScript's random number function. To do this, you'll generate 5,000 random numbers and calculate their average.

This example will use a look, which you'll learn more about in the next chapter. But this is a simple enough example that you should be able to follow along. In this case, the loop will generate the random numbers. You'll be surprised how fast JavaScript can do this.

To begin your script, you will initialize a variable called total. This variable will store a running total of all of the random values, so it's important that it starts at 0:

```
total = 0;
```

Next, begin a loop that will execute 5,000 times. Use a for loop because you want it to execute a fixed number of times:

```
for (i=1; i<=5000; i++) {
```

Within the loop, you will need to create a random number and add its value to total. Here are the statements that do this and continue with the next iteration of the loop:

NOTE

The % symbol in the previous
code is the *modulo operator*,
which gives you the remainder
after dividing one number by
another. Here it is used to find
even multiples of 1,000.

```
    num = Math.random();
    total += num;
}
```

Depending on the speed of your computer, it might take a few seconds to
generate those 5,000 random numbers. Just to be sure something is happening, the script will display a status message after each 1,000 numbers:

```
if (i % 1000 == 0)
    document.write("Generated " + i + " numbers...<br/>");
```

The final part of your script will calculate the average by dividing `total`
by 5,000. Your script can also round the average to three decimal places:

```
average = total / 5000;
average = Math.round(average * 1000) / 1000;
document.write("<h2>Average of 5000 numbers: " + average + "</h2>");
```

To test this script and see just how random those numbers are, combine the
complete script with an HTML document and `<script>` tags. Listing 17.7
shows the complete random number testing script.

LISTING 17.7   A Script to Test JavaScript's Random Number Function

```
<?xml version="1.0" encoding="UTF-8"?>
<!DOCTYPE html PUBLIC "-//W3C//DTD XHTML 1.1//EN"
  "http://www.w3.org/TR/xhtml11/DTD/xhtml11.dtd">

<html xmlns="http://www.w3.org/1999/xhtml" xml:lang="en">
  <head>
    <title>Math Example</title>
  </head>
  <body>
    <h1>Math Example</h1>
    <p>How random are JavaScript's random numbers?
    Let's generate 5000 of them and find out.</p>
    <script type="text/javascript">
    total = 0;
    for (i=1; i<=5000; i++) {
      num = Math.random();
      total += num;
      if (i % 1000 == 0) {
          document.write("Generated " + i + " numbers...<br/>");
        }
      }
    average = total / 5000;
    average = Math.round(average * 1000) / 1000;
    document.write("<h2>Average of 5000 numbers: " + average + "</h2>");
    </script>
</body>
</html>
```

To test the script, load the HTML document into a browser. After a short delay, you should see a result. If it's close to .5, the numbers are reasonably random. My result was .503, as shown in Figure 17.3.

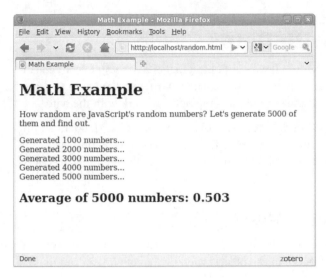

FIGURE 17.3
The random number testing script in action.

> **NOTE**
>
> The average you've used here is called an *arithmetic mean*. This type of average isn't a perfect way to test randomness. Actually, all it tests is the distribution of the numbers above and below .5. For example, if the numbers turned out to be 2,500 .4s and 2,500 .6s, the average would be a perfect .5—but they wouldn't be very random numbers. (Thankfully, JavaScript's random numbers don't have this problem.)

Using the with Keyword

The with keyword is one you haven't seen before. You can use it to make JavaScript programming easier—or at least easier to type.

The with keyword specifies an object, and it is followed by a block of statements enclosed in braces. For each statement in the block, any properties you mention without specifying an object are assumed to be for that object.

As an example, suppose you have a string called lastname. You can use with to perform string operations on it without specifying the name of the string every time:

```
with (lastname) {
    window.alert("length of last name: " + length);
    capname = toUpperCase();
}
```

In this example, the length property and the toUpperCase method refer to the lastname string, although it is only specified once with the with keyword.

Obviously, the with keyword only saves a bit of typing in situations like this. However, you might find it more useful when you're dealing with a DOM object throughout a large procedure, or when you are repeatedly using a built-in object, such as the Math object.

Working with Dates

The Date object is a built-in JavaScript object that enables you to conveniently work with dates and times. You can create a Date object anytime you need to store a date and use the Date object's methods to work with the date.

You encountered one example of a Date object in Chapter 4, "Understanding JavaScript," with the time/date script. The Date object has no properties. To set or obtain values from a Date object, you must use the methods described in the next section.

Creating a Date Object

You can create a Date object using the new keyword. You can also optionally specify the date to store in the object when you create it. You can use any of the following formats:

```
birthday = new Date();
birthday = new Date("November 1, 2010 08:00:00");
birthday = new Date(11,1, 2010);
birthday = new Date(11,1,2010, 8, 0, 0);
```

You can choose any of these formats, depending on which values you want to set. If you use no parameters, as in the first example, the current date is stored in the object. You can then set the values using the set methods, described in the next section.

Setting Date Values

A variety of set methods enable you to set components of a Date object to values:

- ▸ setDate() sets the day of the month.
- ▸ setMonth() sets the month. JavaScript numbers the months from 0 to 11, starting with January (0).
- ▸ setFullYear() sets the year.
- ▸ setTime() sets the time (and the date) by specifying the number of milliseconds since January 1, 1970.
- ▸ setHours(), setMinutes(), and setSeconds() set the time.

As an example, the following statement sets the year of a `Date` object called `holiday` to 2010:

```
holiday.setFullYear(2010);
```

Reading `Date` **Values**

You can use the `get` methods to get values from a `Date` object. This is the only way to obtain these values because they are not available as properties. Here are the available `get` methods for dates:

- ▶ `getDate()` gets the day of the month.

- ▶ `getMonth()` gets the month.

- ▶ `getFullYear()` gets the year.

- ▶ `getTime()` gets the time (and the date) as the number of milliseconds since January 1, 1970.

- ▶ `getHours()`, `getMinutes()`, `getSeconds()`, and `getMilliseconds()` get the components of the time.

Working with Time Zones

Finally, a few functions are available to help your `Date` objects work with local time values and time zones:

- ▶ `getTimeZoneOffset()` function gives you the local time zone's offset from UTC (Coordinated Universal Time, based on the old Greenwich Mean Time standard). In this case, *local* refers to the location of the browser. (Of course, this only works if the user has set his system clock accurately.)

- ▶ `toUTCString()` function converts the `date` object's time value to text, using UTC. This method was introduced in JavaScript 1.2 to replace the `toGMTString` method, which still works but should be avoided.

- ▶ `toLocalString()` function converts the `date` object's time value to text, using local time.

Along with these basic functions, JavaScript 1.2 and later include UTC versions of several of the functions described previously. These are identical to the regular commands, but work with UTC instead of local time:

- ▶ `getUTCDate()` function gets the day of the month in UTC time.

- ▶ `getUTCDay()` function gets the day of the week in UTC time.

NOTE

Along with `setFullYear` and `getFullYear`, which require four-digit years, JavaScript includes `setYear` and `getYear` methods, which use two-digit year values. You should always use the four-digit version to avoid Year 2000 issues.

- ▶ getUTCFullYear() function gets the four-digit year in UTC time.

- ▶ getUTCMonth() function returns the month of the year in UTC time.

- ▶ getUTCHours(), getUTCMinutes(), getUTCSeconds(), and getUTCMilliseconds() return the components of the time in UTC.

- ▶ setUTCDate(), setUTCFullYear(), setUTCMonth(), setUTCHours(), setUTCMinutes(), setUTCSeconds(), and setUTCMilliseconds() set the time in UTC.

Converting Between Date Formats

Two special methods of the Date object enable you to convert between date formats. Instead of using these methods with a Date object you created, you use them with the built-in object Date itself. These include the following:

- ▶ Date.parse()method converts a date string, such as November 1, 2010, to a Date object (number of milliseconds since 1/1/1970).

- ▶ Date.UTC() method does the opposite. It converts a Date object value (number of milliseconds) to a UTC (GMT) time.

Summary

In this chapter, you learned several important features of JavaScript. First, you learned how to use functions to group JavaScript statements and how to call functions and use the values they return. Next, you learned about JavaScript's object-oriented features—defining objects with constructor functions, creating object instances, and working with properties, property values, and methods.

As an example of these object-oriented features, you looked closer at the Math and Date objects built into JavaScript and learned more than you ever wanted to know about random numbers.

Q&A

Q. Many objects in JavaScript, such as DOM objects, include parent and child objects. Can I include child objects in my custom object definitions?

A. Yes. Just create a constructor function for the child object, and then add a property to the parent object that corresponds to it. For example, if you created a `Nicknames` object to store several nicknames for a person in the card file example, you could add it as a child object in the `Card` object's constructor: `this.nick = new Nicknames();`.

Q. Can I create an array of custom objects?

A. Yes. First, create the object definition as usual and define an array with the required number of elements. Then assign a new object to each array element (for example, `cardarray[1] = new Card();`). You can use a loop, described in the next chapter, to assign objects to an entire array at once.

Q. Can I modify all properties of objects?

A. With custom objects, yes—but this varies with built-in objects and DOM objects. For example, you can use the `length` property to find the length of a string, but it is a *read-only property* and cannot be modified.

Q. The random numbers are generated so quickly I can't be sure it's happening at all. Is there a way to slow this process down?

A. Yes. If you add one or more form fields to the example and use them to display the data as it is generated, you'll see a much slower result. It will still be done within a couple of seconds on a fast computer, though.

Workshop

The workshop contains quiz questions and activities to help you solidify your understanding of the material covered. Try to answer all questions before looking at the "Answers" section that follows.

Quiz

1. What JavaScript keyword is used to create an instance of an object?

   a. `object`

   b. `new`

   c. `instance`

2. What is the meaning of the `this` keyword in JavaScript?

   a. The current object.

   b. The current script.

   c. It has no meaning.

3. Which of the following objects *cannot* be used with the `new` keyword?

   a. `Date`

   b. `Math`

   c. `String`

4. How does JavaScript store dates in a `Date` object?

   a. The number of milliseconds since January 1, 1970

   b. The number of days since January 1, 1900

   c. The number of seconds since Netscape's public stock offering

5. What is the range of random numbers generated by the `Math.random` function?

   a. Between `1` and `100`

   b. Between `1` and the number of milliseconds since January 1, 1970

   c. Between `0` and `1`

Answers

1. b. The `new` keyword creates an object instance.

2. a. The `this` keyword refers to the current object.

3. b. The `Math` object is static; you can't create a `Math` object.

4. a. Dates are stored as the number of milliseconds since January 1, 1970.

5. c. JavaScript's random numbers are between `0` and `1`.

Exercises

▶ Modify the `Greet` function to accept two parameters, `who1` and `who2`, and to include both names in a single greeting dialog. Modify Listing 17.2 to use a single function call to the new function.

▶ Modify the definition of the `Card` object to include a property called `email` for the person's email address. Modify the `PrintCard` function in Listing 17.5 to include this property.

▶ Modify the random number script in Listing 17.7 to run three times, calculating a total of 15,000 random numbers, and display separate totals for each set of 5,000. (You'll need to use another `for` loop that encloses most of the script.)

CHAPTER 18

Controlling Flow with Conditions and Loops

Statements in a JavaScript program generally execute in the order in which they appear, one after the other. Because this isn't always practical, most programming languages provide *flow control* statements that let you control the order in which code is executed. Functions, which you learned about in the previous chapter, are one type of flow control—although a function might be defined first thing in your code, its statements can be executed anywhere in the script.

In this chapter, you'll look at two other types of flow control in JavaScript: *conditions*, which allow a choice of different options depending on a value, and *loops*, which allow repetitive statements.

The `if` Statement

One of the most important features of a computer language is the capability to test and compare values. This allows your scripts to behave differently based on the values of variables or based on input from the user.

The `if` statement is the main conditional statement in JavaScript. This statement means much the same in JavaScript as it does in English—for example, here is a typical conditional statement in English:

If the phone rings, answer it.

This statement consists of two parts: a condition (*If the phone rings*) and an action (*answer it*). The `if` statement in JavaScript works much the same way. Here is an example of a basic `if` statement:

```
if (a == 1) window.alert("Found a 1!");
```

WHAT YOU'LL LEARN IN THIS CHAPTER:

▶ How to test variables with the `if` statement

▶ How to use various operators to compare values

▶ How to use logical operators to combine conditions

▶ How to use alternative conditions with `else`

▶ How to create expressions with conditional operators

▶ How to test for multiple conditions

▶ How to perform repeated statements with the `for` loop

▶ How to use `while` for a different type of loop

▶ How to use `do...while` loops

▶ How to create infinite loops (and why you shouldn't)

▶ How to escape from loops and continuing loops

▶ How to loop through an array's properties

This statement includes a condition (if a equals 1) and an action (display a message). This statement checks the variable a and, if it has a value of 1, displays an alert message. Otherwise, it does nothing.

If you use an if statement like the preceding example, you can use a single statement as the action. You can also use multiple statements for the action by enclosing them in braces ({}), as shown here:

```
if (a == 1) {
   window.alert("Found a 1!");
   a = 0;
}
```

This block of statements checks the variable a once again. If it finds a value of 1, it displays a message and sets a back to 0.

Conditional Operators

The action part of an if statement can include any of the JavaScript statements you've already learned (and any others, for that matter), but the condition part of the statement uses its own syntax. This is called a *conditional expression*.

A conditional expression usually includes two values to be compared (in the preceding example, the values were a and 1). These values can be variables, constants, or even expressions in themselves.

Between the two values to be compared is a *conditional operator*. This operator tells JavaScript how to compare the two values. For instance, the == operator is used to test whether the two values are equal. A variety of conditional operators is available:

- ► ==—Is equal to
- ► !=—Is not equal to
- ► <—Is less than
- ► >—Is greater than
- ► >=—Is greater than or equal to
- ► <=—Is less than or equal to

Combining Conditions with Logical Operators

Often, you'll want to check a variable for more than one possible value or check more than one variable at once. JavaScript includes *logical operators*, also known as Boolean operators, for this purpose. For example, the following two statements check different conditions and use the same action:

```
if (phone == "") window.alert("error!");
if (email == "") window.alert("error!");
```

Using a logical operator, you can combine them into a single statement:

```
if ((phone == "") ¦¦ (email == "")) window.alert("Something's Missing!");
```

This statement uses the logical Or operator (¦¦) to combine the conditions. Translated to English, this would be, "If the phone number is blank or the email address is blank, display an error message."

An additional logical operator is the And operator, &&. Consider this statement:

```
if ((phone == "") && (email == "")) window.alert("Both are Missing!");
```

This statement uses &&, so the error message will only be displayed if *both* the email address and phone number variables are blank. (In this particular case, Or is a better choice.)

The third logical operator is the exclamation mark (!), which means Not. It can be used to invert an expression—in other words, a true expression would become false, and a false one would become true. For example, here's a statement that uses the Not operator:

```
if (!(phone == "")) alert("phone is OK");
```

In this statement, the ! (Not) operator inverts the condition, so the action of the if statement is executed only if the phone number variable is *not* blank. The extra parentheses are necessary because all JavaScript conditions must be in parentheses. You could also use the != (Not equal) operator to simplify this statement:

```
if (phone != "") alert("phone is OK");
```

As with the previous statement, this alerts you if the phone number field is not blank.

TIP

If the JavaScript interpreter discovers the answer to a conditional expression before reaching the end, it does not evaluate the rest of the condition. For example, if the first of two conditions separated by the && operator is false, the second is not evaluated. You can take advantage of this to improve the speed of your scripts.

TIP

The logical operators are powerful, but it's easy to accidentally create an impossible condition with them. For example, the condition ((a < 10) && (a > 20)) might look correct at first glance. However, if you read it aloud, you get "If a is less than 10 and a is greater than 20"—an impossibility in our universe. In this case, Or (¦¦) should have been used.

The `else` Keyword

An additional feature of the `if` statement is the `else` keyword. Much like its English equivalent, `else` tells the JavaScript interpreter what to do if the condition isn't true. The following is a simple example of the `else` keyword in action:

```
if (a == 1) {
   alert("Found a 1!");
   a = 0;
} else {
   alert("Incorrect value: " + a);
}
```

This is a modified version of the previous example. This displays a message and resets the variable a if the condition is met. If the condition is not met (if a is not 1), a different message is displayed.

Using Shorthand Conditional Expressions

In addition to the `if` statement, JavaScript provides a shorthand type of conditional expression that you can use to make quick decisions. This uses a peculiar syntax that is also found in other languages, such as C. A conditional expression looks like this:

```
variable = (condition) ? (true action) : (false action);
```

This assigns one of two values to the variable: one if the condition is true, and another if it is false. Here is an example of a conditional expression:

```
value = (a == 1) ? 1 : 0;
```

This statement might look confusing, but it is equivalent to the following `if` statement:

```
if (a == 1) {
   value = 1;
} else {
   value = 0;
}
```

In other words, the value after the question mark (?) will be used if the condition is true, and the value after the colon (:) will be used if the condition is false. The colon represents the `else` portion of this statement and, like the `else` portion of the `if` statement, is optional.

These shorthand expressions can be used anywhere JavaScript expects a value. They provide an easy way to make simple decisions about values. As an example, here's an easy way to display a grammatically correct message about a variable:

```
document.write("Found " + counter +
    ((counter == 1) ? " word." : " words."));
```

This will print the message Found 1 word if the counter variable has a value of 1 and Found 2 words if its value is 2 or greater. This is one of the most common uses for a conditional expression.

Testing Multiple Conditions with `if` and `else`

You can now create an example script using `if` and `else`. In Chapter 4, "Understanding JavaScript," you created a simple script that displays the current date and time. This example will use conditions to display a greeting that depends on the time: "Good morning," "Good afternoon," "Good evening," or "Good day." To accomplish this, you can use a combination of several `if` statements:

```
if (hours < 10)  {
    document.write("Good morning.");
}  else if (hours >= 14 && hours <= 17)  {
    document.write("Good afternoon.");
}  else if (hours >= 17)  {
    document.write("Good evening.");
}  else {
    document.write("Good day.");
}
```

The first statement checks the hours variable for a value less than 10—in other words, it checks whether the current time is before 10:00 a.m. If so, it displays the greeting "Good morning."

The second statement checks whether the time is between 2:00 p.m. and 5:00 p.m. and, if so, displays "Good afternoon." This statement uses else if to indicate that this condition will only be tested if the previous one failed—if it's morning, there's no need to check whether it's afternoon. Similarly, the third statement checks for times after 5:00 p.m. and displays "Good evening."

The final statement uses a simple else, meaning it will be executed if none of the previous conditions matched. This covers the times between 10:00 a.m. and 2:00 p.m. (neglected by the other statements) and displays "Good day."

The HTML File

To try this example in a browser, you'll need an HTML file. We will keep the JavaScript code separate, so Listing 18.1 is the complete HTML file. Save it as `timegreet.html`, but don't load it into the browser until you've prepared the JavaScript file in the next section.

LISTING 18.1   The HTML File for the Time and Greeting Example

```
<?xml version="1.0" encoding="UTF-8"?>
<!DOCTYPE html PUBLIC "-//W3C//DTD XHTML 1.1//EN"
  "http://www.w3.org/TR/xhtml11/DTD/xhtml11.dtd">

<html xmlns="http://www.w3.org/1999/xhtml" xml:lang="en">
  <head>
    <title>Time Greet Example</title>
  </head>
  <body>
    <h1>Current Date and Time</h1>
    <script type="text/javascript" src="timegreet.js" > </script>
</body>
</html>
```

The JavaScript File

Listing 18.2 shows the complete JavaScript file for the time greeting example. This uses the built-in `Date` object functions to find the current date and store it in `hours`, `mins`, and `secs` variables. Next, `document.write` statements display the current time, and the `if` and `else` statements introduced earlier display an appropriate greeting.

LISTING 18.2   A Script to Display the Current Time and a Greeting

```
// Get the current date
now = new Date();
// Split into hours, minutes, seconds
hours = now.getHours();
mins = now.getMinutes();
secs = now.getSeconds();
// Display the time
document.write("<h2>");
document.write(hours + ":" + mins + ":" + secs);
document.write("</h2>");
// Display a greeting
document.write("<p>");
if (hours < 10)  {
    document.write("Good morning.");
} else if (hours >= 14 && hours <= 17) {
```

LISTING 18.2   Continued

```
    document.write("Good afternoon.");
} else if (hours >= 17)  {
    document.write("Good evening.");
} else  {
    document.write("Good day.");
}
document.write("</p>");
```

To try this example, save this file as `timegreet.js`, and then load the `timegreet.html` file into your browser. Figure 18.1 shows the results of this script.

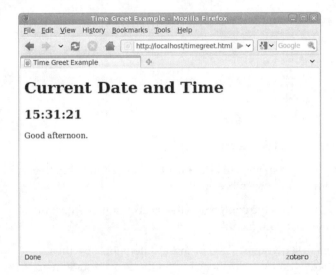

FIGURE 18.1
The output of the time greeting example.

Using Multiple Conditions with switch

In the previous example, you used several `if` statements in a row to test for different conditions. Here is another example of this technique:

```
if (button=="next") {
    window.location="next.html";
} else if (button=="previous") {
    window.location="prev.html";
} else if (button=="home") {
    window.location="home.html";
} else if (button=="back") {
    window.location="menu.html";
}
```

Although this is a compact way of doing things, this method can get messy if each `if` statement has its own block of code with several statements. As an alternative, JavaScript includes the `switch` statement, which enables you to combine several tests of the same variable or expression into a single block of statements. The following shows the same example converted to use `switch`:

```
switch(button) {
    case "next":
        window.location="next.html";
        break;
    case "previous":
        window.location="prev.html";
        break;
case "home":
        window.location="home.html";
        break;
case "back":
        window.location="menu.html";
        break;
default:
        window.alert("Wrong button.");
}
```

NOTE

You can use multiple statements after each `case` statement within the `switch` structure. You don't need to enclose them in braces. If the case matches, the JavaScript interpreter executes statements until it encounters a `break` or the next `case`.

The `switch` statement has several components:

▶ The initial `switch` statement. This statement includes the value to test (in this case, `button`) in parentheses.

▶ Braces (`{` and `}`) enclose the contents of the `switch` statement, similar to a function or an `if` statement.

▶ One or more `case` statements. Each of these statements specifies a value to compare with the value specified in the `switch` statement. If the values match, the statements after the `case` statement are executed. Otherwise, the next case is tried.

▶ The `break` statement is used to end each case. This skips to the end of the `switch`. If `break` is not included, statements in multiple cases might be executed whether they match or not.

▶ Optionally, the `default` case can be included and followed by one or more statements that are executed if none of the other cases were matched.

Using for **Loops**

The for keyword is the first tool to consider for creating loops, much like you saw in the previous chapter during the random number example. A for loop typically uses a variable (called a *counter* or an *index*) to keep track of how many times the loop has executed, and it stops when the counter reaches a certain number. A basic for statement looks like this:

```
for (var = 1; var < 10; var++) { // more code }
```

There are three parameters to the for loop, separated by semicolons:

▶ The first parameter (var = 1 in the example) specifies a variable and assigns an initial value to it. This is called the *initial expression* because it sets up the initial state for the loop.

▶ The second parameter (var < 10 in the example) is a condition that must remain true to keep the loop running. This is called the *condition* of the loop.

▶ The third parameter (var++ in the example) is a statement that executes with each iteration of the loop. This is called the *increment expression* because it is typically used to increment the counter. The increment expression executes at the end of each loop iteration.

After the three parameters are specified, a left brace ({) is used to signal the beginning of a block. A right brace (}) is used at the end of the block. All the statements between the braces will be executed with each iteration of the loop.

The parameters for a for loop might sound a bit confusing, but after you're used to it, you'll use for loops frequently. Here is a simple example of this type of loop:

```
for (i=0; i<10; i++) {
   document.write("This is line " + i + "<br />");
}
```

These statements define a loop that uses the variable i, initializes it with the value of zero, and loops as long as the value of i is less than 10. The increment expression, i++, adds one to the value of i with each iteration of the loop. Because this happens at the end of the loop, the output will list the numbers zero through nine.

TIP

It's a good style convention to
use braces with all loops
whether they contain one statement or many. This makes it
easy to add statements to the
loop later without causing syntax errors.

When a loop includes only a single statement between the braces, as in this
example, you can omit the braces if you want. The following statement
defines the same loop without braces:

```
for (i=0; i<10; i++)
    document.write("This is line " + i + "<br />");
```

The loop in this example contains a `document.write` statement that will be
repeatedly executed. To see just what this loop does, you can add it to a
`<script>` section of an HTML document, as shown in Listing 18.3.

LISTING 18.3   A Loop Using the `for` Keyword

```
<?xml version="1.0" encoding="UTF-8"?>
<!DOCTYPE html PUBLIC "-//W3C//DTD XHTML 1.1//EN"
  "http://www.w3.org/TR/xhtml11/DTD/xhtml11.dtd">

<html xmlns="http://www.w3.org/1999/xhtml" xml:lang="en">
  <head>
    <title>Using a for Loop</title>
  </head>
  <body>
    <h1>Using a for Loop</h1>
    <p>The following is the output of the <strong>for</strong> loop:</p>
    <script type="text/javascript">
    for (i=1;i<10;i++) {
        document.write("This is line " + i + "<br />");
    }
    </script>
</body>
</html>
```

This example displays a message with the loop's counter during each iteration. The output of Listing 18.3 is shown in Figure 18.2.

Notice that the loop was only executed nine times. This is because the conditional is `i<10`. When the counter (`i`) is incremented to `10`, the expression
is no longer true. If you need the loop to count to `10`, you can change the
conditional; either `i<=10` or `i<11` will work fine.

The `for` loop is traditionally used to count from one number to another,
but you can use just about any statement for the initialization, condition,
and increment. However, there's usually a better way to do other types of
loops with the `while` keyword, as described in the next section.

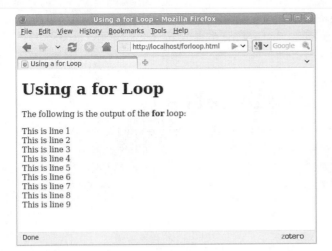

FIGURE 18.2
The results of the for loop example.

Using while **Loops**

Another keyword for loops in JavaScript is while. Unlike for loops, while loops don't necessarily use a variable to count. Instead, they execute as long as a condition is true. In fact, if the condition starts out as false, the statements won't execute at all.

The while statement includes the condition in parentheses, and it is followed by a block of statements within braces, just like a for loop. Here is a simple while loop:

```
while (total < 10) {
    n++;
    total += values[n];
}
```

This loop uses a counter, n, to iterate through the values array. Rather than stopping at a certain count, however, it stops when the total of the values reaches 10.

You might have noticed that you could have done the same thing with a for loop:

```
for (n=0;total < 10; n++) {
    total += values[n];
}
```

As a matter of fact, the for loop is nothing more than a special kind of while loop that handles an initialization and an increment for you. You can generally use `while` for any loop. However, it's best to choose whichever type of loop makes the most sense for the job, or that takes the least amount of typing.

Using `do...while` Loops

JavaScript, like many other programming languages, includes a third type of loop: the `do...while` loop. This type of loop is similar to an ordinary `while` loop, with one difference: The condition is tested at the *end* of the loop rather than the beginning. Here is a typical `do...while` loop:

```
do {
    n++;
    total += values[n];
}
while (total < 10);
```

As you've probably noticed, this is basically an upside-down version of the previous `while` example. There is one difference: With the do loop, the condition is tested at the end of the loop. This means that the statements in the loop will always be executed at least once, even if the condition is never true.

Working with Loops

Although you can use simple `for` and `while` loops for straightforward tasks, there are some considerations you should make when using more complicated loops. In the next sections, we'll look at infinite loops and the `break` and `continue` statements, which give you more control over your loops.

Creating an Infinite Loop

The `for` and `while` loops give you quite a bit of control over the loop. In some cases, this can cause problems if you're not careful. For example, look at the following loop code:

```
while (i < 10) {
    n++;
    values[n] = 0;
}
```

There's a mistake in this example. The condition of the `while` loop refers to the `i` variable, but that variable doesn't actually change during the loop.

This creates an *infinite loop*. The loop will continue executing until the user stops it or until it generates an error of some kind.

Infinite loops can't always be stopped by the user, except by quitting the browser—and some loops can even prevent the browser from quitting or cause a crash.

Obviously, infinite loops are something to avoid. They can also be difficult to spot because JavaScript won't give you an error that actually tells you there is an infinite loop. Thus, each time you create a loop in a script, you should be careful to make sure there's a way out.

Occasionally, you might want to create an infinite loop deliberately. This might include situations when you want your program to execute until the user stops it, or if you are providing an escape route with the break statement, which is introduced in the next section. Here's an easy way to create an infinite loop:

```
while (true) {
```

Because the value true is the conditional, this loop will always find its condition to be true.

Escaping from a Loop

There is one way out of an infinite loop. You can use the break statement during a loop to exit it immediately and continue with the first statement after the loop. Here is a simple example of the use of break:

```
while (true) {
    n++;
    if (values[n] == 1) break;
}
```

Although the while statement is set up as an infinite loop, the if statement checks the corresponding value of an array. If it finds a value of 1, it exits the loop.

When the JavaScript interpreter encounters a break statement, it skips the rest of the loop and continues the script with the first statement after the right brace at the loop's end. You can use the break statement in any type of loop, whether infinite or not. This provides an easy way to exit if an error occurs or if another condition is met.

NOTE

Depending on the browser version in use, an infinite loop might even make the browser stop responding to the user. Be sure you provide an escape route from infinite loops and save your script before you test it just in case.

Continuing a Loop

One more statement is available to help you control the execution of statements in a loop. The `continue` statement skips the rest of the loop, but, unlike `break`, it continues with the next iteration of the loop. Here is a simple example:

```
for (i=1; i<21; i++) {
   if (score[i]==0) continue;
   document.write("Student number ",i, " Score: ", score[i], "\n");
}
```

This script uses a `for` loop to print out scores for 20 students, stored in the `score` array. The `if` statement is used to check for scores with a value of `0`. The script assumes that a score of `0` means that the student didn't take the test, so it continues the loop without printing that score.

Looping Through Object Properties

Yet another type of loop is available in JavaScript. The `for...in` loop is not as flexible as an ordinary `for` or `while` loop. Instead, it is specifically designed to perform an operation on each property of an object.

For example, the `navigator` object contains properties that describe the user's browser. You can use `for...in` to display this object's properties:

```
for (i in navigator) {
    document.write("property: " + i);
    document.write(" value: " + navigator[i] + "<br>");
}
```

Like an ordinary `for` loop, this type of loop uses an index variable (`i` in the example). For each iteration of the loop, the variable is set to the next property of the object. This makes it easy when you need to check or modify each of an object's properties.

▼ TRY IT YOURSELF

Working with Arrays and Loops

To apply your knowledge of loops, you will now create a script that deals with arrays using loops. As you progress through this script, try to imagine how difficult it would be without JavaScript's looping features.

This simple script will prompt the user for a series of names. After all of the names have been entered, it will display the list of names in a numbered list. To begin the script, initialize some variables:

```
names = new Array();
i = 0;
```

The names array will store the names the user enters. You don't know how many names will be entered, so you don't need to specify a dimension for the array. The i variable will be used as a counter in the loops.

Next, use the prompt statement to prompt the user for a series of names. Use a loop to repeat the prompt for each name. You want the user to enter at least one name, so a do loop is ideal:

```
do {
    next = prompt("Enter the Next Name", "");
    if (next > " ") names[i] = next;
    i = i + 1;
    }
    while (next > " ");
```

This loop prompts for a string called next. If a name was entered and isn't blank, it's stored as the next entry in the names array. The i counter is then incremented. The loop repeats until the user doesn't enter a name or clicks Cancel in the prompt dialog.

Next, your script can display the number of names that was entered:

```
document.write("<h2>" + (names.length) + " names entered.</h2>");
```

This statement displays the length property of the names array, surrounded by level 2 header tags for emphasis.

Next, the script should display all the names in the order they were entered. Because the names are in an array, the for...in loop is a good choice:

```
document.write("<ol>");
for (i in names) {
    document.write("<li>" + names[i] + "</li>");
}
document.write("</ol>");
```

Here you have a for...in loop that loops through the names array, assigning the counter i to each index in turn. The script then prints the name between opening and closing <li> tags as an item in an ordered list. Before and after the loop, the script prints beginning and ending <ol> tags.

TIP

If you're interested in making your scripts as short as possible, remember that you could use the increment (++) operator to combine the i = i + 1 statement with the previous statement: names[i++]=1.

▼ TRY IT YOURSELF

Working with Arrays and Loops

continued

You now have everything you need for a working script. Listing 18.4 shows the HTML file for this example, and Listing 18.5 shows the JavaScript file.

LISTING 18.4   A Script to Prompt for Names and Display Them (HTML)

```
<?xml version="1.0" encoding="UTF-8"?>
<!DOCTYPE html PUBLIC "-//W3C//DTD XHTML 1.1//EN"
 "http://www.w3.org/TR/xhtml11/DTD/xhtml11.dtd">

<html xmlns="http://www.w3.org/1999/xhtml" xml:lang="en">
  <head>
    <title>Loops Example</title>
  </head>
  <body>
<h1>Loops Example</h1>
    <p>Enter a series of names and I will display them in a
    numbered list.</p>
    <script type="text/javascript" src="loops.js" > </script>
</body>
</html>
```

LISTING 18.5   A Script to Prompt for Names and Display Them (JavaScript)

```
// create the array
names = new Array();
i = 0;
// loop and prompt for names
do {
    next = window.prompt("Enter the Next Name", "");
    if (next > " ") names[i] = next;
    i = i + 1;
    } while (next > " ");
document.write("<h2>" + (names.length) + " names entered.</h2>");
// display all of the names
document.write("<ol>");
for (i in names) {
    document.write("<li>" + names[i] + "</li>");
}
document.write("</ol>");
```

To try this example, save the JavaScript file as loops.js, and then load the HTML document into a browser. You'll be prompted for one name at a time. Enter several names, and then click Cancel to indicate that you're finished. Figure 18.3 shows what the final results should look like in a browser.

TRY IT YOURSELF ▼

**Working with Arrays
and Loops**
continued

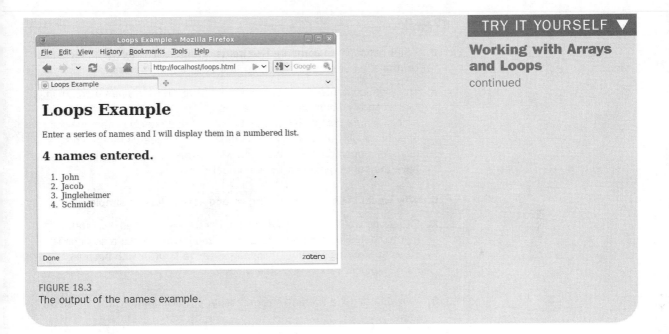

FIGURE 18.3
The output of the names example.

Summary

In this chapter, you learned two ways to control the flow of your scripts. First, you learned how to use the `if` statement to evaluate conditional expressions and react to them. You also learned a shorthand form of conditional expression using the `?` operator and the `switch` statement for working with multiple conditions.

You also learned about JavaScript's looping capabilities using `for`, `while`, and other loops and how to control loops further using the `break` and `continue` statements. Lastly, you looked at the `for...in` loop for working with each property of an object.

Q&A

Q. What happens if I compare two items of different data types (for example, a number and a string) in a conditional expression?

A. The JavaScript interpreter does its best to make the values a common format and compare them. In this case, it would convert them both to strings before comparing. In JavaScript 1.3 and later, you can use the special equality operator === to compare two values and their types—using this operator, the expression will be true only if the expressions have the same value *and* the same data type.

Q. Why would I use `switch` if using `if` and `else` is just as simple?

A. Either one works, so it's your choice. Personally, I find `switch` statements confusing and prefer to use `if`. Your choice might also depend on what other programming languages you're familiar with because some support `switch` and others don't.

Q. Why don't I get a friendly error message if I accidentally use = instead of ==?

A. In some cases, this will result in an error. However, the incorrect version often appears to be a correct statement. For example, in the statement `if (a=1)`, the variable `a` will be assigned the value 1. The `if` statement is considered true, and the value of `a` is lost.

Q. It seems like I could use a `for` loop to replace any of the other loop methods (`while`, `do`, and so on). Why so many choices?

A. You're right. In most cases, a `for` loop will work, and you can do all your loops that way if you want. For that matter, you can use `while` to replace a `for` loop. You can use whichever looping method makes the most sense for your application.

Workshop

The workshop contains quiz questions and exercises to help you solidify your understanding of the material covered. Try to answer all questions before looking at the "Answers" section that follows.

Quiz

1. Which of the following operators means "is not equal to" in JavaScript?

    a. !

    b. !=

    c. <>

2. What does the `switch` statement do?

    a. Tests a variable for a number of different values

    b. Turns a variable on or off

    c. Makes ordinary `if` statements longer and more confusing

3. Which type of JavaScript loop checks the condition at the *end* of the loop?

    a. `for`

    b. `while`

    c. `do...while`

4. Within a loop, what does the `break` statement do?

    a. Crashes the browser

    b. Starts the loop over

    c. Escapes the loop entirely

5. The statement `while (3==3)` is an example of

    a. A typographical error

    b. An infinite loop

    c. An illegal JavaScript statement

Answers

1. b. The != operator means *is not equal to*.

2. a. The switch statement can test the same variable or expression for a number of different values.

3. c. The do...while loop uses a condition at the end of the loop.

4. c. The break statement escapes the loop.

5. b. Because the condition (3==3) will always be true, this statement creates an infinite loop.

Exercises

▶ Modify Listing 18.4 to sort the names in alphabetical order before displaying them. You can use the sort method of the Array object, described in Chapter 16, "Using JavaScript Variables, Strings, and Arrays."

▶ Modify Listing 18.4 to prompt for exactly 10 names. What happens if you click the Cancel button instead of entering a name?

CHAPTER 19
Responding to Events

In your experience with JavaScript so far, most of the scripts you've written have executed in a calm, orderly fashion, moving from the first statement to the last. You've seen a few event handlers used in sample scripts to focus your attention on other aspects of programming, and it is likely that you used your common sense to follow along with the actions. That alone speaks to the relative ease and simplicity of using JavaScript event handlers within your HTML.

In this chapter, you'll learn to use the wide variety of event handlers supported by JavaScript. Rather than executing in order, scripts using event handlers can interact directly with the user. You'll use event handlers in just about every script you write throughout the rest of this book, and in fact they're likely to feature prominently in most scripts you will write, period.

WHAT YOU'LL LEARN IN
THIS CHAPTER:

► How event handlers work
► How event handlers relate to objects
► How to create an event handler
► How to detect mouse and keyboard actions
► How to use onclick to change the appearance of <div>

Understanding Event Handlers

As you learned in Chapter 14, "Getting Started with JavaScript Programming," JavaScript programs don't have to execute in order. You also learned they can detect *events* and react to them. Events are things that happen to the browser—the user clicking a button, the mouse pointer moving, or a web page or image loading from the server.

A wide variety of events enable your scripts to respond to the mouse, the keyboard, and other circumstances. Events are the key method JavaScript uses to make web documents interactive.

The script that you use to detect and respond to an event is called an *event handler*. Event handlers are among the most powerful features of JavaScript. Luckily, they're also among the easiest features to learn and use—often, a useful event handler requires only a single statement.

Objects and Events

As you learned in Chapter 15, "Working with the Document Object Model (DOM)," JavaScript uses a set of objects to store information about the various parts of a web page—buttons, links, images, windows, and so on. An event can often happen in more than one place (for example, the user could click any one of the links on the page), so each event is associated with an object.

Each event has a name. For example, the `onMouseOver` event occurs when the mouse pointer moves over an object on the page. When the pointer moves over a particular link, the `onMouseOver` event is sent to that link's event handler, if it has one.

To define an event handler, you add the word on to the beginning of the event's name. For example, the `onMouseOver` event handler is called when the mouse moves over a link. To define the event handler, you add it to that particular link's `<a>` HTML tag.

Creating an Event Handler

You don't need the `<script>` tag to define an event handler. Instead, you can add an event handler attribute to an individual HTML tag. For example, here is a link that includes an `onMouseOver` event handler:

```
<a href="http://www.google.com/"
   onmouseover="alert('You moved over the link.');">
   This is a link.</a>
```

Note that this is all one `<a>` tag, although it's split into multiple lines. This specifies a statement to be used as the `onMouseOver` event handler for the link. This statement displays an alert message when the mouse moves over the link.

You can use JavaScript statements like the previous one in an event handler, but if you need more than one statement, it's a good idea to use a function instead. Just define the function in the header of the document, and then call the function as the event handler like this:

```
<a href="#bottom" onmouseover="DoIt();">Move the mouse over this link.</a>
```

This example calls a function called `DoIt()` when the user moves the mouse over the link. Using a function is convenient because you can use longer, more readable JavaScript routines as event handlers.

Defining Event Handlers with JavaScript

Rather than specifying an event handler in an HTML document, you can use JavaScript to assign a function as an event handler. This enables you to set event handlers conditionally, turn them on and off, and change the function that handles an event dynamically.

To define an event handler in this way, you first define a function, and then assign the function as an event handler. Event handlers are stored as properties of the document object or another object that can receive an event. For example, these statements define a function called mousealert, and then assign it as the onMouseDown event handler for the document:

```
function mousealert() {
    alert ("You clicked the mouse!");
}
document.onmousedown = mousealert;
```

You can use this technique to set up an event handler for any HTML element, but an additional step is required: You must first find the object corresponding to the element. To do this, use the document.getElementById function. First, define an element in the HTML document and specify an id attribute:

```
<a href="http://www.google.com/" id="link1">
```

Next, in the JavaScript code, find the object and apply the event handler:

```
obj = document.getElementById("link1");
obj.onclick = MyFunction;
```

You can do this for any object as long as you've defined it with a unique id attribute in the HTML file. Using this technique, you can easily assign the same function to handle events for multiple objects without adding clutter to your HTML code.

Supporting Multiple Event Handlers

What if you want more than one thing to happen when you click on an element? For example, suppose you want two functions called update and display to both execute when a button is clicked. You can't assign two functions to the onclick property. One solution is to define a function that calls both functions:

```
function UpdateDisplay() {
    update();
    display();
}
```

TIP

For simple event handlers, you can use two statements if you separate them with a semi-colon. However, in most cases it's easier to use a function to perform the statements.

TIP

Setting up event handlers this way is also a good practice in general: It enables you to use an external JavaScript file to define the function and set up the event, keeping the JavaScript code completely separate from the HTML file.

This isn't always the ideal way to do things. For example, if you're using two third-party scripts and both of them want to add an `onLoad` event to the page, there should be a way to add both. The W3C DOM standard defines a function, `addEventListener`, for this purpose. This function defines a *listener* for a particular event and object, and you can add as many listener functions as you need.

Unfortunately, `addEventListener` is not supported by Internet Explorer, so you have to use a different function, `attachEvent`, in that browser. See Chapter 21, "Using Unobtrusive JavaScript," for a function that combines these two for a cross-browser event-adding script.

Using the `event` Object

When an event occurs, you might need to know more about the event—for example, for a keyboard event, you need to know which key was pressed. The DOM includes an `event` object that provides this information.

To use the `event` object, you can pass it on to your event handler function. For example, this statement defines an `onKeyPress` event that passes the `event` object to a function:

```
<body onkeypress="getkey(event);">
```

You can then define your function to accept the event as a parameter:

```
function getkey(e) {
...
}
```

In Firefox, Safari, Opera, and Chrome, an `event` object is automatically passed to the event handler function, so this will work even if you use JavaScript rather than HTML to define an event handler. In Internet Explorer, the most recent event is stored in the `window.event` object. The previous HTML example passes this object to the event handler function. If you define the event handler with JavaScript, this is not possible, so you need to use some code to find the correct object:

```
function getkey(e) {
    if (!e) e=window.event;
...
}
```

This checks whether the e variable is already defined. If not, it gets the `window.event` object and stores it in e. This ensures that you have a valid `event` object in any browser.

Unfortunately, although both Internet Explorer and non-Internet Explorer browsers support `event` objects, they support different properties. One property that is the same in both browsers is `event.type`, the type of event. This is simply the name of the event, such as `mouseover` for an `onMouseOver` event and `keypress` for an `onKeyPress` event. The following sections list some additional useful properties for each browser.

Internet Explorer `event` Properties

The following are some of the commonly used properties of the `event` object for Internet Explorer:

- **`event.button`**—The mouse button that was pressed. This value is 1 for the left button and usually 2 for the right button.
- **`event.clientX`**—The x-coordinate (column, in pixels) where the event occurred.
- **`event.clientY`**—The y-coordinate (row, in pixels) where the event occurred.
- **`event.altkey`**—A flag that indicates whether the Alt key was pressed during the event.
- **`event.ctrlkey`**—A flag that indicates whether the Ctrl key was pressed.
- **`event.shiftkey`**—A flag that indicates whether the Shift key was pressed.
- **`event.keyCode`**—The key code (in Unicode) for the key that was pressed.
- **`event.srcElement`**—The object where the element occurred.

Non-Internet Explorer `event` Properties

The following are some of the commonly used properties of the `event` object for modern browsers that are not Internet Explorer:

- **`event.modifiers`**—Indicates which modifier keys (Shift, Ctrl, Alt, and so on) were held down during the event. This value is an integer that combines binary values representing the different keys.
- **`event.pageX`**—The x-coordinate of the event within the web page.
- **`event.pageY`**—The y-coordinate of the event within the web page.
- **`event.which`**—The keycode for keyboard events (in Unicode) or the button that was pressed for mouse events (It's best to use the cross-browser `button` property instead.)

NOTE

The event.pageX and event.pageY properties are based on the top-left corner of the element where the event occurred, not always the exact position of the mouse pointer.

TIP

One of the most common uses for the onMouseOver and onMouseOut event handlers is to create *rollovers*—images that change when the mouse moves over them. You'll learn how to create these later in the chapter.

NOTE

The object in this case can be a link. It can also be a form element. You'll learn more about forms in Chapter 26, "Working with Web-Based Forms."

▶ **event.button**—The mouse button that was pressed. This works just like Internet Explorer except that the left button's value is 0 and the right button's value is 2.

▶ **event.target**—The object where the element occurred.

Using Mouse Events

The DOM includes a number of event handlers for detecting mouse actions. Your script can detect the movement of the mouse pointer and when a button is clicked, released, or both. Some of these will be familiar to you already because you have seen them in action in previous chapters.

Over and Out

You've already seen the first and most common event handler, onMouseOver. This handler is called when the mouse pointer moves over a link or other object.

The onMouseOut handler is the opposite—it is called when the mouse pointer moves out of the object's border. Unless something strange happens, this always happens sometime after the onMouseOver event is called.

This handler is particularly useful if your script has made a change when the pointer moved over the object—for example, displaying a message in the status line or changing an image. You can use an onMouseOut handler to undo the action when the pointer moves away.

Ups and Downs (and Clicks)

You can also use events to detect when the mouse button is clicked. The basic event handler for this is onClick. This event handler is called when the mouse button is clicked while positioned over the appropriate object.

For example, you can use the following event handler to display an alert when a link is clicked:

```
<a href="http://www.google.com/"
    onclick="alert('You are about to leave this site.');">
    Go Away</a>
```

In this case, the onClick event handler runs before the linked page is loaded into the browser. This is useful for making links conditional or displaying a disclaimer before launching the linked page.

If your `onClick` event handler returns the `false` value, the link will not be followed. For example, the following is a link that displays a confirmation dialog. If you click Cancel, the link is not followed; if you click OK, the new page is loaded:

```
<a href="http://www.google.com/"
    onclick="return(window.confirm('Are you sure?'));">
    Go Away</a>
```

This example uses the `return` statement to enclose the event handler. This ensures that the `false` value that is returned when the user clicks Cancel is returned from the event handler, which prevents the link from being followed.

The `onDblClick` event handler is similar, but is used only if the user double-clicks on an object. Because links usually require only a single click, you could use this to make a link do two different things depending on the number of clicks. (Needless to say, this could be confusing.) You can also detect double-clicks on images and other objects.

To give you even more control of what happens when the mouse button is pressed, two more events are included:

▶ `onMouseDown` is used when the user presses the mouse button.

▶ `onMouseUp` is used when the user releases the mouse button.

These two events are the two halves of a mouse click. If you want to detect an entire click, use `onClick`. Use `onMouseUp` and `onMouseDown` to detect just one or the other.

To detect which mouse button is pressed, you can use the `button` property of the `event` object. This property is assigned the value 0 or 1 for the left button and 2 for the right button. This property is assigned for `onClick`, `onDblClick`, `onMouseUp`, and `onMouseDown` events.

As an example of these event handlers, you can create a script that displays information about mouse button events and determines which button is pressed. Listing 19.1 shows the mouse event script.

CAUTION

Browsers don't normally detect `onClick` or `onDblClick` events for the right mouse button. If you want to detect the right button, `onMouseDown` is the most reliable way.

LISTING 19.1   The JavaScript File for the Mouse Click Example

```
function mousestatus(e) {
    if (!e) e = window.event;
    btn = e.button;
    whichone = (btn < 2) ? "Left" : "Right";
    message=e.type + " : " + whichone + "\n";
    document.form1.info.value += message;
}
```

LISTING 19.1   Continued

```
obj=document.getElementById("testlink");
obj.onmousedown = mousestatus;
obj.onmouseup = mousestatus;
obj.onclick = mousestatus;
obj.ondblclick = mousestatus;
```

This script includes a function, `mousestatus`, that detects mouse events. This function uses the `button` property of the `event` object to determine which button was pressed. It also uses the `type` property to display the type of event because the function will be used to handle multiple event types.

After the function, the script finds the object for a link with the `id` attribute `testlink` and assigns its `onmousedown`, `onmouseup`, `onclick`, and `ondblclick` events to the `mousestatus` function.

Save this script as click.js. Next, you will need an HTML document to work with the script, as shown in Listing 19.2.

LISTING 19.2   The HTML File for the Mouse Click Example

```
<?xml version="1.0" encoding="UTF-8"?>
<!DOCTYPE html PUBLIC "-//W3C//DTD XHTML 1.1//EN"
  "http://www.w3.org/TR/xhtml11/DTD/xhtml11.dtd">

<html xmlns="http://www.w3.org/1999/xhtml" xml:lang="en">
  <head>
    <title>Mouse Click Text</title>
  </head>
  <body>
    <h1>Mouse Click Test</h1>
    <p>Click the mouse on the test link below. A message
    will indicate which button was clicked.</p>
    <h2><a href="#" id="testlink">Test Link</a></h2>
    <form action="" name="form1">
    <div>
    <textarea rows="10" cols="70" name="info"></textarea>
    </div>
    </form>
    <script type="text/javascript" src="click.js"></script>
</body>
</html>
```

This file defines a test link with the `id` property `testlink`, which is used in the script to assign event handlers. It also defines a form and a textarea used by the script to display the events. To test this document, save it in the same folder as the JavaScript file you created previously and load the HTML document into a browser. The results are shown in Figure 19.1.

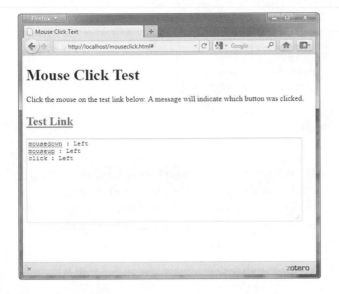

FIGURE 19.1
The mouse click example in action.

NOTE

Notice that a single click of the left mouse button triggers three events: onMouseDown, onMouseUp, and onClick.

Using Keyboard Events

JavaScript can also detect keyboard actions. The main event handler for this purpose is onKeyPress, which occurs when a key is pressed and released or held down. As with mouse buttons, you can detect the down and up parts of the keypress with the onKeyDown and onKeyUp event handlers.

Of course, you might find it useful to know which key the user pressed. You can find this out with the event object, which is sent to your event handler when the event occurs. In Internet Explorer, event.keyCode stores the ASCII character code for the key that was pressed. In non-Internet Explorer browsers, the event.which property stores the ASCII character code for the key that was pressed.

If you'd rather deal with actual characters than key codes, you can use the fromCharCode string method to convert them. This method converts a numeric ASCII code to its corresponding string character. For example, the following statement converts the event.which property to a character and stores it in the key variable:

```
key = String.fromCharCode(event.which);
```

Because different browsers have different ways of returning the key code, displaying key browsers independently is a bit harder. However, you can create a script that displays keys for either browser. The following function will display each key as it is typed:

NOTE

ASCII (American Standard Code for Information Interchange) is the standard numeric code used by most computers to represent characters. It assigns the numbers 0–128 to various characters—for example, the capital letters A through Z are ASCII values 65 to 90.

```
function DisplayKey(e) {
   // which key was pressed?
   if (e.keyCode) keycode=e.keyCode;
      else keycode=e.which;
   character=String.fromCharCode(keycode);
   // find the object for the destination paragraph
   k = document.getElementById("keys");
   // add the character to the paragraph
   k.innerHTML += character;
}
```

NOTE

The final lines in the
DisplayKey function use the
getElementById function and
the innerHTML attribute to display the keys you type within a
paragraph on the page.

The DisplayKey function receives the event object from the event handler and stores it in the variable e. It checks whether the e.keyCode property exists and stores it in the keycode variable if present. Otherwise, it assumes the browser is not Internet Explorer and assigns keycode to the e.which property.

The remaining lines of the function convert the key code to a character and add it to the paragraph in the document with the id attribute keys. Listing 19.3 shows a complete example using this function.

LISTING 19.3   Displaying Typed Characters

```
<?xml version="1.0" encoding="UTF-8"?>
<!DOCTYPE html PUBLIC "-//W3C//DTD XHTML 1.1//EN"
  "http://www.w3.org/TR/xhtml11/DTD/xhtml11.dtd">

<html xmlns="http://www.w3.org/1999/xhtml" xml:lang="en">
  <head>
    <title>Displaying Keypresses</title>
    <script type="text/javascript">
    function DisplayKey(e) {
       // which key was pressed?
       if (e.keyCode) keycode=e.keyCode;
          else keycode=e.which;
       character=String.fromCharCode(keycode);
       // find the object for the destination paragraph
       k = document.getElementById("keys");
       // add the character to the paragraph
       k.innerHTML += character;
    }
    </script>
  </head>
  <body onkeypress="DisplayKey(event)">
    <h1>Displaying Typed Characters</h1>
    <p>This document includes a simple script that displays
    the keys you type in the paragraph below. Type a few keys
    to try it. </p>
    <p id="keys"></p>
</body>
</html>
```

When you load this example, watch the characters you've typed appear in a paragraph of the document. Figure 19.2 shows this example in action.

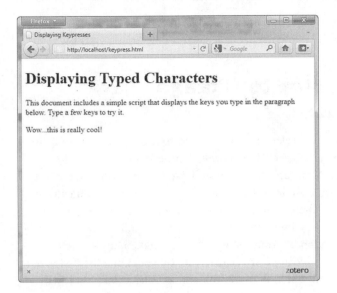

FIGURE 19.2
Displaying the keys that were pressed.

Using the `onLoad` **and** `onUnload` Events

Another event you might use often is `onLoad`. This event occurs when the current page (including all of its images) finishes loading from the server.

The `onLoad` event is related to the `window` object, and to define it, you use an event handler in the `<body>` tag. For example, the following is a `<body>` tag that uses a simple event handler to display an alert when the page finishes loading:

```
<body onload="alert('Loading complete.');">
```

Images can also have an `onLoad` event handler. When you define an `onLoad` event handler for an `<img>` tag, it is triggered as soon as the specified image has completely loaded.

To set an `onLoad` event using JavaScript, you assign a function to the `onload` property of the `window` object:

```
window.onload = MyFunction;
```

You can also specify an onUnload event for the <body> tag. This event will be triggered whenever the browser unloads the current document—this occurs when another page is loaded or when the browser window is closed.

In the next section you'll see an event handler in action, within the context of functionality you're likely to encounter when developing your own sites.

Using onclick to Change <div> Appearance

As you've seen, the onclick event can be used to invoke all sorts of action; you might think of a mouse click as a way to submit a form by clicking on a button, but you can capture this event and use it to provide interactivity within your pages as well. In this example, you will see how you can use the onclick event to show or hide information contained in a <div>. In this case, you are adding interactivity to your page by allowing the user to show previously hidden information when users click on a piece of text. This is referred to as a *piece of text* because, strictly speaking, the text is not a link. That is to say, it will look like a link and act like a link, but it will not be marked up within an <a> tag.

Listing 19.4 provides the complete code for this example, as shown initially in Figure 19.3.

LISTING 19.4   Using onclick to Show or Hide Content

```
<?xml version="1.0" encoding="UTF-8"?>
<!DOCTYPE html PUBLIC "-//W3C//DTD XHTML 1.1//EN"
  "http://www.w3.org/TR/xhtml11/DTD/xhtml11.dtd">

<html xmlns="http://www.w3.org/1999/xhtml" xml:lang="en">
  <head>
    <title>Steptoe Butte</title>
    <style type="text/css">
    a {
       text-decoration: none;
       font-weight: bold;
       color: #7a7abf;
    }
    #hide_e {
       display: none;
    }
    #elevation {
       display: none;
    }
    #hide_p {
       display: none;
```

LISTING 19.4   continued

```
   }
   #photos {
      display: none;
   }
   #show_e {
      display: block;
   }
   #show_p {
      display: block;
   }
   .fakelink {
      cursor:pointer;
      text-decoration: none;
      font-weight: bold;
      color: #E03A3E;
   }
   </style>
</head>
<body>
   <h1>Steptoe Butte</h1>
   <p><img src="steptoebutte.jpg" alt="View from Steptoe Butte"
   style="float:left;margin-right:12px;margin-bottom:6px;border:1px
   solid #000" />Steptoe Butte is a quartzite island jutting out of the
   silty loess of the <a class="tip"
   href="http://en.wikipedia.org/wiki/Palouse">Palouse <span>Learn more
   about the Palouse!</span></a> hills in Whitman County, Washington.
   The rock that forms the butte is over 400 million years old, in
   Contrast with the 15-7 million year old
   <a href="http://en.wikipedia.org/wiki/Columbia_River">Columbia
   River</a> basalts that underlie the rest of the Palouse (such
   "islands" of ancient rock have come to be called buttes, a
   butte being defined as a small hill with a flat top, whose width at
   top does not exceed its height).</p>
   <p>A hotel built by Cashup Davis stood atop Steptoe Butte from
   1888 to 1908, burning down several years after it closed. In 1946,
   Virgil McCroskey donated 120 acres (0.49 km2) of land to form
   Steptoe Butte State Park, which was later increased to over 150
   acres (0.61 km2). Steptoe Butte is currently recognized as a
   National Natural Landmark because of its unique geological
   value. It is named in honor of  <a
   href="http://en.wikipedia.org/wiki/Colonel_Edward_Steptoe">
   Colonel Edward Steptoe</a>.</p>
   <div class="fakelink"
        id="show_e"
        onclick="this.style.display='none';
        document.getElementById('hide_e').style.display='block';
        document.getElementById('elevation').style.display='inline';
   ">&raquo; Show Elevation</div>

   <div class="fakelink"
        id="hide_e"
        onclick="this.style.display='none';
```

LISTING 19.4   Continued

```
            document.getElementById('show_e').style.display='block';
            document.getElementById('elevation').style.display='none';
     ">&raquo; Hide Elevation</div>

     <div id="elevation">3,612 feet (1,101 m), approximately 1,000
     feet (300 m) above the surrounding countryside.</div>

     <div class="fakelink"
          id="show_p"
          onclick="this.style.display='none';
          document.getElementById('hide_p').style.display='block';
          document.getElementById('photos').style.display='inline';
     ">&raquo; Show Photos from the Top of Steptoe Butte</div>

      <div class="fakelink"
           id="hide_p"
           onclick="this.style.display='none';
           document.getElementById('show_p').style.display='block';
           document.getElementById('photos').style.display='none';
      ">&raquo; Hide Photos from the Top of Steptoe Butte</div>

      <div id="photos"><img src="steptoe_sm1.jpg" alt="View
      from Steptoe Butte"style="margin-right: 12px; border: 1px
      solid #000" /><img src="steptoe_sm2.jpg" alt="View from
      Steptoe Butte" style="margin-right: 12px; border: 1px solid
      #000" /><img src="steptoe_sm3.jpg" alt="View from Steptoe
      Butte" style="margin-right: 12px; border: 1px solid #000" />
      </div>

      <p><em>Text from
      <a href="http://en.wikipedia.org/wiki/Steptoe_Butte">
      Wikipedia</a>, photos
      by the author.</em></p>
   </body>
</html>
```

To begin, look at the six entries in the style sheet. The first entry simply styles links that are surrounded by the <a></a> tag pair; these links display as nonunderlined, bold, blue links. You can see these regular links in the two paragraphs of text (and in the line at the bottom of the page) in Figure 19.3.

The next four entries are for specific IDs, and those IDs are all set to be invisible (display: none) when the page initially loads. The two IDs that follow are set to display as block elements when the page initially loads. Again, strictly speaking, these two IDs would not have to be defined as such because it is the default display. The style sheet includes these entries for the purpose of illustrating the differences. If you count the number of <div> elements in Listing 19.4, you will find six in the code: four invisible and two that are visible upon page load.

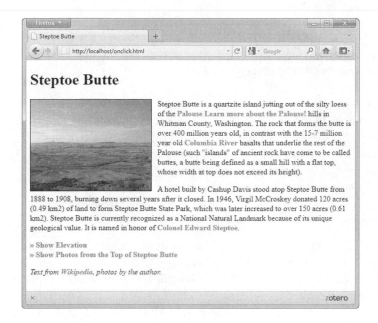

FIGURE 19.3
The initial display of Listing 19.4.

The goal in this example is to change the display value of two IDs when another ID is clicked. But first you have to make sure users realize a piece of text is clickable, and that typically happens when users see their mouse pointers change to reflect a link is present. Although not shown in Figure 19.3, when you look at this example in your browser you will see that the mouse pointer changes to a hand with a finger pointing at a particular link.

This functionality is achieved by defining a class for this particular text; the class is called `fakelink`, as you can see in this snippet of code:

```
<div class="fakelink"
     id="show_e"
     onclick="this.style.display='none';
     document.getElementById('hide_e').style.display='block';
     document.getElementById('elevation').style.display='inline';
">&raquo; Show Elevation</div>
```

The `fakelink` class ensures that the text is rendered as nonunderlined, bold, and red; `cursor: pointer` causes the mouse pointer to change in such a way that users think the text is a link of the type that would normally be enclosed in an `<a></a>` tag. But the really interesting stuff happens when we associate an `onclick` attribute with a `<div>`. In the sample snippet just shown, the value of the `onclick` attribute is a series of commands that change the current value of CSS elements.

Let's look at them separately:

```
this.style.display='none';
document.getElementById('hide_e').style.display='block';
document.getElementById('elevation').style.display='inline';
```

What you are looking at are different JavaScript methods meant to change particular elements. In the first line, the `this` keyword refers to the element itself. In other words, `this` refers to the `<div>` ID called `show_e`. The keyword style refers to the style object; the `style` object contains all the CSS styles that you assign to the element. In this case, we are most interested in the display style. Therefore, `this.style.display` means "the display style of the `show_e` ID," and what we are doing here is setting the value of the display style to none when the text itself is clicked.

But that is not all we are doing because there are three actions that occur within the `onclick` attribute. The other two actions begin with `document.getElementByID()` and include a specific ID name within the parentheses. We use `document.getElementByID()` instead of `this` because the second and third actions set CSS style properties for elements that are not the parent element. As you can see in the snippet, in the second and third actions, we are setting the display property values for the element IDs `hide_e` and `elevation`. All told, when users click the currently visible `<div>` called `show_e`:

▶ The `show_e` `<div>` becomes invisible.

▶ The `hide_e` `<div>` becomes visible and is displayed as a block.

▶ The `elevation` `<div>` becomes visible and is displayed inline.

The result of these actions is shown in Figure 19.4.

There is another set of `<div>` elements in the code in Listing 19.3, the ones that control the visibility of the additional photos. These elements are not affected by the `onclick` actions in the elevation-related elements. That is to say, when you click on either Show Elevation or Hide Elevation, the photo-related `<div>` elements do not change at all. You could show the elevation and not the photos (as seen in Figure 19.4), the photos and not the elevation, or both the elevation and photos at the same time (see Figure 19.5).

This brief example has shown you the very beginning of the layout and interaction possibilities that await you when you master CSS in conjunction with JavaScript events. For example, you can code your pages so that your users can change elements of the style sheet, change to an entirely different style sheet, move blocks of text to other places in the layout, take quizzes or submit forms, and much, much more.

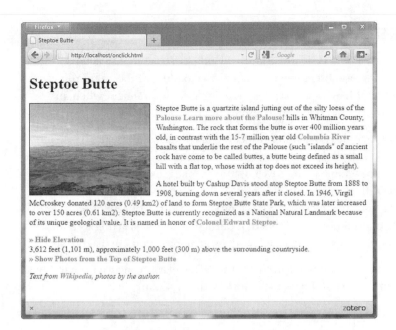

FIGURE 19.4
After clicking "Show Elevation," the visibility of it and other `<div>` elements change based on the commands in the `onclick` attribute.

FIGURE 19.5
The page after clicking both Show Elevation and Show Photos from the Top of Steptoe Butte.

Summary

In this chapter, you've learned to use events to detect mouse actions, keyboard actions, and other events, such as the loading of the page. You can use event handlers to perform a simple JavaScript statement when an event occurs or to call a more complicated function.

JavaScript includes a variety of other events. Many of these are related to forms, which you'll learn more about in Chapter 26. In a longer example at the end of this chapter, you saw how to use onclick to show or hide text in a page with some design elements in it. Some new CSS was introduced: the use of the cursor property. Assigning a cursor property of pointer enabled you to indicate to users that particular text was acting as a link even though it was not enclosed in <a></a> tags as you are used to seeing.

In the next chapter, you'll learn about the objects associated with windows, frames, and layers and how they work with JavaScript.

Q&A

Q. Can you capture mouse or keyboard events on elements other than text, such as images?

A. Yes, these types of events can be applied to actions related to clicking on or rolling over images and text. However, other multimedia objects, such as embedded YouTube videos or Flash files, are not interacted with in the same way, as those objects are played via additional software for which other mouse or keyboard actions are applicable. For instance, if you click on a YouTube video that is embedded in your web page, you are interacting with the YouTube player and no longer your actual web page—that action cannot be captured in the same way.

Q. What happens if I define both `onKeyDown` and `onKeyPress` event handlers? Will they both be called when a key is pressed?

A. The `onKeyDown` event handler is called first. If it returns `true`, the `onKeyPress` event is called. Otherwise, no keypress event is generated.

Q. When I use the `onLoad` event, my event handler sometimes executes before the page is done loading or before some of the graphics. Is there a better way?

A. This is a bug in some older browsers. One solution is to add a slight delay to your script using the `setTimeout` method.

Workshop

The workshop contains quiz questions and exercises to help you solidify your understanding of the material covered. Try to answer all questions before looking at the "Answers" section that follows.

Quiz

1. Which of the following is the correct event handler to detect a mouse click on a link?

    a. `onMouseUp`

    b. `onLink`

    c. `onClick`

2. When does the onLoad event handler for the <body> tag execute?

    a. When an image is finished loading

    b. When the entire page is finished loading

    c. When the user attempts to load another page

3. Which of the following event object properties indicates which key was pressed for an onKeyPress event in Internet Explorer?

    a. event.which

    b. event.keyCode

    c. event.onKeyPress

Answers

1. c. The event handler for a mouse click is onClick.

2. b. The <body> tag's onLoad handler executes when the page and all its images are finished loading.

3. b. In Internet Explorer, the event.keyCode property stores the character code for each key press.

Exercises

▶ Add commands to the onClick attributes in Listing 19.4 so that only one of the <div> elements (the elevation or photos) is visible at a time.

CHAPTER 20
Using Windows and Frames

Now that you've gotten your feet wet with basic JavaScript functionality, let's return to some specific aspects of the Document Object Model (DOM). In this chapter, you'll learn more about some of the most useful objects in the DOM—browser windows and frames—and how JavaScript can interact with them.

Controlling Windows with Objects

In Chapter 15, "Working with the Document Object Model (DOM)," you learned that you can use DOM objects to represent various parts of the browser window and the current HTML document. You also learned that the `history`, `document`, and `location` objects are all children of the `window` object.

In this chapter, you'll take a closer look at the `window` object itself. As you've probably guessed by now, this means you'll be dealing with browser windows. A variation of the `window` object also enables you to work with frames, as you'll see later in this chapter.

The `window` object always refers to the current window (the one containing the script). The `self` keyword is also a synonym for the current window. As you'll learn in the next sections, you can have more than one window on the screen at the same time and can refer to them with different names.

Properties of the `window` Object

Although there is normally a single `window` object, there might be more than one if you are using pop-up windows or frames. As you learned in Chapter 15, the `document`, `history`, and `location` objects are properties (or children) of the `window` object. In addition to these, each `window` object has the following properties:

▶ `window.closed`—Indicates whether the window has been closed. This only makes sense when working with multiple windows because the current window contains the script and cannot be closed without ending the script.

▶ `window.defaultstatus` and `window.status`—The default message for the status line and a temporary message to display on the status line. Some recent browsers disable status line changes by default, so you might not be able to use these.

▶ `window.frames[]`—An array of objects for frames, if the window contains them. You'll learn more about frames later in this chapter.

▶ `window.name`—The name specified for a frame or for a window opened by a script.

▶ `window.opener`—In a window opened by a script, this is a reference to the window containing the script that opened it.

▶ `window.parent`—For a frame, a reference to the parent window containing the frame.

▶ `window.screen`—A child object that stores information about the screen the window is in—its resolution, color depth, and so on.

▶ `window.self`—A synonym for the current `window` object.

▶ `window.top`—A reference to the top-level window when frames are in use.

NOTE

The properties of the `window.screen` object include `height`, `width`, `availHeight`, and `availWidth` (the available height and width rather than total), and `colorDepth`, which indicates the color support of the monitor: 8 for 8-bit color, 32 for 32-bit color, and so on.

Creating a New Window

One of the most convenient uses for the `window` object is to create a new window. You can do this to display a document—for example, a pop-up advertisement or the instructions for a game—without clearing the current window. You can also create windows for specific purposes, such as navigation windows.

You can create a new browser window with the `window.open()` method. A typical statement to open a new window looks like this:

```
WinObj=window.open("URL", "WindowName", "LIST_OF_FEATURES");
```

The following are the components of the `window.open()` statement in the previous example:

▶ The `WinObj` variable is used to store the new `window` object. You can access methods and properties of the new object by using this name.

- ▶ The first parameter of the `window.open()` method is a URL, which will be loaded into the new window. If it's left blank, no web page will be loaded. In this case, you could use JavaScript to fill the window with content.

- ▶ The second parameter specifies a window name (here, `WindowName`). This is assigned to the `window` object's `name` property and is used to refer to the window.

- ▶ The third parameter is a list of optional features, separated by commas. You can customize the new window by choosing whether to include the toolbar, status line, and other features. This enables you to create a variety of "floating" windows, which might look nothing like a typical browser window.

The features available in the third parameter of the `window.open()` method include `width` and `height`, to set the size of the window in pixels, and several features that can be set to either `yes` (1) or `no` (0): `toolbar`, `location`, `directories`, `status`, `menubar`, `scrollbars`, and `resizable`. You can list only the features you want to change from the default.

This example creates a small window with no toolbar or status line:

```
SmallWin = window.open("","small","width=100,height=120,
        toolbar=0,status=0");
```

Opening and Closing Windows

Of course, you can use JavaScript to close windows as well. The `window.close()` method closes a window. Browsers don't normally allow you to close the main browser window without the user's permission; this method's main purpose is for closing windows you have created. For example, this statement closes a window called `updateWindow`:

```
updateWindow.close();
```

As another example, Listing 20.1 shows an HTML document that enables you to open a small new window by pressing a button. You can then press another button to close the new window. The third button attempts to close the current window. Depending on your browser and its settings, this might or might not work (for example, by default, your browser might disallow scripts from closing windows that the script itself did not create or open). If the script does close the window, most browsers will ask for confirmation first.

LISTING 20.1   An HTML Document That Uses JavaScript to Enable You
to Create and Close Windows

```
<?xml version="1.0" encoding="UTF-8"?>
<!DOCTYPE html PUBLIC "-//W3C//DTD XHTML 1.1//EN"
  "http://www.w3.org/TR/xhtml11/DTD/xhtml11.dtd">

<html xmlns="http://www.w3.org/1999/xhtml" xml:lang="en">
  <head>
    <title>Create a New Window</title>
  </head>
  <body>
    <h1>Create a New Window</h1>
    <p>Use the buttons below to open and close windows in JavaScript.</p>
    <form name="winform" action="">
    <p><input type="button" value="Open New Window"
       onclick="NewWin=window.open('','NewWin',
       'toolbar=no,status=no,width=200,height=100');" /></p>
    <p><input type="button" value="Close New Window"
        onclick="NewWin.close();" /></p>
    <p><input type="button" value="Close Main Window"
        onclick="window.close();" /></p>
    </form>
  </body>
</html>
```

This example uses simple event handlers to do its work by providing a different handler for each of the buttons. Figure 20.1 shows the result of
pressing the Open New Window button: It opens a small new window on
top of the main browser window.

FIGURE 20.1
A new browser window opened
with JavaScript.

Moving and Resizing Windows

The DOM also enables you to move or resize windows. You can do this using the following methods for any `window` object:

- ▶ `window.moveTo()` moves the window to a new position. The parameters specify the x (column) and y (row) position.

- ▶ `window.moveBy()` moves the window relative to its current position. The x and y parameters can be positive or negative and are added to the current values to reach the new position.

- ▶ `window.resizeTo()` resizes the window to the width and height specified as parameters.

- ▶ `window.resizeBy()` resizes the window relative to its current size. The parameters are used to modify the current width and height.

As an example, Listing 20.2 shows an HTML document with a simple script that enables you to resize and move the main window based on values entered in a form.

LISTING 20.2   Moving and Resizing the Current Window

```
<?xml version="1.0" encoding="UTF-8"?>
<!DOCTYPE html PUBLIC "-//W3C//DTD XHTML 1.1//EN"
  "http://www.w3.org/TR/xhtml11/DTD/xhtml11.dtd">

<html xmlns="http://www.w3.org/1999/xhtml" xml:lang="en">
  <head>
    <title>Moving and Resizing Windows</title>
    <script type="text/javascript">
    function doIt() {
     if (document.form1.w.value && document.form1.h.value) {
        self.resizeTo(document.form1.w.value, document.form1.h.value);
     }
     if (document.form1.x.value && document.form1.y.value) {
        self.moveTo(document.form1.x.value, document.form1.y.value);
     }
    }
    </script>
  </head>
  <body>
  <h1>Moving and Resizing Windows</h1>
  <form name="form1">
  <p><strong>Resize to:</strong> <br/>
  <input size="5" type="text" name="w" /> pixels wide and <br/>
  <input size="5" type="text" name="h" /> pixels high </p>
  <p><strong>— AND/OR —</strong></p>
  <p><strong>Move to:</strong> <br/>
```

LISTING 20.2   Continued

```
    X-position: <input size="5" type="text" name="x" />
    Y-position: <input size="5" type="text" name="y" /> </p>
    <div><input type="button" value="Change Window"
        onclick="doIt();" /></div>
    </form>
    </body>
</html>
```

In this example, the doIt function is called as an event handler when you click the Change Window button. This function checks whether you have specified width and height values. If you have, it uses the self.resizeTo() method to resize the current window. Similarly, if you have specified x and y values, it uses self.moveTo() to move the window. If you have set both pairs of values, the script will both resize and move your window.

Depending on their settings, some browsers might not allow your script to resize or move the main window. In particular, Firefox can be configured to disallow it. You can enable it by selecting Options from the menu. Select the Content tab, click the Advanced button next to the Enable JavaScript option, and enable or disable the Move or Resize Existing Windows option. Other browsers are likely to have similar options available in the Options or Preferences menus.

Using Timeouts

Sometimes the hardest thing to get a script to do is to do nothing at all—for a specific amount of time. Fortunately, JavaScript includes a built-in function to do this. The window.setTimeout method enables you to specify a time delay and a command that will execute after the delay passes.

You begin a timeout with a call to the setTimeout() method, which has two parameters. The first is a JavaScript statement, or group of statements, enclosed in quotes. The second parameter is the time to wait in milliseconds (thousandths of seconds). For example, the following statement displays an alert dialog box after 10 seconds:

```
ident=window.setTimeout("alert('Time's up!')",10000);
```

A variable (ident in this example) stores an identifier for the timeout. This enables you to set multiple timeouts, each with its own identifier. Before a timeout has elapsed, you can stop it with the clearTimeout() method, specifying the identifier of the timeout to stop:

```
window.clearTimeout(ident);
```

Normally, a timeout only happens once because the statement you specify in the setTimeout statement is only executed once. But often, you'll want your statement to execute over and over. For example, your script might be updating a clock or a countdown and need to execute once per second.

You can make a timeout repeat by issuing the setTimeout() method call again in the function called by the timeout. Listing 20.3 shows an HTML document that demonstrates a repeating timeout.

CAUTION

Like event handlers, timeouts use a JavaScript statement within quotation marks. Make sure that you use a single quote (apostrophe) on each side of each string within the statement, as shown in the preceding example.

LISTING 20.3   Using Timeouts to Update a Page Every Two Seconds

```
<?xml version="1.0" encoding="UTF-8"?>
<!DOCTYPE html PUBLIC "-//W3C//DTD XHTML 1.1//EN"
  "http://www.w3.org/TR/xhtml11/DTD/xhtml11.dtd">

<html xmlns="http://www.w3.org/1999/xhtml" xml:lang="en">
  <head>
    <title>Timeout Example</title>
    <script type="text/javascript">
    var counter = 0;

    // call Update function 2 seconds after first load
    ID=window.setTimeout("Update();",2000);

    function Update() {
       counter++;
       textField = document.getElementById("showText");
       textField.innerHTML = "The counter is now at " + counter;
       // set another timeout for the next count
       ID=window.setTimeout("Update();",2000);
       }
    </script>
    </head>
    <body>
    <h1>Timeout Example</h1>
    <p>The counter will update every two seconds.</p>
    <p>Press RESET or STOP to restart or stop the count.</p>
    <hr/>
    <form name="form1">
    <p id="showText"></p>
    <div><input type="button" value="RESET"
         onclick="counter = 0;" />
        <input type="button" value="STOP"
         onclick="window.clearTimeout(ID);" />
    </div>
    </form>
    </body>
</html>
```

This program displays a message inside a specially named <p> tag every two seconds, including a counter that increments each time. The <p> tag is given an id value of "showText" and the Update() function includes two lines that tells the script that the text should be placed between these two tags:

```
textField = document.getElementById("showText");
textField.innerHTML = "The counter is now at " + counter;
```

The first line creates a variable called textField that holds the value of the element given the id value of "showText". The second line says that given that value, the text about the counter and the counter number should be placed inside the starting and ending tags of the element with the id value of "showText"—that is the purpose of the innerHTML method.

After the script has loaded and begun the counting, you can use the Reset button to start the count over and the Stop button to stop the counting.

This script calls the setTimeout() method when the page loads and again at each update. The Update()function performs the update, adding one to the counter and setting the next timeout. The Reset button sets the counter to zero, and the Stop button demonstrates the clearTimeout() method. Figure 20.2 shows the display of the timeout example after the counter has been running for a while.

FIGURE 20.2

The output of the timeout example.

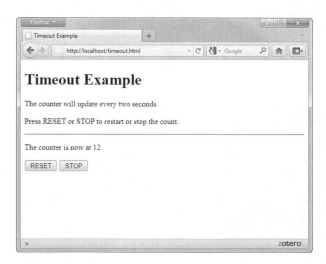

Displaying Dialog Boxes

The window object includes three methods that are useful for displaying messages and interacting with the user. You've already used these in some of your scripts. Here's a summary:

▶ window.alert(*message*) displays an alert dialog box. This dialog box simply gives the user a message.

▶ window.confirm(*message*) displays a confirmation dialog box. This displays a message and includes the OK and Cancel buttons. This method returns true if OK is clicked and false if Cancel is clicked.

▶ window.prompt(*message,default*) displays a message and prompts the user for input. It returns the text entered by the user. If the user does not enter anything, the default value is used.

To use the confirm and prompt methods, use a variable to receive the user's response. For example, this statement displays a prompt and stores the text the user enters in the text variable:

```
text = window.prompt("Enter some text","Default value");
```

As a further illustration of these types of dialog boxes, Listing 20.4 shows an HTML document that uses buttons and event handlers to enable you to test dialog boxes.

LISTING 20.4   An HTML Document That Uses JavaScript to Display
Alerts, Confirmations, and Prompts

```
<?xml version="1.0" encoding="UTF-8"?>
<!DOCTYPE html PUBLIC "-//W3C//DTD XHTML 1.1//EN"
  "http://www.w3.org/TR/xhtml11/DTD/xhtml11.dtd">

<html xmlns="http://www.w3.org/1999/xhtml" xml:lang="en">
  <head>
    <title>Alerts, Confirmations, and Prompts</title>
  </head>
  <body>
  <h1>Alerts, Confirmations, and Prompts</h1>
  <p>Use the buttons below to test dialogs in JavaScript.</p>
  <form name="winform">
  <div>
    <input type="button" value="Display an Alert"
      onclick="window.alert('This is a test alert.')" />
    <input type="button" value="Display a Confirmation"
       onclick="window.confirm('Would you like to confirm?');" />
    <input type="button" value="Display a Prompt"
       onclick="window.prompt('Enter Text:',
```

TIP

You can usually omit the window object when referring to these methods because it is the default context of a script (for example, alert("text")).

LISTING 20.4   Continued

```
                        'This is the default.');" />
  </div>
  </form>
    </body>
</html>
```

This document displays three buttons, and each one uses an event handler to display one of the dialog boxes.

Figure 20.3 shows the script in Listing 20.4 in action. The prompt dialog box is currently displayed and shows the default value.

FIGURE 20.3
The dialog box example's output, including a prompt dialog box.

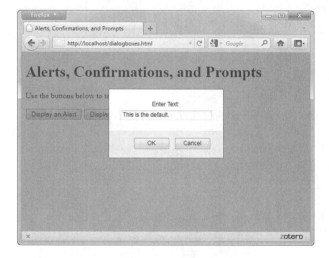

Working with Frames

Browsers also support *frames*, which enable you to divide the browser window into multiple panes. Each frame can contain a separate URL or the output of a script.

You might have visited websites in which the browser window seemingly allowed you to move between several different pages. The truth is that the browser really was allowing you to view several pages at once by separating the browser window into regions that contain separate web pages; each region is known as a *frame*. Of course, from the user's perspective, everything comes together to form a single window of web content, but there are separate pages at work.

A *frame* is a rectangular region within the browser window that displays a web page alongside other pages in other frames. At first glance, Figure 20.4 might look like an ordinary web page, but it is actually two separate HTML pages, both displayed in the same web browser window. Each page is displayed in its own frame, arranged horizontally and separated by the horizontal bar.

FIGURE 20.4
Frames allow more than one web page to be displayed at once.

If frames are used, typically they are used to create a framed site that takes advantage of a static set of navigational links; you can see these links in the top frame of Figure 20.4. When one of the links in this example is clicked, the top frame will not change; a new page will be loaded and displayed in the bottom frame (see Figure 20.5).

FIGURE 20.5
Clicking Products brings up a new bottom page but leaves the top frame the same.

You should be aware that frames have long been a vexed issue in web design. The advantages have never really outweighed the disadvantages, yet due to differences in browser support for HTML and CSS standards, frames were seen as a way to achieve certain goals despite their shortcomings. As a web developer, I do not recommend the use of frames for the following reasons:

▶ Frames go against the fundamental concept of the Web, which is the hypertextual connection between individual instances of web content that can be accessed via a single web address (URL).

▶ Printing parts of a framed site is very difficult; unless you have clicked on the specific frame you want to print, and select Print this Frame from a context menu (if one is available), all that will print is the frameset itself, which will have no content in it.

▶ If a frame lacks proper coding, or if it has proper coding but the code is used for nefarious purposes, a user could get stuck inside a framed site unable to view external content outside of the frame.

▶ Frames have been used historically in lieu of standard, professional, accessible methods of web development and design. There is no reason to choose the lesser option when the better option of CSS layout is available.

▶ For these (and other) reasons, frames have been removed from the HTML5 standard. The antiquated `<frame />`, `<frameset>`, and `<noframes>` tags will simply not be available in the future.

Despite these shortcomings, in the next few sections you will learn how to create a very simple framed site. It is quite likely that you will still encounter framed sites, and you might need to know how to re-create the look and feel of the site but without using frames. In that case, it is important to understand how frames are constructed so you can successfully deconstruct them.

Additionally, you will learn about a type of frame—the `<iframe>`—that does serve an important purpose and will still be present in HTML5.

Building a Frameset

This section shows you how to create the simple framed site shown in Figures 20.4 and 20.5. The contents of each frame were created as ordinary HTML pages. The pages are top.html (for the navigation), home.html, products.html, services.html, and contact.html. These pages don't contain any tags you haven't already seen in other chapters. A special page known as a frameset document was used to put the pages together; in this case, that document is index.html.

Creating a Frameset Document

A *frameset document* is an HTML page that instructs the web browser to split its window into multiple frames and specifies which web page should be displayed in each frame.

A frameset document actually has no content. It only tells the browser which other pages to load and how to arrange them in the browser window. Listing 20.5 shows the frameset document for the sample framed site shown in Figures 20.4 and 20.5.

LISTING 20.5   Frameset Document for the Site Shown in Figures 20.4 and 20.5

```
<?xml version="1.0" encoding="UTF-8"?>
<!DOCTYPE html PUBLIC "-//W3C//DTD XHTML 1.0 Frameset//EN"
  "http://www.w3.org/TR/xhtml11/DTD/xhtml11.dtd">

<html xmlns="http://www.w3.org/1999/xhtml" xml:lang="en">
  <head>
    <title>Sample Framed Site</title>
  </head>

  <frameset rows="50,*">
    <frame src="top.html" name="top" />
    <frame src="home.html" name="main" />
    <noframes>
     <body>
       <h1>Sample Framed Site</h1>
       Your browser does not support frames. Sorry!
     </body>
    </noframes>
  </frameset>
</html>
```

Listing 20.4 uses a <frameset> tag instead of a <body> tag. No tags that would normally be contained in a <body> tag can be within the <frameset> tag. The <frameset> tag in this example includes a rows attribute, meaning that the frames should be arranged on top of each other like the horizontal rows of a table. If you want your frames to be side by side, use a cols attribute (instead of a rows attribute).

You must specify the sizes of the rows or cols, either as precise pixel values or as percentages of the total size of the browser window. You can also

NOTE

It's important to notice that the DTD used in this sample page is not the familiar XHTML 1.1 DTD that you've been using throughout the book. This is because frames are not supported in the standard XHTML 1.1 DTD. Therefore, to validate a page with frames, you must instead use the XHTML 1.0 Frameset DTD, which is a special DTD designed just for pages that use frames.

use an asterisk (*) to indicate that a frame should fill whatever space is available in the window. If more than one frame has an * value, the remaining space will be divided equally between them.

In Listing 20.5, `<frameset rows="50,*">` splits the window vertically into two frames. The top frame will be exactly 50 pixels tall, and the bottom frame will take up all the remaining space in the window. The top frame contains the document `top.html` (see Listing 20.6), and the bottom frame contains `home.html` (see Listing 20.7).

TIP

After the framesets in Listing 20.6, there is a complete web page between the <body> and </body> tags. Notice that the content of this page doesn't appear at all in Figure 20.4 or Figure 20.5. All web browsers that support frames will ignore anything between the <noframes> and </noframes> tags.

All major browsers these days support frames, so the issue of frames compatibility is much less significant now than in years past. Even so, it's easy enough to include the <noframes> tag and cover the few users who might still use ancient browsers—if you use frames at all, that is.

LISTING 20.6   The `top.html` Navigation Bar for the Sample Framed Site

```
<?xml version="1.0" encoding="UTF-8"?>
<!DOCTYPE html PUBLIC "-//W3C//DTD XHTML 1.0 Transitional//EN"
  "http://www.w3.org/TR/xhtml11/DTD/xhtml1-transitional.dtd">

<html xmlns="http://www.w3.org/1999/xhtml" xml:lang="en">
  <head>
    <title>Sample Framed Site</title>
    <style type="text/css">
    body { background-color:#5F9F9F; }
    a { color: #FFFFFF; }
    .main {
       text-align:center;
       color:#FFFFFF;
       font-weight:bold;
       font-size:16pt;
    }
    </style>
  </head>
  <body>
    <div class="main">
      <a href="home.html" target="main">HOME</a> ::
      <a href="products.html" target="main">PRODUCTS</a> ::
      <a href="services.html" target="main">SERVICES</a> ::
      <a href="contact.html" target="main">CONTACT</a>
    </div>
  </body>
</html>
```

LISTING 20.7   The `home.html` Single Content Frame Within the Sample Framed Site

```
<?xml version="1.0" encoding="UTF-8"?>
<!DOCTYPE html PUBLIC "-//W3C//DTD XHTML 1.1//EN"
  "http://www.w3.org/TR/xhtml11/DTD/xhtml11.dtd">

<html xmlns="http://www.w3.org/1999/xhtml" xml:lang="en">
  <head>
    <title>Sample Framed Site</title>
```

LISTING 20.7   Continued

```
  <style type="text/css">
  body { background-color:#5F9F9F; }
  </style>
 </head>
 <body>
   <h1 style="text-align:center">Sample Framed Site: Home</h1>
   <p style="text-align:center">This is an example of the
      "home" page.</p>
 </body>
</html>
```

NOTE

The pages in Listing 20.6 and Listing 20.7 use the XHTML 1.0 Transitional and XHTML 1.1 DTDs, respectively. The XHTML 1.1 DTD is newer and much stricter, but the use of the `target` attribute in Listing 20.6 requires the use of the XHTML 1.0 Transitional DTD for validity; there is nothing in Listing 20.7 that is invalid in XHTML 1.1.

In this example, the top navigation frame has a fixed height of 50 pixels. But because you can't predict the size of the window in which users will view your web page, it is often convenient to use percentages rather than exact pixel values to dictate the size of the rows and columns. For example, to make a left frame 20% of the width of the browser window with a right frame taking up the remaining 80%, you would type the following:

```
<frameset cols="20%,80%">
```

Whenever you specify any frame size in pixels, it's a good idea to include at least one frame in the same frameset with a variable (*) width so that the document can grow to fill a window of any size.

Adding Individual Frames

Within the `<frameset>` and `</frameset>` tags, you should have a `<frame />` tag indicating which HTML document to display in each frame. Note that if you have fewer `<frame />` tags than the number of frames defined in the `<frameset>` tag, any remaining frames will be left blank.

Include a `src` attribute in each `<frame>` tag with the address of the web page to load in that frame. You can put the address of an image file, instead of a web page, if you just want a frame with a single image in it.

Linking Between Frames and Windows

The real power of frames begins to emerge when you give a frame a unique name with the `name` attribute in the `<frame />` tag. You can then make any link on the page change the contents of that frame by using the `target` attribute in an `<a>` tag. For example, Listing 20.6 includes the following tag:

```
<frame src="home.html" name="main" />
```

NOTE

Technically speaking, the name tag is outdated and has been replaced by the id tag.

However, current web browsers still rely on name instead of id when it comes to identifying frames as targets and the use of name is still valid XHTML. So, for now, you need to stick with the name attribute when identifying frames. Of course, it wouldn't hurt to use both attributes.

This code displays the home.html page in that frame when the page loads and names the frame "main".

In the code for the top frame, which is shown in Listing 20.7, you will see the following link:

```
<a href="services.html" target="main">SERVICES</a>
```

When the user clicks this link, services.html is displayed in the frame named main (the lower frame). If the target="main" attribute had been left out, the services.html page would be displayed in the current (top) frame instead.

Modifying Frame Borders

There are HTML attributes that you can use with your frame code to get rid of the frame dividers, make more space in small frames by reducing the size of the margins, and force frames not to have scrollbars. Listing 20.8 shows a modified version of the code in Listing 20.4. The two changes made to the code are the addition of the following attributes to the <frame> tags: scrolling="no" and frameborder="0".

LISTING 20.8   Frameset Document for the Site Shown in Figure 20.6

```
<?xml version="1.0" encoding="UTF-8"?>
<!DOCTYPE html PUBLIC "-//W3C//DTD XHTML 1.0 Frameset//EN"
  "http://www.w3.org/TR/xhtml11/DTD/xhtml11.dtd">

<html xmlns="http://www.w3.org/1999/xhtml" xml:lang="en">
  <head>
    <title>Sample Framed Site</title>
  </head>

  <frameset rows="50,*">
    <frame src="top.html" name="top" scrolling="no" frameborder="0" />
    <frame src="home.html" name="main" scrolling="no" frameborder="0"/>
    <noframes>
     <body>
       <h1>Sample Framed Site</h1>
       Your browser does not support frames. Sorry!
     </body>
    </noframes>
  </frameset>
</html>
```

FIGURE 20.6
This is the page whose code is shown in Listing 20.8 after attributes were added to the `<frame />` tags.

Using JavaScript Objects for Frames

When a window contains multiple frames, each frame is represented in JavaScript by a `frame` object. This object is equivalent to a `window` object, but it is used for dealing specifically with that frame. The `frame` object's name is the same as the `NAME` attribute you give it in the `<frame>` tag.

Remember the `window` and `self` keywords, which refer to the current window? When you are using frames, these keywords refer to the current frame instead. Another keyword, `parent`, enables you to refer to the main window.

Each frame object in a window is a child of the `parent` window object. Suppose you define a set of frames using the following HTML:

```
<frameset rows="*,*" cols="*,*">
<frame name="topleft" src="topleft.html">
<frame name="topright" src="topright.html">
<frame name="bottomleft" src="botleft.html">
<frame name="bottomright" src="botright.html">
</frameset>
```

This simply divides the window into quarters. If you have a JavaScript script in the `topleft.html` file, it would refer to the other windows as `parent.topright`, `parent.bottomleft`, and so on. The keywords `window` and `self` would refer to the `topleft` frame.

> **NOTE**
>
> If you use nested framesets, things are a bit more complicated. `window` still represents the current frame, `parent` represents the frameset containing the current frame, and `top` represents the main frameset that contains all the others.

The `frames` Array

Rather than referring to frames in a document by name, you can use the `frames` array. This array stores information about each of the frames in the document. The frames are indexed starting with zero and beginning with the first `<frame>` tag in the frameset document.

For example, you could refer to the frames defined in the previous example using array references:

▶ `parent.frames[0]` is equivalent to the `topleft` frame.

▶ `parent.frames[1]` is equivalent to the `topright` frame.

▶ `parent.frames[2]` is equivalent to the `bottomleft` frame.

▶ `parent.frames[3]` is equivalent to the `bottomright` frame.

You can refer to a frame using either method interchangeably, and depending on your application, you should use the most convenient method. For example, a document with 10 frames would probably be easier to use by number, but a simple two-frame document is easier to use if the frames have meaningful names.

Using Inline Frames

Inline frames do not have the same usability issues that regular frames do, but inline frames are used for different reasons. Instead of being a pure layout trick, the `<iframe>` is used much like an `<object>` tag—to place a chunk of something within an existing document. In the case of the `<object>` tag, that "something" is usually multimedia. You can use an `<iframe>` to embed an entirely separate HTML document, image, or other source. Listing 20.9 and Listing 20.10 show the code to produce the inline frame shown in Figure 20.7.

LISTING 20.9   XHTML Code to Call an `<iframe>`

```
<?xml version="1.0" encoding="UTF-8"?>
<!DOCTYPE html PUBLIC "-//W3C//DTD XHTML 1.0 Transitional//EN"
  "http://www.w3.org/TR/xhtml1/DTD/xhtml1-transitional.dtd">

<html xmlns="http://www.w3.org/1999/xhtml" xml:lang="en">
  <head>
    <title>Using an iframe</title>
    <style type="text/css">
    body { background-color:#CCCCCC; }
```

LISTING 20.9   Continued

```
    iframe {
       width:500px;
       height:100px;
       border:1px solid black;
       background-color:#FFFFFF;
    }
    </style>
  </head>
  <body  style="background:#CCCCCC">
     <h1 style="text-align:center">Inline Frame Example</h1>
        <div  style="text-align:center">
          <iframe src="iframe_src.html">
          <p>Uh oh...your browser does not support iframes.</p>
          </iframe>
        </div>
  </body>
</html>
```

LISTING 20.10   The Source of the `<iframe>` Called in Listing 20.9

```
<?xml version="1.0" encoding="UTF-8"?>
<!DOCTYPE html PUBLIC "-//W3C//DTD XHTML 1.1//EN"
  "http://www.w3.org/TR/xhtml1/DTD/xhtml11.dtd">

<html xmlns="http://www.w3.org/1999/xhtml" xml:lang="en">
  <head>
    <title>iframe source</title>
    <style type="text/css">
    body { background-color:#FFFFFF; }
    p {
       color: #FF0000;
       font-weight: bold;
    }
    </style>
  </head>
  <body>
     <p>I AM A SOURCE DOCUMENT...inside an iframe.</p>
  </body>
</html>
```

The only XHTML code you haven't yet encountered in Listing 20.9 is the `<iframe>` itself. You can see that it requires a value for the `src` attribute— the source—and that you can use styles to define a width, height, border type, and background color (among other things). Listing 20.10 shows the source of the `<iframe>`, which is just a regular file with some text and styles in it.

FIGURE 20.7
Listing 20.9 calls the inline frame whose code is shown in Listing 20.10.

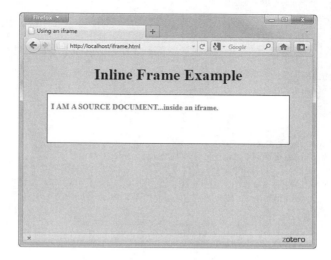

Inline frames are often used to bring in content from other websites. Common uses include serving ads to users from third-party advertising services and using Google's Site Search to display search results to your users (leveraging Google's search technology). Figure 20.8 shows an instance of an <iframe> used to pull search results into a custom site template.

FIGURE 20.8
Using an <iframe> to display Google Custom Search results.

In Figure 20.8, everything in the white area is actually content in an `<iframe>`, with the source being a script on Google's website that runs and then displays content within the template at the Digital Inspiration website. If you look closely at Figure 20.8—and I do not believe you can see it in the figure—you can see a faint gray border around the actual `<iframe>` itself.

Unlike the `<frame />` you learned about earlier in this chapter, the `<iframe>` is here to stay and is still a part of HTML5.

Summary

In this chapter, you've learned how to use the `window` object to work with browser windows and used its properties and methods to set timeouts and display dialog boxes. You've also learned how JavaScript can work with framed documents.

As to the framed documents themselves, you learned how to display more than one page simultaneously by splitting the web browser window into frames. You learned how to use a frameset document to define the size and arrangement of the frames and which web content will be loaded into each frame. You learned how to create links that change the contents of any frame you choose while leaving the other frames unchanged. You also learned about a few optional settings that control the appearance of resizable borders and scrollbars in frames. Finally, you learned how to use the inline frame to display content from your site or other websites.

Table 20.1 summarizes the tags and attributes covered in this chapter.

TABLE 20.1   HTML Tags and Attributes Covered in Chapter 20

Tag/Attribute	Function
`<frame />`	Defines a single frame within a `<frameset>`.
Attributes	
`src="url"`	The URL of the document to be displayed in this frame.
`id="name"`	A name to be used for targeting this frame with the `target` attribute in `<a href>` links; compliant with XHTML.
`name="name"`	A name to be used for targeting this frame with the `target` attribute in `<a href>` links. Will eventually be replaced by `id` but for the time being is still useful because it works in current web browsers.
`scrolling="yes/no/auto"`	Determines whether a frame has scrollbars. Possible values are `yes`, `no`, and `auto`.
`noresize="noresize"`	Prevents the user from resizing this frame (and possibly adjacent frames) with the mouse.
`<frameset>...</frameset>`	Divides the main window into a set of frames that can each display a separate document.
`rows="numrows"`	Splits the window or frameset vertically into a number of rows specified by a number (such as 7), a percentage of the total window width (such as 25%), or an asterisk (*) indicating that a frame should take up all the remaining space or divide the space evenly between frames (if multiple * frames are specified).
`cols="numcols"`	Works similar to `rows`, except that the window or frameset is split horizontally into columns.
`frameborder="1/0"`	Specifies whether to display a border for a frame. Options are 1 (yes) and 0 (no).
`<noframes>...</noframes>`	Provides an alternative document body in `<frameset>` documents for browsers that do not support frames (usually encloses `<body>...</body>`).
`<iframe>...</iframe>`	Creates an inline frame; accepts all the same attributes as does `<frame />` and can be styled with CSS.

Q&A

Q. When a script is running in a window created by another script, how can it refer back to the original window?

A. JavaScript includes the `window.opener` property, which lets you refer to the window that opened the current window.

Q. How can I update two frames at once when the user clicks on a single link?

A. You can do this by using an event handler and including two statements to load URLs into different frames.

Q. Can I display other users' web pages in one frame and my own pages in another frame at the same time? What if those other sites use frames, too?

A. You can load any document from anywhere on the Internet (or an intranet) into a frame. If the document is a frameset, its frames are sized to fit within the existing frame into which you load it.

For example, you could put a list of your favorite links in one frame and use a separate frame to display the pages that those links refer to. This makes it easy to provide links to other sites without risking that someone will get lost and never come back to your own site.

You should also be aware that framing somebody else's pages so that they appear to be part of your own site might get you in legal trouble, so be sure to get explicit written permission from anyone whose pages you plan to put within one of your frames (just as you would if you were putting images or text from their site on your own pages).

Workshop

The workshop contains quiz questions and exercises to help you solidify your understanding of the material covered. Try to answer all questions before looking at the "Answers" section that follows.

Quiz

1. Which of the following methods displays a dialog box with OK and Cancel buttons and waits for a response?

    a. `window.alert`

    b. `window.confirm`

    c. `window.prompt`

2. What does the `window.setTimeout` method do?

    a. Executes a JavaScript statement after a delay

    b. Locks up the browser for the specified amount of time

    c. Sets the amount of time before the browser exits automatically

3. You're working with a document that contains three frames with the names `first`, `second`, and `third`. If a script in the second frame needs to refer to the first frame, what is the correct syntax?

    a. `window.first`

    b. `parent.first`

    c. `frames.first`

4. What `<iframe>` code would produce a borderless `<iframe>` with a white background that encompasses 98% of the width of the page and is 250 pixels high?

Answers

1. b. The `window.confirm` method displays a dialog box with OK and Cancel buttons.

2. a. The `window.setTimeout` method executes a JavaScript statement after a delay.

3. b. The script in the second frame would use `parent.first` to refer to the first frame.

4. Use the following code:

```
<iframe src="some_source.html" style="width:98%;height:250px;
   border:none; background-color:#FFFFFF;">
 <p>Put message here for people not able to see the inline
frame.</p>
</iframe>
```

Exercises

▶ Using timeouts and JavaScript to display date and time (which you learned earlier in this book), create a script to reload automatically every second or two to display a "live" clock.

▶ Think of some ways you can use an `<iframe>` or two in your site—perhaps for an ad or perhaps to leverage the free Google Site Search that you can offer to your users. Leave room in your design for that element.

CHAPTER 21
Using Unobtrusive JavaScript

In this chapter, you'll learn some guidelines for creating scripts and pages that are easy to maintain, easy to use, and follow web standards. This is known as *unobtrusive scripting*: Scripts add features without getting in the way of the user, the developer maintaining the code, or the designer building the layout of the site. You'll also learn how to make sure your scripts will work in multiple browsers and won't stop working when a new browser comes along.

Scripting Best Practices

As you start to develop more complex scripts, it's important to know some scripting *best practices*. These are guidelines for using JavaScript that more experienced programmers have learned the hard way. Here are a few of the benefits of following these best practices:

- ► Your code will be readable and easy to maintain, whether you're turning the page over to someone else or just trying to remember what you did a year ago.

- ► You'll create code that follows standards and won't be crippled by a new version of a particular browser.

- ► You'll create pages that work even without JavaScript.

- ► It will be easy to adapt code you create for one site to another site or project.

- ► Your users will thank you for creating a site that is easy to use and easy to fix when things go wrong.

WHAT YOU'LL LEARN IN THIS CHAPTER:

- ► Best practices for creating unobtrusive scripts
- ► Separating content, presentation, and behavior
- ► Following web standards to create cross-browser scripts
- ► Reading and displaying browser information
- ► Using feature sensing to avoid errors
- ► Supporting non-JavaScript browsers

Whether you're writing an entire AJAX web application or simply enhancing a page with a three-line script, it's useful to know some of the concepts that are regularly considered by those who write complex scripts for a living. The following sections introduce some of these best practices.

Content, Presentation, and Behavior

When you create a web page, or especially an entire site or application, you're dealing with three key areas: *content*, *presentation*, and *behavior*—all of which you've learned about in the previous chapters.

- ▶ *Content* consists of the words that a visitor can read on your pages. You create the content as text and mark it up with HTML to define different classes of content—headings, paragraphs, links, and so on.

- ▶ *Presentation* is the appearance and layout of the words on each page—text formatting, fonts, colors, and graphics. Although it was common in the early days of the Web to create the presentation using HTML only, you can now use Cascading Style Sheets (CSS) to define the presentation.

- ▶ *Behavior* is what happens when you interact with a page—items that highlight when you move over them, forms you can submit, and so on. This is where JavaScript comes in, along with server-side languages such as PHP.

It's a good idea to keep these three areas in mind, especially as you create larger sites. Ideally, you want to keep content, presentation, and behavior separated as much as possible. One good way to do this is to create an external CSS file for the presentation, an external JavaScript file for the behavior, and link them to the HTML document.

Keeping things separated like this makes it easier to maintain a large site—if you need to change the color of the headings, for example, you can make a quick edit to the CSS file without having to look through all of the HTML markup to find the right place to edit. It also makes it easy for you to reuse the same CSS and JavaScript on multiple pages of a site. Last but not least, this will encourage you to use each language where its strengths lie, making your job easier.

Progressive Enhancement

One of the old buzzwords of web design was *graceful degradation*. The idea was that you could build a site that used all the bells and whistles of the latest browsers, as long as it would "gracefully degrade" to work on older browsers. This mostly meant testing on a few older browsers and hoping it worked, and there was always the possibility of problems in browsers that didn't support the latest features.

Ironically, you might expect browsers that lack the latest features to be older, less popular ones, but some of the biggest problems are with brand-new browsers—those included with mobile phones and other new devices, all of which are primitive compared to the latest browsers running on computers.

One new approach to web design that addresses this problem is known as *progressive enhancement*. The idea is to keep the HTML documents as simple as possible so that they'll definitely work in even the most primitive browsers. After you've tested that and made sure the basic functionality is there, you can add features that make the site easier to use or better looking for those with new browsers.

If you add these features unobtrusively, they have little chance of preventing the site from working in its primitive HTML form. Here are some guidelines for progressive enhancement:

- ▶ Enhance the presentation by adding rules to a separate CSS file. Try to avoid using HTML markup strictly for presentation, such as `<em>` for boldface or `<blockquote>` for an indented section.

- ▶ Enhance behavior by adding scripts to an external JavaScript file.

- ▶ Add events without using inline event handlers, as described in Chapter 19, "Responding to Events," and later in this chapter.

- ▶ Use feature sensing, described later this chapter, to ensure that JavaScript code only executes on browsers that support the features it requires.

NOTE

The term *progressive enhancement* first appeared in a presentation and article on this topic by Steve Champeon. The original article, along with many more web design articles, is available on his company's website at http://hesketh.com/.

Adding Event Handlers

In Chapter 19, you learned that there is more than one way to set up an event handler. The simplest way is to add them directly to an HTML tag. For example, this `<body>` tag has an event handler that calls a function called `Startup`.

```
<body onLoad="Startup();">
```

This method still works, but it does mean putting JavaScript code in the HTML page, which means you haven't fully separated content and behavior. To keep things entirely separate, you can set up the event handler in the JavaScript file instead, using syntax like this:

```
window.onload=Startup;
```

Right now, this is usually the best way to set up events: It keeps JavaScript out of the HTML file, and it works in all modern browsers. However, it does have one problem: You can't attach more than one event to the same element of a page. For example, you can't have two different onLoad event handlers that both execute when the page loads.

When you're the only one writing scripts, this is no big deal—you can combine the two into one function. But when you're trying to use two or three third-party scripts on a page, and all of them want to add an onLoad event handler to the body, you have a problem.

The W3C Event Model

To solve this problem and standardize event handling, the W3C created an event model as part of the DOM level 2 standard. This uses a method, addEventListener(), to attach a handler to any event on any element. For example, the following uses the W3C model to set up the same onLoad event handler as the previous examples:

```
window.addEventListener('load', Startup, false);
```

The first parameter of addEventListener() is the event name without the on prefix—load, click, mouseover, and so on. The second parameter specifies the function to handle the event, and the third is an advanced flag that indicates how multiple events should be handled. (false works for most purposes.)

Any number of functions can be attached to an event in this way. Because one event handler doesn't replace another, you use a separate function, removeEventListener(), which uses the same parameters:

```
window.removeEventListener('load', Startup, false);
```

The problem with the W3C model is that Internet Explorer (versions 6, 7 and 8) doesn't support it (it has been introduced in IE9). Instead, it supports a proprietary method, attachEvent(), which does much the same thing. Here's the Startup event handler defined Microsoft-style:

```
window.attachEvent('onload', Startup);
```

The `attachEvent()` method has two parameters. The first is the event, with the on prefix—`onload`, `onclick`, `onmouseover`, and so on. The second is the function that will handle the event. Internet Explorer also supports a `detachEvent()` method with the same parameters for removing an event handler.

Attaching Events the Cross-Browser Way

As you can see, attaching events in this new way is complex and will require different code for different browsers. In most cases, you're better off using the traditional method to attach events, and that method is used in most of this book's examples. However, if you really need to support multiple event handlers, you can use some `if` statements to use either the W3C method or Microsoft's method. For example, the following code adds the `ClickMe()` function as an event for the element with the `id` attribute `btn`:

```
obj = document.getElementById("btn");
if (obj.addEventListener) {
   obj.addEventListener('click',ClickMe,false);
} else if (obj.attachEvent) {
   obj.attachEvent('onclick',ClickMe);
} else {
   obj.onclick=ClickMe;
}
```

This checks for the `addEventListener()` method and uses it if it's found. Otherwise, it checks for the `attachEvent()` method and uses that. If neither is found, it uses the traditional method to attach the event handler. This technique is called *feature sensing* and is explained in detail later this chapter.

Many universal functions are available to compensate for the lack of a consistent way to attach events. If you are using a third-party library, there's a good chance it includes an event function that can simplify this process for you.

Web Standards: Avoid Being Browser Specific

The Web was built on standards, such as the HTML standard developed by the W3C. Now there are a lot of standards involved with JavaScript—CSS, the W3C DOM, and the ECMAScript standard that defines JavaScript's syntax.

Microsoft, the Mozilla Project, Google, and other browser developers such as Opera Software continually improve their browsers' support for web standards, but there are always going to be some browser-specific, nonstandard features, and some parts of the newest standards won't be consistently supported between browsers.

TIP

The Yahoo! UI Library, like many other third-party libraries, includes an event-handling function that can attach events in any browser, attach the same event handler to many objects at once, and other nice features. See http://developer.yahoo.net/yui/ for details, and see Chapter 22, "Using Third-Party Libraries," for information about using various other available libraries.

NOTE

One reason to make sure you follow standards is that your pages can be better interpreted by search engines, which often helps your site get search traffic. Separating content, presentation, and behavior is also good for search engines because they can focus on the HTML content of your site without having to skip over JavaScript or CSS.

Although it's perfectly fine to test your code in multiple browsers and do whatever it takes to get it working, it's a good idea to follow the standards rather than browser-specific techniques when you can. This ensures that your code will work on future browsers that improve their standards support, whereas browser-specific features might disappear in new versions.

Documenting Your Code

As you create more complex scripts, don't forget to include comments in your code to document what it does, especially when some of the code seems confusing or is difficult to get working. It's also a good idea to document all the data structures, variables, and function arguments used in a larger script.

Comments are a good way to organize code, and will help you work on the script in the future. If you're doing this for a living, you'll definitely need to use comments so that others can work on your code as easily as you can.

Usability

While you're adding cool features to your site, don't forget about *usability*— making things as easy, logical, and convenient as possible for users of your site. Although there are many books and websites devoted to usability information, a bit of common sense goes a long way.

For example, suppose you use a drop-down list as the only way to navigate between pages of your site. This is a common use for JavaScript, and it works well, but is it usable? Try comparing it to a simple set of links across the top of a page.

- ▶ The list of links lets you see at a glance what the site contains; the drop-down list requires you to click to see the same list.

- ▶ Users expect links and can spot them quickly—a drop-down list is more likely to be part of a form than a navigation tool, and thus won't be the first thing they look for when they want to navigate your site.

- ▶ Navigating with a link takes a single click—navigating with the drop-down list takes at least two clicks.

Remember to consider the user's point of view whenever you add JavaScript to a site, and be sure you're making the site easier to use—or at least not harder to use. Also, make sure the site is easy to use even without JavaScript; although this might only apply to a small percentage of your users, that percentage is likely to include users of screen readers or other software packages necessary for people with visual impairments.

Design Patterns

If you learn more about usability, you'll undoubtedly see *design patterns* mentioned. This is a computer science term meaning "an optimal solution to a common problem." In web development, design patterns are ways of designing and implementing part of a site that webmasters run into over and over.

For example, if you have a site that displays multiple pages of data, you'll have Next Page and Previous Page links, and perhaps numeric links for each page. This is a common design pattern—a problem many web designers have had to solve, and one with a generally agreed-upon solution. Other common web design patterns include a login form, a search engine, or a list of navigation links for a site.

Of course, you can be completely original and make a search engine, a shopping cart, or a login form that looks nothing like any other, but unless you have a way of making them even easier to use, you're better off following the pattern and giving your users an experience that matches their expectations.

Although you can find some common design patterns just by browsing sites similar to yours and noticing how they solved particular problems, there are also sites that specialize in documenting these patterns, and they're a good place to start if you need ideas on how to make your site work.

Accessibility

One final aspect of usability to consider is *accessibility*—making your site as accessible as possible for all users, including the disabled. For example, blind users might use a text-reading program to read your site, which will ignore images and most scripts. More than just good manners, accessibility is mandated by law in some countries.

The subject of accessibility is complex, but you can get most of the way there by following the philosophy of progressive enhancement: Keep the HTML as simple as possible, keep JavaScript and CSS separate, and make JavaScript an enhancement rather than a requirement for using your site.

TIP

The Yahoo! Developer Network documents a variety of design patterns used on its network of sites, many of which are implemented using JavaScript: http://developer.yahoo.net/ypatterns/.

NOTE

Ensuring that sites function without JavaScript is one of the first steps toward accessibility compliance. For more information on accessibility, see http://www.w3.org/WAI/.

Reading Browser Information

In Chapter 15, "Working with the Document Object Model (DOM)," you learned about the various objects (such as `window` and `document`) that represent portions of the browser window and the current web document. JavaScript also includes an object called `navigator` that you can use to read information about the user's browser.

The `navigator` object isn't part of the DOM, so you can refer to it directly. It includes a number of properties, each of which tells you something about the browser. These include the following:

▶ `navigator.appCodeName` is the browser's internal code name, such as Mozilla.

▶ `navigator.appName` is the browser's name, such as Netscape or Microsoft Internet Explorer.

▶ `navigator.appVersion` is the version of the browser being used—for example, 5.0 (Windows).

▶ `navigator.userAgent` is the user-agent header, a string that the browser sends to the web server when requesting a web page. It includes the entire version information—for example, Mozilla/5.0 (Windows NT 6.1; WOW64; rv:5.0) Gecko/20100101 Firefox/5.0.

▶ `navigator.language` is the language (such as English or Spanish) of the browser. This is stored as a code, such as en_US for U.S. English. This property is supported by Chrome, Firefox, Opera, and Safari.

▶ `navigator.platform` is the computer platform of the current browser. This is a short string, such as Linux i686, Win32, or MacPPC. You can use this to enable any platform-specific features—for example, ActiveX components.

> **NOTE**
>
> As you might have guessed, the navigator object is named after Netscape Navigator, the browser that originally supported JavaScript. Fortunately, this object is also supported by Internet Explorer and most other recent browsers.

Displaying Browser Information

As an example of how to read the `navigator` object's properties, Listing 21.1 shows a script that displays a list of the properties and their values for the current browser.

LISTING 21.1   A Script to Display Information About the Browser

```
<?xml version="1.0" encoding="UTF-8"?>
<!DOCTYPE html PUBLIC "-//W3C//DTD XHTML 1.1//EN"
  "http://www.w3.org/TR/xhtml11/DTD/xhtml11.dtd">

<html xmlns="http://www.w3.org/1999/xhtml" xml:lang="en">
  <head>
```

LISTING 21.1   Continued

```
   <title>Browser Information</title>
 </head>
 <body>
  <h1>Browser Information</h1>
      <p>The <strong>navigator</strong> object contains the
   following information about the browser you are using:</p>
  <script type="text/javascript">
  document.write("<ul>");
  document.write("<li><strong>Code Name:</strong> " +
     navigator.appCodeName);
  document.write("<li><strong>App Name:</strong> " +
     navigator.appName);
  document.write("<li><strong>App Version:</strong> " +
     navigator.appVersion);
  document.write("<li><strong>User Agent:</strong> " +
     navigator.userAgent);
  document.write("<li><strong>Language:</strong> " +
     navigator.language);
  document.write("<li><strong>Platform:</strong> " +
     navigator.platform);
  document.write("</ul>");
   </script>
  </body>
</html>
```

This script includes a basic HTML document. A script is used within the body of the document to display each of the properties of the navigator object using the document.write() statement.

To try this script, load it into the browser of your choice. If you have more than one browser or browser version handy, try it in each one. Firefox's display of the script is shown in Figure 21.1.

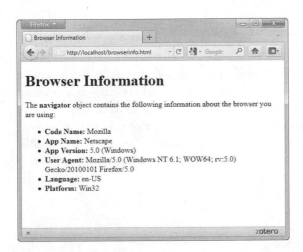

FIGURE 21.1
Firefox displays the browser information script.

Dealing with Dishonest Browsers

If you tried the browser information script in Listing 21.1 using certain versions of Internet Explorer, you probably got a surprise. Figure 21.2 shows how Internet Explorer 6.0 displays the script.

There are several unexpected things about this display. First, the `navigator. language` property is listed as undefined. This isn't much of a surprise because this property isn't supported by Internet Explorer.

More importantly, you'll notice that the word `Mozilla` appears in the Code Name and User Agent fields. The full user agent string reads as follows:

```
Mozilla/4.0 (compatible; MSIE 6.0; Windows 98)
```

FIGURE 21.2
How Internet Explorer 6 displays the browser information script.

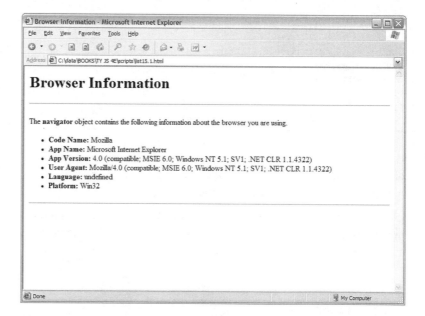

Believe it or not, Microsoft did have a good reason for this. At the height of the browser wars, about the time Netscape 3.0 and IE 3.0 came out, it was becoming common to see "Netscape only" pages. Some webmasters who used features such as frames and JavaScript set their servers to turn away browsers without `Mozilla` in their user agent string. The problem with this was that most of these features were also supported by Internet Explorer.

Microsoft solved this problem in IE 4.0 by making IE's user agent read Mozilla, with the word compatible in parentheses. This allows IE users to view those pages, but still includes enough details to tell web servers which browser is in use.

You've probably already noticed the other problem with Internet Explorer 6.0's user agent string: the portion reading Mozilla/4.0. Not only is IE claiming to be Netscape, but it's also masquerading as version 4.0. Why?

As it turns out, this was another effort by Microsoft to stay one step ahead of the browser wars, although this one doesn't make quite as much sense. Because poorly written scripts were checking specifically for Mozilla/4 for dynamic HTML pages, Microsoft was concerned that its 5.0 version would fail to run these pages. Because changing it now would only create more confusion, this tradition continued with IE 6.0.

Although these are two interesting episodes in the annals of the browser wars, what does all this mean to you? Well, you'll need to be careful when your scripts are trying to differentiate between IE and Netscape and between different versions. You'll need to check for specific combinations instead of merely checking the navigator.appVersion value. Fortunately, there's a better way to handle this, as you'll learn in the next section.

Cross-Browser Scripting

If all those details about detecting different browser versions seem confusing, here's some good news—in most cases, you can write cross-browser scripts without referring to the navigator object at all. This is not only easier, it's better because browser-checking code is often confused by new browser versions and has to be updated each time a new browser is released.

Feature Sensing

Checking browser versions is sometimes called *browser sensing*. The better way of dealing with multiple browsers is called *feature sensing*. In feature sensing, rather than checking for a specific browser, you check for a specific feature. For example, suppose your script needs to use the document.getElementById() function. You can begin a script with an if statement that checks for the existence of this function:

```
if (document.getElementById) {
    // do stuff
}
```

If the `getElementById` function exists, the block of code between the brackets will be executed. Another common way to use feature sensing is at the beginning of a function that will make use of a feature:

```
function changeText() {
    if (!document.getElementById) return;
    // the rest of the function executes if the feature is supported
}
```

You don't need to check for *every* feature before you use it—for example, there's not much point in verifying that the `window` object exists in most cases. You can also assume that the existence of one feature means others are supported: If `getElementById()` is supported, chances are the rest of the W3C DOM functions are supported.

Feature sensing is a very reliable method of keeping your JavaScript unobtrusive—if a browser supports the feature, it works, and if the browser doesn't, your script stays out of the way. It's also much easier than trying to keep track of hundreds of different browser versions and what they support.

Dealing with Browser Quirks

So, if feature sensing is better than browser sensing, why do you still need to know about the `navigator` object? There's one situation where it still comes in handy, although if you're lucky you won't find yourself in that situation.

As you develop a complex script and test it in multiple browsers, you might run across a situation where your perfectly standard code works as it should in one browser and fails to work in another. Assuming you've eliminated the possibility of a problem with your script, you've probably run into a browser bug or a difference in features between browsers at the very least. Here are some tips for this situation:

- ▶ Double-check for a bug in your own code.

- ▶ Search the Web to see whether to the code, and you might sidestep the bug.

- ▶ If the problem is that a feature is missing in one browser, use feature sensing to check for that feature.

- ▶ When all else fails, use the `navigator` object to detect a particular browser and substitute some code that works in that browser. This should be your last resort.

NOTE

Feature sensing is also handy when working with third-party libraries, as discussed in Chapter 22. You can check for the existence of an object or a function belonging to the library to verify that the library file has been loaded before your script uses its features.

TIP

Peter-Paul Koch's QuirksMode, http://www.quirksmode.org, is a good place to start when you're looking for specific information about browser bugs.

Supporting Non-JavaScript Browsers

Some visitors to your site will be using browsers that don't support JavaScript at all. These aren't just a few holdouts using ancient browsers—actually, there are more non-JavaScript browsers than you might think:

▶ Most modern browsers, such as Internet Explorer, Firefox, and Chrome, include an option to turn off JavaScript, and some users do so. More often, the browser might have been set up by their ISP or employer with JavaScript turned off by default, usually in a misguided attempt to increase security.

▶ Some corporate firewalls and personal antivirus software block JavaScript.

▶ Some ad-blocking software mistakenly prevents scripts from working even if they aren't related to advertising.

▶ More and more mobile phones are coming with web browsers these days, and most of these support little to no JavaScript.

▶ Some visually impaired users use special-purpose browsers or text-only browsers that might not support JavaScript.

As you can see, it would be foolish to assume that all your visitors will support JavaScript. Two techniques you can use to make sure these users can still use the site are discussed in the following sections.

Using the `<noscript>` Tag

One way to be friendly to non-JavaScript browsers is to use the `<noscript>` tag. Supported in most modern browsers, this tag displays a message to non-JavaScript browsers. Browsers that support JavaScript ignore the text between the `<noscript>` tags, whereas others display it. Here is a simple example:

```
<noscript>
This page requires JavaScript. You can either switch to a browser
that supports JavaScript, turn your browser's script support on,
or switch to the <a href="nojs.html">Non-JavaScript</a> version of
this page.
</noscript>
```

Although this works, the trouble is that `<noscript>` is not consistently supported by all browsers that support JavaScript. An alternative that avoids `<noscript>` is to send users with JavaScript support to another page. This can be accomplished with a single JavaScript statement:

> **NOTE**
>
> Search engines are another "browser" that will visit your site frequently, and they usually don't pay any attention to JavaScript. If you want search engines to fully index your site, it's critical that you avoid making JavaScript a requirement to navigate the site.

```
<script type="text/javascript">
window.location="JavaScript.html";
</script>
```

This script redirects the user to a different page. If the browser doesn't support JavaScript, of course, the script won't be executed, and the rest of the page can display a warning message to explain the situation.

Keeping JavaScript Optional

Although you can detect JavaScript browsers and display a message to the rest, the best choice is to simply make your scripts unobtrusive. Use JavaScript to enhance rather than as an essential feature; keep JavaScript in separate files and assign event handlers in the JavaScript file rather than in the HTML. Browsers that don't support JavaScript will simply ignore your script.

In those rare cases where you absolutely need JavaScript—for example, an AJAX application or a JavaScript game—you can warn users that JavaScript is required. However, it's a good idea to offer an alternative JavaScript-free way to use your site, especially if it's an e-commerce or business site that your business relies on. Don't turn away customers with lazy programming.

One place you should definitely *not* require JavaScript is in the navigation of your site. Although you can create drop-down menus and other fancy navigation tools using JavaScript, they prevent users' non-JavaScript browsers from viewing all of your site's pages. They also prevent search engines from viewing the entire site, compromising your chances of getting search traffic.

Avoiding Errors

If you've made sure JavaScript is only an enhancement to your site, rather than a requirement, those with browsers that don't support JavaScript for whatever reason will still be able to navigate your site. One last thing to worry about: It's possible for JavaScript to cause an error or confuse these browsers into displaying your page incorrectly.

This is a particular concern with browsers that partially support JavaScript, such as mobile phone browsers. They might interpret a `<script>` tag and start the script, but might not support the full JavaScript language or DOM. Here are some guidelines for avoiding errors:

NOTE

Google's Gmail application (http://mail.google.com), one of the most well-known uses of AJAX, requires JavaScript for its elegant interface. However, Google offers a Basic HTML View that can be used without JavaScript. This allows Google to support older browsers and mobile phones without compromising the user experience for those with modern browsers.

- ► Use a separate JavaScript file for all scripts. This is the best way to guarantee that the browser will ignore your script completely if it does not have JavaScript support.

- ► Use feature sensing whenever your script tries to use the newer DOM features, such as document.getElementById().

- ► Test your pages with your browser's JavaScript support turned off. Make sure nothing looks strange and make sure you can still navigate the site.

TIP

The developer's toolbars for Firefox and Internet Explorer include a convenient way to turn off JavaScript for testing.

As an example of unobtrusive scripting, you can create a script that adds functionality to a page with JavaScript without compromising its performance in older browsers. In this example, you will create a script that creates graphic check boxes as an alternative to regular check boxes.

Let's start with the final result: Figure 21.3 shows this example as it appears in Firefox. The first check box is an ordinary HTML one, and the second is a graphic check box managed by JavaScript.

TRY IT YOURSELF ▼

Creating an Unobtrusive Script

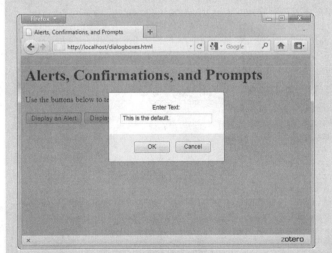

FIGURE 21.3
The graphic check box example in action, with the graphical check box checked.

The graphic check box is just a larger graphic that you can click on to display the checked or unchecked version of the graphic. Although this could just be a simple JavaScript simulation that acts like a check box, it's a bit more sophisticated. Take a look at the HTML for this example in Listing 21.2.

▼ TRY IT YOURSELF

Creating an Unobtrusive Script

continued

LISTING 21.2 The HTML File for the Graphic Check Box Example

```
<?xml version="1.0" encoding="UTF-8"?>
<!DOCTYPE html PUBLIC "-//W3C//DTD XHTML 1.1//EN"
  "http://www.w3.org/TR/xhtml11/DTD/xhtml11.dtd">

<html xmlns="http://www.w3.org/1999/xhtml" xml:lang="en">
  <head>
    <title>Graphic Checkboxes</title>
  </head>
  <body>
    <h1>Graphic Checkbox Example</h1>
    <form name="form1"  method="post" action="">
  <p><input type="checkbox" name="check1" id="check1"/>
  An ordinary checkbox.</p>
  <p><input type="checkbox" name="check2" id="check2"/>
  A graphic checkbox, created with unobtrusive JavaScript.</p>
    </form>
    <script type="text/javascript" src="checkbox.js"></script>
  </body>
</html>
```

If you look closely at the HTML, you'll see that the two check boxes are defined in exactly the same way with the standard `<input>` tag. Rather than substitute for a check box, this script actually replaces the regular check box with the graphic version. The script for this example is shown in Listing 21.3.

LISTING 21.3 The JavaScript File for the Graphic Check Box Example

```
function graphicBox(box) {
   // be unobtrusive
   if (!document.getElementById) return;
   // find the object and its parent
   obj = document.getElementById(box);
   parentobj = obj.parentNode;
   // hide the regular checkbox
   obj.style.visibility = "hidden";
   // create the image element and set its onclick event
   img = document.createElement("img");
   img.onclick = Toggle;
   img.src = "unchecked.gif";
   // save the checkbox id within the image ID
   img.id = "img" + box;
   // display the graphic checkbox
   parentobj.insertBefore(img,obj);
}
function Toggle(e) {
   if (!e) var e=window.event;
   // find the image ID
```

LISTING 21.3   Continued

```
    img = (e.target) ? e.target : e.srcElement;
    // find the checkbox by removing "img" from the image ID
    checkid = img.id.substring(3);
    checkbox = document.getElementById(checkid);
    // "click" the checkbox
    checkbox.click();
    // display the right image for the clicked or unclicked state
    if (checkbox.checked) file = "checked.gif";
       else file="unchecked.gif";
    img.src=file;
}
//replace the second checkbox with a graphic
graphicBox("check2");
```

TRY IT YOURSELF ▼

Creating an Unobtrusive Script

continued

This script has three main components:

▶ The graphicBox() function converts a regular check box to a graphic one. It starts by hiding the existing check box by changing its style.visibility property, and then creates a new image node containing the unchecked.gif graphic and inserts it into the DOM next to the original check box. It gives the image an id attribute containing the text img plus the check box's id attribute to make it easier to find the check box later.

▶ The Toggle() function is specified by graphicBox() as the event handler for the new image's onClick event. This function removes img from the image's id attribute to find the id of the real check box. It executes the click() method on the check box, toggling its value. Finally, it changes the image to unchecked.gif or checked.gif depending on the state of the real check box.

▶ The last line of the script file runs the graphicBox() function to replace the second check box with the id attribute check2.

Using this technique has three important advantages. First, it's an unobtrusive script. The HTML has been kept simple, and browsers that don't support JavaScript will display the ordinary check box. Second, because the real check box is still on the page but hidden, it will work correctly when the form is submitted to a server-side script. Last but not least, you can use it to create any number of graphic check boxes simply by defining regular ones in the HTML file and adding a call to graphicBox() to transform each one.

To try this example, save the JavaScript file as checkbox.js and be sure the HTML file is in the same folder. You'll also need two graphics the same size, unchecked.gif and checked.gif, in the same folder.

Summary

In this chapter, you've learned many guidelines for creating scripts that work in as many browsers as possible and how to avoid errors and headaches when working with different browsers. Most importantly, you learned how you can use JavaScript while keeping your pages small, efficient, and valid with web standards.

Q&A

Q. Is it possible to create 100% unobtrusive JavaScript that can enhance a page without causing any trouble for anyone?

A. Not quite. For example, the unobtrusive script in the Try It Yourself section of this chapter is close—it will work in the latest browsers, and the regular check box will display and work fine in even ancient browsers. However, it can still fail if someone with a modern browser has images turned off: The script will hide the check box because JavaScript is supported, but the image won't be there. This is a rare circumstance, but it's an example of how any feature you add can potentially cause a problem for some small percentage of your users.

Q. Can I detect the user's email address using the `navigator` object or another technique?

A. No, there is no reliable way to detect users' email addresses using JavaScript. (If there were, you would get hundreds of advertisements in your mailbox every day from companies that detected your address as you browsed their pages.) You can use a signed script to obtain the user's email address, but this requires the user's permission and only works in some versions of Netscape.

Workshop

The workshop contains quiz questions and exercises to help you solidify your understanding of the material covered. Try to answer all questions before looking at the "Answers" section that follows.

Quiz

1. Which of the following is the best place to put JavaScript code?

    a. Right in the HTML document

    b. In a separate JavaScript file

    c. In a CSS file

2. Which of the following is something you *can't* do with JavaScript?

    a. Send browsers that don't support a feature to a different page

    b. Send users of Internet Explorer to a different page

    c. Send users of non-JavaScript browsers to a different page

3. Which of the following is the best way to define an event handler that works in all modern browsers?

   a. `<body onLoad="MyFunction()">`

   b. `window.onload=MyFunction;`

   c. `window.attachEvent('load',MyFunction,false);`

Answers

1. b. The best place for JavaScript is in a separate JavaScript file.

2. c. You can't use JavaScript to send users of non-JavaScript browsers to a different page because the script won't be executed at all.

3. b. The code `window.onload=MyFunction;` defines an event handler in all modern browsers. This is better than using an inline event handler as in (a) because it keeps JavaScript out of the HTML document. Option (c) uses the W3C's standard method, but does not work in Internet Explorer.

Exercises

▶ Add several check boxes to the HTML document in Listing 21.2 and add the corresponding function calls to the script in Listing 21.3 to replace all of them with graphic check boxes.

▶ Modify the script in Listing 21.3 to convert all check boxes with a `class` value of `graphic` into graphic check boxes. You can use `getElementsByTagName()` and then check each item for the right `className` property.

CHAPTER 22

Using Third-Party Libraries

Third-party JavaScript libraries, or code libraries written and maintained by another party for easy implementation in your own code, offer many advantages. First and foremost, using these libraries enables you to avoid reinventing the wheel for common tasks. Additionally, these libraries enable you to implement cross-browser scripting and sophisticated user interface elements without first having to become an expert in JavaScript.

WHAT YOU'LL LEARN IN THIS CHAPTER:

▶ Why you might use a third-party JavaScript library

▶ How to download and use one of the more popular third-party JavaScript libraries in your applications

Using Third-Party Libraries

When you use JavaScript's built-in `Math` and `Date` functions, JavaScript does most of the work—you don't have to figure out how to convert dates between formats or calculate a cosine. Third-party libraries are not included with JavaScript, but they serve a similar purpose: enabling you to do complicated things with only a small amount of code.

Using one of these libraries is usually as simple as copying one or more files to your site and including a `<script>` tag in your document to load the library. Several popular JavaScript libraries are discussed in the following sections.

Prototype

Prototype, created by Sam Stephenson, is a JavaScript library that simplifies tasks such as working with DOM objects, dealing with data in forms, and remote scripting (AJAX). By including a single prototype.js file in your document, you have access to many improvements to basic JavaScript.

For example, you've used the `document.getElementById` method to obtain the DOM object for an element within a web page. Prototype includes an

NOTE

Prototype is free, open-source software. You can download it from its official website at http://www.prototypejs.org/. Prototype is also built into the Ruby on Rails framework for the server-side language Ruby—see http://www.rubyonrails.com/ for more information.

NOTE

jQuery's home page is at http://jquery.com/, where you can not only download the latest version, but also gain access to extensive documentation and example code.

The companion UI library can be found at http://jqueryui.com/.

TIP

If you don't want to download and store the jQuery library on your own computer, you can use a remotely hosted version, such as the one by Google. Instead of including a locally hosted .js file in your page head, use the following code:

```
<script
src="http://ajax.googleapis.c
om/ajax/libs/jquery/1.6.2/
jquery.min.js"
type="text/javascript"></
script>
```

In many cases, this provides better performance than hosting your own version, due to Google's servers being optimized for low-latency, massively parallel content delivery.

improved version of this in the $()$ function. Not only is it easier to type, but it is also more sophisticated than the built-in function and supports multiple objects.

Adding Prototype to your pages requires only one file, prototype.js, and one `<script>` tag:

```
<script type="text/javascript" src="prototype.js"></script>
```

jQuery

The first implementation of jQuery was introduced in 2006. What was originally an easy, cross-browser means DOM manipulation has subsequently become a stable, powerful library containing not just DOM manipulation tools, but many additional features that make cross-browser JavaScript coding much more straightforward and productive.

The library is currently up to version 1.6.2 and now also has an additional advanced user interface extensions library that can be used alongside the existing library to rapidly build and deploy rich user interfaces or add a variety of attractive effects to existing components.

Like the Prototype library described previously, jQuery has at its heart a sophisticated, cross-browser method for selection of page elements. The selectors used to obtain elements are based on a combination of simple CSS-like selector styles, so with the CSS techniques you learned in Part III, "Advanced Web Page Design with CSS," you should have no problem getting up to speed with jQuery. For example, if you want to get an element that has an ID of *someElement*, all you do is use the following:

```
$("#someElement")
```

Or to return a collection of elements that have the *someClass* class name, you can simply use the following:

```
$(".someClass")
```

We can very simply get or set values associated with our selected elements. Let's suppose, for example, that we want to hide all elements having the class name hideMe. We can do that, in a fully cross-browser manner, in just one line of code:

```
$(".hideMe").hide();
```

Manipulating HTML and CSS properties is just as straightforward. To append the phrase "powered by jQuery" to all paragraph elements, for example, we would simply write the following:

```
$("p").append(" powered by jQuery");
```

To then change the background color of those same elements, we can manipulate their CSS properties directly:

```
$("p").css("background-color","yellow");
```

Additionally, jQuery includes simple cross-browser methods for determining whether an element has a class, adding and removing classes, getting and setting the text or `innerHTML` of an element, navigating the DOM, getting and setting CSS properties, and handling of easy cross-browser events.

The associated UI library adds a huge range of UI widgets (such as date pickers, sliders, dialogs and progress bars), animation tools, drag-and-drop capabilities, and much more.

Script.aculo.us

By the end of this book, you'll learn to do some useful things with JavaScript, often using complex code. But you can also include impressive effects in your pages using a prebuilt library. This enables you to use impressive effects with only a few lines of code.

Script.aculo.us by Thomas Fuchs is one such library. It includes functions to simplify drag-and-drop tasks, such as rearranging lists of items. It also includes a number of combination effects, which enable you to use highlighting and animated transitions within your pages. For example, a new section of the page can be briefly highlighted in yellow to get the user's attention, or a portion of the page can fade out or slide off the screen.

After you've included the appropriate files, using effects is as easy as using any of JavaScript's built-in methods. For example, the following statements use Script.aculo.us to fade out an element of the page with the `id` value `test`:

```
obj = document.getElementById("test");
new Effect.Fade(obj);
```

Script.aculo.us is built on the Prototype framework described in the previous section and includes all of the functions of Prototype, so you could also simplify this further by using the $ function:

```
new Effect.Fade($("test"));
```

TIP

You can even extend jQuery yourself by writing further plugins or use the thousands already submitted by other developers. Browse http://www.jqueryplugins.com/ to see lots of examples in searchable categories.

NOTE

You will create a script that demonstrates several Script.aculo.us effects in the Try It Yourself section later this chapter.

AJAX Frameworks

AJAX (Asynchronous JavaScript and XML), also known as *remote scripting*, enables JavaScript to communicate with a program running on the web server. This enables JavaScript to do things that were traditionally not possible, such as dynamically loading information from a database or storing data on a server without refreshing a page.

AJAX requires some complex scripting, particularly because the methods you use to communicate with the server vary depending on the browser in use. Fortunately, many libraries have been created to fill the need for a simple way to use AJAX, and you'll try your hand at this later in this book.

NOTE

See Chapter 24, "AJAX: Remote Scripting," for examples of remote scripting, with and without using third-party libraries.

Both jQuery and the Prototype library, described previously, include AJAX features. There are also many dedicated AJAX libraries. One of the most popular is SAJAX (Simple AJAX), an open-source toolkit that makes it easy to use AJAX to communicate with PHP, Perl, and other languages from JavaScript. Visit the SAJAX website for details at http://www.modernmethod.com/sajax.

Other Libraries

There are many more JavaScript libraries out there, and more are appearing all the time as JavaScript is taken more seriously as an application language. Here are some more libraries you might want to explore:

▶ Dojo (http://www.dojotoolkit.org/) is an open-source toolkit that adds power to JavaScript to simplify building applications and user interfaces. It adds features ranging from extra string and math functions to animation and AJAX.

▶ The Yahoo! UI Library (http://developer.yahoo.net/yui/) was developed by Yahoo! and made available to everyone under an open-source license. It includes features for animation, DOM features, event management, and easy-to-use user interface elements such as calendars and sliders.

▶ MochiKit (http://mochikit.com/) is a lightweight library that adds features for working with the DOM, CSS colors, string formatting, and AJAX. It also supports a nice logging mechanism for debugging your scripts.

▶ MooTools (http://mootools.net/) is a compact, modular JavaScript framework enabling you to build powerful, flexible, and cross-browser code using a simple-to-understand, well-documented API (application programming interface).

To see how simple it is to use an external library, you will now create an example script that includes the Script.aculo.us library and use event handlers to demonstrate several of the available effects.

Downloading the Library

To use the library, you will need to download it and copy the files you need to the same folder where you will store your script. You can download the library from the Script.aculo.us website at http://script.aculo.us/downloads.

The download is available as a Zip file. Inside the Zip file you will find a folder following the naming convention of scriptaculous-js-x.x.x where each x stands for part of the version number (the version as of this writing is 1.9.0). You will need the following files from the folders under this folder:

▶ prototype.js (the Prototype library) from the lib folder

▶ effects.js (the effects functions) from the src folder

Copy both of these files to a folder on your computer, and be sure to create your demonstration script in the same folder.

Including the Files

To add the library to your HTML document, simply use <script> tags to include the two JavaScript files you copied from the download:

```
<script type="text/javascript" src="prototype.js"> </script>
<script type="text/javascript" src="effects.js"> </script>
```

If you include these statements as the first things in the <head> section of your document, the library functions will be available to other scripts or event handlers anywhere in the page.

Using Effects

After you have included the library, you simply need to include a bit of JavaScript to trigger the effects. We will use a section of the page wrapped in a <div> tag with the id value test to demonstrate the effects. Each effect is triggered by a simple event handler on a button. For example, this code defines the Fade Out button:

```
<input type="button" value="Fade Out"
    onclick="new Effect.Fade($('test'))">
```

This uses the $ function built into Prototype to obtain the object for the element with the id value test, and then passes it to the Effect.Fade function built into Script.aculo.us.

TRY IT YOURSELF ▼

Adding Effects with a Library

CAUTION

This example was created using version 1.9.0 of the Script.aculo.us library. It should work with later versions, but the library might have changed since this was written. If you have trouble, you might need to use this specific version.

NOTE

The Script.aculo.us download includes many other files, and you can include the entire library if you intend to use all of its features. For this example, you only need the two files described here.

TIP

This example will demonstrate six effects: Fade, Appear, SlideUp, SlideDown, Highlight, and Shake. There are more than 16 effects in the library, plus methods for supporting Drag and Drop and other features. See http://script.aculo.us for details.

▼ TRY IT YOURSELF

Adding Effects with a Library

continued

Building the Script

After you have included the libraries, you can combine them with event handlers and some example text to create a complete demonstration of Script.aculo.us effects. The complete HTML document for this example is shown in Listing 22.1.

LISTING 22.1   The Complete Library Effects Example

```
<?xml version="1.0" encoding="UTF-8"?>
<!DOCTYPE html PUBLIC "-//W3C//DTD XHTML 1.1//EN"
  "http://www.w3.org/TR/xhtml11/DTD/xhtml11.dtd">

<html xmlns="http://www.w3.org/1999/xhtml" xml:lang="en">
  <head>
    <title>Testing script.aculo.us effects</title>
    <script type="text/javascript" src="prototype.js"></script>
    <script type="text/javascript" src="effects.js"></script>
  </head>
  <body>
  <h1>Testing script.aculo.us Effects</h1>
  <form name="form1">
  <input type="button" value="Fade Out"
     onclick="new Effect.Fade($('test'))">
  <input type="button" value="Fade In"
     onclick="new Effect.Appear($('test'))">
  <input type="button" value="Slide Up"
     onclick="new Effect.SlideUp($('test'))">
  <input type="button" value="Slide Down"
     onclick="new Effect.SlideDown($('test'))">
  <input type="button" value="Highlight"
     onclick="new Effect.Highlight($('test'))">
  <input type="button" value="Shake"
     onclick="new Effect.Shake($('test'))">
  </form>
  <div id="test" style="background-color:#CCC;
  margin:20px; padding:10px;">
  <h2>Testing Effects</h2>
  <hr/>
  <p>This section of the document is within a &lt;div&gt; element
  with the <strong>id</strong> value of <strong>test</strong>.
  The event handlers on the buttons above send this object to the
  <a href="http://script.aculo.us/">script.aculo.us</a> library
  to perform effects. Click the buttons to see the effects.</p>
  </div>
  </body>
</html>
```

TRY IT YOURSELF ▼

Adding Effects with a Library
continued

This document starts with two `<script>` tags to include the library's files. The effects are triggered by the event handlers defined for each of the six buttons. The `<div>` section at the end defines the `test` element that will be used to demonstrate the effects.

To try this example, make sure the prototype.js and effects.js files from Script.aculo.us are stored in the same folder as your script, and then load it into a browser. The display should look like Figure 22.1, and you can use the six buttons at the top of the page to trigger effects.

FIGURE 22.1
The library effects example.

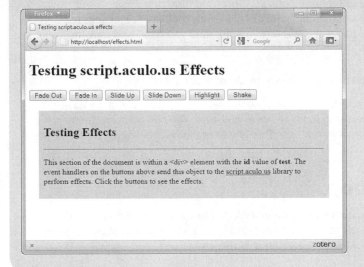

Summary

In this chapter, you learned about some of the many third-party libraries available for JavaScript. These can offer many advantages including easy cross-browser scripting, selection and editing of HTML and CSS values, animation, and more sophisticated user-interface tools such as drag-and-drop.

Q&A

Q. How do I include a third-party JavaScript library into my pages?

A. The process varies slightly from library to library. Usually it's simply a matter of including one or more external .js files into the `<head>` part of your web page. See the documentation supplied with your chosen library for specific details.

Q. Can I use more than one third-party library in the same script?

A. Yes, in theory: If the libraries are well written and designed not to interfere with each other, there should be no problem combining them. In practice, this will depend on the libraries you need and how they were written.

Q. Can I build my own library to simplify scripting?

A. Yes, as you deal with more complicated scripts, you'll find yourself using the same functions over and over. You can combine them into a library for your own use. This is as simple as creating a .js file.

Workshop

The workshop contains quiz questions and exercises to help you solidify your understanding of the material covered. Try to answer all questions before looking at the "Answers" section that follows.

Quiz

1. Which of the following objects *is not* a JavaScript library?

    a. MooTools

    b. Prototype

    c. AJAX

2. How can you extend jQuery yourself?

    a. jQuery can't be extended.

    b. By writing server-side scripts.

    c. By writing a plug-in or using a prewritten one.

3. What other JavaScript third-party library does Script.aculo.us employ?

    a. Prototype

    b. Dojo

    c. jQuery

Answers

1. c. AJAX is a programming technique enabling your scripts to use resources hosted on your server. There are many libraries to help you employ AJAX functionality, but AJAX itself is not a library.

2. c. jQuery has a well documented way to write and use plug-ins.

3. a. Script.aculo.us uses the prototype.js library.

Exercises

▶ Write a simple script using the jQuery library or use an example script from the jQuery website. Run the script using both locally and remotely hosted versions of jQuery. Can you see any difference in performance?

▶ Visit the Script.aculo.us page at http://script.aculo.us/ to find the complete list of effects. Modify Listing 22.1 to add buttons for one or more additional effects.

CHAPTER 23

Greasemonkey: Enhancing the Web with JavaScript

One of the recent trends is that JavaScript is being used in new ways, both inside and outside web browsers. In this chapter, you'll look at Greasemonkey, a Firefox extension that enables you to write scripts to modify the appearance and behavior of sites you visit. User scripts can also work in Internet Explorer, Opera, and Safari with the right add-ons, and Chrome has native support for user scripts.

Introducing Greasemonkey

So far in this book, you've been using JavaScript to work on your own sites. In this chapter, you'll take a break from that and learn about a way to use JavaScript on *other people's sites*. Greasemonkey is an extension for the Firefox browser that enables *user scripts*. These are scripts that run as soon as you load a page and can make changes to the page's DOM.

A user script can be designed to work on all web pages or to only affect particular sites. Here are some of the things user scripts can do:

- ▶ Change the appearance of one or more sites—colors, font size, and so on

- ▶ Change the behavior of one or more sites with JavaScript

- ▶ Fix a bug in a site before the site author does

- ▶ Add a feature to your browser, such as text macros—see the Try It Yourself section later in this chapter for an example

As a simple example, a user script called Linkify is provided with Greasemonkey. It affects all pages you visit and turns unlinked URLs into hyperlinks. In other words, the script looks for any string that resembles a URL in the page, and if it finds a URL that is not enclosed in an <a> tag, it modifies the DOM to add a link to the URL.

Greasemonkey scripts can range from simple ones such as Linkify to complex scripts that add a feature to the browser, rearrange a site to make it more usable, or eliminate annoying features of sites such as pop-up ads.

Keep in mind that Greasemonkey doesn't do anything to the websites you visit—it strictly affects *your personal experience* with the sites. In this way, it's similar to other browser customizations, such as personal style sheets and browser font settings.

Installing Greasemonkey in Firefox

Greasemonkey works in Firefox for Windows, Macintosh, and Linux platforms. You can install it by visiting the http://www.greasespot.net/ and following the Download link. Use the Add To Firefox button to install Greasemonkey (see Figure 23.1). After installation, you might be asked to restart Firefox before Greasemonkey can be used.

> **NOTE**
>
> Greasemonkey was created in 2004 by Aaron Boodman. Its official site is http://www.greasespot.net/. At this writing, the current version of Greasemonkey is 0.9.10.

> **FIGURE 23.1**
> Use the Add To Firefox button to install Greasemonkey.

> **NOTE**
>
> When you first install Greasemonkey, the extension doesn't do anything—you'll need to install one or more user scripts, as described later in this chapter in "Working with User Scripts," to make it useful.

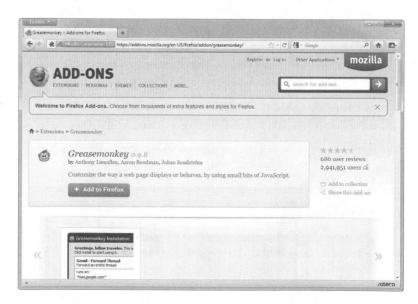

Trixie for Internet Explorer

The Greasemonkey extension was written as a Firefox extension and does not work on other browsers (although user scripts do with the right helpers). Fortunately, there's an alternative for those that prefer Internet Explorer: Trixie is an add-on for Internet Explorer that supports user scripts. Trixie is available free from its official site at http://www.bhelpuri.net/Trixie/. To install Trixie, you will need to make sure that you have the .NET Framework installed.

Trixie supports most of Greasemonkey's features, and user scripts for Greasemonkey often work with Trixie without modification; however, due to differences between Firefox and Internet Explorer, not all Greasemonkey scripts can be run within IE. See the Trixie site for more detailed information on installing and running Trixie.

Other Browsers

User script features have also appeared for other browsers. Along with Trixie for IE, some other browsers can support user scripts:

▶ Opera, the cross-platform browser from Opera Software ASA, has built-in support for user scripts and supports Greasemonkey scripts in many cases. See Opera's site for details at http://www.opera.com/.

▶ From version 4.0, Google's Chrome browser has included native support for Greasemonkey scripts. Behind the scenes, these are converted into Chrome extensions.

▶ Creammonkey is a beta add-on for Apple's Safari browser to support user scripts. You can find it at http://8-p.info/CreamMonkey/index.html.en.

User Script Security

Before you get into user scripting, a word of warning: Don't install a script unless you understand what it's doing or you've obtained it from a trustworthy source. Although the Greasemonkey developers have spent a great deal of time eliminating security holes, it's still possible for a malicious script to cause you trouble—at the very least, it could send information about which sites you visit to a third-party website.

To minimize security risks, be sure you're running the latest version of Greasemonkey or Trixie. Only enable scripts you are actively using and limit scripts you don't trust to specific pages so that they don't run on every page you visit.

Working with User Scripts

User scripts are a whole new way of working with JavaScript—rather than uploading them for use on your website, you install them in the browser for your own personal use. The following sections show you how to find useful scripts and install and manage them.

Finding Scripts

Anyone can write user scripts, and many people have. Greasemonkey sponsors a directory of user scripts at http://userscripts.org/. There you can browse or search for scripts or submit scripts you've written.

The script archive has thousands of scripts available. Along with general-purpose scripts, many of the scripts are designed to add features to—or remove annoying features from—particular sites.

Installing a Script

After you've found a script you want to install, you can install it from the Web:

- ▶ In Firefox with Greasemonkey, open the script in the browser, and then select Tools, Install This User Script from the menu.

- ▶ In IE with Trixie, download the script into the Scripts directory under the Trixie installation folder. By default, this is at Program Files\Bhelpuri\Trixie\Scripts. Then, go to the Tools menu and select Trixie Options (Alt-T, X). This will show the Trixie Options dialog where you can click on the Reload Scripts button and select OK. This will load your new script and enable it.

You can also install a script from a local file. You'll use this technique to install your own script later this chapter.

Managing Scripts

After you've installed one or more scripts with Greasemonkey, you can manage them by selecting Greasemonkey, Manage User Scripts from the Firefox menu. The Manage User Scripts dialog is shown in Figure 23.2.

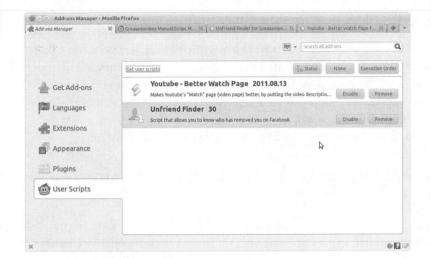

FIGURE 23.2
Managing user scripts in
Greasemonkey.

The user scripts you have available are listed in the right column. Click on a script name to manage it:

▶ Use the Enable/Disable button to enable or disable each script.

▶ Click the Remove button to remove a script.

▶ Right-click and choose Edit to open a script in a text editor. When it is saved, it will immediately take effect on pages you load.

Trixie for IE has a similar dialog. The Trixie Options dialog (Alt-T, X) can be used to manage the scripts you have installed. From this dialog, as shown in Figure 23.3, you can view the scripts installed, enable or disable scripts, or reload scripts. The dialog also shows which sites or pages the script will execute on.

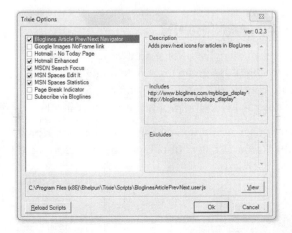

FIGURE 23.3
The Trixie Options dialog.

Testing User Scripts

If you have a script enabled, it will be activated as soon as you load a page that matches one of the Included Pages specified for the script. (The script is run after the page is loaded, but before the onload event.) If you want to make sure Greasemonkey is running, either try one of the scripts available for a script enabled (it will activate as soon as you load a page that matches one download) or type in the simple script in the next section.

Activating and Deactivating Greasemonkey or Trixie

Sometimes when a script is enabled, it will be activated as soon as you load a page that matches one where you'll want to turn off Greasemonkey altogether, especially if one of the scripts you've installed is causing an error. To do this, right-click on the monkey icon in the lower-right corner of the browser window and select the Enabled option to deselect it. The monkey icon changes to a gray sad-faced monkey, and no user scripts will be run at all. You can re-enable it at any time using the same option.

With Trixie for Internet Explorer, use Explorer's Manage Add-Ons menu to disable Trixie.

Creating Your Own User Scripts

You've already learned most of what you need to know to create user scripts since they're written in JavaScript. In this section, you'll create and test a simple script and look at some features you'll use when creating more advanced scripts.

Creating a Simple User Script

One of the best uses for Greasemonkey is to solve annoyances with sites you visit. For example, a site might use green text on an orange background. Although you could contact the webmaster and beg for a color change, user scripting lets you deal with the problem quickly yourself.

As a simple demonstration of user scripting, you can create a user script that changes the text and background colors of paragraphs in sites you visit. Listing 23.1 shows this user script.

LISTING 23.1 A Simple User Script to Change Paragraph Colors

```
// Change the color of each paragraph
var zParagraphs = document.getElementsByTagName("p");
for (var i=0; i<zParagraphs.length; i++) {
   zParagraphs[i].style.backgroundColor="#000000";
   zParagraphs[i].style.color="#ffffff";
}
```

This script uses the `getElementsByTagName()` DOM method to find all the paragraph tags in the current document and store their objects in the `zParagraphs` array. The `for` loop iterates through the array and changes the `style.color` and `style.backgroundColor` properties for each one.

Describing a User Script

Greasemonkey supports *metadata* at the beginning of your script. These are JavaScript comments that aren't executed by the script, but provide information to Greasemonkey. To use this feature, enclose your comments between `// ==UserScript==` and `// ==/UserScript` comments.

The metadata section can contain any of the following directives. All of these are optional, but using them will make your user script easier to install and use.

▶ **@name**—A short name for the script, displayed in Greasemonkey's list of scripts after installation.

▶ **@namespace**—An optional URL for the script author's site. This is used as a namespace for the script: Two scripts can have the same name as long as the namespace is different.

▶ **@description**—A one-line description of the script's purpose.

▶ **@include**—The URL of a site on which the script should be used. You can specify any number of URLs, each in its own `@include` line. You can also use the wildcard * to run the script on all sites or a partial URL with a wildcard to run it on a group of sites.

▶ **@exclude**—The URL of a site on which the script should *not* be used. You can specify a wildcard for `@include`, and then exclude one or more sites that the script is incompatible with. The `@exclude` directive can also use wildcards.

Listing 23.2 shows the color-changing example with a complete set of metadata comments added at the top.

LISTING 23.2   The Color-Changing Script with Metadata Comments

```
// ==UserScript==
// @name        WhiteOnBlack
// @namespace   http://www.thickbook.com/
// @description Display paragraphs in white text on black
// @include     *
// ==/UserScript==
//
// Change the color of each paragraph
var zParagraphs = document.getElementsByTagName("p");
for (var i=0; i<zParagraphs.length; i++) {
   zParagraphs[i].style.backgroundColor="#000000";
   zParagraphs[i].style.color="#ffffff";
}
```

Testing Your Script

Now that you've added the metadata, installing your script is simple. Follow these steps to install the script in Firefox:

1. Save the script file as colors.user.js. The filename must end in .user.js to be recognized as a Greasemonkey script.

2. In Firefox, choose File, Open from the menu.

3. Select your script from the Open File dialog.

4. After the script is displayed in the browser, select Tools, Install This User Script.

5. An alert will display to inform you that the installation was successful. The new user script is now running on all sites.

Both Greasemonkey and Trixie for IE will use the metadata you specified to set the script's included pages, description, and other options when you install it.

After you've installed and enabled the script, any page you load will have its paragraphs displayed in white text on a black background. For example, Figure 23.4 shows the user script's effect on a simple "Hello World" script. Because the body text is enclosed in a <p> tag, it is displayed in white on black.

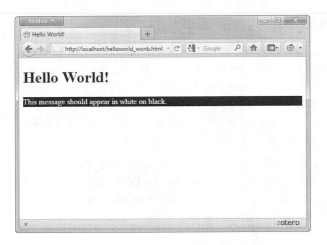

FIGURE 23.4
A basic page altered by the color-changing user script.

NOTE

You probably don't want to make a change this drastic to *all* sites you visit. Instead, you can use @include to make this script affect only one or two sites whose colors you find hard to read. Don't forget that you can also change the colors in the script to your own preference.

Greasemonkey API Functions

You can use all the DOM methods covered in this book to work with pages in user scripts, along with JavaScript's built-in functions. In addition to these, Greasemonkey defines an API (application programming interface) with a few functions that can be used exclusively in user scripts:

▶ **GM_log(*message, level*)**—Inserts a message into the JavaScript console. The *level* parameter indicates the severity of the message: 0 for information, 1 for a warning, and 2 for an error.

▶ **GM_setValue(*variable, value*)**—Sets a variable stored by Greasemonkey. These variables are stored on the local machine. They are specific to the script that set them and can be used in the future by the same script. (These are similar to cookies, but are not sent to a server.)

▶ **GM_getValue(*variable*)**—Retrieves a value previously set with GM_setValue.

▶ **GM_registerMenuCommand(*command, function*)**—Adds a command to the browser menu. These commands appear under Tools, User Script Commands. The *command* parameter is the name listed in the menu, and *function* is a function in your script that the menu selection will activate.

▶ **GM_xmlhttpRequest(*details*)**—Requests a file from a remote server, similar to the AJAX features described in Chapter 24, "AJAX: Remote Scripting." The *details* parameter is an object that can contain a number of properties to control the request. See the Greasemonkey documentation for all the properties you can specify.

Creating a Site-Specific Script

You might want to use a user script to fix a problem or add a feature to a specific site. For example, you might want to remove all of the advertisements that display on your Facebook profile page—there are numerous Greasemonkey scripts at http://userscripts.org/ to address such an issue. To create such custom scripts, in addition to using @include to specify the site's URL, you'll need to know something about the site's DOM.

You can use the DOM Inspector in Firefox (or the similar feature in Internet Explorer's developer toolbar) to browse the DOM for the site and find the objects you want to work with. Depending on how they are marked up, you can access them through the DOM:

▶ If an element has an id attribute, you can simply use document.getElementById() in your script to find its object.

▶ If a nearby element has an id defined, you can use DOM methods to find it—for example, if the parent element has an id, you can use a method such as firstChild() to find the object you need.

▶ If all else fails, you can use document.getElementsByTagName() to find all objects of a certain type—for example, all paragraphs. If you need to refer to a specific one, you can use a loop and check each one for a certain attribute.

As an example, Listing 23.3 shows a simple user script you could use as a site-specific script to automatically fill out certain fields in forms.

LISTING 23.3   A User Script to Fill Out Form Fields Automatically

```
// ==UserScript==
// @name        AutoForm
// @namespace   http://www.thickbook.com/
// @description Fills in forms automatically
// @include     *
// ==/UserScript==
// this function fills out form fields
//
var zTextFields = document.getElementsByTagName("input");
for (var i=0; i<zTextFields.length; i++) {
  thefield=zTextFields[i].name;
  if (!thefield) thefield=zTextFields[i].id;
  // Set up your auto-fill values here
  if (thefield == "yourname") zTextFields[i].value="Your Name Here";
  if (thefield == "phone") zTextFields[i].value="(xxx) xxx-xxxx";
  alert("field:" + thefield + " value: " + zTextFields[i].value);
}
```

This script uses getElementsByTagName() to find all the <input> elements in a document, including text fields. It uses a for loop to examine each one. If it finds a field with the name or id value "yourname" or "phone", it inserts the appropriate value.

To test this script, save it as autoform.user.js and install the user script as described earlier in this chapter. To test it, save Listing 23.4 as form.html and load it into Firefox—it happens to have both of the field names the script looks for. The yourname and phone fields will be automatically filled out with the value shown first in an alert, as shown in Figure 23.5.

LISTING 23.4   An HTML Form to Test AutoForm

```
<?xml version="1.0" encoding="UTF-8"?>
<!DOCTYPE html PUBLIC "-//W3C//DTD XHTML 1.1//EN"
  "http://www.w3.org/TR/xhtml11/DTD/xhtml11.dtd">

<html xmlns="http://www.w3.org/1999/xhtml" xml:lang="en">
  <head>
    <title>Auto-Fill Form Example</title>
  </head>
  <body>
    <h1>Auto-Fill Form Example</h1>
    <p>Please enter the following information:</p>
    <form method="post" action="">
    <p><strong>Name:</strong>
          <input type="text" size="20" name="yourname" /></p>
    <p><strong>Address:</strong>
          <input type="text" size="20" name="address" /></p>
    <p><strong>Phone:</strong>
          <input type="text" size="20" name="phone" /></p>
    <p><input type="button" value="Display" onclick="display();" /></p>
    </form>
  </body>
</html>
```

To make it easy to test, Listing 23.3 doesn't include specific sites in the @include line. To make a true site-specific script, you would need to find out the field names for a particular site, add if statements to the script to fill them out, and use @include to make sure the script only runs on the site.

FIGURE 23.5
The form-filling user script in
action.

Debugging User Scripts

Debugging a user script is much like debugging a regular JavaScript
program—errors are displayed in the JavaScript Console in Firefox or in
an error message in Internet Explorer. Here are a few debugging tips:

▶ As with regular scripts, you can also use the alert() method to display information about what's going on in your script.

▶ The browser may display a line number with an error message, but
when you're working with user scripts, these line numbers are mean-
ingless—they refer neither to lines in your user script nor to the page
you're currently viewing.

▶ Use the GM_log() method described earlier in this chapter to log
information about your script, such as the contents of variables, to
the JavaScript console.

▶ If you're trying to write a cross-browser user script, watch for methods that are browser specific. See Chapter 21, "Using Unobtrusive
JavaScript," for information about cross-browser issues.

▶ Watch for conflicts with any existing scripts on the page.

▶ If you're using multiple user scripts, be sure they don't conflict. Use
unique variable and function names in your scripts.

Most of the issues with user scripts are the same as for regular JavaScript.

Now that you've learned the basics of Greasemonkey, you can try a more complex—and more useful—example of a user script.

If you spend much time on the Web, you'll find yourself needing to fill out web forms often, and you probably type certain things—such as your name or URL—into forms over and over. The user script you create here will let you define macros for use in any text area. When you type a macro keyword (a period followed by a code), and then type another character, the macro keyword will be instantly replaced by the text you've defined. For example, you can define a macro so that every time you type **.cu**, it will expand into the text "See you later."

Listing 23.5 shows the text area macro user script.

TRY IT YOURSELF ▼

Creating a User Script

CAUTION

This script has been tested on Greasemonkey 0.9.10 for Firefox. Because browsers and extensions are always changing, it might stop working at some point.

LISTING 23.5   The Text Area Macro User Script

```
// ==UserScript==
// @name         TextMacro
// @namespace    http://www.thickbook.com/
// @description  expands macros in text areas as you type
// @include      *
// ==/UserScript==
// this function handles the macro replacements
function textmacro(e) {
  // define your macros here
  zmacros = [
    [".mm", "Michael Moncur"],
    [".js", "JavaScript"],
    [".cu", "See you later."]
  ];
  if (!e) var e = window.event;
  // which textarea are we in?
  thisarea= (e.target) ? e.target : e.srcElement;
  // replace text
  for (i=0; i<zmacros.length; i++) {
    vv = thisarea.value;
    vv = vv.replace(zmacros[i][0],zmacros[i][1]);
    thisarea.value=vv;
  }
}
// install the event handlers
var zTextAreas = document.getElementsByTagName("textarea");
for (var i=0; i<zTextAreas.length; i++) {
  if (zTextAreas[i].addEventListener)
    zTextAreas[i].addEventListener("keydown",textmacro,0);
  else if (zTextAreas[i].attachEvent)
    zTextAreas[i].attachEvent("onkeydown",textmacro);
}
```

▼ TRY IT YOURSELF

Creating a User Script
continued

NOTE

To avoid conflicts with existing event handlers within web pages, this example uses the `addEventListener()` method to add the event handler. This method defines an event handler without overwriting existing events. In Internet Explorer, it uses the similar `attachEvent()` method.

TIP

This script runs on all sites by default. If you only want the macros to work on certain sites, you can change the `@include` directive to specify them. If the script causes trouble on some sites, you can exclude them with `@exclude`.

How It Works

This user script begins with the usual comment metadata. The `@include` command specifies a wildcard, `*`, so the script will work on all sites. The actual work is done in the `textmacro` function. This function begins by defining the macros that will be available:

```
zmacros = [
  [".mm", "Michael Moncur"],
  [".js", "JavaScript"],
  [".cu", "See you later."]
];
```

This example defines three macros using a two-dimensional array. To make the script useful to you, define your own. You can have any number of macros—just add a comma after the last macro line and add your items before the closing bracket.

Next, the function uses the `target` property to find the text area in which you're currently typing. Next, it uses a `for` loop to do a search and replace within the text area's `value` property for each of your macros.

The section of code after the `textmacro()` function sets up an event handler for each text area. First, it uses `getElementsByTagName()` to find all the text areas, and then it uses a `for` loop to add an `onkeydown` event handler to each one.

Using This Script

To use this script, first make sure you've installed and enabled Greasemonkey as described earlier this chapter. Save the script as textmacro.user.js. You can then install the user script.

After the script is installed, try loading any page with a text area. You should be able to type a macro, such as `.jd` or `.js`, followed by another character such as a space, within the text area and see it instantly expand into the correct text.

Summary

In this chapter, you've learned how to use Greasemonkey for Firefox—and its counterpart for Internet Explorer, Trixie—to enable user scripting in your browser. You've learned how user scripts work and how to install and manage them. Finally, you created two examples of functioning user scripts.

Q&A

Q. Is there any way to prevent users from using Greasemonkey while viewing my site?

A. Because Greasemonkey affects only the user who installed it, it's usually harmless to allow it. If you still want to prevent its use, this is difficult, but not impossible, and varies with different versions of Greasemonkey. Search the Web to find current solutions.

Q. What if I want to do something more sophisticated, such as modifying Firefox's menu?

A. This capability does not exist in Greasemonkey, but Firefox extensions are also written in JavaScript. In fact, you can compile a user script into a Firefox extension, and then add more advanced features. See http://www.ghacks.net/2009/08/31/greasemonkey-to-firefox-add-on-compiler/ for details.

Q. What happens when a new version of Firefox or Internet Explorer is released?

A. Although I have faith in the Greasemonkey developers, there's no guarantee that this extension will work in future browser versions. If you're concerned about this, you might want to write your own Firefox extension instead.

Q. Are there limits to how much I can modify a page using Greasemonkey?

A. No—in fact, you can yank the entire content of the page's DOM out and replace it with HTML of your choosing using the `innerHTML` property. You'd have to do quite a bit of work to make something as useful as the original page, of course.

Workshop

The workshop contains quiz questions and exercises to help you solidify your understanding of the material covered. Try to answer all questions before looking at the "Answers" section that follows.

Quiz

1. Which of the following offers user scripting for Microsoft Internet Explorer?

    a. Greasemonkey

    b. Microsoft Live Scripting Toolbar

    c. Trixie

2. Which of the following is not a valid Greasemonkey API function?

   a. `GM_log()`

   b. `GM_alert()`

   c. `GM_setValue()`

3. Which is the correct `@include` directive to run a script on both www.google.com and google.com?

   a. `@include *.google.com`

   b. `@include www.google.com.*`

   c. `@include google.com`

Answers

1. c. Trixie is a user script add-on for Internet Explorer.

2. b. There is no `GM_alert()` method, although the standard `alert()` method will work in a user script.

3. a. Using `@include *.google.com` will run the script on any page on any site within the google.com domain.

Exercises

▶ Modify the color-changing user script in Listing 23.2 to use different colors and add another style attribute—for example, use `style.fontSize` to change the font size.

▶ The color-changing example works on paragraphs, but text often appears in other places, such as bullet lists. Modify Listing 23.2 to make the changes to `<li>` tags and paragraphs.

▶ Currently, the macro example in the Try It Yourself section only works on text inputs that use `<textarea>` tags. Modify the script in Listing 23.3 to work on `<input>` tags also. (You'll need to add a second call `getElementsByTagName()` and a loop to add the event handlers.)

AJAX: Remote Scripting

Remote scripting, also known as AJAX (Asynchronous JavaScript and XML), is a browser feature that enables JavaScript to escape its client-side boundaries and work with files on a web server or with server-side programs. In this chapter, you'll learn how AJAX works and create two working examples.

Introducing AJAX

Traditionally, one of the major limitations of JavaScript is that it couldn't communicate with a web server because it is a client-side technology—it stays within the browser. For example, you could create a game in JavaScript, but keeping a list of high scores stored on a server would require submitting a page to a server-side form, which JavaScript could not do (because it wasn't meant to do that).

Speaking purely about user interactions, one of the limitations of web pages in general was that getting data from the user to the server, or from the server to the user, generally required a new page to be loaded and displayed. But in 2011, you likely run across websites every day that enable you to interact with content without loading a new page every time you click or submit a button.

AJAX is the answer to both of these problems. AJAX refers to JavaScript's capability to use a built-in object, XMLHttpRequest, to communicate with a web server without submitting a form or loading a page. This object is supported by Internet Explorer, Firefox, Chrome, and all other modern browsers.

Although the term *AJAX* was coined in 2005, XMLHttpRequest has been supported by browsers for years—it was developed by Microsoft and first appeared in Internet Explorer 5. Nonetheless, it has only recently become a

NOTE

The term *AJAX* first appeared in an online article by Jesse James Garrett of Adaptive Path on February 18, 2005. It still appears here: http://www.adaptivepath.com/ideas/ajax-new-approach-web-applications.

popular way of developing applications because browsers that support it have become more common. Another name for this technique is *remote scripting*.

The JavaScript Client (Front End)

JavaScript traditionally only has one way of communicating with a server—submitting a form. Remote scripting allows for much more versatile communication with the server. The *A* in AJAX stands for *asynchronous*, which means that the browser (and the user) isn't left hanging while waiting for the server to respond. Here's how a typical AJAX request works:

1. The script creates an XMLHttpRequest object and sends it to the web server. The script can continue after sending the request.

2. The server responds by sending the contents of a file or the output of a server-side program.

3. When the response arrives from the server, a JavaScript function is triggered to act on the data.

4. Because the goal is a more responsive user interface, the script usually displays the data from the server using the DOM, eliminating the need for a page refresh.

In practice, this happens quickly, but even with a slow server, it can still work. Also, because the requests are asynchronous, more than one can be in progress at a time.

The Server-Side Script (Back End)

The part of an application that resides on the web server is known as the *back end*. The simplest back end is a static file on the server—JavaScript can request the file with XMLHttpRequest, and then read and act on its contents. More commonly, the back end is a server-side program running in a language such as PHP, Perl, or Ruby.

JavaScript can send data to a server-side program using GET or POST methods, the same two ways an HTML form works. In a GET request, the data is encoded in the URL that loads the program. In a POST request, it is sent separately and can contain more data.

XML

The *X* in AJAX stands for *XML* (Extensible Markup Language), the universal markup language upon which the latest versions of HTML are built. A server-side file or program can send data in XML format, and JavaScript can act on the data using its methods for working with XML. These are similar to the DOM methods you've already used—for example, you can use the `getElementsByTagName()` method to find elements with a particular tag in the data.

Keep in mind that XML is just one way to send data, and not always the easiest. The server could just as easily send plain text, which the script could display, or HTML, which the script could insert into the page using the `innerHTML` property. Some programmers have even used server-side scripts to return data in JavaScript format, which can be easily executed using the `eval` function.

Popular Examples of AJAX

Although typical HTML and JavaScript is used to build web pages and sites, AJAX techniques often result in *web applications*—web-based services that perform work for the user. Here are a few well-known examples of AJAX:

▶ Google's Gmail mail client (http://mail.google.com/) uses AJAX to make a fast-responding email application. You can delete messages and perform other tasks without waiting for a new page to load.

▶ Amazon.com uses AJAX for some functions. For example, if you click on one of the Yes/No voting buttons for a product comment, it sends your vote to the server and a message appears next to the button thanking you, all without loading a page.

▶ Digg (http://www.digg.com) is a site where users can submit news stories and vote to determine which ones are displayed on the front page. The voting happens inside the page next to each story.

These are just a few examples. Subtle bits of remote scripting are appearing all over the Web, and you might not even notice them—you'll just be annoyed a little bit less often at waiting for a page to load.

NOTE

JSON (JavaScript Object Notation) takes the idea of encoding data in JavaScript and formalizes it. See http://www.json.org/ for details and code examples in many languages.

NOTE

See Chapter 22, "Using Third-Party Libraries," for information about using third-party libraries with JavaScript.

AJAX Frameworks and Libraries

Because remote scripting can be complicated, especially considering the browser differences you'll learn about later this chapter, several frameworks and libraries have been developed to simplify AJAX programming.

For starters, three of the libraries described earlier in this book, JQuery, Prototype, and Script.aculo.us, include functions to simplify remote scripting. There are also some dedicated libraries for languages such as PHP, Python, and Ruby.

Some libraries are designed to add server-side functions to JavaScript, whereas others are designed to add JavaScript interactivity to a language like PHP. You'll build a simple library later this chapter that will be used to handle the remote scripting functions for this chapter's examples.

Limitations of AJAX

Remote scripting is a relatively new technology, so there are some things it can't do, and some things to watch out for. Here are some of the limitations and potential problems of AJAX:

- ▶ The script and the XML data or server-side program it requests data from must be on the same domain.

- ▶ Some older browsers and some less common browsers (such as mobile browsers) don't support XMLHttpRequest, so you can't count on its availability for all users.

- ▶ Requiring AJAX might compromise the accessibility of a site for disabled users.

- ▶ Users may still be accustomed to seeing a new page load each time they change something, so there might be a learning curve for them to understand an AJAX application.

As with other advanced uses of JavaScript, the best approach is to be unobtrusive—make sure there's still a way to use the site without AJAX support if possible, and use feature sensing to prevent errors on browsers that don't support it. See Chapter 21, "Using Unobtrusive JavaScript," for more details.

Using XMLHttpRequest

You will now look at how to use XMLHttpRequest to communicate with a server. This might seem a bit complex, but the process is the same for any request. Later, you will create a reusable code library to simplify this process.

Creating a Request

The first step is to create an XMLHttpRequest object. To do this, you use the new keyword, as with other JavaScript objects. The following statement creates a request object in some browsers:

```
ajaxreq = new XMLHttpRequest();
```

The previous example works with Firefox, Chrome, Internet Explorer 7 and 8, and other modern browsers, but not with Internet Explorer 5 or 6. It is up to you whether you want to support these browsers or not because their percentages of use are very low. However, some institutions might be stuck with a lot of IE6 browsers installed at workstations, so your mileage may vary.

From this point forward, the sample code will only support IE7 and beyond (modern browsers), but if you want to support these old browsers, you have to use ActiveX syntax:

```
ajaxreq = new ActiveXObject("Microsoft.XMLHTTP");
```

The library section later this chapter demonstrates how to use the correct method depending on the browser in use. In either case, the variable you use (ajaxreq in the example) stores the XMLHttpRequest object. You'll use the methods of this object to open and send a request, as explained in the following sections.

Opening a URL

The open() method of the XMLHttpRequest object specifies the filename as well as the method in which data will be sent to the server: GET or POST. These are the same methods supported by web forms.

```
ajaxreq.open("GET","filename");
```

For the GET method, the data you send is included in the URL. For example, this command opens the search.php program and sends the value "John" for the query parameter:

```
ajaxreq.open("GET","search.php?query=John");
```

Sending the Request

You use the send() method of the XMLHttpRequest object to send the request to the server. If you are using the POST method, the data to send is the argument for send(). For a GET request, you can use the null value instead:

```
ajaxreq.send(null);
```

Awaiting a Response

After the request is sent, your script will continue without waiting for a result. Because the result could come at any time, you can detect it with an event handler. The XMLHttpRequest object has an onreadystatechange event handler for this purpose. You can create a function to deal with the response and set it as the handler for this event:

```
ajaxreq.onreadystatechange = MyFunc;
```

The request object has a property, readyState, that indicates its status, and this event is triggered whenever the readyState property changes. The values of readyState range from 0 for a new request to 4 for a complete request, so your event-handling function usually needs to watch for a value of 4.

Although the request is complete, it might not have been successful. The status property is set to 200 if the request succeeded or an error code if it failed. The statusText property stores a text explanation of the error or "OK" for success.

Interpreting the Response Data

When the readyState property reaches 4 and the request is complete, the data returned from the server is available to your script in two properties: responseText is the response in raw text form, and responseXML is the response as an XML object. If the data was not in XML format, only the text property will be available.

JavaScript's DOM methods are meant to work on XML, so you can use them with the responseXML property. Later this chapter, you'll use the getElementsByTagName() method to extract data from XML.

Creating a Simple AJAX Library

You should be aware by now that AJAX requests can be a bit complex. To make things easier, you can create an AJAX library. This is a JavaScript file that provides functions that handle making a request and receiving the result, which you can reuse any time you need AJAX functions.

This library will be used in the two examples later this chapter. Listing 24.1 shows the complete AJAX library, including the special case for older browsers.

LISTING 24.1   The AJAX Library

```
// global variables to keep track of the request
// and the function to call when done
var ajaxreq=false, ajaxCallback;
// ajaxRequest: Sets up a request
function ajaxRequest(filename) {
   try {
    // Firefox / IE7 / Others
    ajaxreq= new XMLHttpRequest();
   } catch (error) {
    try {
      // IE 5 / IE 6
      ajaxreq = new ActiveXObject("Microsoft.XMLHTTP");
    } catch (error) {
      return false;
    }
   }
   ajaxreq.open("GET", filename);
   ajaxreq.onreadystatechange = ajaxResponse;
   ajaxreq.send(null);
}
// ajaxResponse: Waits for response and calls a function
function ajaxResponse() {
   if (ajaxreq.readyState !=4) return;
   if (ajaxreq.status==200) {
      // if the request succeeded...
      if (ajaxCallback) ajaxCallback();
   } else alert("Request failed: " + ajaxreq.statusText);
   return true;
}
```

The following sections explain how this library works and how to use it.

The `ajaxRequest` Function

The `ajaxRequest` function handles all the steps necessary to create and send an `XMLHttpRequest`. First, it creates the `XMLHttpRequest` object. As noted before, this requires a different command for older browsers and will cause an error if the wrong one executes, so `try` and `catch` are used to create the request. First the standard method is used, and if it causes an error, the ActiveX method is tried. If that also causes an error, the `ajaxreq` variable is set to `false` to indicate that AJAX is unsupported.

The `ajaxResponse` Function

The `ajaxResponse` function is used as the `onreadystatechange` event handler. This function first checks the `readyState` property for a value of `4`. If it has a different value, the function returns without doing anything.

Next, it checks the `status` property for a value of `200`, which indicates the request was successful. If so, it runs the function stored in the `ajaxCallback` variable. If not, it displays the error message in an alert box.

Using the Library

To use this library, follow these steps:

1. Save the library file as `ajax.js` in the same folder as your HTML documents and scripts.

2. Include the script in your document with a `<script src>` tag. It should be included before any other scripts that use its features.

3. In your script, create a function to be called when the request is complete and set the `ajaxCallback` variable to the function.

4. Call the `ajaxRequest()` function. Its parameter is the filename of the server-side program or file. (This library supports `GET` requests only, so you don't need to specify the method.)

5. Your function specified in `ajaxCallback` will be called when the request completes successfully, and the global variable `ajaxreq` will store the data in its `responseXML` and `responseText` properties.

The two remaining examples in this chapter make use of this library to create AJAX applications.

Creating an AJAX Quiz Using the Library

Now that you have a reusable AJAX library, you can use it to create JavaScript applications that take advantage of remote scripting. This first example displays quiz questions on a page and prompts you for the answers.

Rather than including the questions in the script, this example reads the quiz questions and answers from an XML file on the server as a demonstration of AJAX.

The HTML File

The HTML for this example is straightforward. It defines a simple form with an Answer field and a Submit button, along with some hooks for the script. The HTML for this example is shown in Listing 24.2.

LISTING 24.2   The HTML File for the Quiz Example

```
<?xml version="1.0" encoding="UTF-8"?>
<!DOCTYPE html PUBLIC "-//W3C//DTD XHTML 1.1//EN"
  "http://www.w3.org/TR/xhtml11/DTD/xhtml11.dtd">

<html xmlns="http://www.w3.org/1999/xhtml" xml:lang="en">
  <head>
    <title>Ajax Quiz Test</title>
    <script type="text/javascript" src="ajax.js"></script>
  </head>
  <body>
    <h1>Ajax Quiz Example</h1>
    <form method="post" action="">
    <p><input type="button" value="Start the Quiz" id="startq" /></p>
    <p><strong>Question:</strong>
    <span id="question">[Press Button to Start Quiz]</span></p>
    <p><strong>Answer:</strong>
    <input type="text" name="answer" id="answer" /></p>
    <p><input type="button" value="Submit Answer" id="submit" /></p>
    </form>
    <script type="text/javascript" src="quiz.js"></script>
  </body>
</html>
```

This HTML file includes the following elements:

▶ The <script> tag in the <head> section includes the AJAX library you created in the previous section from the ajax.js file.

CAUTION

Unlike most of the scripts in this book, this example requires a web server. It will not work on a local machine due to browsers' security restrictions on remote scripting.

▶ The `<script>` tag in the `<body>` section includes the `quiz.js` file, which will contain the quiz script.

▶ The `<span id="question">` tag sets up a place for the question to be inserted by the script.

▶ The text field with the `id` value `"answer"` is where the user will answer the question.

▶ The button with the `id` value `"submit"` will submit an answer.

▶ The button with the `id` value `"startq"` will start the quiz.

You can test the HTML document at this time by placing the file on your web server and accessing it via the URL, but the buttons won't work until you add the XML and JavaScript files, as you'll learn about in the next two sections.

The XML File

The XML file for the quiz is shown in Listing 24.3. I've filled it with a few JavaScript questions, but it could easily be adapted for another purpose.

LISTING 24.3   The XML File Containing the Quiz Questions and Answers

```
<?xml version="1.0" ?>
<questions>
    <q>What DOM object contains URL information for the window?</q>
    <a>location</a>
    <q>Which method of the document object finds the
       object for an element?</q>
    <a>getElementById</a>
    <q>If you declare a variable outside a function,
       is it global or local?</q>
    <a>global</a>
    <q>What is the formal standard for the JavaScript language
called?</q>
    <a>ECMAScript</a>
</questions>
```

The `<questions>` tag encloses the entire file and each question and answer are enclosed in `<q>` and `<a>` tags. Remember, this is XML, not HTML— these are not standard HTML tags, but tags that were created for this example. Because this file will be used only by your script, it does not need to follow a standard format.

To use this file, save it as `questions.xml` in the same folder as the HTML document. It will be loaded by the script you create in the next section.

Of course, with a quiz this small, you could have made things easier by storing the questions and answers in a JavaScript array. But imagine a much larger quiz, with thousands of questions, or a server-side program that pulls questions from a database, or even a hundred different files with different quizzes to choose from, and you can see the benefit of using a separate XML file.

The JavaScript File

Because you have a separate library to handle the complexities of making an AJAX request and receiving the response, the script for this example only needs to deal with the action for the quiz itself. Listing 24.4 shows the JavaScript file for this example.

LISTING 24.4   The JavaScript File for the Quiz Example

```
// global variable qn is the current question number
var qn=0;
// load the questions from the XML file
function getQuestions() {
   obj=document.getElementById("question");
   obj.firstChild.nodeValue="(please wait)";
   ajaxCallback = nextQuestion;
   ajaxRequest("questions.xml");
}
// display the next question
function nextQuestion() {
   questions = ajaxreq.responseXML.getElementsByTagName("q");
   obj=document.getElementById("question");
   if (qn < questions.length) {
      q = questions[qn].firstChild.nodeValue;
      obj.firstChild.nodeValue=q;
   } else {
      obj.firstChild.nodeValue="(no more questions)";
   }
}
// check the user's answer
function checkAnswer() {
   answers = ajaxreq.responseXML.getElementsByTagName("a");
   a = answers[qn].firstChild.nodeValue;
   answerfield = document.getElementById("answer");
   if (a == answerfield.value) {
      alert("Correct!");
   }
   else {
      alert("Incorrect. The correct answer is: " + a);
```

LISTING 24.4   Continued

```
    }
    qn = qn + 1;
    answerfield.value="";
    nextQuestion();
}
// Set up the event handlers for the buttons
obj=document.getElementById("startq");
obj.onclick=getQuestions;
ans=document.getElementById("submit");
ans.onclick=checkAnswer;
```

This script consists of the following:

▶ The first `var` statement defines a global variable, qn, which will keep track of which question is currently displayed. It is initially set to zero for the first question.

▶ The `getQuestions()` function is called when the user clicks the Start Quiz button. This function uses the AJAX library to request the contents of the `questions.xml` file. It sets the `ajaxCallback` variable to the `nextQuestion()` function.

▶ The `nextQuestion()` function is called when the AJAX request is complete. This function uses the `getElementsByTagName()` method on the `responseXML` property to find all the questions (`<q>` tags) and store them in the `questions` array.

▶ The `checkAnswer()` function is called when the user submits an answer. It uses `getElementsByTagName()` to store the answers (`<a>` tags) in the `answers` array, and then compares the answer for the current question with the user's answer and displays an alert indicating whether they were right or wrong.

▶ The script commands after this function set up two event handlers. One attaches the `getQuestions()` function to the Start Quiz button to set up the quiz; the other attaches the `checkAnswer()` function to the Submit button.

Testing the Quiz

To try this example, you'll need all four files in the same folder: ajax.js (the AJAX library), quiz.js (the quiz functions), questions.xml (the questions), and the HTML document. All but the HTML document need to have the correct filenames so they will work correctly. Also, remember that because it uses AJAX, this example requires a web server.

Figure 24.1 shows the quiz in action. The second question has just been answered.

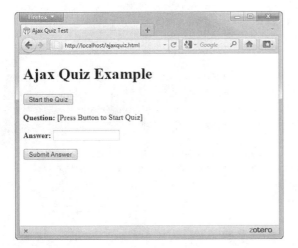

FIGURE 24.1
The quiz example loaded in a web browser.

Debugging AJAX Applications

Dealing with remote scripting means working with several languages at once—JavaScript, server-side languages such as PHP, XML, and of course HTML. Thus, when you find an error, it can be difficult to track down. Here are some tips for debugging AJAX applications:

▶ Be sure all filenames are correct and that all files for your application are in the same folder on the server.

▶ If you are using a server-side language, test it without the script: Load it in the browser and make sure it works; try passing variables to it in the URL and checking the results.

▶ Check the `statusText` property for the results of your request—an `alert` message is helpful here. It is often a clear message such as "File not found" that might explain the problem.

▶ If you're using a third-party AJAX library, check its documentation— many libraries have built-in debugging features you can enable to examine what's going on.

Making a Live Search Form

CAUTION

Once again, because it uses AJAX, this example requires a web server. You'll also need PHP to be installed, which it is by default by the vast majority of hosting services.

One of the most impressive demonstrations of AJAX is *live search*: Whereas a normal search form requires that you click a button and wait for a page to load to see the results, a live search displays results within the page immediately as you type in the search field. As you type letters or press the backspace key, the results are updated instantly to make it easy to find the result you need.

Using the AJAX library you created earlier, live search is not too hard to implement. This example will use a PHP program on the server to provide the search results, and can be easily adapted to any search application.

The HTML Form

The HTML for this example simply defines a search field and leaves some room for the dynamic results. The HTML document is shown in Listing 24.5.

LISTING 24.5   The HTML File for the Live Search Example

```
<?xml version="1.0" encoding="UTF-8"?>
<!DOCTYPE html PUBLIC "-//W3C//DTD XHTML 1.1//EN"
  "http://www.w3.org/TR/xhtml11/DTD/xhtml11.dtd">

<html xmlns="http://www.w3.org/1999/xhtml" xml:lang="en">
  <head>
    <title>Ajax Live Search Example</title>
    <script type="text/javascript" src="ajax.js"></script>
  </head>
  <body>
    <h1>Ajax Live Search Example</h1>
    <form method="get" action="">
     <p><strong>Search for:</strong>
       <input type="text" size="40" id="searchlive" /></p>
      <div id="results">
      <ul id="list">
        <li>[Search results will display here.]</li>
      </ul>
      </div>
     </form>
    <script type="text/javascript" src="search.js"></script>
  </body>
</html>
```

This HTML document includes the following:

▶ The <script> tag in the <head> section includes the AJAX library, ajax.js.

▶ The <script> tag in the <body> section includes the search.js script, which you'll create next.

▶ The `<input>` element with the id value `"searchlive"` is where you'll type your search query.

▶ The `<div>` element with the id value `"results"` will act as a container for the dynamically fetched results. A bulleted list is created with a `<ul>` tag; this will be replaced with a list of results when you start typing.

The PHP Back End

Next, you'll need a server-side program to produce the search results. This PHP program includes a list of names stored in an array. It will respond to a JavaScript query with the names that match what the user has typed so far. The names will be returned in XML format. For example, here is the output of the PHP program when searching for "smith":

```
<names>
<name>John Smith</name>
<name>Jane Smith</name>
</names>
```

Although the list of names is stored within the PHP program here for simplicity, in a real application it would more likely be stored in a database—and this script could easily be adapted to work with a database containing thousands of names. The PHP program is shown in Listing 24.6.

LISTING 24.6 The PHP Code for the Live Search Example

```php
<?php
  header("Content-type: text/xml");
  $names = array (
    "John Smith", "John Jones", "Jane Smith", "Jane Tillman",
    "Abraham Lincoln", "Sally Johnson", "Kilgore Trout",
    "Bob Atkinson", "Joe Cool", "Dorothy Barnes",
    "Elizabeth Carlson", "Frank Dixon", "Gertrude East",
    "Harvey Frank", "Inigo Montoya", "Jeff Austin",
    "Lynn Arlington", "Michael Washington", "Nancy West" );
if (!$query) {
    $query=$_GET['query'];
}
echo "<?xml version=\"1.0\" ?>\n";
echo "<names>\n";
while (list($k,$v)=each($names)) {
    if (stristr($v,$query)) {
       echo "<name>$v</name>\n";
    }
}
echo "</names>\n";
?>
```

TRY IT YOURSELF ▼

Making a Live Search Form

continued

▼ TRY IT YOURSELF

Making a Live Search Form

continued

NOTE

If you want to learn more about PHP, try *Sams Teach Yourself PHP, MySQL and Apache All-in-One* (ISBN: 067232976X).

This chapter is too small to teach you PHP, but here's a summary of how this program works:

▶ The `header` statement sends a header indicating that the output is in XML format. This is required for `XMLHttpRequest` to correctly use the `responseXML` property.

▶ The `$names` array stores the list of names. You can use a much longer list of names without changing the rest of the code.

▶ The program looks for a `GET` variable called `query` and uses a loop to output all the names that match the query.

▶ Because PHP can be embedded in an HTML file, the `<?php` and `?>` tags indicate that the code between them should be interpreted as PHP.

Save the PHP program as search.php in the same folder as the HTML file. You can test it by typing a query such as **search.php?query=John** in the browser's URL field. Use the View Source command to view the XML result.

The JavaScript Front End

Finally, the JavaScript for this example is shown in Listing 24.7.

LISTING 24.7   The JavaScript File for the Live Search Example

```javascript
// global variable to manage the timeout
var t;
// Start a timeout with each keypress
function StartSearch() {
    if (t) window.clearTimeout(t);
    t = window.setTimeout("LiveSearch()",200);
}
// Perform the search
function LiveSearch() {
    // assemble the PHP filename
    query = document.getElementById("searchlive").value;
    filename = "search.php?query=" + query;
    // DisplayResults will handle the Ajax response
    ajaxCallback = DisplayResults;
    // Send the Ajax request
    ajaxRequest(filename);
}
// Display search results
function DisplayResults() {
    // remove old list
    ul = document.getElementById("list");
    div = document.getElementById("results");
    div.removeChild(ul);
```

TRY IT YOURSELF ▼

Making a Live Search Form

continued

LISTING 24.7   Continued

```
   // make a new list
   ul = document.createElement("ul");
   ul.id="list";
   names = ajaxreq.responseXML.getElementsByTagName("name");
   for (i = 0; i < names.length; i++) {
      li = document.createElement("li");
      name = names[i].firstChild.nodeValue;
      text = document.createTextNode(name);
      li.appendChild(text);
      ul.appendChild(li);
   }
   if (names.length==0) {
      li = document.createElement("li");
      li.appendChild(document.createTextNode("No results"));
      ul.appendChild(li);
   }
   // display the new list
   div.appendChild(ul);
}
// set up event handler
obj=document.getElementById("searchlive");
obj.onkeydown = StartSearch;
```

This script includes the following components:

- ▶ A global variable, t, is defined. This will store a pointer to the timeout used later in the script.

- ▶ The StartSearch() function is called when the user presses a key. This function uses setTimeout() to call the LiveSearch() function after a 200-millisecond delay. The delay is necessary so that the key the user types has time to appear in the search field.

- ▶ The LiveSearch() function assembles a filename that combines search.php with the query in the search field and launches an AJAX request using the library's ajaxRequest() function.

- ▶ The DisplayResults() function is called when the AJAX request is complete. It deletes the bulleted list from the <div id="results"> section, and then assembles a new list using the W3C DOM and the AJAX results. If there were no results, it displays a "No results" message in the list.

- ▶ The final lines of the script set the StartSearch() function up as an event handler for the onkeydown event of the search field.

▼ TRY IT YOURSELF

Making a Live Search Form

continued

FIGURE 24.2
The live search example as displayed in the browser.

Making It All Work

To try this example, you'll need three files on a web server: ajax.js (the library), search.js (the search script), and the HTML file. Figure 24.2 shows this example in action.

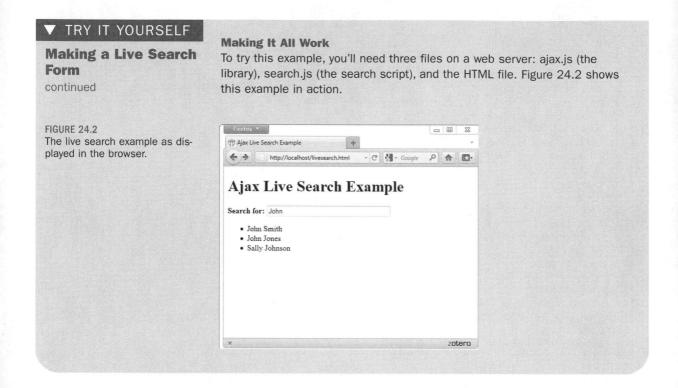

Summary

In this chapter, you've learned how AJAX, or remote scripting, allows JavaScript to communicate with a web server. You created a reusable AJAX library that can be used to create any number of AJAX applications, and you created an example using an XML file. Finally, you created a live search form using AJAX and PHP.

Q&A

Q. What happens if the server is slow, or never responds to the request?

A. This is another reason you should use AJAX as an optional feature—whether caused by the server or by the user's connection, there will be times when a request is slow to respond or never responds. In this case, the callback function will be called late or not at all. This can cause trouble with overlapping requests; for example, in the live search example, an erratic server might cause the responses for the first few characters typed to come in a few seconds apart, confusing the user. You can remedy this by checking the `readyState` property to make sure a request is not already in progress before you start another one.

Q. In the live search example, why is the `onkeydown` event handler necessary? Wouldn't the `onchange` event be easier to use?

A. Although `onchange` tells you when a form field has changed, it is not triggered until the user moves on to a different field—it doesn't work for "live" search, so you have to watch for key presses instead. The `onkeypress` handler would work, but in some browsers it doesn't detect the Backspace key, and it's nice to have the search update when you backspace to shorten the query.

Workshop

The workshop contains quiz questions and exercises to help you solidify your understanding of the material covered. Try to answer all questions before looking at the "Answers" section that follows.

Quiz

1. Which of the following is the *A* in *AJAX*?

    a. Advanced

    b. Asynchronous

    c. Application

2. Which property of an `XMLHttpRequest` object indicates whether the request was successful?

   a. `status`

   b. `readyState`

   c. `success`

3. True or False: To support old versions of Internet Explorer, you must create an ActiveX object rather than an `XMLHttpRequest` object when using AJAX.

Answers

1. b. AJAX stands for Asynchronous JavaScript and XML.

2. a. The `status` property indicates whether the request was successful; `readyState` indicates whether the request is complete, but does not indicate success.

3. True. Internet Explorer 5 and 6 require ActiveX, whereas versions of Internet Explorer after version 7 support the `XMLHttpRequest` object natively.

Exercises

► Build your own XML file of questions and answers on your favorite topic and try it with the quiz example.

► Use the AJAX library to add an AJAX feature to your site or create a simple example of your own.

CHAPTER 25
Creating Print-Friendly Web Pages

If you've ever used an online mapping tool such as MapQuest or Google Maps, you've no doubt experienced the need to print a web page. Similarly, the proliferation of coupons offered only online, purchase receipts for items from online resellers, and web-based flight check-in and the ability to print boarding passes from your home computer have increased the need for print-friendly pages. It's true, not all web pages are designed entirely for viewing on the screen!

You might not realize this, but it's possible to specifically design and offer print-friendly versions of your pages for users who want to print a copy for offline reading—something that Google Maps offers after showing you the on-screen version of content. CSS makes it easy to create web pages that will change appearance based on how they are viewed. In this chapter, you learn how to create such pages.

WHAT YOU'LL LEARN IN THIS CHAPTER:

► What makes a page print-friendly
► How to apply a media-specific style sheet
► How to create a style sheet for print pages
► How to view your web page in print preview mode

▼ TRY IT YOURSELF

Reviewing Your Content for Print-Friendliness

As you work your way through this chapter, consider any of your own web pages that might look good in print. Then think about what you would want to change about them to make them look even better on the printed page. Here are some ideas to consider:

▶ Even against warnings in previous chapters, do you have pages that use a patterned background image or an unusual background color with contrasting text? This kind of page can be difficult to print because of the background, so you might consider offering a print version of the page that doesn't use a custom background image or color and simply uses black text. When preparing a page for printing, stick to black text on a white background if possible.

▶ Do your pages include lots of links? If so, you might consider changing the appearance of links for printing so that they don't stand out— remove any underlining, for example. Remember, you can't click a piece of paper!

▶ Finally, is every image on your page absolutely essential? Colorful images cost valuable ink to print on most printers, so you might consider leaving some, if not all, images out of your print-friendly pages.

What Makes a Page Print-Friendly?

It's important to point out that some web pages are print-friendly already. If your pages use white backgrounds with dark contrasting text and few images, you might not even need to concern yourself with a special print-friendly version. On the other hand, pages with dark backgrounds, dynamic links, and several images might prove to be unwieldy for the average printer.

The main things to keep in mind as you consider what it takes to make your pages more print-friendly are the limitations imposed by the medium. In other words, what is it about a printed page that makes it uniquely different from a computer screen? The obvious difference is size—a printed page is at a fixed size, typically 8 ½ by 11 inches, whereas the size of screens can vary greatly. In addition to size, printed pages also have color limitations (even on color printers). Very few users want to waste the ink required to print a full-color background when they really just want to print the text on the page.

Most users also aren't interested in printing more than the text that serves as the focus on the page. For example, Figure 25.1 shows a travel route mapped out from Independence, Missouri to Oregon City, Oregon (an approximation of the historic Oregon Trail).

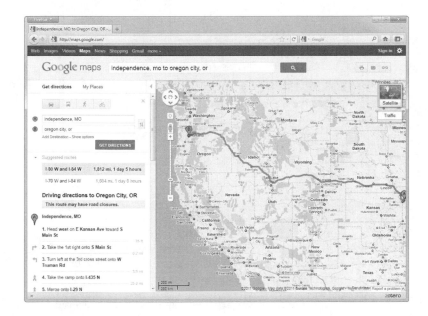

FIGURE 25.1
This page isn't very print-friendly due to the form inputs and large image with its own display controls.

The page shown in Figure 25.1 contains form input fields, a large image that can itself be controlled (moved, zoomed, and so on), and other ancillary items that you come to expect in web content. Above the map appears a set of Actions that you can perform, one of which is a link to print the page. At this point, you might wonder why you can't just click the Print button on your web browser. You certainly can do this, but that command prints the page as it is shown on your screen—complete with the form input fields and graphical elements, when all you really want to know are the turns you need to make when driving this route.

If you click the Print link in the body of the page, your web browser will display a page (see Figure 25.2) that Google has formatted specifically to be printed.

As shown in the figure, the print-friendly version of this page represents a significant improvement over the original, at least from the perspective of a printer. All the form inputs and images were removed.

FIGURE 25.2
The print-friendly version of the page isolates the text of the driving instructions so that it can be printed by itself.

NOTE

If the font of printer-specific pages is sans serif, some web designers recommend changing the font to serif, which is considered easier to read in print. If you use a sans serif font on your pages, it's up to you to decide whether you want to maintain the core look of a page when it's printed—which means you don't change the font to serif.

In the spirit of giving you a better grasp on what, specifically, to consider as you move toward creating print-friendly pages, following is a list of changes you should at least consider:

▶ Remove the background of the page, which effectively gives the printed page a white background.

▶ Change text colors to black; it's okay to have some color in the text but black is preferred.

▶ Make sure that the font size is large enough that the page can be easily read when printed. You might have to test some different sizes.

▶ Remove link formatting or simply revert to a basic underlined link. Some designers like to retain an underline just so that a visitor knows that a link exists in the original page.

▶ Remove any and all nonessential images. This typically includes any images that aren't critical to conveying the content in the page, such as navigation buttons, most ads, and animated images.

In addition to these suggestions, you might find it useful to add a byline with information about the author of the page, along with a URL for the page and copyright information. This is information that could potentially get lost after the user leaves your website and has only the printed version of the page in hand.

You probably don't need to make these changes to your pages just yet. The idea is to plant the seed of what constitutes a print-friendly page so that you can do a better job of creating a printer-specific style sheet. That's right: It's possible to create a style sheet that is applied to pages only when they are printed. You learn this in the next section.

Applying a Media-Specific Style Sheet

Figure 25.1 showed how a small printer icon with a link enables you to view a special print-friendly version of a page. This type of icon is popular on many news sites, and it's an important feature because you otherwise might not want to hassle with printing a page and wasting paper and ink on the graphics and ads that accompany articles. Although the printer icon and link approach is intuitive and works great, there is an option that does not require these specific links to print-friendly content.

This option involves using a print-specific style sheet that is automatically applied to a page when the user elects to print the page. CSS supports the concept of *media-specific style sheets*, which are style sheets that target a particular medium, such as the screen or printer. CSS doesn't stop with those two forms of media, however. Check out the following list of specific media types that CSS 2 enables you to support with a unique style sheet:

▶ **all**—For all devices

▶ **aural**—For speech synthesizers (called *speech* in CSS 1 media types)

▶ **braille**—For Braille tactile feedback devices

▶ **embossed**—For paged Braille printers

▶ **handheld**—For handheld devices with limited screen size and bandwidth

▶ **print**—For printed material and documents viewed on screen in Print Preview mode

▶ **projection**—For projected presentations

▶ **screen**—For color computer screens

▶ **tty**—For devices using a fixed-pitch character grid (such as a terminal, teletype, or handheld devices with limited displays)

▶ **tv**—For television-type devices, which are typically low resolution, color and have limited ability to scroll

Perhaps the most interesting of these media is the aural type, which allows for web pages that can be read aloud or otherwise listened to. Clearly, the architects of CSS envision a Web with a much broader reach than we currently think of as we design pages primarily for computer screens. Although you probably don't need to worry too much about aural web page design just yet, it serves as a good heads-up as to what might be on the horizon.

The good news about style sheets as applied to other media is that they don't require you to learn anything new. Okay, maybe in the case of aural web pages you'll need to learn a few new tricks, but for now you can use the same style properties you've already learned to create print-specific style sheets. The trick is knowing how to apply a style sheet for a particular medium.

If you recall, the `<link />` tag is used to link an external style sheet to a web page. This tag supports an attribute named `media` that you haven't seen yet. This attribute is used to specify the name of the medium to which the style sheet applies. By default, this attribute is set to `all`, which means that an external style sheet will be used for all media if you don't specify otherwise. The other acceptable attribute values correspond to the list of media provided in the previous list.

Establishing a print-specific style sheet for a web page involves using two `<link />` tags, one for the printer and one for each remaining medium. Following is code that handles this task:

```
<link rel="stylesheet" type="text/css" href="standard.css" media="all" />
<link rel="stylesheet" type="text/css" href="for_print.css" media="print" />
```

In this example, two style sheets are linked into a web page. The first sheet targets all media by setting the `media` attribute to `all`. If you did nothing else, the `standard.css` style sheet would apply to all media. However, the presence of the second style sheet results in the `for_print.css` style sheet being used to print the page.

You can specify multiple media types in a single `<link />` tag by separating the types with a comma, like this:

```
<link rel="stylesheet" type="text/css" href="for_pp.css"
      media="print, projector" />
```

This code results in the `for_pp.css` style sheet applying solely to the `print` and `projector` media types and nothing else.

NOTE

You can also use the `@import` command to link media-specific style sheets. For example, the following code works just like the previous `<link />` code:

```
@import url(player.css) all;
@import url(player_print.css)
print;
```

CAUTION

You might have been tempted to specify `media="screen"` in the first linked style sheet in the previous code. Although this would work for viewing the page in a normal web browser, it would cause problems if a user viewed the page using a handheld browser or any of the other types of media. In other words, a style sheet applies only to the specific media types mentioned in the `media` attribute and nothing more.

Designing a Style Sheet for Print Pages

Using the recommended list of modifications required for a print-friendly web page, it's time to take a stab at creating a print-friendly style sheet. Let's first look at a page that is displayed using a normal (screen) style sheet (see Figure 25.3).

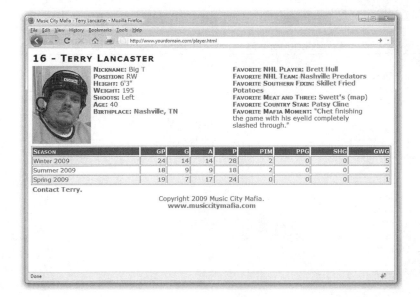

FIGURE 25.3
A CSS-styled page as viewed in a normal web browser.

TIP

You can specify a media type for your style sheets even if you aren't linking to external versions. The `<style>` tag also uses the same `media` attribute as the `<link />` tag.

This figure reveals how the page looks in a normal web browser. In reality, this page isn't too far from being print-ready, but it could still benefit from some improvements.

The following changes can help make this web page more print-friendly:

▶ Change the color of all text to black.

▶ Remove link formatting (bold and color).

▶ Stack the two player information sections vertically because they are unlikely to fit horizontally on the printed page.

▶ Remove the contact link entirely.

The first two changes to the normal style sheet are straightforward; they primarily involve changing or undoing existing styles. The third change,

however, requires a bit of thought. Because you know that printed pages
are a fixed size, you should use absolute positioning for all the elements on
the printed page. This makes it much easier to place the content sections
exactly where you want them. Finally, the last item on the list is very easy
to accommodate by simply setting the `display` style property of the `con-
tact` element to `none`.

Listing 25.1 shows the CSS code for the `player_print.css` style sheet,
which incorporates these changes into a style sheet that is perfectly suited
for printing hockey player pages.

LISTING 25.1   CSS Code for the Print-Specific Hockey Player Style Sheet

```
body {
  font-family:Verdana, Arial;
  font-size:12pt;
  color:black;
}

div {
  padding:3px;
}

div.title {
  font-size:18pt;
  font-weight:bold;
  font-variant:small-caps;
  letter-spacing:2px;
  position:absolute;
  left:0in;
  top:0in;
}

div.image {
  position:absolute;
  left:0in;
  top:0.5in;
}

div.info {
  position:absolute;
  left:1.75in;
  top:0.5in;
}

div.favorites {
  position:absolute;
  left:1.75in;
  top:2in;
}
```

LISTING 25.1   Continued

```
div.footer {
  position:absolute;
  text-align:left;
  left:0in;
  top:9in;
}

table.stats {
  width:100%;
  text-align:right;
  font-size:11pt;
  position:absolute;
  left:0in;
  top:3.75in;
}

div.contact {
  display:none;
}

.label {
  font-weight:bold;
  font-variant:small-caps;
}

tr.heading {
  font-variant:small-caps;
  background-color:black;
  color:white;
}

tr.light {
  background-color:white;
}

tr.dark {
  background-color:#EEEEEE;
}

th.season, td.season {
  text-align:left;
}

a, a:link, a:visited {
  color:black;
  font-weight:normal;
  text-decoration:none;
}
```

Probably the neatest thing about this code is how it uses inches (in) as the unit of measure for all the absolute positioning code. This makes sense when you consider that we think of printed pages in terms of inches, not pixels. If you study the code carefully, you'll notice that the text is all black, all special style formatting has been removed from the links, and content sections are now absolutely positioned (so that they appear exactly where you want them).

Viewing a Web Page in Print Preview

Figure 25.4 shows the print-friendly version of a hockey player page as it appears in a browser's Print Preview window.

FIGURE 25.4
You can use Print Preview to view the print-friendly version of a web page before you print it.

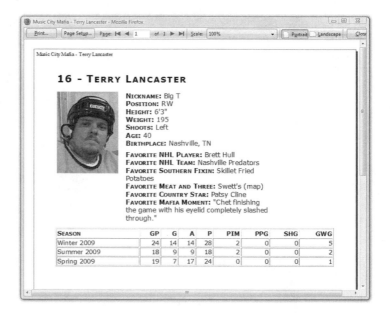

If Figure 25.4 had shown the entire page—all 11 inches of height and then some—you would have noticed that the print-friendly version of the page now includes the footer at the very bottom of the page (see Figure 25.5).

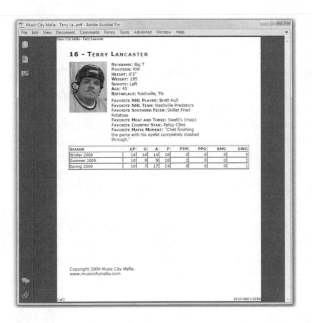

Just to show you how print-friendly pages can be used in a practical situation, check out Figure 25.5. This figure shows the same hockey player page as a PDF document that can be viewed in Adobe Acrobat Reader.

Adobe's virtual printer can be used to "print" the hockey player web page to a PDF document. You might also find PDF converters such as DoPDF (http://www.dopdf.com/) will work for you for at a lower cost than the Adobe Acrobat software. Printing to a PDF effectively creates a version of the print-friendly web page in a format that can be easily shared electronically for printing.

NOTE

To learn more about Acrobat, visit http://www.adobe.com/products/acrobat/.

Summary

This chapter focused on a practical application of CSS that solves a common need: printing web pages. You began the chapter by learning what exactly constitutes a print-friendly web page. From there, you learned about the mechanism built into CSS that allows a page to distinguish between the media in which it is being rendered, and then you learned how to select a style sheet accordingly. And finally, you created a print-specific style sheet that was used to style a page just for printing. Although most users prefer viewing a page on a large computer screen to reading it on paper, there are times when a printed web page is a necessity. Be sure to give your web page visitors the utmost in flexibility by offering print-friendly pages.

Q&A

Q. Can I use the `media` attribute of the `<link />` tag to create a style sheet specifically for viewing a web page on a handheld device?

A. Yes. By setting the `media` attribute of the `<link />` tag to `handheld`, you specifically target handheld devices with a style sheet. You will likely see all mobile websites eventually shift toward this approach to serve mobile pages, as opposed to using specialized markup languages such as WML (Wireless Markup Language).

Q. Do I still need to provide printer icons on my pages so that they can be printed?

A. No. The linked style sheet technique you learned about in this chapter allows you to support print-friendly web pages without any special links on the page. However, if you want to enable the user to view a print-friendly version of a page in a browser, you can link to another version of the page that uses the print-specific style sheet as its main (browser) style sheet. Or you can provide some "fine print" on the page that instructs the user to use the browser's Print Preview feature to view the print-friendly version of the page.

Workshop

The workshop contains quiz questions and activities to help you solidify your understanding of the material covered. Try to answer all questions before looking at the "Answers" section that follows.

Quiz

1. Does having a button to a print-friendly page mean the page is actually print-friendly?

2. What happens to an external style sheet that is linked to a page without any `media` attribute specified?

3. How would you link a style sheet named `freestyle.css` to a page so that it applies only when the page is viewed on a television?

Answers

1. No—you still have to link to a page with a specific style sheet applied to the content so that it appears print-friendly.

2. The `media` attribute assumes its default value of `all`, which causes the style sheet to target all media types.

3. Use the following in the `<head>` section of your HTML:

```
<link rel="stylesheet" type="text/css" href="freestyle.css" media="tv"
/>
```

Exercises

▶ Create a print-friendly style sheet for a page that has a fair number of colors and images. Be sure to add an extra `<link />` tag to the page that links in the print-specific style sheet.

▶ If you're feeling really ambitious, try using the `handheld` value of the `<link />` tag's `media` attribute to create a handheld-specific version of one of your web pages. The concept is the same as creating a print-friendly page, except in this case you're dealing with an extremely constrained screen size instead of a printed page. You can test the page by publishing it and then opening it on a mobile phone or handheld browser.

CHAPTER 26
Working with Web-Based Forms

To this point, pretty much everything in this book has focused on getting information out to others. But you can also use your web pages to gather information from the people who read them.

Web forms enable you to receive feedback, orders, or other information from the users who visit your web pages. If you've ever used a search engine such as Google, Yahoo!, or Bing, you're familiar with HTML forms—those single field entry forms with one button that, when pressed, give you all the information you are looking for and then some. Product order forms are also an extremely popular use of forms; if you've ordered anything from Amazon.com or purchased something from an eBay seller, you've used forms. In this chapter, you learn how to create your own forms, but you learn only how to create the front-end of those forms. Working with the back-end of forms requires the knowledge of a programming language and is beyond the scope of this book. However, in some instances JavaScript can play a role in form processing, such as rudimentary form content delivery and validation.

How HTML Forms Work

An HTML form is part of a web page that includes areas where users can enter information to be sent back to you, sent to another email address that you specify, sent to a database that you manage, or sent to another system altogether such as a third-party management system for your forms such as Salesforce.com.

Before you learn the HTML tags that are used to make your own forms, you should at least conceptually understand how the information from those forms makes its way back to you. The actual behind-the-scenes (the *server-side*

NOTE

PHP is the most popular server-side programming language; it's supported by any web-hosting provider worth its salt. You can learn more about PHP at http://www.php.net/ or you can just dive right in to learning this programming language (plus database interactivity) from the ground up in *PHP, MySQL and Apache All in One* (ISBN: 067232976X). Although several other books on PHP and related technologies are available, I am partial to this one because I wrote it. It is geared toward absolute beginners with PHP or any other programming language.

NOTE

There is a way to send form data without a server-side script, and you'll learn about that method—which uses a mailto link in the `action` attribute of the `<form>`—later in this chapter. But as you try that, be aware that it can produce inconsistent results; individual web browsers, as well as personal security settings, can cause that action to respond differently than what you intended.

or *back-end*) process requires knowledge of at least one programming language or at least the ability to follow specific instructions when using someone else's server-side script to handle the form input. At that point in the process, you should either work with someone who has the technical knowledge, or you should learn the basics on your own. Simple form-processing is not difficult at all and it is likely that your web-hosting provider has several back-end scripts that you can use with minimal customization.

Forms include a button for the user to submit the form; that button can be an image that you create yourself or a standard HTML form button that is created when a form `<input>` tag is created and given a `type` value of `submit`. When someone clicks a form submission button, all the information typed in the form is sent to a URL that you specify in the `action` attribute of the `<form>` tag. That URL should point to a specific script that will process your form, sending the form contents via email or performing another step in an interactive process (such as requesting results from a search engine or placing items in an online shopping cart).

After you start thinking about doing more with form content than simply emailing results to yourself, additional technical knowledge is required. For example, if you want to create an online store that accepts credit cards and processes transactions, there are some well-established practices for doing so, all geared toward ensuring the security of your customers' data. That is not an operation that you'll want to enter into lightly; you'll need more knowledge than this book provides.

Before you put a form online, you should look in the user guide for your web-hosting provider and see what they offer in the way of form-processing scripts. You are likely to find a readily available Perl or PHP script that you can use with only minimal configuration.

Creating a Form

Every form must begin with a `<form>` tag, which can be located anywhere in the body of the HTML document. The `<form>` tag normally has three attributes, `name`, `method` and `action`:

```
<form name="form1" method="post" action="/myprocessingscript.php">
```

The most common `method` is `post`, which sends the form entry results as a document. In some situations, you might need to use `method="get"`, which submits the results as part of the URL header instead. For example, `get` is sometimes used when submitting queries to search engines from a web form. Because you're not yet an expert on forms, just use `post` unless your web-hosting provider's documentation tells you to do otherwise.

The `action` attribute specifies the address to which to send the form data. You have two options here:

- ▶ You can type the location of a form-processing program or script on a web server and the form data will then be sent to that program.

- ▶ You can type `mailto:` followed by your email address and the form data will be sent directly to you whenever someone fills out the form. However, this approach is completely dependent on the user's computer being properly configured with an email client. People accessing your site from a public computer without an email client will be left out in the cold.

```
<form method="post" action="mailto:me@mysite.com">
```

Each form in your HTML page is represented in JavaScript by a `form` object, which has the same name as the `name` attribute in the `<form>` tag you used to define it.

Alternatively, you can use the `forms` array to refer to forms. This array includes an item for each form element, indexed starting with 0. For example, if the first form in a document has the name `form1`, you can refer to it in one of two ways:

```
document.form1
document.forms[0]
```

Along with the elements, each `form` object also has a list of properties, most of which are defined by the corresponding `<form>` tag. You can also set these from within JavaScript. They include the following:

- ▶ `action` is the form's `action` attribute, or the program to which the form data will be submitted.

- ▶ `encoding` is the `MIME` type of the form, specified with the `enctype` attribute. In most cases, this is not needed (unless you are uploading a file with the form).

- ▶ `length` is the number of elements in the form. You cannot change this property.

- ▶ `method` is the method used to submit the form, either `GET` or `POST`. This determines the data format used to send the form result to a CGI script and does not affect JavaScript.

▶ target specifies the window in which the result of the form (from the CGI script) will be displayed. Normally, this is done in the main window, replacing the form itself, but you can use this attribute to work with pop-up windows or frames.

The form created in Listing 26.1 and shown in Figure 26.1 includes just about every type of user input component you can currently use on HTML forms. Refer to this listing and figure as you read the following explanations of each type of input element.

LISTING 26.1   A Form with Various User-Input Components

```
<?xml version="1.0" encoding="UTF-8"?>
<!DOCTYPE html PUBLIC "-//W3C//DTD XHTML 1.1//EN"
  "http://www.w3.org/TR/xhtml11/DTD/xhtml11.dtd">

<html xmlns="http://www.w3.org/1999/xhtml" xml:lang="en">
  <head>
    <title>Guest Book</title>

    <style type="text/css">
      .formlabel {
         font-weight:bold;
         width: 250px;
         margin-bottom: 12px;
         float: left;
         text-align: left;
         clear: left;
      }
      .formfield {
         font-weight:normal;
         margin-bottom: 12px;
         float: left;
         text-align: left;
      }

      input, textarea, select {
         border: 1px solid black;
      }
    </style>
  </head>
  <body>
    <h1>My Guest Book</h1>
          <p>Please sign my guest book. Thanks!</p>
    <form name="gbForm" method="post" action="URL_to_script">

    <div class="formlabel">What is your name?</div>
    <div  class="formfield"><input type="text" name="name"
       size="50" /></div>

    <div class="formlabel">What is your e-mail address?</div>
    <div class="formfield"><input type="text" name="email"
```

LISTING 26.1   Continued

```
    size="50" /></div>

<div class="formlabel">Please check all that apply:</div>
<div class="formfield">
   <input type="checkbox" name="website_response[]" value="I
   really like your Web site." />I really like your Web site.<br />
   <input type="checkbox" name="website_response[]" value="One
   of the best sites I've seen." />One of the best sites I've
   seen.<br />
   <input type="checkbox" name="website_response[]" value="I sure
   wish my site looked as good as yours." />I sure wish my site
   looked as good as yours.<br />
   <input type="checkbox" name="website_response[]" value="I have
   no taste and I'm pretty dense, so your site didn't do much for
   me." />I  have no taste and I'm pretty dense, so your site
   didn't do much for me.<br />
</div>

<div  class="formlabel">Choose the one thing you love best about my
web site:</div>
<div class="formfield">
   <input type="radio" name="lovebest" value="me" />That gorgeous
   picture of you.<br />
   <input type="radio" name="lovebest" value="cats" />All the
   beautiful pictures of your cats.<br />
   <input type="radio" name="lovebest" value="childhood" />The
   inspiring recap of your suburban childhood.<br />
   <input type="radio" name="lovebest" value="treasures" />The
   detailed list of all your Elvis memorabilia.<br />
</div>

<div class="formlabel">If my web site were a book, how many copies
would it sell?</div>
<div class="formfield">
  <select size="3" name="sales">
    <option value="Millions, for sure." selected="selected">Millions,
      for sure.</option>
    <option value="100,000+ (would be Oprah's favorite)">100,000+
      (would be Oprah's favorite)</option>
    <option value="Thousands (an under-appreciated classic)">
      Thousands (an under-appreciated classic)</option>
    <option value="Very few: not banal enough for today's
      public">Very few: not banal enough for today's
      public.</option>
    <option value="Sell? None. Everyone will download it
      for free.">Sell? None. Everyone will download it for
      free.</option>
  </select>
</div>

<div class="formlabel">How can I improve my web site?</div>
<div class="formfield">
  <select name="suggestion">
    <option value="Couldn't be better." selected="selected">Couldn't
```

LISTING 26.1   Continued

```
          be better.</option>
        <option value="More about the cats.">More about the
          cats.</option>
        <option value="More about the family.">More about the
          family.</option>
        <option value="More about Elvis.">More about Elvis.</option>
      </select>
    </div>

    <div class="formlabel">Feel free to type more praise,
      gift offers, etc. below:</div>
    <div class="formfield">
      <textarea name="comments" rows="4" cols="55"></textarea>
    </div>

    <div style="float:left;">
      <input type="submit" value="Click Here to Submit" />
      <input type="reset" value="Erase and Start Over" />
    </div>
    </form>
  </body>
</html>
```

FIGURE 26.1
The code shown in Listing 26.1
uses nearly every type of HTML
form input element.

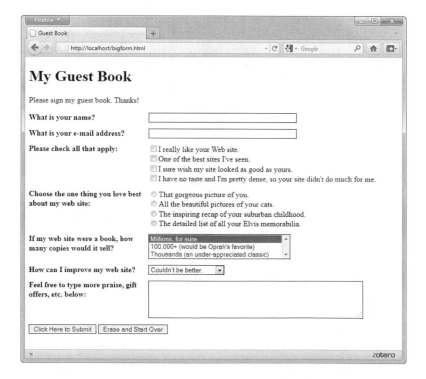

The code in Listing 26.1 uses a `<form>` tag that contains quite a few `<input />` tags. Each `<input />` tag corresponds to a specific user input component, such as a check box or radio button. The input, select, and text area elements contain borders in the style sheet, so it is easy to see the outline of the elements in the form. Keep in mind that you can apply all sorts of CSS to those elements.

The next few sections dig into the `<input />` and other form-related tags in detail.

Accepting Text Input

To ask the user for a specific piece of information within a form, use the `<input />` tag. This tag must fall between the `<form>` and `</form>` tags, but it can be anywhere on the page in relation to text, images, and other HTML tags. For example, to ask for someone's name, you could type the following text followed immediately by an `<input />` field:

```
<p>What's your name? <input type="text" size="50"
     maxlength="100" name="user_name" /></p>
```

The `type` attribute indicates what type of form element to display—a simple, one-line text entry box in this case. (Each element type is discussed individually in this chapter.)

The `size` attribute indicates approximately how many characters wide the text input box should be. If you are using a proportionally spaced font, the width of the input will vary depending on what the user enters. If the input is too long to fit in the box, most web browsers will automatically scroll the text to the left.

The `maxlength` attribute determines the number of characters the user is allowed to type into the text box. If a user tries to type beyond the specified length, the extra characters won't appear. You can specify a length that is longer, shorter, or the same as the physical size of the text box. The `size` and `maxlength` attributes are used only for `type="text"` because other input types (check boxes, radio buttons, and so on) have fixed sizes.

Naming Each Piece of Form Data

No matter what type an input element is, you must give a name to the data it gathers. You can use any name you like for each input item, as long as each one on the form is different (except in the case of radio buttons and

> **TIP**
>
> If you want the user to enter text without the text being displayed on the screen, you can use `<input type="password" />` instead of `<input type="text" />`. Asterisks (***) are then displayed in place of the text the user types. The `size`, `maxlength`, and `name` attributes work exactly the same for `type="password"` as they do for `type="text"`. Keep in mind that this technique of hiding a password provides only visual protection; there is no encryption or other protection associated with the password being transmitted.

NOTE

Form-processing scripts are oversimplified here for the sake of explanation within the scope of this book. The exact appearance (or name) of the variables made available to your processing script depends on the programming language of that script. But conceptually, it's valid to say that the name of the input element becomes the name of the variable and the value of the input element becomes that variable's value on the back-end.

check boxes, which are discussed later in this chapter). When the form is processed by a back-end script, each data item is identified by name. This name becomes a variable, which is filled with a value. The value is either what the user typed in the form or the value associated with the element the user selected.

For example, if a user enters **Jane Doe** in the text box defined previously, a variable is sent to the form processing script; the variable is `user_name` and the value of the variable is `Jane Doe`. Form-processing scripts work with these types of variable names and values.

To use this (or other) text fields in JavaScript, remember that the text object uses the `name` attribute; you would refer to the value of the field in the previous snippet as:

```
document.formname.user_name.value
```

Additional examples of name/value pairs are covered throughout this chapter.

Including Hidden Data in Forms

Want to send certain data items to the server script that processes a form but don't want the user to see those data items? Use an `<input />` tag with a `type="hidden"` attribute. This attribute has no effect on the display; it just adds any name and value you specify to the form results when they are submitted.

If you are using a form-processing script provided by your web-hosting provider, you might use this attribute to tell a script where to email the form results. For example, including the following code will email the results to me@mysite.com after the form has been submitted:

```
<input type="hidden" name="mailto" value="me@mysite.com" />
```

You might sometimes see scripts using hidden input elements to carry additional data that might be useful when you receive the results of the form submission; some examples of hidden form fields include an email address and a subject for the email. If you are using a script provided by your web hosting provider, consult the documentation provided with that script for additional details about potential required hidden fields.

Exploring Form Input Controls

Various input controls are available for retrieving information from the user. You've already seen one text-entry option, and the next few sections introduce you to most of the remaining form-input options you can use to design forms.

Check Boxes

The simplest input type is a *check box*, which appears as a small square. Users can click checkboxes to select or deselect one or more items in a group. For example, the checkboxes listed in Listing 26.1 display after a label that reads "Please check all that apply," implying that the user could indeed check all that apply.

The HTML for the check boxes in Listing 26.1 shows that the value of the name attribute is the same for all of them: website_response[].

```
<input type="checkbox" name="website_response[]" value="I
   really like your Web site." />I really like your Web site.<br />
<input type="checkbox" name="website_response[]" value="One
   of the best sites I've seen." />One of the best sites I've
   seen.<br />
<input type="checkbox" name="website_response[]" value="I sure
   wish my site looked as good as yours." />I sure wish my site
   looked as good as yours.<br />
<input type="checkbox" name="website_response[]" value="I have
   no taste and I'm pretty dense, so your site didn't do much for
   me." />I  have no taste and I'm pretty dense, so your site
   didn't do much for me.<br />
```

The use of the brackets in the name attribute ([]) indicates to the processing script that a series of values will be placed into this one variable, instead of just one value (well, it might just be one value if the user only selects one check box). If a user selects the first check box, the text string "I really like your Web site." will be placed in the website_response[] bucket. If the user selects the third checkbox, the text string "I sure wish my site looked as good as yours." will also be put into the website_response[] bucket. The processing script will then work with that variable as an array of data rather just a single entry.

However, you might see groups of check boxes that do use individual names for the variables in the group. For example, the following is another way of writing the check box group:

TIP

If you find that the label for an input element is displayed too close to the element, just add a space between the close of the `<input />` tag and the start of the label text, like this:

```
<input type="checkbox"
name="mini" /> Mini Piano
Stool
```

```
<input type="checkbox" name="liked_site" value="yes" /> I really like
    your Web site.<br />
<input type="checkbox" name="best_site" value="yes" /> One of the best
    Sites I've seen.<br />
<input type="checkbox" name="my_site_sucks" value="yes" />I sure wish my
    site looked as good as yours.<br />
<input type="checkbox" name="am_dense" value="yes" />I have no taste and
    I'm pretty dense, so your site didn't do much for me.<br />
```

In the previous check boxes, the variable name of the first check box is "liked_site" and the value (if checked) is "yes".

If you want a check box to be checked by default when the form is rendered by the web browser, include the checked attribute. For example, the following code creates two check boxes and the first is checked by default:

```
<input type="checkbox" name="website_response[]" value="I
    really like your Web site." checked="checked" />I really like
    your Web site.<br />
<input type="checkbox" name="website_response[]" value="One
    of the best sites I've seen." />One of the best sites I've
    seen.<br />
```

The check box labeled "I really like your site." is checked by default in this example. The user would have to click the check box to indicate they had another opinion of your site. The check box marked "One of the best I've seen." would be unchecked to begin with, so the user would have to click it to turn it on. Check boxes that are not selected do not appear in the form output at all.

If you want to handle values from the checkbox object in JavaScript, the object has the following four properties:

▶ name is the name of the check box and also the object name.

▶ value is the "true" value for the check box—usually on. This value is used by server-side programs to indicate whether the check box was checked. In JavaScript, you should use the checked property instead.

▶ defaultChecked is the default status of the check box, assigned by the checked attribute in HTML.

▶ checked is the current value. This is a Boolean value: true for checked and false for unchecked.

To manipulate the check box or use its value, you use the checked property. For example, this statement turns on a check box called same_address in a form named order:

```
document.order.same.checked = true;
```

The check box has a single method: `click()`. This method simulates a click on the box. It also has a single event, `onClick`, which occurs whenever the check box is clicked. This happens whether the box was turned on or off, so you'll need to examine the `checked` property via JavaScript to see what action really happened.

Radio Buttons

Radio buttons, for which only one choice can be selected at a time, are almost as simple to implement as check boxes. The simplest use of a radio button is for yes/no questions or for voting when only one candidate can be selected.

To create a radio button, just use `type="radio"` and give each option its own `<input />` tag. Use the same `name` for all the radio buttons in a group, but don't use the `[]` that you used with the check box:

```
<input type="radio" name="vote" value="yes" checked="checked" /> Yes<br />
<input type="radio" name="vote" value="no" /> No <br/>
```

The `value` can be any name or code you choose. If you include the `checked` attribute, that button is selected by default. No more than one radio button with the same `name` can be checked.

When designing your form and choosing between checkboxes and radio buttons, ask yourself, "Is the question being asked one that could be answered only one way?" If so, use a radio button.

As for scripting, radio buttons are similar to check boxes, except that an entire group of them shares a single name and a single object. You can refer to the following properties of the `radio` object:

▶ `name` is the name common to the radio buttons.

▶ `length` is the number of radio buttons in the group.

To access the individual buttons in JavaScript, you treat the `radio` object as an array. The buttons are indexed, starting with `0`. Each individual button has the following properties:

▶ `value` is the value assigned to the button.

▶ `defaultChecked` indicates the value of the `checked` attribute and the default state of the button.

▶ `checked` is the current state.

NOTE

Radio buttons are named for their similarity to the buttons on old pushbutton radios. Those buttons used a mechanical arrangement so that when you pushed one button in, the others popped out.

For example, you can check the first radio button in the `radio1` group on the `form1` form with this statement:

```
document.form1.radio1[0].checked = true;
```

However, if you do this, be sure you set the other values to `false` as needed. This is not done automatically. You can use the `click()` method to do both of these in one step.

Like a check box, radio buttons have a `click()` method and an `onClick` event handler. Each radio button can have a separate statement for this event.

Selection Lists

Both *scrolling lists* and *pull-down pick lists* are created with the `<select>` tag. You use this tag together with the `<option>` tag, as the following example shows (taken from Listing 26.1):

```
<select size="3" name="sales">
   <option value="Millions, for sure." selected="selected">Millions,
      for sure.</option>
   <option value="100,000+ (would be Oprah's favorite)">100,000+
      (would be Oprah's favorite)</option>
   <option value="Thousands (an under-appreciated classic)">Thousands
      (an under-appreciated classic)</option>
       <option value="Very few: not banal enough for today's public">Very
       few: not banal enough for today's public.</option>
   <option value="Sell? None. Everyone will download it for free.">Sell?
      None. Everyone will download it for free.</option>
</select>
```

No HTML tags other than `<option>` and `</option>` should appear between the `<select>` and `</select>` tags.

Unlike the `text` input type, the `size` attribute here determines how many items show at once on the selection list. If `size="2"` were used in the preceding code, only the first two options would be visible and a scrollbar would appear next to the list so the user could scroll down to see the third option.

Including the `multiple` attribute enables users to select more than one option at a time; the `selected` attribute makes an option initially selected by default. When the form is submitted, the text specified in the `value` attribute for each option accompanies the selected option.

TIP

If you leave out the `size` attribute or specify `size="1"`, the list creates a drop-down pick list. Pick lists don't allow for multiple choices; they are logically equivalent to a group of radio buttons. The following example shows another way to choose yes or no for a question:

```
<select name="vote">
  <option
value="yes">Yes</option>
  <option
value="no">No</option>
</select>
```

The object for selection lists is the `select` object. The object itself has the following properties:

▶ `name` is the name of the selection list.

▶ `length` is the number of options in the list.

▶ `options` is the array of options. Each selectable option has an entry in this array.

▶ `selectedIndex` returns the index value of the currently selected item. You can use this to check the value easily. In a multiple-selection list, this indicates the first selected item.

The `options` array has a single property of its own, `length`, which indicates the number of selections. In addition, each item in the `options` array has the following properties:

▶ `index` is the index into the array.

▶ `defaultSelected` indicates the state of the `selected` attribute.

▶ `selected` is the current state of the option. Setting this property to `true` selects the option. The user can select multiple options if the `multiple` attribute is included in the `<select>` tag.

▶ `name` is the value of the `name` attribute. This is used by the server.

▶ `text` is the text that is displayed in the option.

The `select` object has two methods—`blur()` and `focus()`—which perform the same purposes as the corresponding methods for `text` objects. The event handlers are `onBlur`, `onFocus`, and `onChange`, also similar to other objects.

Reading the value of a selected item is a two-step process. You first use the `selectedIndex` property, and then use the `value` property to find the value of the selected choice. Here's an example:

```
ind = document.mvform.choice.selectedIndex;
val = document.mvform.choice.options[ind].value;
```

This uses the `ind` variable to store the selected index, and then assigns the `val` variable to the value of the selected choice. Things are a bit more complicated with a multiple selection; you have to test each option's `selected` attribute separately.

> **NOTE**
>
> You can change selection lists dynamically—for example, choosing a product in one list could control which options are available in another list. You can also add and delete options from the list.

Text Fields and Text Areas

The `<input type="text">` attribute mentioned earlier this chapter allows the user to enter only a single line of text. When you want to allow multiple lines of text in a single input item, use the `<textarea>` and `</textarea>` tags to create a text area instead of just a text field. Any text you include between these two tags is displayed as the default entry. Here's an example:

```
<textarea name="comments" rows="4" cols="20">Your
     message here.</textarea>
```

As you probably guessed, the `rows` and `cols` attributes control the number of rows and columns of text that fit in the input box. The `cols` attribute is a little less exact than `rows` and approximates the number of characters that fit in a row of text. Text area boxes do have a scrollbar, however, so the user can enter more text than what fits in the display area.

The `text` and `textarea` objects also have a few methods you can use:

- ▶ `focus()` sets the focus to the field. This positions the cursor in the field and makes it the current field.

- ▶ `blur()` is the opposite; it removes the focus from the field.

- ▶ `select()` selects the text in the field, just as a user can do with the mouse. All of the text is selected; there is no way to select part of the text.

You can also use event handlers to detect when the value of a text field changes. The `text` and `textarea` objects support the following event handlers:

- ▶ The `onFocus` event happens when the text field gains focus.

- ▶ The `onBlur` event happens when the text field loses focus.

- ▶ The `onChange` event happens when the user changes the text in the field and then moves out of it.

- ▶ The `onSelect` event happens when the user selects some or all of the text in the field. Unfortunately, there's no way to tell exactly which part of the text was selected. (If the text is selected with the `select()` method described previously, this event is not triggered.)

If used, these event handlers should be included in the `<input>` tag declaration. For example, the following is a text field including an `onChange` event that displays an alert:

```
<input type="text" name="text1" onChange="window.alert('Changed.');" />
```

Submitting Form Data

Forms typically include a button that submits the form data to a script on the server or invokes a JavaScript action. You can put any label you like on the submit button with the `value` attribute:

```
<input type="submit" value="Place My Order Now!" />
```

A gray button will be sized to fit the label you put in the `value` attribute. When the user clicks it, all data items on the form are sent to the email address or script specified in the form's `action` attribute.

You can also include a Reset button that clears all entries on the form so users can start over if they change their minds or make mistakes. Use the following:

```
<input type="reset" value="Clear This Form and Start Over" />
```

If the standard Submit and Reset buttons look a little bland to you, remember that you can style them using CSS. If that's not good enough, you'll be glad to know that there is an easy way to substitute your own graphics for these buttons. To use an image of your choice for a Submit button, use the following:

```
<input type="image" src="button.gif" alt="Order Now!" />
```

The `button.gif` image will display on the page and the form will be submitted when a user clicks the `button.gif` image. You can also include any attributes normally used with the `<img />` tag, such as `alt` and `style`.

The form element also includes a generic button type. When using `type="button"` in the `<input />` tag, you will get a button that performs no action on its own but can have an action assigned to it using a JavaScript event handler.

Using JavaScript for Form Events

The `form` object has two methods: `submit()` and `reset()`. You can use these methods to submit the data or reset the form yourself, without requiring the user to press a button. One reason for this is to submit the form when the user clicks an image or performs another action that would not usually submit the form.

The `form` object has two event handlers, `onSubmit` and `onReset`. You can specify a group of JavaScript statements or a function call for these events within the `<form>` tag that defines the form.

CAUTION

If you use the `submit()` method to send data to a server or by email, most browsers will prompt the user to verify that he wants to submit the information. There's no way to do this behind the user's back.

If you specify a statement or a function for the `onSubmit` event, the statement is called before the data is submitted to the server-side script. You can prevent the submission from happening by returning a value of `false` from the `onSubmit` event handler. If the statement returns `true`, the data will be submitted. In the same fashion, you can prevent a Reset button from working with an `onReset` event handler.

Accessing Form Elements with JavaScript

NOTE

Both forms and elements can be referred to by their own names or as indices in the `forms` and `elements` arrays. For clarity, the examples in this chapter use individual form and element names rather than array references. You'll also find it easier to use names in your own scripts.

The most important property of the `form` object is the `elements` array, which contains an object for each of the form elements. You can refer to an element by its own name or by its index in the array. For example, the following two expressions both refer to the first element in the form shown in Listing 26.1:

```
document.gbForm.elements[0]
document.gbForm.name
```

If you do refer to forms and elements as arrays, you can use the `length` property to determine the number of objects in the array: `document.forms.length` is the number of forms in a document, and `document.gbForm.elements.length` is the number of elements in the `gbForm` form.

You can also access form elements using the W3C DOM. In this case, you use an `id` attribute on the form element in the HTML document, and use the `document.getElementById()` method to find the object for the form. For example, this statement finds the object for the text field called `name` and stores it in the `name` variable:

```
name = document.getElementById("name");
```

This enables you to quickly access a form element without first finding the `form` object. You can assign an `id` to the `<form>` tag and find the corresponding object if you need to work with the form's properties and methods.

Displaying Data from a Form

As a simple example of using forms, Listing 26.2 shows a form with name, address, and phone number fields, as well as a JavaScript function that displays the data from the form in a pop-up window.

LISTING 26.2   A Form That Displays Data in a Pop-up Window

```
<?xml version="1.0" encoding="UTF-8"?>
<!DOCTYPE html PUBLIC "-//W3C//DTD XHTML 1.1//EN"
  "http://www.w3.org/TR/xhtml11/DTD/xhtml11.dtd">

<html xmlns="http://www.w3.org/1999/xhtml" xml:lang="en">
  <head>
    <title>Form Display Example</title>
    <script type="text/javascript">
    function display() {
      dispWin = window.open('','NewWin',
      'toolbar=no,status=no,width=300,height=200')
      message = "<ul><li><strong>NAME: </strong>" +
      document.form1.name.value;
      message += "<li><strong>ADDRESS: </strong>" +
      document.form1.address.value;
      message += "<li><strong>PHONE: </strong>" +
      document.form1.phone.value + "</ul>";
      dispWin.document.write(message);
    }
    </script>
  </head>
  <body>
    <h1>Form Display Example</h1>
        <p>Enter the following information. When you press the Display
  button, the data you entered will be displayed in a pop-up.</p>
    <form name="form1" method="get" action="">
    <p>NAME: <input type="text" name="name" size="50" /></p>
    <p>ADDRESS: <input type="text" name="address" size="50" /></p>
    <p>PHONE: <input type="text" name="phone" size="50" /></p>
    <p><input type="button" value="Display" onclick="display();" /></p>
    </form>
  </body>
</html>
```

Here is a breakdown of how this HTML document and script work:

- ▸ The <script> section in the document's header defines a function
  called display() that opens a new window and displays the information from the form.

- ▸ The <form> tag begins the form. Because this form is handled entirely by JavaScript, the form action and method have no value.

- ▸ The <input /> tags define the form's three fields: yourname,
  address, and phone. The last <input /> tag defines the Display button, which is set to run the display() function.

Figure 26.2 shows this form in action. The Display button has been pressed, and the pop-up window shows the results.

FIGURE 26.2

Displaying data from a form in a pop-up window.

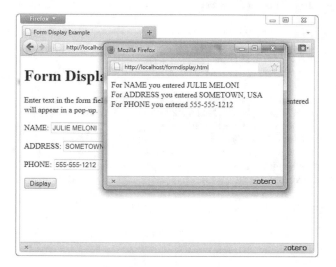

Sending Form Results by Email

One easy way to use a form is to send the results by email. You can do this without using any JavaScript, although you could use JavaScript to validate the information entered (as you'll learn later in this chapter).

To send a form's results by email, you use the `mailto:` action in the form's `action` attribute. Listing 26.3 is a modified version of the name and address form from Listing 26.2 that sends the results by email.

LISTING 26.3   Sending a Form's Results by Email

```
<?xml version="1.0" encoding="UTF-8"?>
<!DOCTYPE html PUBLIC "-//W3C//DTD XHTML 1.1//EN"
  "http://www.w3.org/TR/xhtml11/DTD/xhtml11.dtd">

<html xmlns="http://www.w3.org/1999/xhtml" xml:lang="en">
  <head>
    <title>Form Submit Example</title>
  </head>
  <body>
    <h1>Form Submit Example</h1>
        <p>Enter the following information. When you press the Send
  button, the data you entered will be send via e-mail.</p>
    <form name="form1" method="post" action="mailto:user@domain.com"
          enctype="text/plain">
```

LISTING 26.3   Continued

```
      <p>NAME: <input type="text" name="name" size="50" /></p>
      <p>ADDRESS: <input type="text" name="address" size="50" /></p>
      <p>PHONE: <input type="text" name="phone" size="50" /></p>
      <p><input type="submit" value="Submit Form" /></p>
      </form>
  </body>
</html>
```

To use this form, change `user@domain.com` in the `action` attribute of the `<form>` tag to your email address. Notice the `enctype="text/plain"` attribute in the `<form>` tag. This ensures that the information in the email message will be in a readable plain-text format rather than encoded.

Although this provides a quick and dirty way of retrieving data from a form, the disadvantage of this technique is that it is highly browser dependent. Whether it will work for each user of your page depends on the configuration of her browser and email client.

CAUTION

Because this technique does not consistently work on all browsers, I don't recommend you use it. Some browsers will invoke your mail client; others will send the form data via your browser-based email account. This example is offered more as an example of a process you *could* use JavaScript to accomplish and might see in many scripts you find on the web. For a more reliable way of sending form results, you can use a server-side form-to-email script; your hosting provider will likely have one or more available for your use.

One of JavaScript's most useful purposes is validating forms. This means using a script to verify that the information entered is valid—for example, that no fields are blank and that the data is in the right format.

You can use JavaScript to validate a form whether it's submitted by email or to a server-side script or is simply used by a script. Listing 26.4 is a version of the name and address form that includes validation.

TRY IT YOURSELF ▼

Validating a Form

LISTING 26.4   A Form with a Validation Script

```
<?xml version="1.0" encoding="UTF-8"?>
<!DOCTYPE html PUBLIC "-//W3C//DTD XHTML 1.1//EN"
  "http://www.w3.org/TR/xhtml11/DTD/xhtml11.dtd">

<html xmlns="http://www.w3.org/1999/xhtml" xml:lang="en">
  <head>
    <title>Form Submit Example</title>
    <script type="text/javascript">
    function validate() {
      if (document.form1.name.value.length < 1) {
         alert("Please enter your full name.");
         return false;
      }
      if (document.form1.address.value.length < 3) {
         alert("Please enter your address.");
         return false;
      }
```

▼ TRY IT YOURSELF

Validating a Form
continued

LISTING 26.4   Continued

```
        if (document.form1.phone.value.length < 3) {
            alert("Please enter your phone number.");
            return false;
        }
        return true;
    }
    </script>
</head>
<body>
    <h1>Form Submit Example</h1>
        <p>Enter the following information. When you press the Send
    button, the data you entered will be send via e-mail.</p>
        <form name="form1" method="post" action="mailto:user@domain.com"
            enctype="text/plain" onsubmit="return validate();">
        <p>NAME: <input type="text" name="name" size="50" /></p>
        <p>ADDRESS: <input type="text" name="address" size="50" /></p>
        <p>PHONE: <input type="text" name="phone" size="50" /></p>
        <p><input type="submit" value="Submit Form" /></p>
        </form>
</body>
</html>
```

NOTE

The validation in this script is basic—you could go further and ensure that the phone field contains only numbers and the right amount of digits by using JavaScript's string features described in Chapter 16, "Using JavaScript Variables, Strings, and Arrays."

TIP

You can also use the onchange event handler in each form field to call a validation routine. This allows the field to be validated before the Submit button is pressed.

This form uses a function called validate() to check the data in each of the form fields. Each if statement in this function checks a field's length. If the field is long enough to be valid, the form can be submitted; otherwise, the submission is stopped and an alert message is displayed.

This form is set up to send its results by email, as in Listing 26.3. If you want to use this feature, be sure to read the information about email forms earlier in this chapter and change user@domain.com to your desired email address.

The <form> tag uses an onsubmit event handler to call the validate() function. The return keyword ensures that the value returned by validate() will determine whether the form is submitted.

Figure 26.3 shows this script in action. The form has been filled out except for the name, and a dialog box indicates that the name needs to be entered.

TRY IT YOURSELF ▼

Validating a Form
continued

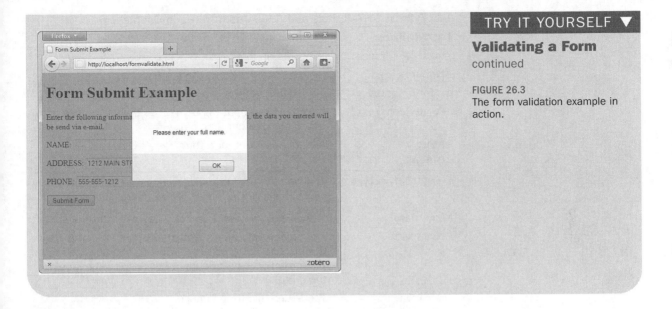

FIGURE 26.3
The form validation example in action.

Summary

This chapter demonstrated how to create HTML forms, which allow your visitors to provide information to you.

You learned about all the major form elements and how form-processing scripts interpret the names and value attributes of those elements. When you are ready to try a back-end form processing script, you're now well-versed in the front-end details.

You also learned how form elements can be used with JavaScript. You learned about the form object and the objects for the various form elements and used them in several sample scripts.

We stopped short of doing anything in-depth with that information because form handling requires an external script to process that form. You did learn one way to send simple form data by email and how to use JavaScript to validate a form before it is submitted.

Table 26.1 summarizes the HTML tags and attributes covered in this chapter.

TABLE 26.1   HTML Tags and Attributes Covered in Chapter 26

Tag/Attribute	Function
`<form>...</form>`	Indicates an input form.
Attributes	
`action="scripturl"`	The address of the script to process this form input.
`method="post/get"`	How the form input will be sent to the server. Normally set to `post`, rather than `get`.
`<input />`	An input element for a form.
Attributes	
`type="controltype"`	The type for this input widget. Possible values are `check-box`, `hidden`, `radio`, `reset`, `submit`, `text`, and `image`.
`name="name"`	The unique name of this item, as passed to the script.
`value="value"`	The default value for a text or hidden item. For a check box or radio button, it's the value to be submitted with the form. For reset or submit buttons, it's the label for the button itself.
`src="imageurl"`	The source file for an image.
`checked="checked"`	For check boxes and radio buttons. Indicates that this item is checked.
`size="width"`	The width, in characters, of a text input region.
`maxlength= "maxlength"`	The maximum number of characters that can be entered into a text region.
`<textarea>... </textarea>`	Indicates a multiline text entry form element. Default text can be included.
Attributes	
`name="name"`	The name to be passed to the script.
`rows="numrows"`	The number of rows this text area displays.
`cols="numchars"`	The number of columns (characters) this text area displays.
`<select>...</select>`	Creates a menu or scrolling list of possible items.
Attributes	
`name="name"`	The name that is passed to the script.
`size="numelements"`	The number of elements to display. If `size` is indicated, the selection becomes a scrolling list. If no `size` is given, the selection is a drop-down pick list.
`multiple="multiple"`	Allows multiple selections from the list.
`<option>...</option>`	Indicates a possible item within a `<select>` element.
Attributes	
`selected="selected"`	With this attribute included, the `<option>` will be selected by default in the list.
`value="value"`	The value to submit if this `<option>` is selected when the form is submitted.

Q&A

Q. If I use JavaScript to add validation and other features to my form, can users with non-JavaScript browsers still use the form?

A. Yes, if you're careful. Be sure to use a Submit button rather than the `submit` action. Also, the server-side script might receive nonvalidated data, so be sure to include the same validation in the CGI script. Non-JavaScript users will be able to use the form, but won't receive instant feedback about their errors.

Q. Is there any way to create a large number of text fields without dealing with different names for all of them?

A. Yes. If you use the same name for several elements in the form, their objects will form an array. For example, if you defined 20 text fields with the name `member`, you could refer to them as `member[0]` through `member[19]`. This also works with other types of form elements.

Q. Is there a way to place the cursor on a particular field when the form is loaded or after my validation routine displays an error message?

A. Yes. You can use the field's `focus()` method to send the cursor there. To do this when the page loads, you can use the `onLoad` method in the `<body>` tag. However, there is no way to place the cursor in a particular position within the field.

Workshop

The workshop contains quiz questions and activities to help you solidify your understanding of the material covered. Try to answer all questions before looking at the "Answers" section that follows.

Quiz

1. What HTML code would you use to create a guestbook form that asks someone for his name and gender? Assume that you have a form-processing script set up at `/scripts/formscript` and that you need to include the following hidden input element to tell the script where to send the form results:

   ```
   <input type="hidden" name="mailto" value="you@yoursite.com" />
   ```

2. If you created an image named `submit.gif`, how would you use it as the Submit button for the form you created in Question 1?

3. Which of these attributes of a `<form>` tag determines where the data will be sent?

   a. `action`

   b. `method`

   c. `name`

4. Where do you place the `onsubmit` event handler to validate a form?

    a. In the `<body>` tag

    b. In the `<form>` tag

    c. In the `<input />` tag for the Submit button

Answers

1. You would use HTML code similar to the following (with the appropriate DOCTYPE and other structural markup, of course):

```
<form name="form1" method="post" action="/scripts/formscript">
<input type="hidden" name="mailto" value="you@yoursite.com" />
<p>Your Name: <input type="text" name="name" size="50" /></p>
<p>Your Gender:
<input type="radio" name="gender" value="male" /> male
<input type="radio" name="gender" value="female" /> female
<input type="radio" name="gender" value="mind your business" />
    mind your business </p>
<p><input type="submit" value="Submit Form" /></p>
</form>
```

2. Replace the following code:

```
<input type="submit" value="Submit Form" />
```

with this code:

```
<input type="image" src="submit.gif" />
```

3. a. The `action` attribute determines where the data is sent.

4. b. You place the `onsubmit` event handler in the `<form>` tag.

Exercises

▶ Create a form using all the different types of input elements and selection lists to make sure you understand how each of them works.

▶ Change the `validate` function in Listing 26.4 so that after a message is displayed indicating that a field is wrong, the cursor is moved to that field. (Use the `focus` method for the appropriate form element.)

▶ Add a text field to the form in Listing 26.4 for an email address. Add a feature to the `validate` function that verifies that the email address is at least five characters and that it contains the @ symbol.

▶ Investigate the form-handling options at your web-hosting provider and use a script made available to you by the web-hosting provider to process the form you created in the previous exercise.

CHAPTER 27

Organizing and Managing a Website

The bulk of this book has led you through the design and creation of your own web content, from text to graphics and multimedia, as well as the implementation of basic JavaScript functionality for enhanced user interaction. Along the way I've noted some of the ways you can think about the lifecycle of that content, but in this chapter you'll learn how to look at your work as a whole.

This chapter shows you how to think about organizing and presenting multiple web pages so that visitors will be able to navigate among them without confusion. You'll also learn about ways to make your website memorable enough to visit again and again. Web developers use the term *sticky* to describe pages that people don't want to leave. Hopefully this chapter will help you to make your websites downright gooey!

Because websites can be (and usually should be) updated frequently, it's essential to create pages that can be easily maintained. This chapter shows you how to add comments and other documentation to your pages so that you—or anyone else on your staff—can understand and modify your pages, and also introduces you to version control so that you can innovate individually or as part of a team without overwriting work that you might want to save.

WHAT YOU'LL LEARN IN THIS CHAPTER:

- ▶ How to determine when one page is enough to handle all your content
- ▶ How to organize a simple site
- ▶ How to organize a larger site
- ▶ How to write maintainable code
- ▶ How to get started with version control

▼ TRY IT YOURSELF

Evaluating Your Organization

By this point in the book, you should have enough HTML, CSS, and JavaScript knowledge to produce most of your website. You probably have created a number of pages already and perhaps even published them online.

As you read this chapter, think about how your pages are organized now and how you can improve that organization. Have you used comments in your HTML and JavaScript or created a document showing your organization for future website maintainers? If not, this would be a good time to start. Along the way, don't be surprised if you decide to do a redesign that involves changing almost all of your pages—the results are likely to be well worth the effort!

When One Page Is Enough

Building and organizing an attractive and effective website doesn't always need to be a complex task. If you are creating a web presence for a single entity (such as a local event) that requires only a brief amount of very specific information, you can effectively present that information on a single page without a lot of flashy graphics. In fact, there are several positive features to a single-page web presence:

- ▶ All the information on the site downloads quicker than on more extensive sites.

- ▶ The whole site can be printed on paper with a single print command, even if it is several paper pages long.

- ▶ Visitors can easily save the site on their hard drives for future reference, especially if it uses a minimum of graphics.

- ▶ Links between different parts of the same page usually respond more quickly than links to other pages.

Figure 27.1 shows the first part of a web page that serves its intended audience better as a single lengthy page than it would as a multipage site. The page begins, as most introductory pages should, with a succinct explanation of what the page is about and who would want to read it. A detailed table of contents allows visitors to skip directly to the reference material in which they are most interested. It contains about eight paper pages worth of text explaining how to begin the process of buying a house—something a visitor might think about printing out and reading later, perhaps while also taking notes.

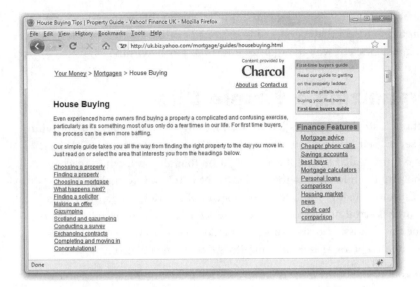

FIGURE 27.1
A good table of contents can make a lengthy page easy to navigate.

As Figure 27.2 shows, each short section of the page is followed by a link leading back to the table of contents, so navigating around the page feels much the same as navigating around a multipage site. Because the contents of the page are intended as a handy reference, visitors will definitely prefer the convenience of bookmarking or saving a single page instead of several separate pages.

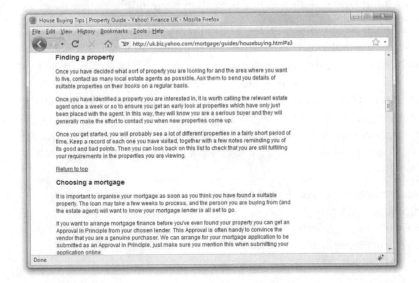

FIGURE 27.2
Always provide a link back to the table of contents after each section of a long web page.

Having seen all the fancy graphics and layouts in this book, you might be tempted to forget that a good, old-fashioned outline is often the clearest and most efficient way to organize long web pages within a site.

Organizing a Simple Site

Although single-page sites have their place, most companies and individuals serve their readers better by dividing their site into short, quick-read pages surrounded by graphical navigation that allows them to reach almost all the information they could want within a few clicks. Furthermore, using multiple pages instead of a series of very long pages minimizes scrolling around on the page, which can be especially bothersome for visitors who are using mobile devices to view the site or who have relatively low-resolution monitors (less than 800×600).

The goal of the home page is simply to make the organization visible on the Internet, but also—and more importantly—act as a portal to the information contained within the site itself. The main page of a site should provide the user with enough information to provide a clear picture of the organization, as well as traditional address and telephone contact information and an email address to contact with questions or feedback. It should also provide clear pathways into the highly structured information that should be contained on other pages in the site. The main page shown in Figure 27.3 provides examples of all these good features: basic information, contact information, and paths to information for multiple audiences.

One of the most common mistakes beginning website developers make is creating pages that look different than other pages on the site. Another equally serious mistake is using the same, publicly available clip art that thousands of other web authors are also using. Remember that on the Internet, one click can take you around the world. The only way to make your pages memorable and recognizable as a cohesive site is to make all your pages adhere to a unique, unmistakable visual theme. In other words, strive for uniqueness as compared to other websites, yet uniformity within the site itself.

As an example of how uniformity can help make a site more cohesive, think about large, popular sites you might have visited, such as ESPN.com. If you visit the MLB section at ESPN.com (see Figure 27.4) and the NFL section (see Figure 27.5), you'll notice a very similar structure.

TIP

Regardless of how large your site is, it's a good idea to carefully organize your resources. For example, place the images for your web pages in a separate folder named `images`. Similarly, if you have files that are available for download, place them in a folder called `downloads`. This makes it much easier to keep track of web page resources based on their particular types (HTML pages, GIF images, and so on). Additionally, if you organize your site into sections, such as Company, Products, Press, and so on, put the individual pages into similarly named directories (`company`, `products`, `press`, and so on) for the same organizational reasons.

FIGURE 27.3
This university main page uses a basic design, minimal but useful graphics, and clear structure to entice users to explore for more information.

FIGURE 27.4
The MLB section at ESPN.com.

In both examples, you see navigation elements at the top of the page (including some sub-navigation elements), a large area in the middle of the page for the featured item graphic, a rectangle on the right side containing links to top stories at the moment, and a second rectangle under the top stories links for the display of an advertisement. The only difference between the MLB section and the NFL section is the color scheme: The MLB section is part of a predominantly blue color scheme, whereas the NFL section is predominantly green. However, in both sections, you know that if you want to read the popular news stories, you look to the right of the page. If you want to navigate to another section in the site or to the site's main page, you look to a navigational element in the top left of the page.

These consistent elements help ensure your users will be able to navigate throughout your content with confidence. From a maintenance perspective, the consistent structural template enables you to reuse pieces of the code. This code reuse typically happens through dynamic server-side programming outside the scope of this book, but in general it means that instead of copying and pasting the same HTML and JavaScript over and over, that client-side code only exists in one place and is applied dynamically to the content. Therefore, instead of making changes to thousands of files, you would only need to make a change once.

Organizing a Larger Site

For complex sites, sophisticated layout and graphics can help organize and improve the look of your site when used consistently throughout all of your pages. To see how you can make aesthetics and organization work hand-in-hand, let's look at examples of navigation (and thus underlying organization) for a few sites that present a large volume of information to several different audiences.

Figure 27.6 shows the main page of Amazon.com, specifically with the side navigation selected. Amazon is in the business of selling products, plain and simple. Therefore, it makes sense for Amazon to show product categories as the main navigational elements, as shown in this figure.

FIGURE 27.6
Amazon.com shows product categories as primary navigation elements.

Although Amazon is in the business of selling products, it still has to provide information regarding who it is, how to contact it, and other ancillary yet important information to enhance the business-to-consumer relationship. Links to this sort of information appear in the footer, or bottom portion, of the Amazon.com website—outside of the viewing area of this screenshot. When creating your site template, you must determine the most important content areas and how to organize that content; also, remember to provide users with basic information—especially if that information will enhance your image and make the user feel as if you value what they have to say.

The next example is of a secondary page within the Starbucks.com website. All of the pages in the Starbucks.com website follow one of the common types of presenting navigation and subnavigation: a horizontal strip for main navigation, with secondary elements for that section placed in a vertical column on the left. As shown in Figure 27.7, the section the user is currently browsing (About Us) is highlighted. This visual indicator helps users orient themselves within the site. Using a visual indicator is a useful tactic because your users might arrive at a page via a search engine or by a link from another website. After your users arrive, you want them to feel at home—or at least feel as if they know where they are in relation to your site—once they get there.

FIGURE 27.7
This Starbucks.com secondary page shows a main navigation element selected with secondary navigation on the left side of the page.

As you can see by the different main navigation elements—Our Coffees, Our Stores, Starbucks Card, At Home, For Business, About Us, and Shop Online—the Starbucks website has to serve the needs of many different types of people coming to the website for many different reasons. As you organize your own site content, determine the information that is most important to you, as well as that which is most important to your users, and create a navigation scheme that finds a happy medium between the two.

Figure 27.8 shows another example of a navigation style, this time with a twist on the standard top navigation/left-side navigation scheme. In this example, the left-side navigation (secondary navigation in this case) also appears in a drop-down menu under the main navigation (refer to Chapter 11, "Using CSS to Do More with Lists, Text, and Navigation," for information on how to do something like this). Hovering the mouse over any of the other main navigation elements shows similar menus. This scheme enables users to have an entire site map at their fingertips because they would be able to reach any place in the site within one click of any other page.

FIGURE 27.8
The BAWSI.org website shows sub-navigation attached to each main navigation element.

You will also notice that the Overview link in the side navigation window is styled a bit differently—with heavier purple text—than the other links in the window, indicating to visitors what page they are on. This visual detail, similar to what you saw on the Starbucks site, is an unobtrusive way to provide users with a sense of where they are within the current navigational scheme.

There are many different types of navigation styles and ways of indicating to users just where they are and where they might want to go next. Keep in mind the following fact: Studies have repeatedly shown that people become confused and annoyed when presented with more than seven choices at a time, and people feel most comfortable with five or fewer choices. Therefore, you should avoid presenting more than five links (either in a list or as graphical icons) next to one another if at all possible and definitely avoid presenting more than seven at once. Amazon.com gets a pass here because it is an Internet superstore and users expect a lot of "departments" in which to shop when they get there. But when you need to present more than seven links in a navigation list, break them into multiple lists with a separate heading for each of the five to seven items, as you saw in the Amazon.com example in Figure 27.6.

It will also help your readers navigate your site without confusion if you avoid putting any page more than two (or, at most, three) links away from the main page. You should also always send readers back to a main category page (or the home page) after they've read a subsidiary page. In other words, try to design somewhat of a flat link structure in which most pages are no more than one or two links deep. You don't want visitors to have to rely heavily, if at all, on their browsers' Back buttons to navigate through your site.

Writing Maintainable Code

If you've ever done any programming before reading this book, you already know how important it is to write code that can be maintained—that is, you or someone else should be able look at your code later and not be utterly confused by it. The challenge is to make your code as immediately understandable as possible. There will come a time when you'll look back on a page that you wrote and you won't have a clue what you were thinking or why you wrote the code the way you did. Fortunately, there is a way to combat this problem of apparent memory loss!

Documenting Code with Comments

Whenever you develop an HTML page or JavaScript snippet, keep in mind that you or someone else will almost certainly need to make changes to it someday. Simple text web pages are usually easy to read and revise, but complex pages with graphics, tables, and other layout tricks can be quite difficult to decipher.

To see what I'm talking about, visit just about any page in a web browser and view its source code. Using Internet Explorer, click the View menu, and then click Source. Using Firefox, click the View menu, and then click Page Source. You might see a jumbled bunch of code that is tough to decipher as pure HTML. This might be due to the fact that the markup has been generated dynamically by content management software systems. Or

NOTE

To include comments in a JavaScript script, put `//` at the beginning of each comment line. (No closing tag is needed for JavaScript comments.) In style sheets, start comments with `/*` and end them with `*/`.

The HTML `<!--` and `-->` tags will not work properly in scripts or style sheets!

You can and should, however, include one `<!--` tag just after a `<script>` or `<style>` tag, with a `-->` tag just before the matching `</script>` or `</style>`. This hides the script or style commands from older browsers that would otherwise treat them as regular text and display them on the page.

it might be due to the fact that its human maintainer has not paid attention to structure, ease of reading, code commenting, and other methods for making the code readable by humans. For the sake of maintaining your own pages, I encourage you to impose a little more order on your HTML markup. The same goes for your JavaScript: Proper indentation is your (and your future development partner's) friend.

As you have seen in several different chapters throughout this book, you can enclose comments to yourself or your coauthors between <!-- and --> tags. These comments will not appear on the web page when viewed with a browser but can be read by anyone who examines the HTML code in a text editor or via web browser's View Source (or View Page Source) function. The following example provides a little refresher just to show you how a comment is coded:

```
<!-- This image needs to be updated daily. -->
<img src="headline.jpg" alt="Today's Headline" />
```

As this code reveals, the comment just before the <img /> tag provides a clue as to how the image is used. When someone reads this code, he knows immediately that this is an image that must be updated every day. The text in the comment is completely ignored by web browsers.

TIP

One handy usage of comments is to hide parts of a web page that are currently under construction. Rather than making the text and graphics visible and explaining that they're under construction, you can hide them from view entirely with some carefully placed opening and closing comment tags around the HTML you do not want to appear. This is a great way to work on portions of a page gradually and show only the end result to the world when you're finished.

TRY IT YOURSELF ▼

Commenting Your Code

It will be well worth your time now to go through all the web pages, scripts, and style sheets you've created so far and add any comments that you or others might find helpful when revising them in the future. Here's what to do:

1. Put a comment explaining any fancy formatting or layout techniques before the tags that make it happen.

2. Use a comment just before an <img /> tag to briefly describe any important graphic whose function isn't obvious from the alt message.

3. Consider using a comment (or several comments) to summarize how the cells of a <table> are supposed to fit together visually.

4. If you use hexadecimal color codes (such as <div style="color: #8040B0">), insert a comment indicating what the color actually is (bluish-purple).

5. Place a comment near a JavaScript function that explains the purpose of that function.

6. Indent your comments to help them stand out and make both the comments and the HTML or JavaScript easier to read. Don't forget to use indentation in the HTML and JavaScript itself to make it more readable, too, as we'll discuss in the next section.

Indenting Code for Clarity

I have a confession. Throughout the book I've been carefully indoctrinating you into an HTML code development style without really letting on. It's time to spill the beans. You've no doubt noticed a consistent pattern with respect to the indentation of all the HTML code in the book. More specifically, each child tag is indented to the right two spaces from its parent tag. Furthermore, content within a tag that spans more than one line is indented within the tag.

The best way to learn the value of indentation is to see some HTML code without it. You know how the song goes—"you don't know what you've got 'til it's gone." Anyway, here's a very simple table coded without any indentation:

```
<table>
<tr><td>Cell One</td><td>Cell Two</td></tr>
<tr><td>Cell Three</td><td>Cell Four</td></tr>
</table>
```

Not only is there no indentation, there also is no delineation between rows and columns within the table. Now compare this code with the following code, which describes the same table:

```
<table>
  <tr>
    <td>Cell One</td>
    <td>Cell Two</td>
  </tr>
  <tr>
    <td>Cell Three</td>
    <td>Cell Four</td>
  </tr>
</table>
```

This heavily indented code makes it plainly obvious how the rows and columns are divided up via <tr> and <td> tags.

Consistent indentation might even be more important than comments when it comes to making your HTML code understandable and maintainable. And you don't have to buy into this specific indentation strategy. If you'd rather use three or four spaces instead of two, that's fine. And if you want to tighten things up a bit and not indent content within a tag, that also works. The main thing to take from this is that it's important to develop a coding style of your own and then ruthlessly stick to it.

Thinking About Version Control

If you've ever used Google Docs, you have encountered a form of version control; in Google Docs, Google automatically saves revisions of your work

TIP

If you work with other people or plan on working with other people developing web pages, you should consider getting together as a group to formulate a consistent coding style. That way everyone is on the same page, pun intended.

as you are typing. This is different than simply automatically saving your work (although it does that, too) because you can revert to any revision along the way. You might have encountered this concept when using popular blog-authoring software such as Blogger or WordPress, or even when editing wikis—both of these also enable users to revise their work without overwriting, and thus deleting for all time, the previous work.

You might be wondering, "Well, what does that have to do with code? You're talking about documents." The answer is simple: Just as you might want to revert to a previous edition of an article or letter, you might want to revert to a previous edition of your code. This could be because you followed a good idea to the end, and the code just proved untenable, but you don't want to start over entirely—just at a certain point along your revision path.

There is more to version control than just revision history. When you start using version control systems to maintain your code, you will hear terms like:

▶ **Commit/check-in and checkout**—When you put an object into the code repository, you are committing that file; when you checkout a file, you are grabbing it from the repository (where all the current and historical versions are stored) and working on it until you are ready to commit or check-in the file again.

▶ **Branch**—The files you have under version control can branch or fork at any point, thus creating two or more development paths. Suppose you want to try some new display layouts or form interactivity but you don't want an existing site to appear modified in any way. You might have started with one master set of files but then forked this set of files for the new site, continuing to develop them independently. If you continued developing the original set of files, that would be working with the *trunk*.

▶ **Change/diff**—This is just the term (change OR diff) for a modification made under version control. You might also hear diff used as a verb, as in "I diffed the files," to refer to the action of comparing two versions of an object. (There is an underlying UNIX command called *diff*.)

There are many more terms than just these few listed here, but if you can conceptualize the repository, the (local) working copy, and the process of checking in and checking out files, you are well on your way to implementing version control for your digital objects.

Using a Version Control System

Although there are several different version control systems available for use—some free and open source and some proprietary—two of the most popular systems are Subversion (http://subversion.apache.org) and Git (http://git-scm.com). If you have a web hosting service that enables you to install Subversion, you can create your own repository and use a Subversion client to connect to it.

But an increasingly popular tool is Git, which is a decentralized approach to version control and also offers numerous tools and hosting options for users who want to get started with a repository but don't necessarily want/need/ understand all the extra installation and maintenance overhead that goes with it. One such hosting option for Git repositories is GitHub (http:// github.org), which allows users to create accounts and store and maintain as many code repositories for free as they would like (as long as they are open source), while also providing paid solutions for users who would like to maintain private code repositories.

For anyone wanting to get started with version control, I recommend Git and GitHub for its relative ease of use and free, cross-platform tools for use. The GitHub Help site would be a great place to start: http://help.github.com/. An added benefit of the already-free GitHub account is the ability to use Gist (http://gist.github.com), which is a way to share code snippets (or whole pages) with others, while these snippets themselves are git repositories and thus versioned and forkable in their own right. GitHub repositories, including Gists, are both excellent ways to get started with version control of your work.

Summary

This chapter has given you examples and explanations to help you organize your web pages into a coherent site that is informative, attractive, and easy to navigate. Web users have grown to become quite savvy in terms of expecting well-designed websites, and they will quickly abandon your site if they experience a poor design that is difficult to navigate.

This chapter also discussed the importance of making your code easy to maintain by adding comments and indentation. Comments are important not only as a reminder for you when you revisit code later but also as instruction if someone else should inherit your code. Indentation might seem like an aesthetic issue, but it can truly help you to quickly analyze and understand the structure of a web page at a glance. Because you are likely soon to need code management tools either for yourself or yourself plus other developers in your group, you were introduced to a few concepts in version control. Version control enables you to innovate without losing your solid, production-quality work and also provides more opportunities for other developers to work within your code base.

Q&A

Q. I've seen pages that ask viewers to change the width of their browser window or adjust other settings before proceeding beyond the home page. Why do they do this?

A. The snarky response is that the site creators do not care about their users. Never force your users to do something differently than they are doing with their browsers, and especially never, ever resize the browser automatically. Those are some of the biggest usability no-no's. When sites tell you to change your settings, it is because the site creators think they can offer a better presentation if they're given that specific control over the size of users' windows or fonts. Of course, few people bother to change their settings when told to do so (as they shouldn't), so these sites often look weird or unreadable. You'll be much better off using the tips you learn in this book to make your site readable and attractive using any window size and using a wide variety of browser settings. The better organized your site is, the more usable it will be for visitors.

Q. Will lots of comments and spaces make my pages load slower when someone views them?

A. The size of a little extra text in your pages is negligible when compared to other, chunkier web page resources (such as images and multimedia). Besides, slower dial-up modem connections typically do a decent job of compressing text when transmitting it, so adding spaces to format your HTML doesn't usually change the transfer time at all. You'd have to type hundreds of comment words to cause even one extra second of delay in loading a page. And keep in mind that with the broadband connections (cable, DSL, and so on) that many people now have, text travels extremely fast. It's the graphics that slow pages down, so squeeze your images as tightly as you can, but use text comments freely.

Workshop

The workshop contains quiz questions and activities to help you solidify your understanding of the material covered. Try to answer all questions before looking at the "Answers" section that follows.

Quiz

1. What are three ways to ensure all your pages form a single cohesive website?

2. What two types of information should always be included on your home page?

3. You want to say, "Don't change this image of me. It's my only chance at immortality," to future editors of a web page, but you don't want users who view the page to see that message. How would you do it?

Answers

1. Use consistent background, colors, fonts, and styles. Repeat the same link words or graphics on the top of the page that the link leads to. Repeat the same small header, buttons, or other element on every page of the site.

2. Use enough identifying information so that users can immediately see the name of the site and what it is about. Also, whatever the most important message you want to convey to your intended audience is, state it directly and concisely. Whether it's your mission statement or trademarked marketing slogan, make sure that it is in plain view here.

3. Put the following comment immediately before the `<img />` tag:

```
<!-- Don't change this image of me.
     It's my only chance at immortality. -->
```

Exercises

▶ Grab a pencil (the oldfangled kind) and sketch out your website as a bunch of little rectangles with arrows between them. Sketch a rough overview of what each page will look like by putting squiggles where the text goes and doodles where the images go. Each arrow should start at a doodle icon that corresponds to the navigation button for the page the arrow leads to. Even if you have the latest whiz-bang website management tools (which are often more work than just creating the site itself), sketching your site by hand can give you a much more intuitive grasp of which pages on your site will be easy to get to and how the layout of adjacent pages will work together—all before you invest time in writing the actual HTML to connect the pages together. Believe it or not, I still sketch out websites like this when I'm first designing them. Sometimes you can't beat a pencil and paper!

▶ Open the HTML files that make up your current website, and check them all for comments and code indentation. Are there areas in which the code needs to be explained to anyone who might look at it in the future? If so, add explanatory comments. Is it difficult for you to tell the hierarchy of your code? Is it difficult to see headings and sections? If so, indent your HTML so that the structure matches the hierarchy and thus enables you to jump quickly to the section you need to edit.

CHAPTER 28

Helping People Find Your Web Pages

Your web pages are ultimately only as useful as they are accessible—if no one can find your pages, your hard work in creating a useful architecture, providing interesting content, and coding them correctly will be for naught. The additional HTML tags you'll discover in this chapter won't make any visible difference in your web pages, but they are extremely important in that they will help your audience more easily find your web pages.

For most website creators, this might be the easiest—but most important— chapter in the book. You'll learn how to add elements to your pages and how to construct your site architecture in such a way as to increase the possibility that search engines will return links to your site when someone searches for words related to your topic or company; this is called *search engine optimization* (SEO).

Contrary to what you might hear from companies who try to sell SEO services to you, there are no magic secrets that guarantee you'll be at the top of every list of search results. However, there is a set of *free* best practices that you can do on your own to make sure your site is as easy to find as possible.

Publicizing Your Website

Presumably, you want your website to attract someone's attention or you wouldn't bother to create it in the first place. However, if you are placing your pages only on a local network or corporate intranet, or you are distributing your site exclusively on removable storage media, helping users find your pages might not be much of a problem. But if you are adding the content of your website to the billions of other pages of content indexed by search engines, bringing your intended audience to your site is a very big challenge indeed.

WHAT YOU'LL LEARN IN THIS CHAPTER:

▶ How to publicize your website

▶ How to list your pages with the major search sites

▶ How to optimize your site for search engines

To tackle this problem, you need a basic understanding of how most people decide which pages they will look at. There are basically three ways people become aware of your website:

▶ Somebody tells them about it and gives them the address; they enter that address directly into their web browser.

▶ They follow a link to your site from someone else's site, an aggregator and recommendation service such as Digg or Reddit, or from a link or mention on a social networking site such as Facebook, Twitter, or Google+.

▶ They find your site indexed in the databases that power the Google, Bing, or Yahoo! search engines (among others).

You can increase your website traffic with a little time and effort. To increase the number of people who hear about you through word-of-mouth, well, use your mouth—and every other channel of communication available to you. If you have an existing contact database or mailing list, announce your website to those people. Add the site address to your business cards or company literature. If you have the money, go buy TV and radio ads broadcasting your Internet address. In short, do the marketing thing. Good old-fashioned word-of-mouth marketing is still the best thing going, even on the Internet—we just have more and more tools available to us online.

NOTE

A very popular, high traffic, and well-respected site (due to their accuracy and added value) for tips for interacting in social networking spaces, especially for the business user, is Mashable: http://www.mashable.com/.

Increasing the number of incoming links to your site from other sites is also pretty straightforward—although that doesn't mean it isn't a lot of work. If there are specialized directories on your topic, either online or in print, be sure you are listed. Participate in social networking, including the implementation of Facebook fan pages (if applicable) for your service or business. Create a Twitter account to broadcast news and connect with customers—again, if that is applicable to your online presence. Go into the spaces where your customers might be, such as blogs that comment on your particular topic of interest, and participate in those communities. That is not to say that you should find a forum on your topic or service and spam its users with links to your site. Act as an expert in your given field, offering advice and recommendations along with your own site URL. There's not much I can say in this chapter to help you with that, except to go out and do it.

The main thing I can help you with is making sure your content has been gathered and indexed correctly by search engines. It's a fair assumption that if your content isn't in Google's databases, you're in trouble.

Search engines are basically huge databases that index as much content on the Internet as possible—including videos and other rich media. They use automated processing to search sites, using programs called *robots* or *spiders* to search pages for content and build the databases. After the content is indexed, the search applications themselves use highly sophisticated techniques of ranking pages to determine which content to display first, second, third, and so on when a user enters a search term.

When the search engine processes a user query, it looks for content that contains the key words and phrases that the user is looking for. But it is not a simple match, as in "if this page contains this phrase, return it as a result," because content is ranked according to frequency and context of the keywords and phrases, as well as the number of links from other sites that lend credibility to it. This chapter will teach you a few ways to ensure that your content appears appropriately in the search engine, based on the content and context you provide.

Listing Your Pages with the Major Search Sites

If you want users to find your pages, you absolutely must submit a request to each of the major search sites to index your pages. Even though search engines index web content automatically, this is the best way to ensure your site has a presence on their sites. Each of these sites has a form for you to fill out with the URL address, a brief description of the site, and, in some cases, a category or list of keywords with which your listing should be associated. These forms are easy to fill out; you can easily complete all of them in an hour with time left over to list yourself at one or two specialized directories you might have found as well. (How do you find the specialized directories? Through the major search sites, of course!)

Even though listing with the major search engines is easy and quick, it can be a bit confusing: Each search engine uses different terminology to identify where you should click to register your pages. The following list might save you some frustration; it includes the addresses of some popular search engines which will include your site for free, along with the exact wording of the link you should click to register:

▶ **Google**—Visit http://www.google.com/addurl/, enter the address of your site and a brief description, and then enter the squiggly verification text, called a *CAPTCHA*, (or Completely Automated Public Turing test to tell Computers and Humans Apart) shown on the page. Then click the Add URL button to add your site to Google.

Before You List Your Pages

But wait! Before you rush off this minute to submit your listing requests, read the rest of this chapter. Otherwise, you'll have a very serious problem, and you will have already lost your best opportunity to solve it.

To see what I mean, imagine this scenario: You publish a page selling automatic cockroach flatteners. I am an Internet user who has a roach problem, and I'm allergic to bug spray. I open my laptop, brush the roaches off the keyboard, log on to my favorite search site, and enter *cockroach* as a search term. The search engine promptly presents me with a list of the first 10 out of 10,400,000 web pages containing the word *cockroach*. You have submitted your listing request, so you know that your page is somewhere on that list.

Did I mention that I'm rich? And did I mention that two roaches are mating on my foot? You even offer same-day delivery in my area. Do you want your page to be number 3 on the list or number 8,542? Okay, now you understand the problem. Just getting listed in a search engine isn't enough—you need to work your way up the rankings.

TIP

There are sites that provide one form that automatically submits itself to all the major search engines, plus several minor search engines. These sites—such as http://www.scrubtheweb.com/, http://www.submitexpress.com/, and http://www.hypersubmit.com/—are popular examples of sites that attempt to sell you a premium service that lists you in many other directories and indexes as well. Depending on your target audience, these services might or might not be of value, but I strongly recommend that you go directly to the major search sites listed on the right and use their forms to submit your requests to be listed. That way you can be sure to answer the questions (which are slightly different at every site) accurately, and you will know exactly how your site listing will appear at each search engine.

▶ **Yahoo! Search**—Visit http://siteexplorer.search.yahoo.com/submit, click on Submit a Website or Webpage, enter the address of your site, and then click the Submit URL button.

▶ **Bing**—Visit http://www.bing.com/docs/submit.aspx, enter the verification text, enter the address of your site, and then click the Submit URL button.

▶ **AllTheWeb**—AllTheWeb search results are provided by Yahoo! Search, so just be sure to submit your site to Yahoo! Search, as explained previously.

▶ **AltaVista**—AltaVista search results are also provided by Yahoo! Search, so just be sure to submit your site to Yahoo!. Search, as explained previously.

Providing Hints for Search Engines

Fact: There is absolutely nothing you can do to guarantee that your site will appear in the top 10 search results for a particular word or phrase in any major search engine (short of buying ad space from the search site, that is). After all, if there were such guarantees, why couldn't everyone else who wants to be number one on the list do it, too? What you can do is avoid being last on the list and give yourself as good a chance as anyone else of being first; this is called SEO, or optimizing the content and structure of your pages so that search engines will favor your pages over others.

Each search engine uses a different method for determining which pages are likely to be most relevant and should therefore be sorted to the top of a search result list. You don't need to get too hung up on the differences, though, because they all use some combination of the same basic criteria. The following list includes almost everything any search engine considers when trying to evaluate which pages best match one or more keywords:

▶ Do keywords appear in the `<title>` tag of the page?

▶ Do keywords appear in the first few lines of the page?

▶ Do keywords appear in a `<meta />` tag in the page?

▶ Do keywords appear in `<h1>` headings in the page?

▶ Do keywords appear in the names of image files and `alt` text for images in the page?

▶ How many other pages within the website link to the page?

▶ How many other pages in other websites link to the page? How many other pages link to those pages?

▶ How many times have users chosen this page from a previous search list result?

Clearly, the most important thing you can do to improve your position is to consider the keywords your intended audience are most likely to enter. I'd recommend that you not concern yourself with common, single-word searches like *food*; the lists they generate are usually so long that trying to make it to the top is like playing the lottery. Focus instead on uncommon words and two- or three-word combinations that are most likely to indicate relevance to your topic (for instance, *Southern home-style cooking* instead of simply *food*). Make sure that those terms and phrases occur several times on your page and be certain to put the most important ones in the `<title>` tag and the first heading or introductory paragraph.

Of all the search-engine evaluation criteria just listed, the use of `<meta />` tags is probably the least understood. Some people rave about `<meta />` tags as if using them could instantly move you to the top of every search list. Other people dismiss `<meta />` tags as ineffective and useless. Neither of these extremes is true.

A `<meta />` *tag* is a general-purpose tag you can put in the `<head>` portion of any document to specify some information about the page that doesn't belong in the `<body>` text. Most major search engines look at `<meta />` tags to provide them with a short description of your page and some keywords to identify what your page is about. For example, your automatic cockroach flattener order form might include the following two tags:

```
<meta name="description"
     content="Order the SuperSquish cockroach flattener." />
<meta name="keywords"
     content="cockroach,roaches,kill,squish,supersquish" />
```

The first tag in this example ensures that the search engine has an accurate description of the page to present on its search results list. The second `<meta />` tag slightly increases your page's ranking on the list whenever any of your specified keywords are included in a search query.

You should always include <meta /> tags with name="description" and name="keywords" attributes in any page that you want to be indexed by a search engine. Doing so might not have a dramatic effect on your position in search lists, and not all search engines look for <meta /> tags, but it can only help.

To give you a concrete example of how to improve search engine results, consider the page shown in Listing 28.1.

This page *should* be easy to find because it deals with a specific topic and includes several occurrences of some uncommon technical terms for which users interested in this subject would be likely to search. However, there are several things you could do to improve the chances of this page appearing high on a search engine results list.

LISTING 28.1   A Page That Will Have Little Visibility During an Internet Site Search

```
<?xml version="1.0" encoding="UTF-8"?>
<!DOCTYPE html PUBLIC "-//W3C//DTD XHTML 1.1//EN"
  "http://www.w3.org/TR/xhtml11/DTD/xhtml11.dtd">

<html xmlns="http://www.w3.org/1999/xhtml" xml:lang="en">
  <head>
    <title>Fractal Central</title>
  </head>

  <body>
    <div style="text-align:center">
      <img  src="fractalaccent.gif" alt="a fractal" />
    </div>
    <div style="width:133px; float:left; padding:6px;
              text-align:center; border-width:4px;
              border-style:ridge">
    Discover the latest software, books and more at our
    online store.<br />
      <a href="orderform.html"><img src="orderform.gif"
        alt="Order Form" style="border-style:none" /></a>
    </div>
    <div  style="float:left; padding:6px">
      <h2>A Comprehensive Guide to the<br />
      Art and Science of Chaos and Complexity</h2>
      <p>What's that? You say you're hearing about
      "fractals" and "chaos" all over the place, but still
      aren't too sure what they are? How about a quick
      summary of some key concepts:</p>
      <ol>
        <li>Even the simplest systems become deeply
        complex and richly beautiful when a process is
        "iterated" over and over, using the results
```

LISTING 28.1   Continued

```
            of each step as the starting point of the next.
            This is how Nature creates a magnificently
            detailed 300-foot redwood tree from a seed
            the size of your fingernail.</li>
            <li>Most "iterated systems" are easily simulated
            on computers, but only a few are predictable and
            controllable. Why? Because a tiny influence, like
            a "butterfly flapping its wings," can be strangely
            amplified to have major consequences such as
            completely changing tomorrow's weather in a distant
            part of the world.</li>
            <li>Fractals can be magnified forever without loss
            of detail, so mathematics that relies on straight
            lines is useless with them. However, they give us
            a new concept called "fractal dimension" which
            can measure the texture and complexity of anything
            from coastlines to storm clouds.</li>
            <li>While fractals win prizes at graphics shows,
            their chaotic patterns pop up in every branch of
            science. Physicists find beautiful artwork coming
            out of their plotters. "Strange attractors" with
            fractal turbulence appear in celestial mechanics.
            Biologists diagnose "dynamical diseases" when
            fractal rhythms fall out of sync. Even pure
            mathematicians go on tour with dazzling videos of their
            research.</li>
          </ol>
          <p>Think all these folks may be on to something?</p>
        </div>
        <div style="text-align:center">
          <a href="http://netletter.com/nonsense/">
            <img src="findout.gif" alt="Find Out More"
                style="border-style:none" /></a>
        </div>
      </body>
    </html>
```

Now compare the page in Listing 28.1 with the changes made to the page in Listing 28.2. The two pages look almost the same, but to search robots and search engines, these two pages appear quite different. The following list summarizes what was changed in the page and how those changes affected indexing:

▶ Important search terms were added to the `<title>` tag and the first heading on the page. The original page didn't even include the word *fractal* in either of these two key positions.

▶ `<meta />` tags were added to assist search engines with a description and keywords.

▶ A very descriptive `alt` attribute was added to the first `<img />` tag. Not all search engines read and index `alt` text, but some do.

▶ The quotation marks around technical terms (such as `"fractal"` and `"iterated"`) were removed because some search engines consider *"fractal"* to be a different word than *fractal*. The quotation marks were replaced with the character entity `&quot;`, which search robots simply disregard. This is also a good idea because XHTML urges web developers to use the `&quot;` entity instead of quotation marks anyway.

▶ The keyword *fractal* was added twice to the text in the order-form box.

It is impossible to quantify how much more frequently users searching for information on fractals and chaos were able to find the page shown in Listing 28.2 versus the page shown in Listing 28.1, but it's a sure bet that the changes could only improve the page's visibility to search engines. As is often the case, the improvements made for the benefit of the search spiders probably made the page's subject easier for humans to recognize and understand as well. This makes optimizing a page for search engines a win-win effort!

LISTING 28.2   An Improvement on the Page in LISTING 28.1

```
<?xml version="1.0" encoding="UTF-8"?>
<!DOCTYPE html PUBLIC "-//W3C//DTD XHTML 1.1//EN"
  "http://www.w3.org/TR/xhtml11/DTD/xhtml11.dtd">

<html xmlns="http://www.w3.org/1999/xhtml" xml:lang="en">
  <head>
    <title>Fractal Central: A Guide to Fractals, Chaos,
           and Complexity</title>
    <meta name="description" content="A comprehensive guide
          to fractal geometry, chaos science and complexity
          theory." />
    <meta name="keywords"  content="fractal,fractals,chaos
          science,chaos theory,fractal geometry,complexity,
          complexity theory" />
  </head>

  <body>
    <div style="text-align:center">
      <img  src="fractalaccent.gif" alt=" Fractal Central: A
          Guide to Fractals, Chaos, and Complexity " />
    </div>
    <div style="width:133px; float:left; padding:6px;
                text-align:center; border-width:4px;
                border-style:ridge">
      Discover the latest fractal software, books and
      more at the  <span style="font-weight:bold">Fractal
      Central</span> online store <br />
```

LISTING 28.2   Continued

```html
      <a href="orderform.html"><img src="orderform.gif"
        alt="Order Form" style="border-style:none" /></a>
          </div>
    <div  style="float:left; padding:6px">
      <h2>A Comprehensive Guide to the<br />
      Art and Science of Chaos and Complexity</h2>
      <p>What's that? You say you're hearing about
      &quot;fractals&quot; and &quot;chaos&quot; all
      over the place, but still aren't too sure what
      they are? How about a quick summary of some key
      concepts:</p>
      <ol>
        <li>Even the simplest systems become deeply
        complex and richly beautiful when a process is
        &quot;iterated&quot; over and over, using the
        Results of each step as the starting point of
        the next. This is how Nature creates a magnificently
        detailed 300-foot redwood tree from a seed
        the size of your fingernail.</li>
        <li>Most &quot;iterated systems&quot; are easily
        simulated on computers, but only a few are predictable
        and controllable. Why? Because a tiny influence, like
        a &quot;butterfly flapping its wings, &quot; can be
        strangely amplified to have major consequences such as
        completely changing tomorrow's weather in a distant
        part of the world.</li>
        <li>Fractals can be magnified forever without loss
        of detail, so mathematics that relies on straight
        lines is useless with them. However, they give us
        a new concept called &quot;fractal dimension&quot;
        which can measure the texture and complexity of
        anything from coastlines to storm clouds.</li>
        <li>While fractals win prizes at graphics shows,
        their chaotic patterns pop up in every branch of
        science. Physicists find beautiful artwork coming
        out of their plotters. &quot;Strange attractors&quot;
        with fractal turbulence appear in celestial mechanics.
        Biologists diagnose &quot;dynamical diseases&quot;
        when fractal rhythms fall out of sync. Even pure
        mathematicians go on tour with dazzling videos of their
        research.</li>
      </ol>
      <p>Think all these folks may be on to something?</p>
    </div>
    <div style="text-align:center">
      <a href="http://netletter.com/nonsense/">
        <img src="findout.gif" alt="Find Out More"
            style="border-style:none" /></a>
    </div>
  </body>
</html>
```

These changes will go a long way toward making the content of this site more likely to be appropriately indexed. In addition to good, indexed content, remember that the quality of content—as well as the number of other sites linking to yours—is important as well.

Additional Tips for Search Engine Optimization

The most important tip I can give you regarding SEO is to not pay an SEO company to perform your SEO tasks if that company promises specific results for you. If a company promises that your site will be the number one result in a Google search, run for the hills and take your checkbook with you—no one can promise that because the search algorithms have so many variables that the number one result might change several times over the course of a given week. That is not to say that all SEO companies are scam artists. Some legitimate site content and architect consultants who perform SEO tasks get lumped in with the spammers who send unsolicited email, such as this:

```
"Dear google.com, I visited your website and noticed that you are not
 listed in most of the major search engines and directories..."
```

This sample e-mail is used as an example in Google's own guidelines for webmasters, along with the note to "reserve the same skepticism for unsolicited email about search engines as you do for burn-fat-at-night diet pills or requests to help transfer funds from deposed dictators." Yes, someone actually sent Google a spam e-mail about how to increase their search ranking...in Google. For more good advice from Google, visit http://www.google.com/webmasters/.

Here are some additional actions you can take, for free, to optimize your content for search engines:

▶ Use accurate page titles. Your titles should be brief, but descriptive and unique. Do not try to stuff your titles with keywords.

▶ Create human-friendly URLs, such as those with words in them that users can easily remember. It is a lot easier to remember—and it's easier for search engines to index in a relevant way—a URL such as http://www.mycompany.com/products/super_widget.html compared to something like http://www.mycompany.com?c=p&id=4&id=49f8sd7345fea.

▶ Create URLs that reflect your directory structure. This assumes you have a directory structure in the first place, which you should.

▶ When possible, use text—not graphical elements—for navigation.

▶ If you have content several levels deep, use a breadcrumb trail so that users can find their way back home. A breadcrumb trail also provides search engines with more words to index. For example, if you are looking at a recipe for biscuits in the Southern Cooking category of a food-related website, the breadcrumb trail for this particular page might look like this:

Home > Southern Cooking > Recipes > Biscuits

▶ Within the content of your page, use headings (<h1>, <h2>, <h3>) appropriately.

In addition to providing rich and useful content for your users, you should follow these tips to increase your site's prominence in page rankings.

Summary

This chapter covered some extremely important territory by exploring how to provide hints to search engines (such as Google, Bing, and Yahoo!) so that users can find your pages more easily. You also saw an example of the HTML behind a perfectly reasonable web page *redone* to make it more search engine friendly. Finally, you learned a few more tips to optimize the indexing of your site overall.

Table 28.1 lists the tags and attributes covered in this chapter.

TABLE 28.1   HTML Tags and Attributes Covered in Chapter 28

Tag/Attribute	Function
<meta />	Indicates meta-information about this document (information about the document itself). Most commonly used to add a page description and to designate keywords. Used in the document <head>.
Attributes	
name="name"	Can be used to specify which type of information about the document is in the content attribute. For example, name="keywords" means that keywords for the page are in content.
content="value"	The actual message or value for the information specified in http-equiv or name. For example, if the http-equiv attribute is set to refresh, the content attribute should be set to the number of seconds to wait, followed by a semicolon and the address of the page to load.

Q&A

Q. I have lots of pages in my site. Do I need to fill out a separate form for each page at each search site?

A. No. If you submit just your home page (which is presumably linked to all the other pages), the search spiders will crawl through all the links on the page (and all the links on the linked pages, and so on) until they have indexed all the pages on your site.

Q. I submitted a request to be listed with a search engine, but when I search for my page, my page never comes up—not even when I enter my company's unique name. What can I do?

A. Most of the big search engines offer a form you can fill out to instantly check whether a specific address is included in their database. If you find that it isn't included, you can submit another request form. Sometimes it takes days or even weeks for the spiders to get around to indexing your pages after you submit a request.

Q. When I put keywords in a `<meta />` tag, do I need to include every possible variation of spelling and capitalization?

A. Don't worry about capitalization; almost all searches are entered in all lowercase letters. Do include any obvious variations or common spelling errors as separate keywords. Although simple in concept, there are more advanced strategies available when it comes to manipulating the `<meta />` tag than I've been able to cover in this chapter. Visit http://en.wikipedia.org/wiki/Meta_element for good information on the various attributes of this tag and how to use it.

Q. I've heard that I can use the `<meta />` tag to make a page automatically reload itself every few seconds or minutes. Is this true?

A. Yes, but there's no point in doing that unless you have some sort of program or script set up on your web server to provide new information on the page. And if that is the case, the chances are good that you can go about that refresh in a different way using AJAX (see Chapter 24, "AJAX: Remote Scripting," for basic information on AJAX). For usability reasons, the use of `<meta />` to refresh content is frowned upon by the W3C and users in general.

Workshop

The workshop contains quiz questions and activities to help you solidify your understanding of the material covered. Try to answer all questions before looking at the "Answers" section that follows.

Quiz

1. If you publish a page about puppy adoption, how could you help make sure that the page can be found by users who enter *puppy*, *dog*, and/or *adoption* at all the major Internet search sites?

2. Suppose you decide to paste your keywords hundreds of times in your HTML code, using a white font on a white background, so that your readers cannot see them. How would search engine spiders deal with this?

3. Is it better to throw all your content in one directory or to organize it into several directories?

Answers

1. Make sure that *puppy*, *dog*, and *adoption* all occur frequently on your main page (as they probably already do) and title your page something along the lines of Puppy Dog Adoption. While you're at it, put the following `<meta />` tags in the `<head>` portion of the page:

```
<meta name="description"
content="dog adoption information and services" />
<meta name="keywords" content="puppy, dog, adoption" />
```

Publish your page online, and then visit the site submittal page for each major search engine (listed earlier in the chapter) to fill out the site submission forms.

2. Search engine spiders would ignore the duplications and possibly black-list you from their index and label you as a spammer.

3. Definitely organize your content into several directories. This will provide easier maintenance of your content, but will also give you the opportunity to create human-readable URLs with directory structures that make sense. It also creates a navigational breadcrumb trail.

Exercises

▶ You've reached the end of the book. If you have a site that is ready for the world to see, review the content and structure for the best possible optimizations, and then submit the address to all the major search engines.

INDEX

Q - R

S

FREE Online Edition

Your purchase of **Sams Teach Yourself HTML, CSS, and JavaScript All in One** includes access to a free online edition for 45 days through the Safari Books Online subscription service. Nearly every [imprint] book is available online through Safari Books Online, along with more than 5,000 other technical books and videos from publishers such as Addison-Wesley Professional, Cisco Press, Exam Cram, IBM Press, O'Reilly, Prentice Hall, and Que.

SAFARI BOOKS ONLINE allows you to search for a specific answer, cut and paste code, download chapters, and stay current with emerging technologies.

Activate your FREE Online Edition at www.informit.com/safarifree

> **STEP 1:** Enter the coupon code: AWWUQGA

> **STEP 2:** New Safari users, complete the brief registration form.
> Safari subscribers, just log in.

If you have difficulty registering on Safari or accessing the online edition, please e-mail customer-service@safaribooksonline.com

12|11